REFLECTIONS *on the* HUMAN VENTURE

REFLECTIONS *on the* HUMAN VENTURE

HADLEY CANTRIL

AND

CHARLES H. BUMSTEAD

NEW YORK UNIVERSITY PRESS
1960

© 1960 by New York University

Library of Congress Catalog Card Number: 59–15237

Manufactured in the United States of America

By Arrangement with Washington Square Press, Inc.

Permission to reprint selections from the following works is gratefully acknowledged:

Conrad Aiken, "Music I Heard with You," from *Collected Poems,* copyright 1953 by Conrad Aiken; reprinted by permission of Oxford University Press, Inc., and Brandt and Brandt.

The Study of Human Abilities: The Jen Wu Chih *of Liu Shao* (New Haven: American Oriental Society, 1937); reprinted by permission of the American Oriental Society.

W. H. Auden, "New Year Letter (January 1, 1940)," and "True Enough," from *The Collected Poetry of W. H. Auden,* copyright 1941 and 1945 by W. H. Auden; reprinted by permission of Random House, Inc., and Faber and Faber, Ltd., London.

Chester I. Barnard, *Organization and Management,* copyright 1948 by The President and Fellows of Harvard College; reprinted by permission of Harvard University Press.

Baudelaire, *My Heart Laid Bare and Other Prose Writings,* Peter Quennel, ed., Norman Cameron, trans.; reprinted by permission of the publishers, The Vanguard Press, and Weidenfeld and Nicolson, Ltd., London.

Martin Buber, *I and Thou,* Ronald Gregor Smith, trans.; reprinted by permission of Charles Scribner's Sons, and T. and T. Clark, Edinburgh.

A Handbook of Marxism, Emile Burns, ed.; reprinted by permission of International Publishers.

Witter Bynner, *THE WAY OF LIFE According to Laotzu,* copyright 1944 by Witter Bynner; reprinted by permission of The John Day Company, Inc., publisher.

G. K. Chesterton, "Science and the Savages," from *Heretics;* reprinted by permission of The Bodley Head, Ltd., London.

iv

For our girls:
Nancy and Mab, Thelma and Mavis

Preface

We have frequently been troubled by the fact that both students and laymen find so many books in psychology not only insufferably dull but also unconvincing and unrewarding. The views of human nature provided by the psychologist for the student or for the inquiring layman often seem to offend his sense of the dignity of man by their narrow intellectualism, while many generalizations stemming from segmented research seem either downright implausible or inconsequential. Somewhere along the line too much of human experience has been left out of account.

The characteristics and qualities that make human experience what it is must first be recognized before they can be described and then dealt with. It is the sensitive novelist, poet, or prophet who seems so far to have done best in combining such recognition with faithful description.

Hence, many books which deal with "human nature" at the level of scientific conceptualization do not seem to ring true. They do not seem to describe or to explain satisfactorily the process of living as the reader knows it in terms of his own immediate, firsthand experience. The result is that both the student and the layman frequently indicate that they can learn more about "human nature" from reading good literature than from taking courses in psychology. And they are probably right.

It is our hope that the readings brought together here with our own textual material will contribute to the development of a more adequate understanding of human living so that people everywhere may have some guideposts for enhancing the quality of their own lives. Sincerely achieved revelations and descriptions of human experience from any source—from the poet, novelist, dramatist, or prophet—receive a respectful hearing. By means of such readings an individual may be able to increase the range and accuracy of his sensitivity to the qualities of his own experience, and become more aware of the value-overtones with which all experience is charged.

The material included is drawn from the work of sensitive, impressionistic writers and from other observers whom we feel have shown themselves to be keen reporters of the human enterprise. We hope the selections will at least illustrate the richness and variety of experience which the psychologist must take into account in constructing any adequate explanatory system. For the awareness of some of the aspects and complexities of on-going experience, described so vividly by many of the passages cited here, may help keep the breath of life in psychology itself, pointing to new dimensions of experience which the psychologist may have neglected. We do not discuss or dissect each of the readings as such, since the reader will enjoy them more if critical analysis is kept to a minimum.

The scope of this book, then, is quite different from that of most books in psychology. It does not purport in any way to be a "text" or to cover the entire range of psychological phenomena, although we hope the book may be a useful supplement to introductory courses in psychology. We also operate on the assumption that a good education yields a comprehension of a few basic principles and a knowledge of the way they apply to a variety of specific situations. And, finally, what we call the "transactional" approach to psychology, which will be sketched in our textual material, has given a different slicing of the subject matter of psychology than do more orthodox approaches. For these reasons the reader will not find, for example, a chapter on individual differences, although a general treatment of this topic is implicit in the materials presented. On the other hand, the nature and functions of faith, religious experience, and prayer—subjects rarely treated in books of psychology—are considered in the final chapter. Since a basic theme of "transactional" psychology is the interdependence of all aspects of experience, it is particularly difficult to write about. For we can discuss only one thing at a time, trying to remind ourselves in the process that what we are talking about depends upon many other things we are *not* at present talking about. It is difficult at best to select an excerpt without doing violence to the meaning or losing the "feel" or the beauty of the whole work. And it is often most unfair to quote an author who originally wrote in a language that has had to be translated for English readers. "Poetry," says Robert Frost, "is what gets lost in translation." Since many of the passages illustrate almost all aspects of a transaction of living, placement within the structure of the book is often somewhat arbitrary.

If the idea which culminated in this book is valid, we hope others will improve upon it. If so, it will have fulfilled one of its major functions.

In a single volume we can only include a tiny sample of selections from literature and from the writings of other observers. Our hope is that we have a sufficient variety of excerpts to illustrate at least the potentialities of such observing and writing for providing us a better systematic understanding of man. Selections are necessarily limited to a very few of the passages we have run across in our own reading and have liked because we feel they express well some insight, some psychological process, or imply an interpretation we endorse. For every selection included, we reluctantly left out at least three others in order to keep this book within manageable proportions. Certainly we do not claim that the collection of readings included here is the best that might be produced. Every reader will no doubt think of favorite passages not included.

The psychologist who tries to write textual material interspersed among passages written by gifted novelists and poets has a discouraging task. In preparing the textual material here, we have sometimes been unhappily aware that our own words had to be sandwiched in between examples of magnificent prose. So we beg the reader's indulgence, referring him to William Faulkner's basis for rating authors, "their splendid failure to do the impossible."

Anyone who had the good fortune to know the late Adelbert Ames, Jr., will recognize how much of his thinking permeates these pages. We are indebted to Mary Chase Morrison for her help in the selection of some passages of poetry included here and to René and Erika Fülöp-Miller for their help. The title was suggested by Tad Cantril. We have used a few selections already contained in *The Practical Cogitator* edited by Charles P. Curtis, Jr. and Ferris Greenslet. Beatrice Miers and Helen Jane Belcher prepared the manuscript and we are most grateful to them. Finally, we are indebted to the Rockefeller

Foundation and the Quaker Hill Foundation, whose assistance made it possible for us to spend several summers together.

H. C.

C. H. B.

Princeton, New Jersey

Before the manuscript of this book went to press, my beloved friend and co-author, Charles Bumstead, died of a heart attack.

H. C.

Contents

REFLECTIONS *on the* HUMAN VENTURE

1

Science, Humanism, and Man[*]

> ". . . the test of truth is that it satisfies the touchstones of human experience. . . ." —OEHSER

THE COMPLEMENTARITY OF SCIENCE AND HUMANISM

"The proper study of mankind is man, says man," says James Thurber. Because of the great technological advances of the past few decades men's lives have become more and more closely involved with each other, and so it seems that the most crucial problems of the second half of the twentieth century will be those of man's relation to man. Solutions to these problems obviously can only advance insofar as we increase our understanding of "human nature."

Without underestimating the progress toward understanding human living which scientists, including psychologists, have made in recent years the present writers feel that the sciences, and especially psychology, can be enormously enriched, and their constructs acquire greater applicability to the problems of living, if they pay closer attention to the insights so frequently provided in the humanities. For the humanists also are basically concerned with the nature of human experience and with the communication of all its nuances. Hence a poem, a painting, or a prayer should be regarded as a psychological datum just as much as the establishment of a sensory threshold in the laboratory or the measurement of an I.Q. It is interesting and relevant here to note the definition *Webster's New International Dictionary* gives of the word "fact":

[*] Notes to this chapter begin on p. 327.

"That which has actual existence, whether subjectively or objectively considered; any event, mental or physical; an occurrence, quality, or relation, the reality of which is manifest in experience or may be inferred with certainty. . . ."

And just as the psychologist should benefit from the humanist, so should science and particularly psychology give humanism new dimensions by magnifying the potential values with which it may deal and by enabling the poet, the musician, the painter, or the prophet to find some inspiration and direction in the "facts" the scientist discovers and the constructs he creates.

The first-order data of human living, whether sought by the poet or the scientist—the nature of naïve on-going experience and behavior—seem unattainable or at least unreportable. As Amiel put it: "To speak is to disperse and scatter. Words isolate and localize life in a single point; they touch only the circumference of being; they analyze, they treat one thing at a time." [1] If it is true that experiencing *as* experiencing, living *as* living, is unreportable and unanalyzable without destroying its "reality," it is perhaps true that humanism gives us the closest approach to the raw, descriptive data we desire. "True poetry is truer than science, because it is synthetic, and seizes at once what the combination of all the sciences is able at most to obtain as a final result." [2]

A most important point, then, to understand clearly at the outset is that experience *as* experience, as it occurs independently of any purpose to describe or analyze it, is almost inaccessible both to the humanist and to the psychologist. Naïve, on-going human experience seems unreportable, ineffable. But it is the men and women we call "humanists" who seem to come closest to capturing and conveying these ineffable, unconceptualizable experiences. Hence we return to them over and over again in trying to get a toe hold on our own awareness, or in trying to lift ourselves up to more satisfying levels of experience. This point is nicely illustrated by a passage from Robert Henri's *The Art Spirit:*

There are moments in our lives, there are moments in a day, when we seem to see beyond the usual—become clairvoyant. We reach then into reality. Such are the moments of our greatest happiness. Such are the moments of our greatest wisdom.

It is in the nature of all people to have these experiences; but in our time and under the conditions of our lives it is only a rare few who are able to continue in the experience and find expression for it.

At such times there is a song going on within us, a song to which we listen. It fills us with surprise. We marvel at it. We would continue to hear it. But few are capable of holding themselves in the state of listening to their own song. Intellectuality steps in and as the song within us is of the utmost sensitiveness, it retires in the presence of the cold, material intellect. It is aristocratic and will not associate itself with the commonplace—and we fall back and become our ordinary selves. Yet we live in the memory of these songs which in moments of intellectual inadvertence have been possible to us. They are the pinnacles of our experience and it is the desire to express these intimate sensations, this song from within, which motivates the masters of all art. [3]

Just as the young infant cannot report the nature of his experiential world in verbal terms, so the adult, while doing the work of the world, is not able to describe and report the process of events he is experiencing. There is much evidence to indicate that when an individual's purpose is to describe and report experience then the very structure and flow of experience itself is altered. The process of living seems most satisfactorily conceptualized as a single, undivided, unitary, but extremely complex process which no single symbol is capable of expressing. Description is necessarily analytical and successive. As soon as one starts to speak or to write, something is left out. In short, one is already dealing with fictions, abstractions, or concepts at least one step removed from first-order data. Furthermore, every person has experiences which he feels are wholly incapable of communication to others.

Vivid descriptions of human experience by non-scientists may therefore supply protocol data with which the scientist may begin his task of cross-examining nature in his attempt to arrive at a set of constructs in terms of which he can summarize, understand, "explain," and better predict the process of human living. For the scientist, who seeks a purely rational conception of our existence, must analyze, classify, and make use of abstractions and concepts— fictions which may be useful and fruitful, but nevertheless still fictions. Whitehead has reminded us that: "Matter-of-fact is an abstraction, arrived at by confining thought to purely formal relations which masquerade as the final reality. This is why science, in its perfection, relapses into the study of differential equations. The concrete world has slipped through the meshes of the scientific net." [4]

The function of concepts and abstractions was noted by Havelock Ellis: ". . . our thinking would itself be fluid if it were not that by fiction we obtain imaginary standpoints and boundaries by which to gain control of the flow of reality. It is the special art and object of thinking to attain existence by quite other methods than that of existence itself. . . . Our conceptions, our conventional signs, have a fictive function to perform; thinking in its lower grades is comparable to paper money, and in its higher forms it is a kind of poetry." [5]

And no matter how fashionable or respectable concepts of *value* and *valuing* are within the domain of science from one decade to another, psychologists must lend an ear to those humanists who have made the study and expression of values their work. For in the pursuit of the ultimate ends of living, what we know as reason, logic, or intelligence may all play a very minor role, leaving out as they do the feeling-tones and values which permeate the totality of human experience. Here are some sample observations of what an orthodox "scientific account" leaves out:

> When you understand all about the sun, and all about the atmosphere, and all about the radiation of the earth, you may still miss the radiance of the sunset.   (WHITEHEAD.)

> When we are told that the leaves of a plant are occupied in decomposing carbonic acid, and preparing oxygen for us, we begin to look upon it with some such indifference as a gasometer. It has become a machine . . . , its emanation of inherent light is no longer pure.
>   (RUSKIN.)

As everyone knows, experience from the first-person point of view—from *your* point of view—is pervaded by feelings and value-overtones that are in a sense unlimited by space and time, even though they are only called into play in the here and now. These feelings and value-overtones must be carefully differentiated from what the psychologist generally calls emotions and, more often than not, refers to as emotions brought about by reflex action. The feelings and value-overtones of experience are what provide man's experience with its peculiarly "human" qualities. And these feelings and value-overtones, as already noted, must be carefully distinguished from our rational thought processes.

THE ORCHESTRATION OF LIVING

The life of each one of us might be likened to a symphony. Thousands of occurrences are orchestrated into what we call experience—or better, experiencing, since experience is always ongoing. Sometimes the flow is smooth and harmonious, sometimes rough and discordant; basic themes repeat themselves periodically in the midst of continued development with varied and new overtones. The span from birth to death has movements with a certain emphasis in each; sometimes the melody is carried by one or a few instruments easily detectable but more often the effect is produced by a variety of instruments with the sound of each lost in the total orchestration.

While the basic themes of each life-symphony may be given in bold outline by our unique heredity, still the final score written is one which we definitely help to compose as we go along. We build a pattern as we progress, a pattern from which it becomes increasingly difficult to deviate. Some sounds and arrangements we filter out since they would spoil our composition. Sometimes our tempo is fast and sprightly, at other times slow and stately. Some of us compose in a style that follows compositions we are familiar with or that are accepted for our day; others of us boldly deviate and become more idiosyncratic and radical. For each of us the symphony that constitutes our living is uniquely ours. And only parts of it are heard from time to time by others as it is heard by ourselves. Much of it we ourselves can hear only when we are with other human beings.

A Beethoven or a Mozart has the genius to communicate to others a whole symphony he hears himself. Similarly, some individuals possess a rare talent to communicate in words the totality of their experiences in such a way that a concrete event has an aura of universality and universals are reflected in concreteness. Such individuals provide "cues," "insights" which the psychologist cannot afford to ignore. And, of course, the reverse of this proposition is equally true if we assume that the humanist also seeks to understand human living. Thus, although the methods of science provide one of our most productive ways of knowing, science, at least as ordinarily conceived and carried on, is limited in the nature of the problems it can attack. For example, science seems unable to answer alone the question of what the goal or goals of human beings *should be*. And the psychologist, particularly, needs to understand much more precisely than he does now the role the ineffable value-aspects of experience play in determining our purposes, both immediate and ultimate, and the role they play in all human behavior not governed by reflexes or simple homeostatic principles. For this reason, if for no other, we should pay attention to what is revealed through other avenues to "truth," to modes of inquiry that differ from those of science. Most human beings carry on their living, their learning, their observing, outside the scope of the scientist's laboratory or constructs. Hence they are relatively unencumbered by the need to be consistent in terms of an established set of abstractions.

It is generally recognized that some poets, artists, novelists, prophets, or other observers possess an unusual sensitivity to the non-rational aspects of living. Although psychology has by no means failed to investigate these abstracted aspects of human experience and although non-scientific writers have by no means confined their attention to them, there does seem to have been a difference in the interest in and appreciation for the role of feelings and values among humanists and scientists, at least in western culture.

There is, of course, no intention here of implying either that man is wholly "rational" or wholly "irrational," or that psychology has dealt exclusively with rational processes and poetry (in the generic sense) exclusively with feelings. Nor do we intend to convey the impression that poets experience "pure" feeling while scientists are devoid of feelings. Both psychology and poetry reveal important truths about the whole of human living, including its intellectual and non-intellectual aspects. But the emphasis has been different. And the recognition of this fact should provide some balance to anyone interested in learning from both.

If the first-order data of human experiencings are ineffable, how close can we come to accurate description? It would seem that the relative simplicity and "wholeness" of the young child, *if* he were capable of vivid and accurate communication, might supply the closest approximation to the unattainable ideal. Among those capable of graphic description, it is apparently those who have retained or can recapture some measure of the child's outlook on the world who provide data which approximate what we desire through their written work or their symbolic creations. These data, for the scientist, may serve as protocol statements, as starting points for formulating hypotheses, selecting variables, conducting experiments, and building theories. By including such data in his inquiry the scientist may better erect a set of constructs, a systematic theory which can pass from the immediately given "facts" and the unique aspects of a concrete situation to the understanding of a much wider range of relevant "facts." Some descriptions of and some discussions of the nature of childhood experiences illustrate what we are referring to.

Can you remember how acute your sensations were, how intensely you felt about everything, when you were a child? The rapture of raspberries and cream, the horror of fish, the hell of castor oil! And the torture of having to get up and recite before the whole class! The inexpressible joy of sitting next to the driver, with the smell of horse sweat and leather in one's nostrils, the white road stretching away to infinity, and the fields of corn and cabbages slowly turning, as the buggy rolled past, slowly opening and shutting like enormous fans! When you're a child, your mind is a kind of saturated solution of feeling, a suspension of all the thrills—but in a latent state, in a condition of indeterminacy. Sometimes it's external circumstances that act as the crystallizing agent, sometimes it's your own imagination. You want some special kind of thrill, and you deliberately work away at yourself until you get it—a bright pink crystal of pleasure, for example, a green or bruise-colored lump of fear; for fear, of course, is a thrill like any other; fear is a hideous kind of fun.

(ALDOUS HUXLEY, *The Genius and the Goddess.*) [6]

Only artists and children have the gift of vividly appreciating images. For these privileged beings, an image represents *something else:* a dream that they recall, a miraculous voyage, a minute of salvation. This appreciation, by the way, has nothing in common with the "appreciation" of certain art-lovers who merely collect agreeable chattels. The "appreciation" of the collector is vitiated by too great variety, or by other influences. The child and the artist continually discover new themes in a single image; and their appreciation is variegated by the manner in which the charm of an image shifts and presents itself to them in new forms.　　　　　(CHARLES BAUDELAIRE, *My Heart Laid Bare and Other Prose Writings.*) [7]

Now, convalescence is a sort of return to childhood. The convalescent enjoys, as the child does, the faculty of taking a lively interest in everything, even in the apparently most trivial things. Let us return, if we can, by a retrospective effort of the imagination, to our youngest, most matutinal impressions. We shall recognise that they had a remarkable affinity with the highly coloured impressions that we received, later on, after a physical illness—provided that this illness did no damage to our mental or spiritual faculties. For the child everything is *new;* he is always *exhilarated.* Nothing more closely resembles what is called inspiration than the joy of a child absorbing form and colour. I shall venture to go further, and assert that inspiration has something in common with cerebral congestion, and that every sublime thought is accompanied by a nervous shock, of greater or less violence, which reaches even the brain.

The nerves of the man of genius are strong; those of a child are weak. In the former reason plays a considerable role; in the latter almost the whole being is occupied by sensibility. Nevertheless, genius is simply *childhood rediscovered* by an act of will; childhood now endowed, for its self-expression, with the organs of a man and that analytical power that enables a man to put order into the automatically amassed sum of physical experiences.

This deep and joyful appreciation of life is the explanation of the fixed and animally ecstatic gaze of a child confronted by what is *new*—whatever it may be, a face or a landscape, light, gilding, colours, shot silks, the magic of a woman's beauty enhanced by her labours at the dressing-table.

A friend of mine once told me that when he was very small he used to watch his father dressing, and would gaze, in wonderment mixed with delight, at the muscles of the arms, the graduated shades of faint pink and yellow in the skin, and the bluish network of veins. The picture of life's outward appearances was already filling the child with deep respect, and laying hold of his very brain. Already he was obsessed and possessed by the contemplation of form. Predestination was precociously showing the tip of its nose. . . .　　　　　(BAUDELAIRE, *ibid.*) [8]

Both the inquiries of the "scientist" and the compositions of the "non-scientist" yield protocols of human experience in one form or another. It is the conditions under which these arise and what is done with them that, in part, distinguish science from poetry. The protocols of the psychologist are likely to come into existence under experimental conditions from a "subject" who, because of the instructions he has received or the particular purpose which brings him to the situation, pays attention to some special aspect of his total experience and reports only on that. The protocols of the non-scientific observer, on the other hand, come into existence in a more natural, non-laboratory situation as part of the rediscovery of "reality," our awareness of which has so often been dulled by familiarity and by our analytical activity.

The humanist is generally content to stop at this level, at the revelation of his discovery or rediscovery of reality in some concrete situation. The scientist, on the other hand, only begins at this level and proceeds through several stages of analysis, abstraction, and conceptualization in his attempt to arrive at concepts which have greatest applicability to a variety of specific, experiential occurrences. The humanist usually rests his case on his own personal insight. In an age when "science" seems to be in the saddle, the humanist may feel overly modest about his insights and may even unnecessarily feel a need to apologize for them. Both the humanist and the scientist must be quite clear that the invaluable contribution the humanist makes is in giving us insights concerning universal truths and sentiments with reference to concrete experiences: giving both the universal and the particular a significance neither could have without the context of the other.

And so we return to the purpose of this volume. If we are interested in understanding "human nature," in comprehending the process of human living, an attempt to synthesize information presented both through literature and through the work of psychologists would seem to be in order. This book represents a step in that direction. It is essentially a collection of excerpts from multifarious sources—essays, poems, biographies, novels, diaries, dramas, prayers—all of which are concerned with the human enterprise, either directly or indirectly, immediately or remotely. For psychology, we feel, should begin with and return to the process of human living in its full orchestration, a process within which differentiations have to be made, but within which no true divisions exist. By erecting a conceptual framework broad enough to encompass both the findings of the science of psychology and the findings of the humanist, it is hoped that a theory of human living will emerge which is intrinsically reasonable and genuinely useful.

We should perhaps remind ourselves in passing that no book or combination of books can provide final solutions. For the very marks of the scientific movement are its devotion to experimentation in a universe that is open-ended, always in process, always changing. Scientific theories must always retain their hypothetical status. The scientific endeavor, although a self-correcting one, never reaches finalities, ultimate truths, or absolute knowledge. For absolutes are themselves always human creations.

SCIENTIFIC AND HUMANISTIC WAYS OF KNOWING

We must first gain perspective on our task. To what degree can man understand himself? Are there limits to man's knowings? Can man know more about "the outside world" than about his own nature? What is the nature and function of scientific inquiry? What are its advantages and limitations? Are there alternative ways of gaining reliable knowledge, and if so, what are their advantages and limitations? These are some of the questions to pose as you read the second group of excerpts.

. . . I like to say that there is no scientific method as such, but that the most vital feature of the scientist's procedure has been merely to do his utmost with his mind, *no holds barred*. This means in particular that no special privileges are accorded to authority or to tradition, that personal prejudices and predilections are carefully guarded against, that one makes continued check to assure oneself that one is not making mistakes, and that any line of inquiry will be followed that appears at all promising. All of these rules are applicable to any situation in which one has to obtain the right answer and all of them are only manifestations of intelligence. The so-called scientific method is merely a special case of the method of intelligence, and any apparently unique characteristics are to be explained by the nature of the subject matter rather than ascribed to the nature of the method itself.

(P. W. BRIDGMAN, *New Vistas for Intelligence*.) [9]

For poetry does not explain our experience. If we begin by thinking that it ought to "explain" the human predicament, we shall quickly see that it does not, and we shall end up thinking that therefore it has no meaning at all. . . . But poetry is at once more modest and, in the great poets, more profound. It is the art of apprehending and concentrating our experience in the mysterious limitations of form.

Philosophy even in the strict sense may be the material of poetry, but poets are not chiefly philosophers. A poet whose main passion is to get his doctrine—or his personality or his local color—into his poems is trying to justify a medium in which he lacks confidence. There is a division of purpose, and the arrogance of facile "solutions" that thinks it can get along without experience. The poet had better write his poetry first; examine it; then decide what he thinks. The poetry may not reveal all that he thinks; it will reveal all he thinks that is any good —for poetry. Poetry is one test of ideas; it is ideas tested by experience, by the act of direct apprehension.

(ALLEN TATE, *Preface to Reactionary Essays on Poetry and Ideas* [1936].) [10]

"You appear, then, to intimate," returned I, "that the more one knows, the worse one observes."

"Certainly," said Goethe, "when the knowledge that is handed down is combined with errors. As soon as anybody belongs to a certain narrow creed in science, every unprejudiced and true perception is gone. The decided Vulcanist always sees through the spectacles of a Vulcanist; and every Neptunist, and every professor of the newest elevation-theory, through his own. The contemplation of the world, with all these theorists, has lost its innocence, the objects no longer appear in their natural purity. If these learned men, then, give an account of their observations, we obtain, notwithstanding their love of truth as individuals, no actual truth with reference to the objects; we always get the taste of a strong subjective mixture.

"I am, however, far from maintaining that an unprejudiced correct knowledge is a drawback to observation. I am much more inclined to support the old truth, that we have only eyes and ears for what we know. The musician by profession hears, in an orchestral performance, every instrument and every single tone; whilst one unacquainted with the art is wrapped up in the massive effect of the whole. A man merely bent upon enjoyment sees in a green or flowery meadow only a pleasant plain, whilst the eye of a botanist discovers an endless detail of the most varied plants and grasses.

"All have their measure and goal; and, as it has been said in my *Goetz von Berlichingen,* that the son, from pure learning, does not know his own father, so in science do we find people who can neither see nor hear, through sheer learning and hypothesis. Such people look at once within; they are so occupied by what is revolving in themselves, that they are like a man in a passion, who passes his dearest friends in the street without seeing them. The observation of nature requires a certain purity of mind that cannot be disturbed or preoccupied by anything. The beetle on the flower does not escape the child; he has devoted all his senses to a single simple interest; and it never strikes him that at the same moment something remarkable may be going on in the formation of the clouds to distract his glances in that direction."

"Then," returned I, "children and the child-like would be good hod-men in science."

"Would to God!" exclaimed Goethe, "we were all nothing more than good hod-men. It is just because we will be more, and carry about with us a great apparatus of philosophy and hypothesis, that we spoil all."

(*Conversations of Goethe with Eckermann*.) [11]

A permanent disadvantage of the study of folk-lore and kindred subjects is that the man of science can hardly be in the nature of things very frequently a man of the world. He is a student of nature; he is scarcely ever a student of human nature. And even where this difficulty is overcome, and he is in some sense a student of human nature, this is only a very faint beginning of the painful progress towards being human. For the study of primitive race and religion stands apart in one important respect from all, or nearly all, the ordinary scientific studies. A man can understand astronomy only by being an astronomer; he can understand entomology only by being an entomologist (or, perhaps, an insect); but he can understand a great deal of anthropology merely by being a man. He is himself the animal which he studies. Hence arises the fact which strikes the eye everywhere in the records of ethnology and folk-lore—the fact that the same frigid and detached spirit which leads to success in the study of astronomy or botany leads to disaster in the study of mythology or human origins. It is necessary to cease to be a man in order to do justice to a microbe; it is not necessary to cease to be a man in order to do justice to men. That same suppression of sympathies, that same waving away of intuitions or guess-work which makes a man preternaturally clever in dealing with the stomach of a spider, will make him preternaturally stupid in dealing with the heart of man. He is making himself inhuman in order to understand humanity. An ignorance of the other world is boasted by many men of science; but in this matter their defect arises, not from ignorance of the other world, but from ignorance of this world. For the secrets about which anthropologists concern themselves can be best learnt, not from books or voyages, but from the ordinary commerce of man with man. The secret of why some savage tribe worships monkeys or the moon is not to be found even by travelling among those savages and taking down their answers in a note-book, although the cleverest man may pursue this course. The answer to the riddle is in England; it is in London; nay, it is in his own heart. When a man has discovered why men in Bond Street wear black hats he will at the same moment have discovered why men in Timbuctoo wear red feathers. The mystery in the heart of some savage war-dance should not be studied in books of scientific travel; it should be studied at a subscription ball. If a man desires to find out the origins of religions, let him not go to the Sandwich Islands; let him go to church. If a man wishes to know the origin of human society, to know what society, philosophically speaking, really is, let him not go into the British Museum; let him go into society.

(G. K. CHESTERTON, *Science and the Savages.*) [12]

The impression is to the writer what experimentation is to the scientist, with this difference, however, that for the scientist the labor of the intellect precedes and for the artist it follows.

(*The Maxims of Marcel Proust.*) [13]

Yet many truths concerning the creature retained I from these (learned) men, and saw the reason thereof from calculations, the succession of times, and the visible testimonies of the stars; and compared them with the saying of Manichaeus, which in his frenzy he had written most largely on these subjects; but discovered not any account of the solstices, or equinoxes, or the eclipses of the greater lights, nor whatever of this sort I had learned in the books of secular philosophy. But I was commanded to believe; and yet it corresponded not with what had been established by calculations and my own sight, but was quite contrary.

Doth then, O Lord God of truth, whoso knoweth these things, therefore please Thee? Surely unhappy is he who knoweth all these, and knoweth not Thee; but happy whoso knoweth Thee, though he know not these. And whoso knoweth both Thee and them is not the happier for them, but for Thee only, if, knowing Thee, he glorifies Thee as God, and is thankful, and becomes not vain in his imaginations. For as he is better off who knows how to possess a tree, and return thanks to Thee for the use thereof, although he know not how many cubits high it is, or how wide it spreads, than he that can measure it, and count all its boughs, and neither owns it, nor knows or loves its Creator: so a believer, whose all this world of wealth is, and who having nothing, yet possesseth all things, by cleaving unto Thee, whom all things serve, though he know not even the circles of the Great Bear, yet it is folly to doubt but he is in a better state than one who can measure the heavens, and number the stars, and poise the elements, yet neglecteth Thee who hast made all things in number, weight, and measure.

(*The Confessions of Saint Augustine.*) [14]

From my first school year to my last I found intolerable those lesson-hours in which poems were taken and treated. That a poem should be brought nearer to me by being explained I felt to be something hateful and silly. The talk about it did nothing but destroy in me the feeling of being possessed by the work of the poet. A poem, I felt, and so I feel still, does not need to be explained; it must be felt, be experienced. Consequently in these lessons I was a very inattentive scholar, yes, even a scholar in opposition. Instead of following the lesson, I read here, there, and everywhere in the reading-book, and intoxicated myself, without a guide, in those poems and extracts which I found most attractive. I had a feeling of having shut my shop-windows so as to keep out the noise in the streets.

(ALBERT SCHWEITZER, *Memoirs of Childhood and Youth.*) [15]

April 7, 1866.— If philosophy is the art of understanding it is evident that it must begin by saturating itself with facts and realities, and that premature abstraction kills it, just as the abuse of fasting destroys the body at the age of growth. Besides, we only understand that which is already within us. To understand is to possess the thing understood, first by sympathy and then by intelligence. Instead, then, of first dismembering and dissecting the object to be conceived, we should begin by laying hold of it in its *ensemble*, then in its formation, last of all in its parts. The procedure is the same, whether we study a watch or a plant, a work of art or a character. We must study, respect, and question what we want to know, instead of massacring it. We must assimilate ourselves to things and surrender ourselves to them; we must open our minds with docility to their influence, and steep ourselves in their spirit and their distinctive form, before we offer violence to them by dissecting them.

(*Amiel's Journal.*) [16]

SCIENTIFIC INQUIRY: THE TRANSACTIONAL PERSPECTIVE

Scientific inquiry, just as any other inquiry, is undertaken to solve a problem. The scientist's purpose is to increase his understanding of a certain range of phenomena. When he meets a hitch or obstacle to his understanding, he attempts to formulate intellectual concepts which will explain away the problem. He abstracts out of the total situation those aspects except for which, in his judgment, the problem would not exist. Before a problem can be transmuted into experimentally verifiable hypotheses, it is necessary to make a judgment concerning the relevant variables. The variables selected will depend upon the particular way in which the problem has been formulated.

Sometimes the most important step in scientific inquiry—creatively formulating the problem for scientific investigation—is overlooked. Einstein and Infeld have pointed out that "the formulation of a problem is often more essential than its solution, which may be merely a matter of mathematical or experimental skill. To raise new questions, new possibilities, to regard old problems from a new angle, requires creative imagination and marks real advance in science." [17] Unless a problem is so formulated that its investigation affords the possibility of going beyond what is already scientifically established, succeeding steps in scientific inquiry are barren and futile.

The Greek historian Polybius (201–120 B.C.) observed that "in their proverb 'The starting point is half the whole,' the Ancients recommended the payment of the utmost attention in any given case to the achievement of a good start; and what is commonly regarded as an exaggerated statement on their part really errs, in my opinion, by falling short of the truth. It may be asserted with confidence that the starting point is not 'half the whole' but that it extends right to the end. It is quite impossible to make a good start in anything without, in anticipation, mentally embracing the completion of the project or realizing in what sphere and to what purpose and for what reason the action is projected. It is equally impossible adequately to summarize any given course of events without, in the process, referring to the starting point and showing whence and how and why that point has led up to the actual transactions of the moment. Starting points must accordingly be regarded as extending not merely to the middle but to the end, and the utmost attention ought, in consequence, to be paid to starting points by both writers and readers of Universal History." [18]

After the problem has been formulated, those relevant variables which seem most important are defined in such a way that they can be used as experimental variables. The next step is that of actual experimental design: working out methods for bringing the selected variables into relationships appropriate for the problem and selecting or devising techniques for manipulating the variables and interpreting the data. The experimental investigation is then carried through and scientific conceptualizations modified in the light of the experimental outcomes. The original problem can now be reformulated in the light of the new data and conceptualization, and the process of inquiry repeated. As pointed out before, the entire process of scientific inquiry is a self-correcting, never-ending one. [19]

Whitehead has noted that "no science can be more secure than the unconscious metaphysics which it tacitly presupposes." [20] It is obviously impossible to disclose that of which we are unaware. So we should try to spell out in some detail those presuppositions and postulates of which we are aware, with which we begin, and which shape our inquiry throughout. Postulations arise not only from a field of inquiry, but also as statements of conditions under which work is done or will be done within the field of inquiry. They are always open to re-examination.

The next set of passages is concerned, then, with what have been called the self-actional, interactional, and transactional levels or modes of observation and inquiry. The passages from Polybius, who seems to have used the exact equivalent of the term "transaction" over 2000 years ago, show what considerations led Polybius to describe his historical method as he did. The passages from Dewey and Bentley give the essential characteristics of the self-actional, interactional, and transactional modes of inquiry, while the succeeding excerpts reflect the spirit of the transactional view.

We might first illustrate what we mean by a story of three baseball umpires who were discussing their profession. The first one said, "Some's balls and some's strikes and I calls 'em as they is." The second one said, "Some's balls and some's strikes and I calls 'em as I sees 'em." While the third one said, "Some's balls and some's strikes but they ain't nothin' till I calls 'em."

> Little thinks, in the field, yon red-cloaked clown
> Of thee from the hill-top looking down;
> The heifer that lows in the upland farm,
> Far-heard, lows not thine ear to charm;

The sexton, tolling his bell at noon,
Deems not that great Napoleon
Stops his horse, and lists with delight,
Whilst his files sweep round yon Alpine height;
Nor knowest thou what argument
Thy life to thy neighbor's creed has lent.
All are needed by each one;
Nothing is fair or good alone.
I thought the sparrow's note from heaven,
Singing at dawn on the alder bough;
I brought him home, in his nest, at even;
He sings the song, but it cheers not now,
For I did not bring home the river and sky;—
He sang to my ear,—they sang to my eye.
The delicate shells lay on the shore;
The bubbles of the latest wave
Fresh pearls to their enamel gave,
And the bellowing of the savage sea
Greeted their safe escape to me.
I wiped away the weeds and foam,
I fetched my sea-born treasures home;
But the poor, unsightly, noisome things
Had left their beauty on the shore
With the sun and the sand and the wild uproar.
The lover watched his graceful maid,
As 'mid the virgin train she strayed,
Nor knew her beauty's best attire
Was woven still by the snow-white choir.
At last she came to his hermitage,
Like the bird from the woodlands to the cage;—
The gay enchantment was undone,
A gentle wife, but fairy none.
Then I said, 'I covet truth;
Beauty is unripe childhood's cheat;
I leave it behind with the games of youth:'—
As I spoke, beneath my feet
The ground-pine curled its pretty wreath,
Running over the club-moss burrs;
I inhaled the violet's breath;
Around me stood the oaks and firs;
Pine-cones and acorns lay on the ground;
Over me soared the eternal sky,

Full of light and of deity;
Again I say, again I heard,
The rolling river, the morning bird;—
Beauty through my senses stole;
I yielded myself to the perfect whole.

(RALPH WALDO EMERSON, *Each and All.*) [21]

. . . The Romans, on the other hand, subjected not merely a portion, but practically the whole of the habitable world, and founded a power of such pre-eminence that no contemporary could resist it and posterity could not hope to surpass it. It is the object of the present work to throw light upon this phenomenon,* and also to demonstrate the numerous and important advantages offered to serious students by the "transactional branch" ** of history.

. . . In previous periods the transactions of the habitable world took place in separate compartments, in which the projects attempted, the results attained, and the localities involved were unrelated. But from this date onward history acquires an organic character, the transactions of Italy and North Africa become involved with those of Hellas and Asia, and all the currents set toward a single goal.

. . . That mighty revolutionary, whose pawns are human lives, has never before achieved such an astonishing *tour de force* as she has staged for the benefit of our generation; yet the monographs of the historical specialists give no inkling of the whole picture, and if any reader supposes that a survey of the leading countries in isolation from one another, or rather, the contemplation of their respective local chronicles, can have given him an intuition into the scheme of the world in its general arrangement and setting, I must hasten to expose his fallacy. To my mind, the persuasion that an acquaintance with local history will give a fair perspective of the whole phenomenon is as erroneous as the notion that the contemplation of the *disjecta membra* of a once living and beautiful organism is equivalent to the direct observation of the organism itself in all the energy and beauty of life. I fancy that anyone who maintained such a position would speedily admit the ludicrous enormity of his error if the organism could be revealed to him by some magician who had reconstituted it, at a stroke, in its original perfection of form and grace of vitality. While the part may conceivably offer a hint of the whole, it cannot possibly yield an exact and certain

* The Greek text of this sentence is corrupt. [ED.]

** In Greek πραγματικός τρόπος—a technical term adopted if not coined by Polybius to characterize his own work. The substantive πράξεις from which πραγματικός is derived, is exactly equivalent to the word "transactions" as used by English historians a century ago. [ED.]

knowledge of it; and the inference is that the specialists have a singularly small contribution to offer toward a true understanding of world history. The study of general contacts and relations and of general resemblances and differences is the only avenue to a general perspective, without which neither profit nor pleasure can be extracted from historical research. (POLYBIUS OF MEGALOPOLIS [ca. 201–120 B.C.], translated by Arnold J. Toynbee.) [22]

With this much of introductory display let us now set down in broad outlines three levels of the organization and presentation of inquiry in the order of their historical appearance, understanding, however, as is the way with evolutions generally, that something of the old, and often much of it, survives within or alongside the new. We name these three levels, those of Self-action, Interaction, and Transaction. These levels are all human behaviors in and with respect to the world, and they are all presentations of the world itself as men report it. We shall permit ourselves as a temporary convenience the irregular use of hyphenization in these names as a means of emphasizing the issues involved in their various applications. This is comparable to a free use of capitalization or of quotation marks, and to the ordinary use of italics for stress. It has the particular value that it enables us to stress the inner confusions in the names as currently used.

Self-action: where things are viewed as acting under their own powers.

Inter-action: where thing is balanced against thing in causal interconnection.

Trans-action: where systems of description and naming are employed to deal with aspects and phases of action, without final attribution to "elements" or other presumptively detachable or independent "entities," "essences," or "realities," and without isolation of presumptively detachable "relations" from such detachable "elements."

These provisional characterizations will be followed in a later chapter by alternatives showing the variety of points of view from which the issues that are involved must be approached. The reader will note that, while names are given as if for the events observed, the characterizations are in terms of selective observation, under the use of phrasings such as "are viewed," "is balanced against," and "are employed." These are the two aspects of the naming-named transaction, for which a running exhibit is thus given, pending clarification as the discussion advances.

The character of the primitive stage of Self-action can be established easily and clearly by a thousand illustrations, past and present—all confident in themselves as factual report in their times, without suspicion of the way in which later generations would reduce them to the status of naïve and simple-minded guesswork.

For Trans-action at the latest end of the development we can show a clean status, not as assertion of its existence, but as a growing manner of observation of high efficiency at the proper time and place, now rapidly advancing to prominence in the growth of knowledge.

As for Inter-action, it furnished the dominant pattern of scientific procedure up to the beginning of the last generation. However, as a natural result of its successes, there grew up alongside it a large crop of imitations and debasements—weeds now ripe for the hoe. To avoid very possible misunderstandings, it is desirable to give a sub-classification of the main types of procedure that may from time to time present themselves as, or be appraised as, interactions. We find:

(*a*) Independently formulated systems working efficiently, such as Newtonian mechanics.

(*b*) Provisionally separated segments of inquiry given an inter-actional form for convenience of study, though with underlying recognition that their results are subject to reinterpretation in wider systems of description; such, for example, as the investigation of certain inter-actions of tissues and organs within the skin of an organism, while remembering, nevertheless, that the "organism-as-a-whole" transactionally viewed (with perhaps also along with it a still wider transactional observation of the "organism-in-environment-as-a-whole") must come into account before final reports are reached.

(*c*) Abuses of (*a*) such as often occurred when, before the Einstein development, efforts were made to force all knowledge under the mechanistic control of the Newtonian system.

(*d*) Grosser abuses much too common today, in which mixtures of self-actional "entities" and inter-actional "particles" are used to produce inter-actional explanations and interpretations *ad lib.*: as when selves are said to inter-act with each other or with environmental objects; when small portions of organisms are said to inter-act with environmental objects as in the traditional theories of sensation; when minds and portions of matter in separate realms are brought by the epistemologies into pseudo-interactional forms; or, probably worst of all, when a word's meaning is severed from the word's actual presence in man's behavior, like a sort of word-soul from a word-body.

(JOHN DEWEY and ARTHUR F. BENTLEY, *Knowing and the Known.*) [23]

To reduce the occasion for some of the ordinary forms of misunderstanding, and to avoid frequent reminder of them in the text, attention is now called to certain positions common in whole or in large degree to current epistemologies, psychologies, and sociologies. These are positions which are *not* shared by us, and which may *in no case* be read into our work whether pro or con by persons who wish properly to appraise it.

1. We employ no basic differentiation of subject *vs.* object, any more than of soul *vs.* body, of mind *vs.* matter, or of self *vs.* not-self.

2. We introduce no knower to confront what is known as if in a different, or superior, realm of being or action; nor any known or knowable as of a different realm to stand over against the knower.

3. We tolerate no "entities" or "realities" of any kind, intruding as if from behind or beyond the knowing-known events, with power to interfere, whether to distort or to correct.

4. We introduce no "faculties" or other operators (however disguised) of an organism's behaviors, but require for all investigation direct observation and usable reports of events, without which, or without the effort to obtain which, all proposed procedure is to be rejected as profitless for the type of enterprise we here undertake.

5. In especial we recognize no names that pretend to be expressions of "inner" thoughts, any more than we recognize names that pretend to be compulsions exercised upon us by "outer" objects.

6. We reject the "no man's land" of words imagined to lie between the organism and its environmental objects in the fashion of most current logics, and require, instead, definite locations for all naming behaviors as organic-environmental transactions under observation.

7. We tolerate no finalities of meaning parading as "ultimate" truth or "absolute" knowledge, and give such purported finalities no recognition whatever under our postulation of natural system for man in the world.

8. To sum up: Since we are concerned with what is inquired into and is in process of knowing as cosmic event, we have no interest in any form of hypostatized underpinning. Any statement that is or can be made about a knower, self, mind, or subject—or about a known thing, an object, or a cosmos—must, so far as we are concerned, be made on the basis, and in terms, of aspects of event which inquiry, as itself a cosmic event, finds taking place.

(JOHN DEWEY and ARTHUR F. BENTLEY, *ibid.*) [24]

> . . . How hard it is to set aside
> Terror, concupiscence and pride,
> Learn who and where and how we are,
> The children of a modest star.

Frail, backward, clinging to the granite
Skirts of a sensible old planet,
Our placid and suburban nurse
In SITTER's swelling universe.
How hard to stretch imagination
To live according to our station.
For we are all insulted by
The mere suggestion that we die
Each moment and that each great I
Is but a process in a process
Within a field that never closes;
As proper people find it strange
That we are changed by what we change,
That no event can happen twice
And that no two existences
Can ever be alike; we'd rather
Be perfect copies of our father,
Prefer our *idées fixes* to be
True of a fixed Reality.

(W. H. AUDEN, *New Year Letter*.) [25]

THE FIRST-PERSON POINT OF VIEW

If we are to understand human experiencing, we must first of all get descriptions of it. Experiencing is an event both private and personal: it can therefore only be fully accounted for when it is approached from the point of view of the person "having" the experience. Psychology, then, in addition to any other type of statement it may employ, must rely on statements made from the standpoint of the individual's own "reality-world," from the first-person point of view.

One may well ask: "If the event named 'experiencing' is private and personal, how can we be sure of communicating effectively with others, and how can science be social?" These are good questions and the answers are not easy. Experiencing, however, is not an isolated event, but typically occurs in conjunction with other behavioral events which can be perceived by others. Our overt behavior must be symbolic so that "meaning" can be conveyed to others. Still, as we shall see in a later chapter, every communication involves a good deal of guessing and a good deal of faith.

When a psychologist reports his work to his colleagues, what he does, essentially, is to make a prediction concerning what they will experience if they perform certain operations under certain conditions. Yet statements of this sort are not fully adequate for an understanding of experience. A psychologist, or any scientist, is of course also experiencing. When he makes operational statements, he abstracts from his own personal experience those aspects which he believes others can, under certain conditions, also experience. Any person, scientist or not, who talks about experiencing and perceiving as if he himself were not a participant in the experiential event, as if his perceiving were wholly "objective," is mouthing absurdities. The necessity of including first-person statements in a study of human experience will be emphasized and clarified in the next chapter. The following passages suggest the importance of taking into account the first-person view and indicate how recognition of the uniqueness of any individual's experience can help clarify misunderstandings among people, as well as misunderstandings about the nature of the "outside world."

Every reader reads himself. The writer's work is merely a kind of optical instrument that makes it possible for the reader to discern what, without this book, he would perhaps never have seen in himself.

(*The Maxims of Marcel Proust.*) [26]

When we wish to correct with advantage, and to show another that he errs, we must notice from what side he views the matter, for on that side it is usually true, and admit that truth to him, but reveal to him the side on which it is false. He is satisfied with that, for he sees that he was not mistaken, and that he only failed to see all sides. Now, no one is offended at not seeing everything; but one does not like to be mistaken, and that perhaps arises from the fact that man naturally cannot see everything, and that naturally he cannot err in the side he looks at, since the perceptions of our senses are always true.

(BLAISE PASCAL, *Pensées.*) [27]

A man who looks out of an open window never sees as much as a man who looks at a window that is shut. There is nothing deeper, more mysterious, more fertile, more murky or more dazzling than a window lit by a candle. What one can see in the light of day is always less interesting than what happens behind a pane of glass. In this black or lustrous pit lives life. Here life dreams, life suffers.

Beyond the wave-crests of the roofs I see a woman of mature age, already wrinkled, a poor woman who always stoops over something and never goes out. From her face, clothes and movements—from almost nothing at all—I have recreated this woman's story, or her legend, rather; and sometimes I narrate it to myself, weeping.

If it had been a poor old man, I would have recreated his legend just as easily.

And I go to bed, proud of having lived and suffered in others but myself.

Perhaps you will say to me: "Are you sure that your legend is true?" How does it matter what the reality outside of myself may be, if it has helped me to live, and to feel that I am, and what I am?

(CHARLES BAUDELAIRE, *My Heart Laid Bare
and Other Prose Writings.*) [28]

. . . Oedipus, for example, or Lear, or even Jesus or Gandhi—you could make a roaring farce out of any of them. It's just a question of describing your characters from the outside, without sympathy and in violent but unpoetical language. In real life farce exists only for spectators, never for the actors. What *they* participate in is either a tragedy or a complicated and more or less painful psychological drama.

(ALDOUS HUXLEY, *The Genius and the Goddess.*) [29]

These are really the thoughts of all men in all ages and lands, they are
    not original with me,
If they are not yours as much as mine they are nothing, or next to
    nothing.   (WALT WHITMAN, *Song of Myself.*) [30]

UNITED NATIONS, N. Y., March 24—To the average citizen of the Western world, the Secretariat building of the United Nations is a skyscraper—pure and simple. In Iran, it is a ship, and no nonsense about it.

This and like discoveries about Eastern reactions to Western symbols pose plenty of headaches these days for the production corps on the films, called "Screen Magazines," turned out regularly on various phases of United Nations activities. For instance:

An American working for the United States Information Service in Iran was approached recently by a native who reported that he had just seen three short films on the proceedings at the United Nations head-quarters in New York.

"What do the delegates eat?" asked the puzzled Iranian. . . .

Table-Sitting Mystifies Iranians

The American did a bit of interviewing. Iranian audiences, he learned, can conceive of only one reason why any group of people would spend hours sitting at a table—to dine. And they are mystified about the pro-fusion of documents they see served up at these photographed sessions, instead of steaming platters.

The nautical aspect of the Secretariat building is equally easy to grasp, once the train of Iranian thought is traced. Outside Teheran, most Iranians have never seen a building higher than two stories. Obviously, the monolith shown to them in films cannot possibly be a building. They have never seen a ship, either, but they have heard about them.

When the camera, based on the Long Island City side of the East River, was focused on the United Nations headquarters and showed vessels steaming past the building, recognition dawned. And since the soaring column of marble and glass in the background appeared to float upon the water, it was also, indisputably, another but queer kind of ship, Iranians thought.

Troubles of the film production crews do not end here, in their efforts to spread understanding throughout the world of what the United Nations is and what it does.

Substitutions Made

Take the problem of depicting the passing of time, in terms that popu-lations anywhere may grasp. For the Western world, it is merely a matter of a close-up of a clock dial, with the hands moving forward steadily. But millions in the Orient never have seen a clock. Therefore the "cut" order is given. Falling leaves are substituted, and the idea is conveyed.

There are manifold other traps for the unwary Westerner in his ap-proach to the East, the film makers can testify. Suppose they resort to a shot of an owl to suggest wisdom. Audiences in the East would be convulsed. For in the lands of the rising sun, the adage "as wise as an owl" has for centuries been reversed to "as stupid as an owl."

The harassed film men are meeting these hurdles as they come. Re-ports from their field representatives who have sat in with baffled East-ern audiences as the films were run off have given them decisive point-ers. It is clear now that three versions of each "Screen Magazine" are necessary—one for the Western world, one for the Middle East, and one for Southeast Asia.

For the latter two, the speed of the reels must be appreciably reduced. The pace of the normal film is much too fast for the population of these areas. Moreover, many objects that are commonplace to Westerners must be clipped as unrecognizable in the Middle and Far East.

U.N. Delegates Help

Fortunately, the film production unit has first-class help at hand. United Nations delegates from the countries concerned have responded readily to appeals for their help in editing the "Screen Magazines" for home consumption. Seated in the tiny preview theatre in the basement of the Secretariat, they scan the Western versions over and over, suggesting eliminations at this or that point and proposing the type of symbols that will be familiar and quickly grasped by their own people. It is slow work, but rewarding.

For the less literate, more primitive populations of the earth, the film men have abandoned motion pictures in favor of the slower, more rudimentary film strips.

Actually a modern version of the old "magic lantern," these slides, joined as a film, can be run off as slowly or rapidly as the operator desires. He has only to flip a tiny lever to move them forward or back, as he discourses on such popular themes as the proper method of planting any local crop or the correct way to bathe the baby. . . .

(KATHLEEN McLAUGHLIN, in the New York *Times,*
March 25, 1953.) [31]

A point made earlier should be re-emphasized. If we put our confidence in the transactional mode of inquiry, and if we believe that human living as human living is an indivisible process, how is it possible to increase our scientific understanding of human nature?

Obviously, experimentation is a test of formulation and requires abstracting the aspects to be investigated from the total situation. The psychologist is faced with the task of intellectualizing the reasons why man's experience and behavior are what they are. This task involves abstractions and concepts the psychologist creates. Since he must dissect the total process of living in order to gain a toe hold for understanding, it is important that he be aware how many steps his abstractions are removed from his first-order data.

The abstracted variables which the psychologist uses do not exist in their own right as independent, God-given entities, and he must be careful not to reify anything as an entity simply because it has been given a proper name. In designing experimental situations, it is disastrous to leave out the "subjective" variables involved in normal experiencing, and the psychologist must be on his guard not to do so lest his experimental results have little significance. Recognizing these difficulties, the best procedure would seem to be to begin with first-person examinations of concrete transactions of living for the purpose of identifying as far as possible all the characteristics of the transaction *except for which* it would not be what it is. These abstracted aspects may *then* serve as, or suggest, manipulable experimental variables to be investigated in terms of their interdependencies and particular modes of participation in the total situation.

Abstracting, conceptualizing, tearing asunder what appears to be united and interdependent is an indispensable feature of scientific inquiry—necessary and fruitful if carefully and wisely done. The next passages emphasize the necessity for, and the limitations and functions of, abstractions, concepts, and theories for the scientific enterprise, and for thinking in general.

The advantage of confining attention to a definite group of abstractions is that you confine your thoughts to clear-cut definite things, with clear-cut definite relations. Accordingly, if you have a logical head, you can deduce a variety of conclusions respecting the relationships between these abstract entities. Furthermore, if the abstractions are well-founded, that is to say, if they do not abstract from everything that is important in experience, the scientific thought which confines itself to these abstractions will arrive at a variety of important truths relating to our experience of nature. We all know those clear-cut trenchant intellects, immovably encased in a hard shell of abstractions. They hold you to their abstractions by the sheer grip of personality.

The disadvantage of exclusive attention to a group of abstractions, however well-founded, is that, by the nature of the case, you have abstracted from the remainder of things. In so far as the excluded things are important in your experience, your modes of thought are not fitted to deal with them. You cannot think without abstractions; accordingly, it is of the utmost importance to be vigilant in critically revising your *modes* of abstraction. It is here that philosophy finds its niche as essential to the healthy progress of society. It is the critic of abstractions. A civilisation which cannot burst through its current abstractions is doomed to sterility after a very limited period of progress. An active school of philosophy is quite as important for the locomotion of ideas, as is an active school of railway engineers for the locomotion of fuel.

(ALFRED NORTH WHITEHEAD, *Science and the Modern World*.) [32]

1. Theories are not final because, though they must fit the facts approximately, they serve to change the facts, not only by making it possible to discover new facts which must then be taken into account, but by modifying what we conceive to be a fact. For a fact is not a thing or event, it is a statement about a thing or event, and it is impossible, or nearly so, to make a statement without implying some theory of events—what is "important," for instance. Thus every statement of fact is an abstraction. It refers to some aspect only of events. Take the fact that "John Doe paid Richard Roe ten dollars." This refers to an event (or series of events). It might be possible to write two pages of facts about that event but most of them would be entirely without interest. Yet if you will listen to the court evidence when there is litigation about whether John Doe paid Richard Roe, you will find that some of the uninteresting facts in these supposed two pages suddenly have become very interesting and important. However, no one by the most extended statement conceivably possible for a human being could completely describe this event.

The observed aspects of things or events about which statements of fact are made are called phenomena. Thus a fact is a statement of an idea, something conceived in the mind, about a phenomenon, an observed aspect of a thing or event. Such an idea is also known as a concept. Thus theories are made up of concepts as statements of fact and must fit the concepts that are "current," "accepted," or "established," depending upon the level of discourse. Ordinarily, however, we do not use the word "concept" to cover a simple idea about a detail or "single" event.

The kind of facts just discussed are "concrete." They concern us in the ordinary routine of life. They are what workmen use, and what clerks handling vouchers are occupied with. Executives have relatively little to do with them, but hate to admit it except when in the mood to say they "can't be bothered with detail."

2. A statement of fact may be not only what we conceive to be a thing or single event, but about a whole collection of events regarded with respect to a particular aspect of them. This general fact is an aggregate of many similar facts. "A million men voted yesterday" is such a fact. This also is a concept but a more "dignified" one than those relat-

ing to "simple" facts." Poincaré said that all generalization is a hypothesis.* It can only be stated on the basis of inference from complex
evidence largely indirect. No one ever saw a million men vote or even
more than a very small fraction of that number voting. What a million
men did depends upon what you mean by man (it does not in this case
include boy, for example, but may include women), what you mean by
voting (are "repeaters" included or excluded?), and many other things,
such as "who said so?" Thus this fact is constructed from ordinary facts
observable by individuals, with the aid of an elaborate theory or set of
theories. It is a fact secured by evidence, the validity of which is determined by some theory.

These are the facts of a kind which chiefly concerns executives. They
often like to believe them concrete, for "facts are facts." The more positively we believe a generalization to be true, the more "real," the more
"concrete" the fact seems to be. To the man who won the election of a
million votes it is a very concrete event. Still he hopes it will not be
necessary "to go behind the returns."

3. There are other ideas or concepts which are not facts in the sense
that they can be directly inferred from evidence of observation and
theory, but which are products of general knowledge, theories, experience, the sense of things, imagination. They are constructed out of whole
cloth, as it were, though not arbitrarily and with no reference to experience, to help give an explanation, that is, to help make a theory. They
are likely to be deemed good if the theory works, that is, if the theory
explains particular and general facts satisfactorily. The question whether
such concepts are true or false often makes no sense, and as to some of
the most useful it can be asserted that they never can be proven true
or false.** Their function is to organize ideas and facts. This is the
kind of thing I mean by "concept" or "construct" in *The Functions*.

The use of such concepts or leading ideas is to furnish the framework
of a theory, that is, a workable explanation of a vast number of facts.
It is necessary to have such a framework to get "basing points," as it
were, some place to start getting order out of bewildering chaos and
to have enough rigidity—"consistency"—to keep things in order long
enough at least to consider them. It is necessary to have more than one
such concept to make a theory. If the reader will regard a fundamental
concept as merely an important way of looking at things, he will understand that a complex set of facts requires more than one way of looking

---

* H. Poincaré, "Science and Hypothesis" in *The Foundations of Science* (New
York, The Science Press, 1929), p. 133.
** H. Poincaré, *passim*.

at things—different angles of view, more than one dimension. I call a set of fundamental concepts furnishing the framework of a theory a "conceptual scheme." It is not complete. Like most such things, this conceptual scheme will have to evolve in the process of using what we have.

Fundamental concepts may be regarded as of two kinds: those which are structural, and those which are dynamic. The first relates to general aspects of the subject that are relatively stable, fixed. The dynamic kind relates to the general ideas as to "how it works," of movement or change. The distinction is more or less arbitrary but convenient. Thus in the theory of the human body structural concepts make up the science of anatomy, and dynamic concepts relate to physiology, notwithstanding that the structural parts of the body are always changing, and much of the physiology may be regarded as comparatively stable—circulation of the blood, for example. In social matters I look upon the structural concepts as stable in the sense that a whirlpool is stable. They are statements of stable relationships between incessantly successive series of acts giving a sense, a feeling, of something fixed.

(CHESTER I. BARNARD, *Organization and Management.*) [33]

The intellectual is constantly betrayed by his own vanity. God-like, he blandly assumes that he can express everything in words; whereas the things one loves, lives, and dies for are not, in the last analysis, completely expressible in words. To write or to speak is almost inevitably to lie a little. It is an attempt to clothe an intangible in a tangible form; to compress an immeasurable into a mold. And in the act of compression, how Truth is mangled and torn! The writer is the eternal Procrustes who must fit his unhappy guests, his ideas, to his set bed of words. And in the process, it is inevitable that the ideas have their legs chopped off, or pulled out of joint, in order to fit the rigid frame.

(ANNE MORROW LINDBERGH, *The Wave of the Future.*) [34]

We go ahead now with an attempt to conceptualize the process of human living, guided by clues from the humanist as well as from the transactional mode of scientific inquiry. Let us consider first the process of perceiving.

2

Man and the World
Around Him*

|| "We make objective what fer-
|| ments in us."   —AMIEL

Even the simplest conceivable occasion of living appears to be tremendously complicated when we stop to think about it. In describing or talking about experience, everything needs to be said at once because of the complex interdependencies involved. Yet one is forced to consider one aspect at a time, reserving the right to discuss its functional role in the total process at some later time.

Perhaps the most obvious distinction which can be made within the process of living is that between knowing and doing. Man is a knower and a doer, an experiencer and a behaver. Although somewhat arbitrary, this distinction seems to be a reasonable and sensible one. For living would not be living if we could experience and know but were unable to act; or, on the other hand, if we could act but not experience the consequences of action or know in what terms to act. Living is knowing-doing and doing-knowing if it is living at all. And yet the distinction between experiencing and behaving is useful; it "rings true" to our common sense and it is

* Notes to this chapter begin on p. 329.

31

necessary for the scientist to abstract "subprocesses" for investigation, even if it tears apart interdependent, intertwining aspects of living.

Our concern here is with the aspect of living we call perceiving, and the interdependent relationship of perceiving to other aspects of living.

Every waking moment involves perceiving, and perceiving never occurs independently of other related processes. The take-off point for scientific investigation must always be perceiving as it is encountered in concrete, real-life situations. Of course, the psychologist must abstract perceiving from the total on-going situation for purposes of investigation, and he must sometimes investigate perceiving under abnormal conditions.

From our knowledge of perceiving up to now, it appears that it has the following major characteristics: (1) the facts of perceiving always show up in concrete situations which include a specific individual participant with a unique personal history who is functioning from a unique space-time position; (2) perceiving constructs for the individual his outside world of objects which he tends to believe exists in its own right and independently of his participation in the transactions of living. By constructing an outside world the process of perceiving simultaneously differentiates the *I* from the *not-I*, the self from the not-self.

While perceiving is always a function of the unique person, the participant, certain aspects of experiential events tend to be attributed to something external to ourselves. The outside world as we experience it—objects, people, events and sequences of events, colors, sounds, tastes, etc.—are products of the perceptual process.

We consider perceiving as an aspect of living through which each individual participates in constructing from his own experience a reality-world in and through which he strives to carry out his purposes and achieve his satisfactions. This functional definition tells us something about the role played by perceiving in living, but it reveals little concerning the process itself, the difficulties involved in studying perceiving, the important variables within the process, or how perceiving develops. Later sections of this chapter deal with these matters.

The following passages illustrate some of the characteristics of perceiving and set the stage for further consideration of its nature and significance.

> This life's five windows of the soul
> Distorts the Heavens from pole to pole,
> And leads you to believe a lie
> When you see with, not thro', the eye
> That was born in a night, to perish in a night,
> When the soul slept in the beams of light.
> (WILLIAM BLAKE, "The Everlasting Gospel.") [1]

These sensations are projected by the mind so as to clothe appropriate bodies in external nature. Thus the bodies are perceived as with qualities which in reality do not belong to them, qualities which in fact are purely the offspring of the mind. Thus nature gets credit which should in truth be reserved for ourselves: the rose for its scent: the nightingale for his song: and the sun for his radiance. The poets are entirely mistaken. They should address their lyrics to themselves, and should turn them into odes of self-congratulation on the excellency of the human mind. Nature is a dull affair, soundless, scentless, colourless; merely the hurrying of material, endlessly, meaninglessly.

(ALFRED NORTH WHITEHEAD, *Science and the Modern World*.) [2]

Our natural tendency is to adjust all our representations, to test them by comparison with reality, and to render them free from contradiction. This is the most natural and obvious method, and it appears to be the only way of advancing a scientific theory of knowledge. This would hold true even if our mental constructs were direct reflections of reality. But the customary modes and results of thought already contain so many subjective and fictional elements that it is not surprising if thought also strikes out along other lines. It must be remembered that the object of the world of ideas as a whole is not the portrayal of reality—this would be an utterly impossible task—but rather to provide us with an *instrument for finding our way about more easily in this world*. Subjective processes of thought inhere in the entire structure of cosmic phenomena. They represent the highest and ultimate results of organic development, and the world of ideas is the fine flower of the whole cosmic process; but for that very reason it is not a copy of it in the ordinary sense. Logical processes are a part of the cosmic process and have as their more immediate object the preservation and enrichment of the life of organisms; they should serve as instruments for enabling them to attain to a more complete life; they serve as intermediaries between living beings. The world of ideas is an edifice well calculated to fulfil this purpose; but to regard it for that reason as a copy is to indulge in a hasty and unjustifiable comparison. Not even elementary sensations are copies of reality; they are rather mere gauges for measuring the changes in reality.   (HANS VAHINGER, *The Philosophy of "As If."*) [3]

And now, I said, let me show in a figure how far our nature is enlightened or unenlightened:—Behold! human beings living in an underground den, which has a mouth open toward the light and reaching all along the den; here they have been from their childhood, and have their legs and necks chained so that they cannot move, and can only see before them, being prevented by the chains from turning round their heads. Above and behind them a fire is blazing at a distance, and between the fire and the prisoners there is a raised way; and you will see, if you look, a low wall built along the way, like the screen which marionette players have in front of them, over which they show the puppets.

I see.

And do you see, I said, men passing along the wall carrying all sorts of vessels, and statues and figures of animals made of wood and stone and various materials, which appear over the wall? Some of them are talking, others silent.

You have shown me a strange image, and they are strange prisoners.

Like ourselves, I replied; and they see only their own shadows, or the shadows of one another, which the fire throws on the opposite wall of the cave?

True, he said; how could they see anything but the shadows if they were never allowed to move their heads?

And of the objects which are being carried in like manner they would only see the shadows?

Yes, he said.

And if they were able to converse with one another, would they not suppose that they were naming what was actually before them? *

Very true.

And suppose further that the prison had an echo which came from the other side, would they not be sure to fancy when one of the passers-by spoke that the voice which they heard came from the passing shadow?

No question, he replied.

[* The text is uncertain: The meaning may be "would they not suppose what they saw to be the real things?" G.]

To them, I said, the truth would be literally nothing but the shadows of the images.

That is certain.

And now look again, and see what will naturally follow if the prisoners are released and disabused of their error. At first, when any of them is liberated and compelled suddenly to stand up and turn his neck round and walk and look toward the light, he will suffer sharp pains; the glare will distress him, and he will be unable to see the realities of which in his former state he had seen the shadows; and then conceive some one saying to him, that what he saw before was an illusion, but that now, when he is approaching nearer to being and his eye is turned toward more real existence, he has a clearer vision,—what will be his reply? And you may further imagine that his instructor is pointing to the objects as they pass and requiring him to name them,—will he not be perplexed? Will he not fancy that the shadows which he formerly saw are truer than the objects which are now shown to him?

Far truer.

And if he is compelled to look straight at the light, will he not have a pain in his eyes which will make him turn away to take refuge in the objects of vision which he can see, and which he will conceive to be in reality clearer than the things which are now being shown to him?

True, he said.   (*The Dialogues of Plato.*) [4]

Enquire of the philosophers, and they will tell you that this matter of perception is still more, indeed desperately complicated. They may even assure you that there is no such thing as pure perception, that it has no story of its own to tell, that it is a part, and a part only, of that active and energetic faculty we call thought, and that it involves memory and anticipation, forethought and afterthought. You place a rose before a mirror. The mirror reflects the rose, but has no knowledge of it, is not even aware of it. Well, the eye has no more knowledge, no more awareness, no more consciousness of the rose than has the mirror. In a word, to separate the seen from the seer is allowed to be finally and utterly impossible. We are, as Niels Bohr expressed it, "both spectators and actors in the great drama of existence." For we must not think of thought as passive, as arising out of perceptions, as steam rises from heated water, but as an activity, a doing, a going out towards, as grasping and manipulating the data of sense. It is this activity, or energy which is at once the characteristic of mind and its chief mystery. The senses, then, do not give us knowledge. An active, inner principle, wholly independent of the senses is essential to the process of obtaining it.

(W. MACNEILE DIXON, *The Human Situation.*) [5]

Life holds hardly any interest except on the days when the dust of reality is mingled with magic sand . . . when some ordinary incident of life becomes a springboard for the imagination. Then a whole promontory of the inaccessible world rises from the mists of fancy and enters our life, where, like the awakened sleeper, we see the individuals of whom we had dreamed so ardently that we thought we should never see them except in dreams.   (*The Maxims of Marcel Proust.*) [6]

Once upon a time, in a kingdom by the sea, there lived a little Princess named Lenore. She was ten years old, going on eleven. One day Lenore fell ill of a surfeit of raspberry tarts and took to her bed.

The Royal Physician came to see her and took her temperature and felt her pulse and made her stick out her tongue. The Royal Physician was worried. He sent for the King, Lenore's father, and the King came to see her.

"I will get you anything your heart desires," the King said. "Is there anything your heart desires?"

"Yes," said the Princess. "I want the moon. If I can have the moon, I will be well again."

Now the King had a great many wise men who always got for him anything he wanted, so he told his daughter that she could have the moon. Then he went to the throne room and pulled a bell cord, three long pulls and a short pull, and presently the Lord High Chamberlain came into the room.

The Lord High Chamberlain was a large, fat man who wore thick glasses which made his eyes seem twice as big as they really were. This made the Lord High Chamberlain seem twice as wise as he really was.

"I want you to get the moon," said the King. "The Princess Lenore wants the moon. If she can have the moon, she will get well again."

"The moon?" exclaimed the Lord High Chamberlain, his eyes widening. This made him look four times as wise as he really was.

"Yes, the moon," said the King. "M-o-o-n, moon. Get it tonight, tomorrow at the latest."

The Lord High Chamberlain wiped his forehead with a handkerchief and then blew his nose loudly. "I have got a great many things for you in my time, your Majesty," he said. "It just happens that I have with me a list of the things I have got for you in my time." He pulled a long scroll of parchment out of his pocket. "Let me see, now." He glanced at the list, frowning. "I have got ivory, apes, and peacocks, rubies, opals, and emeralds, black orchids, pink elephants, and blue poodles, gold bugs, scarabs, and flies in amber, hummingbirds' tongues, angels' feathers, and unicorns' horns, giants, midgets, and mermaids, frankincense, ambergris, and myrrh, troubadors, minstrels, and dancing women, a pound of butter, two dozen eggs, and a sack of sugar—sorry, my wife wrote that in there."

"I don't remember any blue poodles," said the King.

"It says blue poodles right here on the list, and they are checked off with a little check mark," said the Lord High Chamberlain. "So there must have been blue poodles. You just forget."

"Never mind the blue poodles," said the King. "What I want now is the moon."

"I have sent as far as Samarkand and Araby and Zanzibar to get things for you, your Majesty," said the Lord High Chamberlain. "But the moon is out of the question. It is 35,000 miles away and it is bigger than the room the Princess lies in. Furthermore, it is made of molten copper. I cannot get the moon for you. Blue poodles, yes; the moon, no."

The King flew into a rage and told the Lord High Chamberlain to leave the room and to send the Royal Wizard to the throne room.

The Royal Wizard was a little, thin man with a long face. He wore a high red peaked hat covered with silver stars, and a long blue robe covered with golden owls. His face grew very pale when the King told him that he wanted the moon for his little daughter, and that he expected the Royal Wizard to get it.

"I have worked a great deal of magic for you in my time, your Majesty," said the Royal Wizard. "As a matter of fact, I just happen to have in my pocket a list of the wizardries I have performed for you." He drew a paper from a deep pocket of his robe. "It begins: 'Dear Royal Wizard: I am returning herewith the so-called philosopher's stone which you claimed—' no, that isn't it." The Royal Wizard brought a long scroll of parchment from another pocket of his robe. "Here it is," he said. "Now, let's see. I have squeezed blood out of turnips for you, and turnips out of blood. I have produced rabbits out of silk hats, and silk hats out of rabbits. I have conjured up flowers, tambourines, and doves out of nowhere, and nowhere out of flowers, tambourines, and doves. I have brought you divining rods, magic wands, and crystal spheres in which to behold the future. I have compounded philters, unguents, and potions, to cure heartbreak, surfeit, and ringing in the ears. I have made you my own special mixture of walkbane, nightshade, and eagles' tears, to ward off witches, demons, and things that go bump in the night. I have given you seven league boots, the golden touch, and a cloak of invisibility—"

"It didn't work," said the King. "The cloak of invisibility didn't work."

"Yes, it did," said the Royal Wizard.

"No, it didn't," said the King. "I kept bumping into things, the same as ever."

"The cloak is supposed to make you invisible," said the Royal Wizard. "It is not supposed to keep you from bumping into things."

"All I know is, I kept bumping into things," said the King.

The Royal Wizard looked at his list again. "I got you," he said, "horns from Elfland, sand from the Sandman, and gold from the rainbow. Also a spool of thread, a paper of needles, and a lump of beeswax—sorry, those are things my wife wrote down for me to get her."

"What I want you to do now," said the King, "is to get me the moon. The Princess Lenore wants the moon, and when she gets it, she will be well again."

"Nobody can get the moon," said the Royal Wizard. "It is 150,000 miles away, and it is made of green cheese, and it is twice as big as this palace."

The King flew into another rage and sent the Royal Wizard back to his cave. Then he rang a gong and summoned the Royal Mathematician.

The Royal Mathematician was a bald-headed, nearsighted man, with a skullcap on his head and a pencil behind each ear. He wore a black suit with white numbers on it.

"I don't want to hear a long list of all the things you have figured out for me since 1907," the King said to him. "I want you to figure out right now how to get the moon for the Princess Lenore. When she gets the moon, she will be well again."

"I am glad you mentioned all the things I have figured out for you since 1907," said the Royal Mathematician. "It so happens that I have a list of them with me."

He pulled a long scroll of parchment out of a pocket and looked at it. "Now let me see. I have figured out for you the distance between the horns of a dilemma, night and day, and A and Z. I have computed how far is Up, how long it takes to get to Away, and what becomes of Gone. I have discovered the length of the sea serpent, the price of the priceless, and the square of the hippopotamus. I know where you are when you are at Sixes and Sevens, how much Is you have to have to make an Are, and how many birds you can catch with the salt in the ocean— 187,786,132, if it would interest you to know."

"There aren't that many birds," said the King.

"I didn't say there were," said the Royal Mathematician. "I said if there were."

"I don't want to hear about seven hundred million imaginary birds," said the King. "I want you to get the moon for the Princess Lenore."

"The moon is 300,000 miles away," said the Royal Mathematician. "It is round and flat like a coin, only it is made of asbestos, and it is half the size of this kingdom. Furthermore, it is pasted on the sky. Nobody can get the moon."

The King flew into still another rage and sent the Royal Mathematician away. Then he rang for the Court Jester. The Jester came bounding into the throne room in his motley and his cap and bells, and sat at the foot of the throne.

"What can I do for you, your Majesty?" asked the Court Jester.

"Nobody can do anything for me," said the King mournfully. "The Princess Lenore wants the moon, and she cannot be well till she gets it, but nobody can get it for her. Every time I ask anybody for the moon, it gets larger and farther away. There is nothing you can do for me except play on your lute. Something sad."

"How big do they say the moon is," asked the Court Jester, "and how far away?"

"The Lord High Chamberlain says it is 35,000 miles away, and bigger than the Princess Lenore's room," said the King. "The Royal Wizard says it is 150,000 miles away, and twice as big as this palace. The Royal Mathematician says it is 300,000 miles away, and half the size of this kingdom."

The Court Jester strummed on his lute for a little while. "They are all wise men," he said, "and so they must all be right. If they are all right, then the moon must be just as large and as far away as each person thinks it is. The thing to do is find out how big the Princess Lenore thinks it is, and how far away."

"I never thought of that," said the King.

"I will go and ask her, your Majesty," said the Court Jester. And he crept softly into the little girl's room.

The Princess Lenore was awake, and she was glad to see the Court Jester, but her face was very pale and her voice very weak.

"Have you brought the moon to me?" she asked.

"Not yet," said the Court Jester, "but I will get it for you right away. How big do you think it is?"

"It is just a little smaller than my thumbnail," she said, "for when I hold my thumbnail up at the moon, it just covers it."

"And how far away is it?" asked the Court Jester.

"It is not as high as the big tree outside my window," said the Princess, "for sometimes it gets caught in the top branches."

"It will be very easy to get the moon for you," said the Court Jester. "I will climb the tree tonight when it gets caught in the top branches and bring it to you."

Then he thought of something else. "What is the moon made of, Princess?" he asked.

"Oh," she said, "it's made of gold, of course, silly."

The Court Jester left the Princess Lenore's room and went to see the Royal Goldsmith. He had the Royal Goldsmith make a tiny round golden moon just a little smaller than the thumbnail of the Princess Lenore. Then he had him string it on a golden chain so that the Princess could wear it around her neck.

"What is this thing I have made?" asked the Royal Goldsmith when he had finished it.

"You have made the moon," said the Court Jester. "That is the moon."

"But the moon," said the Royal Goldsmith, "is 500,000 miles away and is made of bronze and is round like a marble."

"That's what you think," said the Court Jester as he went away with the moon.

The Court Jester took the moon to the Princess Lenore, and she was overjoyed. The next day she was well again and could get up and go out in the gardens to play.

But the King's worries were not yet over. He knew that the moon would shine in the sky again that night, and he did not want the Princess Lenore to see it. If she did, she would know that the moon she wore on a chain around her neck was not the real moon.

So the King sent for the Lord High Chamberlain and said, "We must keep the Princess Lenore from seeing the moon when it shines in the sky tonight. Think of something."

The Lord High Chamberlain tapped his forehead with his fingers thoughtfully and said, "I know just the thing. We can make some dark glasses for the Princess Lenore. We can make them so dark that she will not be able to see the moon when it shines in the sky."

This made the King very angry, and he shook his head from side to side. "If she wore dark glasses, she would bump into things," he said, "and then she would be ill again." So he sent the Lord High Chamberlain away and called the Royal Wizard.

"We must hide the moon," said the King, "so that the Princess Lenore will not see it when it shines in the sky tonight. How are we going to do that?"

The Royal Wizard stood on his hands and then he stood on his head and then he stood on his feet again. "I know what we can do," he said. "We can stretch some black velvet curtains on poles. The curtains will cover all the palace gardens like a circus tent, and the Princess Lenore will not be able to see through them, so she will not see the moon in the sky."

The King was so angry at this that he waved his arms around. "Black velvet curtains would keep out the air," he said. "The Princess Lenore would not be able to breathe, and she would be ill again." So he sent the Royal Wizard away and summoned the Royal Mathematician.

"We must do something," said the King, "so that the Princess Lenore will not see the moon when it shines in the sky tonight. If you know so much, figure out a way to do that."

The Royal Mathematician walked around in a circle, and then he walked around in a square, and then he stood still. "I have it!" he said. "We can set off fireworks in the gardens every night. We will make a lot of silver fountains and golden cascades, and when they go off, they will fill the sky with so many sparks that it will be as light as day and the Princess Lenore will not be able to see the moon."

The King flew into such a rage that he began jumping up and down. "Fireworks would keep the Princess Lenore awake," he said. "She would not get any sleep at all and she would be ill again." So the King sent the Royal Mathematician away.

When he looked up again, it was dark outside and he saw the bright rim of the moon just peeping over the horizon. He jumped up in a great fright and rang for the Court Jester. The Court Jester came bounding into the room and sat down at the foot of the throne.

"What can I do for you, your Majesty?" he asked.

"Nobody can do anything for me," said the King, mournfully. "The moon is coming up again. It will shine into the Princess Lenore's bedroom, and she will know it is still in the sky and that she does not wear it on a golden chain around her neck. Play me something on your lute, something very sad, for when the Princess sees the moon, she will be ill again."

The Court Jester strummed on his lute. "What do your wise men say?" he asked.

"They can think of no way to hide the moon that will not make the Princess Lenore ill," said the King.

The Court Jester played another song, very softly. "Your wise men know everything," he said, "and if they cannot hide the moon, then it cannot be hidden."

The King put his head in his hands again and sighed. Suddenly he jumped up from his throne and pointed to the windows. "Look!" he cried. "The moon is already shining into the Princess Lenore's bedroom. Who can explain how the moon can be shining in the sky when it is hanging on a golden chain around her neck?"

The Court Jester stopped playing on his lute. "Who could explain how to get the moon when your wise men said it was too large and too far away? It was the Princess Lenore. Therefore the Princess Lenore is wiser than your wise men and knows more about the moon than they do. So I will ask *her*." And before the King could stop him, the Court Jester slipped quietly out of the throne room and up the wide marble staircase to the Princess Lenore's bedroom.

The Princess was lying in bed, but she was wide awake and she was looking out the window at the moon shining in the sky. Shining in her hand was the moon the Court Jester had got for her. He looked very sad, and there seemed to be tears in his eyes.

"Tell me, Princess Lenore," he said mournfully, "how can the moon be shining in the sky when it is hanging on a golden chain around your neck?"

The Princess looked at him and laughed. "That is easy, silly," she said. "When I lose a tooth, a new one grows in its place, doesn't it?"

"Of course," said the Court Jester. "And when the unicorn loses his horn in the forest, a new one grows in the middle of his forehead."

"That is right," said the Princess. "And when the Royal Gardener cuts the flowers in the garden, other flowers come to take their place."

"I should have thought of that," said the Court Jester, "for it is the same way with the daylight."

"And it is the same way with the moon," said the Princess Lenore. "I guess it is the same way with everything." Her voice became very low and faded away, and the Court Jester saw that she was asleep. Gently he tucked the covers in around the sleeping Princess.

But before he left the room, he went over to the window and winked at the moon, for it seemed to the Court Jester that the moon had winked at him.   (JAMES THURBER, *Many Moons.*) [7]

Perceiving, then, is always a process which includes an actively participating unique person. Individuals will tend to have common perceptions to the extent that there is overlapping in their life histories, their purposes, or the situations in which they are pursuing their purposes. This makes communication and social activity possible.

Difficulties in the study of perceiving are manifold. The ever-presence of perceiving and its apparent naturalness tend to obscure basic problems hidden underneath. The belief that objects exist apart from us and independent of our transactions with them makes it tempting to say, "I see objects the way I do because that's the way they are." Another difficulty has already been mentioned—that perceiving is a strictly private affair and its study must be designed to recognize this fact. Even the scientist who studies perceiving is himself perceiving; he enters the transaction as a creative participant, not as a detached, wholly passive, "objective" spectator.[8]

SOME VARIABLES IN THE PERCEPTUAL PROCESS

The *trans*actional point of view differs from the more usual *inter*actional analysis of perceiving, an analysis which implies independent entities with an organism on one side and an objectively definable environment on the other with interaction occurring between the two. It also differs from the usual cause-and-effect analysis with its implication of independent entities and one-way relationships. Instead, "except-for" analysis is undertaken: we try to abstract out of any occasion of living all the essential factors of the total process, i.e., those *except for which* the process or event would not occur as it does. Each essential factor so abstracted is not regarded as the only cause, but merely as one aspect which makes a difference in the total process.

Some of the most important essential factors relevant to the study of perceiving are:

(1) A living, functioning unique *individual.*

(2) An *external environment,* not the environment as perceived, but as it is conceived by the physical scientists (e.g., physical objects with physical properties).

(3) *Impingements,* physical energies to which the organism has some sensitivity (e.g., light, sound, etc.).

(4) *Physiological excitation,* that is, actual stimulation of peripheral nerve endings and transmission of neural impulses within the nervous system, and other related organismic processes.

(5) *Awareness,* experience, or consciousness. This is difficult to define, but is directly "given" as far as the perceiver is concerned.

(6) *Unconscious factors,* such as beliefs, biases, fears, or aspirations which do not enter directly into the awareness of the perceiver, but which he is nevertheless taking account of. Furthermore, perceiving always seems to involve an unconscious process of weighing and choosing among a large number of cues which may often be contradictory.

(7) *Assumptions,* a psychological concept which refers to the effects of previous transactions as they have been "registered," modified, and brought forward through time, and participate in the present occasion.

(8) *Purpose,* another psychological concept which refers to an individual's conscious desire for or expectation of certain consequences of an action or series of actions.

(9) *Action,* which includes the effects of previous actions as they are reflected in assumptions, as well as contemplated future action.

THE PREDICTIVE FUNCTION OF PERCEIVING

A most important characteristic of perceiving is that our "awareness" is meaningful. To put it differently, perceiving is a process through which a particular person attributes *significances* to himself, to his immediate environmental situation, and to their relationship. This means that a central problem of investigation involves studying the correspondence between the significances we assume are "out there" and the significances actually encountered "out there" as we act to carry out our purposes. The process by which correspondence between these two sets of significances is approached or attained is of special importance. [9]

It is inconceivable that perceiving should serve no useful function in carrying forward the process of living, that it should be completely independent of and unrelated to other processes. Perceiving yields a world of outside objects, events, and people with characteristics and locations in space and time: this is our environment, the world in and through which behavioral events occur. Our actions reflect our perceptions. Our perception of a pencil lying on a desk two feet away provides us with a prediction, a prognostic directive, as to what probably will happen if we act in a particular way—that is, if we reach to pick up the pencil at the place where we perceive it to be.

Why have we said above "*probably* will happen"? Why not say "*certainly* will happen"? Most of us assume that for any given set of impingements on the organism (commonly called a stimulus configuration) there is no *one* set of external circumstances in terms of which this set of impingements must be accounted for. This is

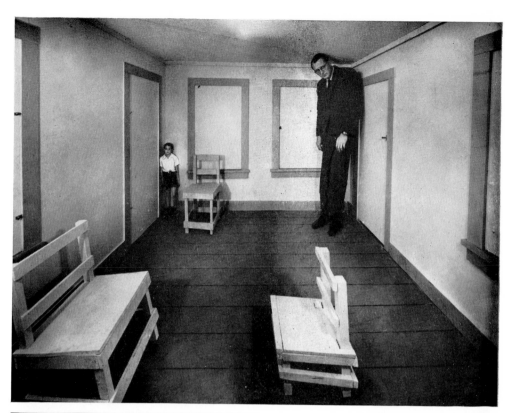

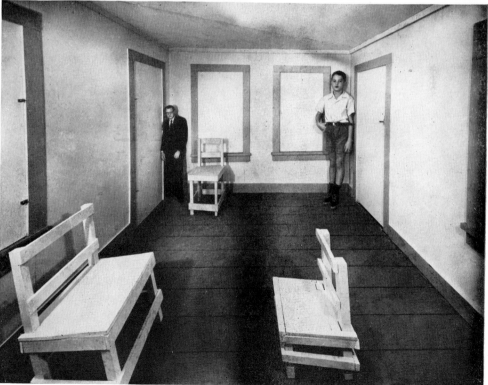

Photographs by Eric Schaal, courtesy LIFE Magazine. Copyright 1950 by Time Inc.

not true. Strictly speaking, various environmental circumstances can give rise to exactly the same pattern of impingements on the organism. For example, the distorted room shown is so constructed that each part subtends the same angle that would be subtended by the equivalent part of a common, cubical room when viewed with one eye from a certain point. One could build a great variety of distorted rooms that would seem normal in shape when one eye was at the prescribed observation point. A controlled experiment, utilizing two different distorted rooms and a normal, cubical room, has shown that people cannot tell the rooms apart and see nothing unusual in their appearance, even though the shapes of all three rooms have been described to them in advance.[10] Equivalence can also be demonstrated with binocular distorted rooms of different shapes and sizes when viewed with both eyes from the proper positions. Furthermore, evidence from investigations involving the so-called visual cues of size, brightness, overlay, parallax, binocular disparity, etc., point to the same conclusion.

It has also been shown that if a person is highly prejudiced against a certain race, then all people of that race will tend to look alike to him. Similarly, if a person has had very little experience with a certain kind of object or person, he may be unable to discriminate between objects or people of that kind. For example, one of the present writers some years ago was teaching a summer-school class in which there were three young ladies who had just come from China, and who seemed to him as alike as three peas in a pod. After the first lecture they came up and said, "Professor, you're a psychologist and we wonder if there is any way you can help us to tell one American from another, for they all look just alike to us."

Perceiving, then, can never be an absolute disclosure of reality; instead it reveals only a possibility, a "best bet" as to what and where the external objects are and what their characteristics are. What is perceived is somehow "chosen" from among almost limitless possibilities. Thus, the perceptual process operates selectively as a filter and the "best bet" seems to be based on the individual's unique past experience as it relates to his presently functioning purposes. Our "best bets" can only be tested through action. Our actions are successful (i.e., we are not surprised, disappointed, or frustrated) insofar as the significances which occur when we do act correspond to those occurring in the process of perceiving the situation.

No one knows, and no one is ever likely to know, what the characteristics are of the very first perceiving in which an unborn or newly-born human organism is a participant. It does not seem reasonable to suppose that the experienced world of the young infant is a big, booming, buzzing confusion, as William James believed. It is much more likely that the awareness of the infant, although not completely chaotic, is essentially meaningless and without significance. A baby's sense impressions are, perhaps, essentially like cryptograms which have no significance until they are caught up in a system which brings them into relation with behavioral events and gives them a functional role to play, or like the instrument panel of a modern airplane when seen by a person from a primitive land. Evidence indicates that the perceptual world and the purposeful behavior of the infant develop together, each expanding, limiting, and affecting the other as the child matures and carves out a world for himself in the process of experiencing–doing and doing–experiencing which constitute living. This point has been beautifully expressed by Martin Buber:

Every child that is coming into being rests, like all life that is coming into being, in the womb of the great mother, the undivided primal world that precedes form. From her, too, we are separated, and enter into personal life, slipping free only in the dark hours to be close to her again; night by night this happens to the healthy man. But this separation does not occur suddenly and catastrophically like the separation from the bodily mother; time is granted to the child to exchange a spiritual connexion, that is, *relation,* for the natural connexion with the world that he gradually loses. He has stepped out of the glowing darkness of chaos into the cool light of creation. But he does not possess it yet; he must first draw it truly out, he must make it into a reality for himself, he must find for himself his own world by seeing and hearing and touching and shaping it. Creation reveals, in meeting, its essential nature as form. It does not spill itself into expectant senses, but rises up to meet the grasping senses. That which will eventually play as an accustomed object around the man who is fully developed, must be wooed and won by the developing man in strenuous action. For no *thing* is a ready-made part of an experience; only in the strength, acting and being acted upon, of what is over against men, is anything made accessible. Like primitive man the child lives between sleep and sleep (a great part of his waking hours is also sleep) in the flash and counter-flash of meeting.[11]

The significances which constitute our perceiving, then, are a function of our past transactions as we have tried to carry out our purposes. They provide us with probabilities on the basis of which we may act in the future.

A CLASSIFICATION OF SIGNIFICANCES

No matter what the source of the significances, it may be useful to distinguish between certain classes of significances: (1) Thing, Object, or Person significances; (2) Sequential significances; (3) Action significances; (4) Evaluative significances.

The term "thing significances" refers to the world of objects and people as we experience them "out there," as possessing their own attributes and as occupying certain space-time positions. We tend to develop norms or standards (expectancies) concerning characteristic sizes, shapes, and other attributed properties of objects. The significances attributed to people have a special importance which we will consider in a later chapter concerned with our relationship to others.

The term "sequential significances" refers to the fact that we perceive events in a sequential relationship, where one event follows another: the brake pedal is pressed and the car slows down; the sun rises and it gets warmer; the switch is flipped and the light comes on. Perceiving is continuous and we are able to relate one perceived event to another. One important sequential significance is that of cause-and-effect: all of us tend, under certain circumstances, to attribute causal significance to some perceived events or objects which are spatially or temporarily proximate to other perceived events or objects. Thus, a stranger who has been seen at night near a store which was robbed during the night may be called up for questioning; a President of the United States is unlikely to be re-elected if his term of office coincides with a severe economic depression.

In order to increase the reliability of sequential expectancies, man has created artifacts—tools and devices of prodigious variety, which he tries to standardize so they will perform the same way in repeated instances. In order to enable persons to anticipate reliably sequences in social behavior, man has adopted norms, customs, rituals, and laws.

"Action significances" are a form of sequential significances, but their importance warrants placing them in a special category. For perceptual events which accompany and follow our own actions have special significance for us and for the process of perceiving. All of us build up sequential expectancies—"If I do this, that will happen"—which may or may not be confirmed when we act. By testing these assumptions or expectancies through action and modifying them accordingly, we come to participate more effectively in chains of sequential events related to our purposes.

The term "evaluative significances" calls attention to the fact that human beings, as they participate in the transactions of living, are often faced with alternatives between which they must choose. As we weigh possible courses of action, we evaluate them on the basis of the probability that each will bring forth the consequences we intend—that is, will result in certain satisfactions or help us avoid certain threats. This complicated process involves the weighing of subsidiary probabilities in each of the other classes of significances. For our satisfaction will depend on how accurately we have sized up the objects or people in the situation, how well we have guessed what the sequence of events will be, and how effective our action has been.

Some of our valuings involve choosing, among various ends that might be pursued, the one that will yield us the value-satisfactions we seek. Other valuings involve the selection, from among alternative routes, of a way to reach the goal that has been chosen. These two kinds of evaluative significances, their interrelationship, and their role in arriving at decisions, choices, or judgments will be considered more fully in chapter V.

Perceiving, then, provides us with significances which serve as predictions of further significances we will probably encounter as we act in and by means of the world around us. And the significances which occur in perceiving are often those which have been found through previous transactions to have been effective in furthering the pursuit of goals. Living results in a set of expectancies or assumptions, a sort of weighted average of the registered consequences of past transactions. These play a vital role in determining what significances occur in the present occasion. Perceiving is rooted in the past history of the individual participant and supplies prognostic directives for future action.

The following passages illustrate some of the points just discussed—the necessity of including a "first-person" approach in the study of perceiving, the role played by beliefs, assumptions and standards based on past transactions as they participate in present perceivings, the various classes of significances experienced, and the orientation of perceiving toward the future.

An objective fact, such as a sense impression, differs according to the psychological state in which one encounters it. And suffering is as powerful a transformer of reality as drunkenness.

(*The Maxims of Marcel Proust.*) [12]

I must be mad, or very tired,
When the curve of a blue bay beyond a railroad track
Is shrill and sweet to me like the sudden springing of a tune,
And the sight of a white church above thin trees in a city square
Amazes my eyes as though it were the Parthenon.
Clear, reticent, superbly final,
With the pillars of its portico refined to a cautious elegance,
It dominates the weak trees,
And the shot of its spire
Is cool, and candid,
Rising into an unresisting sky.
Strange meeting-house

Pausing a moment upon a squalid hill-top.
I watch the spire sweeping the sky,
I am dizzy with the movement of the sky,
I might be watching a mast
With its royals set full
Straining before a two-reef breeze.
I might be sighting a tea-clipper,
Tacking into the blue bay,
Just back from Canton
With her hold full of green and blue porcelain,
And a Chinese coolie leaning over the rail
Gazing at the white spire
With dull, sea-spent eyes.

(AMY LOWELL, "Meeting-House Hill.") [13]

The brain is wider than the sky,
  For, put them side by side,
The one the other will include
  With ease, and you beside.

The brain is deeper than the sea,
  For, hold them, blue to blue,
The one the other will absorb,
  As sponges, buckets do.

The brain is just the weight of God,
  For, lift them, pound for pound,
And they will differ, if they do,
  As syllable from sound.
(EMILY DICKINSON, "The Brain Is Wider than the Sky.") [14]

That which comes after always has a close relationship to what has gone before. For it is not like some enumeration of items separately taken and following a mere inevitable sequence, but there is a rational connection; and just as existing things have been combined in a harmonious order, so also all that comes into being bears the stamp not of a mere succession but of a wonderful relationship.
(MARCUS AURELIUS, *Communings with Himself.*) [15]

Master Pangloss . . . could prove to admiration that there is no effect without a cause, and in this best of all possible worlds the baron's castle was the most magnificent of all castles, and my lady the best of all possible baronesses.

"It is demonstrable," said he, "that things cannot be otherwise than they are; for as all things have been created for some end, they must necessarily be created for the best end. Observe, for instance, the nose is formed for spectacles; therefore we wear spectacles. The legs are visibly designed for stockings; accordingly we wear stockings. Stones were made to be hewn and to construct castles; therefore my lord has a magnificent castle; for the greatest baron in the province ought to be the best lodged. Swine were intended to be eaten; therefore we eat pork all the year round. And they who assert that everything is *right*, do not express themselves correctly; they should say that everything is *best*."
(VOLTAIRE, *Candide or the Optimist.*) [16]

How important our fantasies and expectations are for the right interpretation of danger is proved by the following incident during the last war. It happened on a beautiful summer afternoon in 1941 when I was playing tennis somewhere in Holland. Next to us German officers were playing the same game, dressed in the same kind of shirts and shorts. The only difference was the language, the German spoken with the harsh voices of our hated conquerors.

Suddenly, fighter planes of the R.A.F. came out of the sky, swooping low over the courts. We were cheering with our rackets, greeting our allies and eventual liberators. But our Nazi neighbors were gripped by panic; they threw themselves to the ground in a corner of the tennis field, until the danger had passed. For them it was the enemy, for us the friend, although the eventual objective danger was the same for all.

(JOOST A. M. MEERLOO, *Patterns of Panic.*) [17]

Facts are facts, nailed down, fastened to stay.
And facts are feathers, foam, flying phantoms.
Niagara is a fact or a little bluebird cheeping in a flight
   over the Falls—
Chirping to itself: What have we here?
               And how come?

The stone humps of old mountains
Sag and lift in a line to the sky.
The sunsets come with long shadowprints.
The six-cylinder go-getters ask:
   What time is it?
Who were the Aztecs and the
     Zunis anyhow?
   What do I care about Cahokia?
   Where do we go from here?
   What are the facts?

Facts stay fastened; facts are phantom.
An old one-horse plow is a fact.
A new farm tractor is a fact.
Facts stay fastened; facts fly with bird wings.
Blood and sweat are facts, and
The commands of imagination, the looks back and ahead,
The spirals, pivots, landing places, fadeaways,
The signal lights and dark stars of civilizations.

Now the head of a man, his eyes, are facts.
He sees in his head, as in looking glasses,
A cathedral, ship, bridge, railroad—a skyscraper—
And the plans are drawn, the blueprints fixed,

The design and the line, the shape written clear.
So fact moves from fact to fact, weaves, intersects.
Then come more, then come blood and sweat.
Then come pain and death, lifting and groaning,
And a crying out loud, between paydays.
Then the last ghost on the job walks.
The job stands up, the joined stresses of facts,
The cathedral, ship, bridge, railroad—the skyscraper—
Speaks a living hello to the open sky,
Stretches forth as an acknowledgement:
　"The big job is done.
　By God, we made it."
Facts stay fastened; facts fly with phantom bird wings.
　　　　　　　　(CARL SANDBURG, *Good Morning, America*.) [18]

　　The Vision of Christ that thou dost see
　　Is my vision's greatest enemy.
　　Thine has a great hook nose like thine;
　　Mine has a snub nose like to mine.
　　Thine is the Friend of all Mankind;
　　Mine speaks in parables to the blind.
　　Thine loves the same world that mine hates;
　　Thy heaven doors are my hell gates.
　　Socrates taught what Meletus
　　Loath'd as a nation's bitterest curse,
　　And Caiaphas was in his own mind
　　A benefactor to mankind.
　　Both read the Bible day and night,
　　But thou read'st black where I read white.
　　　　　　　(WILLIAM BLAKE, "The Everlasting Gospel.") [19]

CONSTANCY AND CHANGE IN PERCEIVING

All of us are aware that despite ever-changing impingements on
our sense organs our perceived world remains relatively constant
and stable. Although there are continual changes within the transactional relationship of person and environment, perceived objects
tend to remain the same in terms of their size, shape, color, and
other attributed properties. Obviously, unless the world in and
through which we behave were relatively constant and stable,
effective action would be almost impossible. It must be added,

however, that perceptual constancy is mediated through functionally effective behaving, since perceiving and behaving are inseparably related processes. In transactional inquiry, we must remember, perceiving and doing are treated as two abstracted aspects of an undivided, continuing process of living.

As already emphasized, an individual's present transaction is meaningful because of assumptions he brings to the situation. It is inevitable that his present world should be interpreted in terms of his world of the past. When relatively stable assumptions which have resulted from relatively stable, consistent, and effective behavior in similar past transactions function in a present transaction resembling the past, relative perceptual constancy must occur.

The usefulness of a high degree of constancy is undeniable. However, if nature never repeats exactly, if the only permanence is change, constancy cannot be absolute. Constancy and stability cease to have functional value as change occurs, as one participates in situations which are new. In this case, ineffective actions bring about alterations of assumptions which, in turn, tend to bring about new constancies more appropriate to the changes occurring. Thus, constancy is seen as an abstraction from continuity, both constancy and change being relative terms. In perceiving there is a never-ending process of preserving some constancy within change and some change within constancy.

Before ending this sketchy treatment of perceiving, one other matter should be mentioned. In the earlier part of this chapter, the external reference of perceiving was emphasized—that is, objects and people are experienced as "out there," apart from us. "Outthereness" implies a reference point; the "not-I" aspect of perceiving implies an "I" aspect; significance implies significance *to* or *for* someone. Thus, as we express the perceptual phase of our transactions we say, "*I* see a lamp," "*I* hear a bird singing," "*I* taste garlic in this salad," "If *I* kick him, he'll probably kick *me*," and so forth. Although perceiving is always oriented outward, an aspect of it also always has reference to the "I" or "self" as an active participant, whether expressed or not. Martin Buber was cognizant of the gradual emergence of the "I" aspect of perceiving when he wrote, ". . . the body maturing into a person was hitherto distinguished, as bearer of its perceptions and executor of its impulses, from the world round about. But this distinction was simply a juxtaposition brought about by its seeing its way in the situation, and not an absolute severance of *I* and its object. But now the separated *I* emerges, transformed. Shrunk from substance and fullness to a functional point, to a subject which experiences and uses, *I* approaches and takes possession of all *It* existing 'in and for itself,' and forms in conjunction with it the other primary word. The man who has become conscious of *I*, that is, the man who says *I-It*, stands before things, but not over against them in the flow of mutual action." [20]

Perceiving, then, includes not only a *thatness* (thing) at a *there-ness* (place) *now* (time) but also an *I-ness*, an aspect of awareness reflecting the internal organismic processes which are participating in the transaction. Most perceiving, however, is not very self-conscious; the "I" significance is not focal or prominent in awareness, but generally serves as a background for the more prominent object significances. Certain transactions, however, bring the "I" aspect of perceiving into the foreground of the total pattern of significances, as for example the high degree of self-consciousness which occurs in "stage-fright."

Practitioners of Yoga and others have reported that with practice at concentration one becomes unaware of any sense of effort and of any distinction between the "I" and the "not-I." Furthermore, there seem to be moments in the experience of every adult when there is complete unself-consciousness and perception in any ordinary sense disappears or merges into a sense of identification with a totality. The first of the following selections gives short excerpts indicating some of the teachings of Yoga concerned with banishing the usual distinction between the "I" and the outside world. The second selection, from *Amiel's Journal*, suggests that as death approaches "everything is within everything."

Section I

2. *Yoga* is the suppression of the transformations of the thinking principle. . . .
5. The transformations are five-fold, and are painful or not-painful. . . .
12. Their suppression is secured by application and non-attachment.
13. Application is the effort towards that state.

14. It stands on firm ground, when practised for a long time, without intermission, and with perfect devotion.

15. The consciousness of having mastered (every desire) in the case of one who does not thirst for objects perceptible or scriptural, is non-attachment. . . .

30. Disease, Dullness, Doubt, Carelessness, Sloth, Worldly-mindedness, False notion, Missing the point, and Instability, are the causes of distracting the mind, and they are the obstacles.

31. Pain, Despair, Nervousness, Inspiration, Expiration, are the accompaniments of the causes of distraction. . . .

Section II

6. The sense of being is the blending together, as it were, of the power that knows, with the instruments thereof. . . .

29. Forbearance, Observance, Posture, Regulation of breath, Abstraction, Contemplation, Absorption and Trance, are the eight accessories to *Yoga*. . . .

54. Abstraction is, as it were, the imitation by the senses, of the thinking principle, by withdrawing themselves from their objects.

55. Then follows the greatest mastery over the senses.

(M. N. DVIVEDI, *The Yoga-Sutras of Patanjali*.) [21]

February 15, 1881.—I have, very reluctantly, given up my lecture at the university, and sent for my doctor. On my chimney-piece are the flowers which —— has sent me. Letters from London, Paris, Lausanne, Neuchâtel . . . They seem to me like wreaths thrown into a grave.

Mentally I say farewell to all the distant friends whom I shall never see again.

February 18, 1881.—Misty weather. A fairly good night. Still, the emaciation goes on. That is to say, the vulture allows me some respite, but he still hovers over his prey. The possibility of resuming my official work seems like a dream to me.

Although just now the sense of ghostly remoteness from life which I so often have is absent, I feel myself a prisoner for good, a hopeless invalid. This vague intermediate state, which is neither death nor life, has its sweetness, because if it implies renunciation, still it allows of thought. It is a reverie without pain, peaceful and meditative. Surrounded with affection and with books, I float down the stream of time, as once I glided over the Dutch canals, smoothly and noiselessly. It is as though I were once more on board the *Treckschute*. Scarcely can one hear even the soft ripple of the water furrowed by the barge, or the hoof of the towing horse trotting along the sandy path. A journey under these conditions has something fantastic in it. One is not sure whether one still exists, still belongs to earth. It is like the *manes*, the shadows, flitting through the twilight of the *inania regna*. Existence has become fluid. From the standpoint of complete personal renunciation I watch the passage of my impressions, my dreams, thoughts, and memories. . . . It is a mood of fixed contemplation akin to that which we attribute to the seraphim. It takes no interest in the individual self, but only in the specimen monad, the sample of the general history of mind. Everything is in everything, and the consciousness examines what it has before it. Nothing is either great or small. The mind adopts all modes, and everything is acceptable to it. In this state its relations with the body, with the outer world, and with other individuals, fade out of sight. *Selbst-bewusstsein* becomes once more impersonal *Bewusstsein*, and before personality can be reacquired, pain, duty, and will must be brought into action.

Are these oscillations between the personal and the impersonal, between pantheism and theism, between Spinoza and Leibnitz, to be regretted? No, for it is the one state which makes us conscious of the other. And as man is capable of ranging the two domains, why should he mutilate himself? (*Amiel's Journal.*) [22]

As one participates in the transactions of living, assumptions concerning the self are formed as well as assumptions concerning the external world. These assumptions are all interrelated. A "self-image" takes form and characteristics are attributed to the self—talents, abilities, capacities, etc.—no matter what significances one may have in the transactions of others. One may hesitate to act in a situation in which the "out-thereness" significances are unambiguous but in which one perceives oneself as lacking the necessary capacity for coping with the situation. We might, then, further extend our tentative definitions of perceiving by saying that perceiving is the process through which a particular person attributes significances to his immediate environmental situation and to himself and to their relationship.

What has been said earlier with respect to the continuity, constancy, and stability of environmental significances applies equally to self-significances. Unless one's self-image, the characteristics one attributes to oneself, had some degree of constancy and stability, one's relationship with a constant environment could not possibly be effective. The following excerpts express the continuity and relative constancy of the self through long periods of time.

> His aging nature is the same
> As when childhood wore his name
> In an atmosphere of love
> And to itself appeared enough:
> Only now when he has come
> In walking distance of his tomb,
> He at last discovers who
> He had always been to whom
> He so often was untrue.
>   (W. H. AUDEN, "True Enough.") [23]

Having pried through the strata, analysed to a hair, counsell'd
  with doctors and calculated close,
I find no sweeter fat than sticks to my own bones.

In all people I see myself, none more and not one a barleycorn less,
And the good or bad I say of myself I say of them.

I know I am solid and sound,
To me the converging objects of the universe perpetually flow,
All are written to me, and I must get what the writing means.

I know I am deathless,
I know this orbit of mine cannot be swept by a carpenter's compass,
I know I shall not pass like a child's carlacue cut with a burnt stick
  at night.

I know I am august,
I do not trouble my spirit to vindicate itself or be understood,
I see that the elementary laws never apologise,
(I reckon I behave no prouder than the level I plant my house by,
  after all).

I exist as I am, that is enough,
If no other in the world would be aware I sit content,
And if each and all be aware I sit content.

One world is aware and by far the largest to me, and that is myself,
And whether I come to my own to-day or in ten thousand or ten
   million years,
I can cheerfully take it now, or with equal cheerfulness I can wait.

My foothold is tenon'd and mortis'd in granite,
I laugh at what you call dissolution,
And I know the amplitude of time.

(WALT WHITMAN, "Song of Myself.") [24]

Perhaps, then, both constancy and change refer to the related-ness of the self and the not-self, with action providing the concrete, operational definition of the relatedness. The outside world, the self, and their relationship manifest both constancy and change as they participate in the perceptual aspect of living.

A SUMMING UP

Here is a summary of the more important principles or proposi-tions which have emerged in this chapter.

(1) Perceiving is an abstracted aspect of the process of living. All perceiving, furthermore, is abstractive in nature.

(2) The facts of perceiving always present themselves in con-crete situations which include an actively participating individual with a unique history who is functioning within a unique space-time position.

(3) Perceiving constructs for the individual an outside world of objects, people, and events which he tends to believe exist in their own right independently of his participation. The process of per-ceiving also contributes to the construction of an "I" or self which is regarded as different from and independent of the outside world.

(4) Perceiving can never be an absolute disclosure of what "is." Rather, the significances which occur in perceiving are "best bets" based on the effects of past transactions as they relate to present purposes. The perceptual process operates selectively, choosing among the possibilities presented by the particular set of impinge-ments from outside.

(5) Two or more individuals can never perceive identically, and they perceive similarly only to the extent that the registered effects of their past transactions and present purposes are similar.

(6) There is a basic tendency to treat whatever is perceived as both concrete and absolute, despite its abstract and relative character. Yet this is necessary if rapid and effective action is to occur.

(7) Perceiving is neither an environmental event nor a personal event, but rather an aspect of the total person-environment transaction. The impingements and the externality play an indispensable role in the process by supplying a range of possible perceivings and the individual plays an indispensable role by functioning selectively within the range of possibilities.

* * *

Attention is always a function of intention. The selective operation of the perceptual process in choosing among the possibilities available must go on in terms of the relevance of the unique situation to the purposes and values of the experiencing individual. While present and past are involved in perceiving, its chief value comes from its orientation toward the future. Action cannot be instantaneous, and perceiving serves the function of predicting the future. Our purposive action serves as a test of the hypotheses furnished by our perceivings. We are motivated and behave in terms of the world as we perceive it, and the world as we perceive it is in large measure a product of our past and present motivations and behavior.

We turn, then, to a consideration of that abstracted aspect of living usually labeled "motivation." We shall be concerned with man's goals, with the abstracted and conceptualized aspects of the process of living which seem to account for man's ceaseless striving and for the fact that man's behavior appears to be directed and sustained through time and space in relation to an anticipated future. We are not leaving behind the perceptual aspect of living. We are merely shifting our attention to a related and interdependent aspect which must be taken into account if we are to understand the whole enterprise.

3

Man's Strivings:
Change within Order*

> "The struggle alone pleases us,
> not the victory."　　—PASCAL

As we experience our own behavior "from the inside," it generally seems more or less reasonable and necessary at the time. When we look back on some of the things we have done, they may appear to have been unfortunate or even ridiculous, yet at the moment of their occurrence they probably seemed to us to be the best things to do under what we thought were the limitations and opportunities of the circumstances. Otherwise we would have done something else. What we do is usually purposeful and relevant in terms of the total person-environment transaction of the moment as *we* see it.

Man feels that he is not a puppet, not pushed around and wholly enslaved by external forces, but he also feels that he cannot wholly escape their influence. Rather, within limits, he feels that he initiates, directs, and sustains his behavior in striving to achieve his goals. He therefore feels some responsibility for his own behavior. Man feels that he is often faced with alternatives—alternative goals or alternative means of achieving goals—and that he makes choices on the basis of which he acts.

What, then, do people strive for? What goals exist for human beings? At first glance it appears that human beings seek an almost infinite variety of objects, activities, or experiences, ranging from

---

* Notes to this chapter begin on p. 330.

food and water to houses and yachts, from friendship and recognition to political power and a peaceful world, from playing golf to climbing Mount Everest.

What we seek, as psychologists, is to abstract the common features of the bewildering variety of individual human purposes and decide what are the more fundamental aspirations and goals operative in each individual in every culture and at all times. Then some scheme can be erected within which the great diversity of human purposes may be seen as examples of more fundamental, universal human strivings.

One hypothesis holds that all living things strive to maintain their organization or their form in the face of internal and external disruptive agencies. The tendency of an organism to maintain its equilibrium and its physiological integrity has been called "homeostasis." [1] For example, the body tends to maintain a steady temperature and if this is upset self-regulating processes of the body tend to restore it to normal. Similarly, the alkalinity of the blood and the sugar concentration in the blood are restored to their usual levels if upset by vigorous exercise or other disruptive factors. If bodily welfare is threatened by bacterial attack, defensive and protective bodily processes are thrown into operation.

The concept of homeostasis has been an important and productive one for biologists and physiologists. But can it be extrapolated to man's psychological life? Some psychologists have accepted the concept of homeostasis and used it to explain all aspects of man's psychological life. At this level, it has been interpreted to mean that all behaving tends toward tension-reduction or that all behaving is understandable as an attempt to preserve not the physical organism, but the phenomenal self—that is, everything which an individual experiences as part of or characteristic of himself. From this point of view, every act of an individual is seen as designed either to restore the psychological "field" to a state of relative equilibrium through need-satisfaction, or to preserve or to fortify the individual's concept of himself.

This view of basic human motivation may seem plausible, for a great deal of human and animal behavior does seem to be an attempt to reach a state of relative equilibrium. Human beings seek to satisfy their felt needs, to overcome obstacles and frustrations, to solve problems, and to resolve doubts. And it may seem reasonable to interpret human strivings for fashionable clothes, for recognition, for social position, etc., as subsidiary purposes, contributing to the attainment or enhancement of self-respect and self-esteem.

Before examining this doctrine in more detail for its adequacy in accounting for the directionality and on-goingness of human behavior, some statements about human living written by non-psychologists who have keenly observed themselves and others may be helpful. The first of the following two groups of readings emphasizes the oppositions within human existence, while the second group is more especially concerned with the goals which human beings strive to attain. All of the selections, we feel, have implications for an intrinsically reasonable theory of motivation.

It has been borne in upon the simplest souls in all ages, as clearly as upon philosophers, that if a creative and beneficent principle is at work in the world, a destructive and apparently maleficent principle is also at work, equal in power, equal in the extent of its dominion. Save to the eye of faith the universe displays a dual personality, kindly and cruel, philanthropic and inhuman. If God is in evidence, Satan is also in evidence. Ormuz and Ahriman are in array against each other, the powers of light and darkness, of organisation and disorganisation, construction and destruction, health and disease, life and death. Who has not heard in the rhythm of nature the threatening note, the deep, disquieting roll of her thunder? There is terror in the world as well as beauty, horrors are mingled with its sublimities. It both captivates and alarms. Within the swirling vortex, the endless coming and going of events, within the circumference of the greater motions, the convulsions in the heavens and upheavals in the fevered earth, there are on the human level corresponding upheavals and convulsions, alarms and excursions, everlasting changes and perturbations.

> So between the starry dome
>   And the floor of plains and seas,
> I have never felt at home,
>   Never wholly been at ease.

Such is the world as we know it, and such the conditions of existence: nor can the most soaring imagination provide us with an alternative model, or even assure us of its possibility. Things as they are wear the countenance of fate, the unbending brow of necessity, and who are we to quarrel with the gods?

It has occurred to few philosophers that the discords may be a factor in the scheme, that the situation may have its advantages, a brighter side, and may be even a necessary condition of existence. They have seldom reflected that this clash of opposites may have brought it about that we have a universe at all, and that we ourselves, its offspring, are in being, that from this dark soil of conflict creation sprang. So far we may advance with assurance, the disharmony has at least banished an otherwise incurable and intolerable monotony. But for these oppositions in nature and human life, "the world-wide warfare of the eternal Two," nothing had taken place, all were still, sunk in a motiveless, motionless stagnation. The busy scene of events had been a desert of idleness. Movement implies resistance, high implies low, and light, darkness. If there be no East there is no West, if there be no North there can be no South Pole. There are good kind souls who suppose it possible to have good without evil. But liking involves disliking, and approval disapproval. The antithesis is everlasting and unavoidable. From the clash of opposites has arisen the world with all its varieties, its infinite diversity of creatures. They are our fathers and mothers, these Twain,

> . . . out of which Earth and Heaven were born.
> And from their mingling thence are poured abroad
> The multitudinous birth of mortal things,
> Knit in all forms, and wonderful to see.

In the tension of the opposites is the mainspring of the Cosmos, manifested in organic nature, as in all the circumstances and interests dispersed through the wide ways of men. Out of their great debate arise politics, art and philosophy, for the same duality is present in the central keep of the mind itself, where there is always "a pro and a con," in the conflicting thoughts, the bright and dark angels that sway the course of history. You meet the cut and thrust of these duellists in the collision of wills, the quarrels and animosities, the exchanges and repartees, the sinnerhoods and sainthoods. *Idem semper sentire, nihil sentire.* To feel always the same is to feel nothing. If all things were alike, all men alike, all thoughts alike, what pleasure, what interest, what anything could there be? As the harmonies of the painter or musician arise out of the blending of the colours and the notes, so the mixing and mingling of its elements give to the world its values. "All beings have souls," said the Italian mathematician, Cardan, "even in plants the passions of Love and Hate are at work." "Could differences be abolished sweet love were slain," as the Greek poet expressed it. And our own Blake put the matter also in a sentence. "Without Contraries is no progression. Attraction and Repulsion, Reason and Energy, Love and Hate are necessary to human existence."

(W. MACNEILE DIXON, The Human Situation.) [2]

By one of those eternal contrasts which redress the balance of things, the romance peoples, who excel in the practical matters of life, care nothing for the philosophy of it; while the Germans, who know very little about the practice of life, are masters of its theory. Every living being seeks instinctively to complete itself; this is the secret law according to which that nation whose sense of life is fullest and keenest, drifts most readily toward a mathematical rigidity of theory. Matter and form are the eternal oppositions, and the mathematical intellects are often attracted by the facts of life, just as the sensuous minds are often drawn toward the study of abstract law. Thus strangely enough, what we think we are is just what we are not: what we desire to be is what suits us least; our theories condemn us, and our practice gives the lie to our theories. And the contradiction is an advantage, for it is the source of conflict, of movement, and therefore a condition of progress. Every life is an inward struggle, every struggle supposes two contrary forces; nothing real is simple, and whatever thinks itself simple is in reality the farthest from simplicity. Therefore it would seem that every state is a moment in a series; every being a compromise between contraries. In concrete dialectic we have the key which opens to us the understanding of beings in the series of beings, of states in the series of moments; and it is in dynamics that we have the explanation of equilibrium. Every situation is an *equilibrium* of forces; every life is a *struggle* between opposing forces working within the limits of a certain equilibrium.

(Amiel's Journal.) [3]

The first time we ever saw a large, heavy airplane drop swiftly out of the sky for a landing, we thought the maneuver had an element of madness in it. We haven't changed our opinion much in thirty years. During that time, to be sure, a great many planes have dropped down and landed successfully, and the feat is now generally considered to be practicable, even natural. Anyone who, like us, professes to find something implausible in it is himself thought to be mad. The other morning, after the Convair dived into the East River, an official of the Civil Aeronautics Board said that the plane was "on course and every circumstance was normal"—a true statement, aeronautically speaking. It was one of those statements, though, that illuminate the new normalcy, and it encouraged us to examine the affair more closely, to see how far the world has drifted toward accepting the miraculous as the common-place. Put yourself, for a moment, at the Convair's controls and let us take a look at this day's normalcy. The speed of a Convair, approaching an airport, is about a hundred and forty miles an hour, or better than two miles a minute. We don't know the weight of the plane, but let us say that it is heavier than a grand piano. There are passengers aboard. The morning is dark, drizzly. The skies they are ashen and sober. You are in the overcast. Below, visibility is half a mile. (A few minutes ago it was a mile, but things have changed rather suddenly.) If your forward speed is two miles per minute and you can see half a mile after you get out of the overcast, that means you'll be able to see what you're in for in the next fifteen seconds. At the proper moment, you break out of the overcast and, if you have normal curiosity, you look around to see what's cooking. What you see, of course, is Queens—an awful shock at any time, and on this day of rain, smoke, and shifting winds a truly staggering shock. You are close to earth now, doing two miles a minute, every circumstance is normal, and you have a fifteen-second spread between what you *can* see and what you can't. What you hope to see, of course, is Runway 22 rising gently to kiss your wheels, but, as the passenger from Bath so aptly put it, "When I felt water splashing over my feet, I knew it wasn't an airport."

Airplane design has, it seems to us, been fairly static, and designers have docilely accepted the fixed-wing plane as the sensible and natural form. Improvements have been made in it, safety devices have been added, and strict rules govern its flight. But we'd like to see plane de-signers start playing with ideas less rigid than those that now absorb their fancy. The curse of flight is speed. Or, rather, the curse of flight is that no opportunity exists for dawdling. And so weather is still an enormous factor in air travel. Planes encountering fog are diverted to other airports, and set their passengers down hundreds of miles from where they want to be. In very bad weather, planes are not per-mitted to leave the ground at all. There are still plenty of people who refuse to fly simply because they don't like to proceed at two miles a minute through thick conditions. Before flight becomes what it ought to be, a new sort of plane will have to be created—perhaps a cross between a helicopter and a fixed-wing machine. Its virtue will be that its power can be used either to propel it rapidly forward or to sustain it vertically. So armed, this airplane will be able to face bad weather with equanimity, and when a pall of melancholy hangs over Queens, this plane will be seen creeping slowly down through the overcast and making a painstaking inspection of Runway 22, instead of coming in like a grand piano.

The above remarks on flying drew a fine letter from a T.W.A. captain. His observations reveal a man so well adjusted to this life that they deserve being published. It isn't every day that you encounter a serene personality, either on land or in the sky. The captain did not take exception to our rather sour view of heavier-than-air flight; he merely testified that the acceptance of aerial hazards made him feel "time-fitted" to his profession and "apt to our second of history." (Stylist as well as pilot.)

> To move at a high rate of speed; to feel less secure the closer I come to earth and man; to be able to look ahead with some certainty for 15 seconds;—these factors characterize life in the world today. For most people this constitutes a constant hardship, including rebellion and fretfulness against life. I suspect that by not merely accepting an unforeseeable future, but by building it into my life I may come closer to living a "normal" 20th-century life than those who must still struggle against it.

Well, there you have birdman and philosopher rolled into one—the contemplative pilot, full of semicolons, perfectly sympathetic to modern urgencies, a man with a built-in unforeseeable future who has surrendered himself to his speedy century as proudly and passionately as a bride to her lover. He would be our choice of a pilot if we had to go anywhere by air. Happily, however, our own mind is quiet today, and we shall travel afoot in the Park, time-fitted to the life of a weekly hack, unfretful, grateful for the next fifteen seconds.

The mental poise of this airline pilot in the middle of difficult flight shows man's spirit maintaining a small but significant lead over his instrument panel. Our own earth-bound life, we realize, is schizophrenic. Half the time we feel blissfully wedded to the modern scene, in love with its every mood, amused by its every joke, imperturbable in the face of its threat, bent on enjoying it to the hilt. The other half of the time we are the fusspot moralist, suspicious of all progress, resentful of change, determined to right wrongs, correct injustices, and save the world even if we have to blow it to pieces in the process. These two characters war incessantly in us, and probably in most men. First one is on top, then the other—body and soul always ravaged by the internal slugging match. We envy Captain X, who has come out a whole man instead of a divided one and who is at peace with his environment. We envy all who fly with him through the great sky.

(E. B. WHITE, *"Heavier than Air."*) [4]

The struggle alone pleases us, not the victory. We love to see animals fighting, not the victor infuriated over the vanquished. We would only see the victorious end; and, as soon as it comes, we are satiated. It is the same in play, and the same in the search for truth. In disputes we like to see the clash of opinions, but not at all to contemplate truth when found. To observe it with pleasure, we have to see it emerge out of strife. So in the passions, there is pleasure in seeing the collision of two contraries; but when one acquires the mastery, it becomes only brutality. We never seek things for themselves, but for the search.

(BLAISE PASCAL, *Pensées.*) [5]

We do not rest satisfied with the present. We anticipate the future as too slow in coming, as if in order to hasten its course; or we recall the past, to stop its too rapid flight. So imprudent are we that we wander in the times which are not ours, and do not think of the only one which belongs to us; and so idle are we that we dream of those times which are no more, and thoughtlessly overlook that which alone exists. For the present is generally painful to us. We conceal it from our sight, because it troubles us; and if it be delightful to us, we regret to see it pass away. We try to sustain it by the future, and think of arranging matters which are not in our power, for a time which we have no certainty of reaching.

Let each one examine his thoughts, and he will find them all occupied with the past and the future. We scarcely ever think of the present; and if we think of it, it is only to take light from it to arrange the future. The present is never our end. The past and the present are our means; the future alone is our end. So we never live, but we hope to live; and, as we are always preparing to be happy, it is inevitable we should never be so. (BLAISE PASCAL, *ibid.*) [6]

This day before dawn I ascended a hill and look'd at the crowded heaven,
And I said to my spirit, *When we become the enfolders of those orbs, and the pleasure and knowledge of everything in them, shall we be fill'd and satisfied then?*
And my spirit said, *No, we but level that lift to pass and continue beyond.* (WALT WHITMAN, "Song of Myself.") [7]

A man approaching me in East Thirty-fourth Street, in the thick of noon, had so queer a look in his eye, such a fudgy and fearful expression, I stopped him.

"Quo vadis?" I asked

"You mean me?" he said, sheepishly.

"Yes, sure. Quo vadis?" I repeated. "Where the hell are you going?"

"I won't tell you, because you wouldn't understand," he replied.

"Well then," I said, "I'll put it this way: quo vadimus? Where are either of us going?"

He seemed stunned. A woman, shopping, bumped lightly against him. At length he spoke, in a clear, low, frightened voice.

"I'll tell you where I'm going. I'm on my way to the Crowbar Building, Forty-first and Park, in Pershing Square, named after General Pershing in the Grand Central zone, zone as in Zonite, because I forgot to tell Miss Cortwright to leave a note for Mr. Josefson when he comes in, telling him he should tell the engraver to vignette the halftone on page forty-three of the salesman's instruction book that Irwain, Weasey, Weasey & Button are getting out for the Fretherby-Quigley Company, which is to go to all their salesmen on the road."

"What do the salesmen sell?" I said, quietly.

"They sell a new kind of shorthand course, called the Quigley Method of Intensive Speedwriting."

"Very good," I said. "That's just the kind of errand I imagined you to be on. As I understand it, recapitulating, you are on your way to the Crowbar Building, Forty-first and Park, in Pershing Square named after General Pershing, hero of the song, 'Many a cootie came over from France in General Pershing's underpants,' in the Grand Central zone, zone as in Zonite, because you forgot to tell Miss Cortwright to leave a note for Mr. Josefson when he comes in, telling him he should tell the engraver to vignette the halftone on page forty-three of a booklet that Irwain, Weasey, Weasey & Button are getting out for the Fretherby-Quigley Company, instructing their salesmen how to approach people to sell the Quigley Method of Intensive Speedwriting, which in turn will enable girls like Miss Cortwright to take Mr. Josefson's dictation when he has to send a memo to the engraver telling him not to forget to vignette a halftone in a booklet telling salesmen how to sell shorthand courses. Is that correct?"

"That's where I'm going," said the man.

"Well aren't you ashamed of yourself!" I cried.

"I don't know whether I am or not," he said, with a slight touch of indignation.

"Listen, my friend," I went on, fixing him with my eye, "all you really want is a decent meal when it comes mealtime, isn't it?"

"And a warm place to sleep when it comes night," he added quickly, almost eagerly.

"Exactly, and a warm place to sleep when it comes night. All right then, don't you think that you, who just want a decent meal when it comes mealtime, and a warm place to sleep when it comes night—don't you think you are pretty far from the main issue if you're on your way to tell a Miss Cortwright to leave a note for a Mr. Josefson telling him to . . ."

He motioned me with his hand to stop. "You needn't go on. Yes, I'm far from the issue, sir," he said. "But I do not know what to do. It must be something about the age—what do they call it, the 'machine' age? This Miss Cortwright . . . I don't know. This Josefson . . . I don't know. Nice people, I suppose. It is all so complex. I just drifted into it."

"Exactly," I said. "And it's getting worse, mind you. I predict a bright future for complexity in this country. Did it ever occur to you that there's no limit to how complicated things can get, on account of one thing always leading to another? Did you ever stop to consider how the Cortwrights lead to the Josefsons, and how the Josefsons lead to the engravers? Paths of glory, leading to the engravers, my man. Did you ever stop to think what might happen if people by accident forgot where the whole thing started?"

The man shook his head, very slightly. His eyes were bright but out of focus. I went on, sternly.

"Only the other evening," I said, "I stopped a man on Broadway who had in his face the same look that I detected in your face a moment ago. To him, too, I said: 'Quo vadis?' And he, too, told me a story much like yours. He told me, my friend, that he was on his way to see a Mr. Fitch in the Para-Mutuel Building, who wanted to get permission to make a talking picture of an airplane towing a glider in which was seated a man listening to a radio which was receiving a colored dialogue between two men named Amos and Andy who were talking together in order to advertise a toothpaste and the name of the toothpaste was . . ."

"Pepsodent," put in my man.

"Yes, Pepsodent. And that man—all he really wanted, when you came right down to it, was a decent meal when it came mealtime."

"And a warm place to sleep when it came night," added my friend, hurriedly.

"Exactly."

There was a pause in our conversation at this point. Cars passed back and forth in the street. Women shoppers brushed lightly against us— women who were on their way to buy fringes for lampshades, women who were on their way to buy printed silk, women who were on their way to buy the hooks that hold the rods that hold the curtains. Suddenly my friend addressed me.

"Now *you* tell *me* where *you're* going," he said, sharply.

"Ha, not on your life—you don't catch me that way," I cried. "I'm not telling you where I'm going."

"I suppose you're going fishing," said the man, smirking.

"Smirk again and I'll smack you," I said. "I always smack smirkers." He smirked. I smacked him.

"Now ask me where I'm going!" I said, holding him by the arm.

"I bet I can guess where you're going. I bet you're a writer, on his way to write something. I know your type. You're going to write a story about 'complexity'—about meeting a man in East Thirty-fourth Street who was on his way to the Crowbar Building in Pershing Square, named after General Pershing in the Grand Central zone, zone as in Zonite, because he forgot to tell Miss Cortwright to leave a note for Mr. Josefson to tell the engraver to vignette the halftone . . ."

"Don't repeat it," I said, breaking down. "That's exactly where I'm going."

". . . so a person like Miss Cortwright will have something to read, and not understand, when she isn't busy with dictation," he said, finishing up.

"That's it."

"And all you want is a decent meal when it comes mealtime, isn't it?" asked my friend.

"And a warm place to sleep when it comes night," I added quickly, almost eagerly.

"Sure, I know," he said. "Well, vale!"

"Vale, kid!" I replied. And we continued on our lonely and imponderable ways.   (E. B. WHITE, *"Quo Vadimus?"*) [8]

Certain questions are disturbing my soul, and I beg of you to solve them. For instance, you say that you desire man to unlearn certain of his old customs, and to regulate his will according to the dictates of science and of sane thought. But how know you that man not only *can*, but *must*, change? What leads you to suppose that the human will stands in need of being regulated? In short, how come you to feel certain that such regulation of man's will would bring him any advantage, or that if he refrained from flying in the face of his real, his normal interests (as guaranteed by the deductions of reason and of arithmetic) such a course would *really* be good for him, or require to be made the law for all humanity? So far all this is only a proposition put forward by yourselves—a mere law (we must suppose) that has been made by logicians rather than by humanity as a whole. Perhaps you think me mad, gentlemen? Well, if so, I plead guilty; I quite agree with you. Man is essentially a constructive animal—an animal for ever destined to strive towards a goal, and to apply himself to the pursuit of engineering, in the shape of ceaseless attempts to build a road which shall lead him to an unknown destination. But that is just why man so often *turns aside* from the road. He turns aside for the reason that he is *constrained* to attempt the journey; he turns aside because, being at once foolish and an independent agent, he sometimes takes it into his head that, though the road in question may eventually bring him to a destination of some sort, that destination always lies ahead of him. Consequently, as an irresponsible child, he is led at times to disregard his trade as an engineer, and to give himself up to that fatal indolence which, as we know, is the mother of all vices. Man loves to construct and to lay out roads—of that there can be no question; but why does he also love so passionately to bring about general ruin and chaos? Answer me that. First of all, however, I myself have a word or two to say about it. May not his passion for bringing about general disorder (a passion which, we must admit, allows of no dispute) arise from the fact that he has an instinctive dread of *completely* attaining his end, and so of finishing his building operations? May it not be the truth that only from a distance, and not from close at hand, does he love the edifice which he is erecting? That is to say, may it not be that he loves to create it, but not to *live* in it—only to hand it over, when completed, to *les animaux domestiques*, in the shape of ants, sheep, and so forth?

Ants are creatures of quite a different taste. They are constantly constructing marvellous edifices, but ones that shall be for ever indestructible. From the antheap all respectable ants take their origin and in it (probably) they meet their end. This does credit alike to their continuity and to their perseverance. On the other hand, man is a frivolous, a specious creature, and, like a chessplayer, cares more for the process of attaining his goal than for the goal itself. Besides, who knows (for it never does to be too sure) that the aim which man strives for upon earth may not be contained in this ceaseless continuation of the process of attainment (that is to say, in the process which is comprised in the living of life) rather than in the aim itself, which, of course, is contained in the formula that twice two make four? Yet, gentlemen, this formula is not life at all; it is only the beginning of death! At all events men have always been afraid to think that twice two make four, and I am afraid of it too. Can it be, therefore, that, though man is for ever working to attain this formula, and though, in his search for it, he sails all the seas and sacrifices his whole life to the acquisition of his end, he fears *really* to succeed in the quest, for the reason that, if he were suddenly to come upon the formula, he would feel that he had nothing left to look for? Workmen, on completing their weekly tasks, receive their wages, and betake themselves to the tavern to make merry. Such is their weekly diversion. But whither can man in the mass betake himself? It is plain that he feels ill at ease when the end of his labour has really been reached. That is to say, he loves to attain, but not *completely* to attain; which, of course, is an exceedingly ridiculous *trait* in his character, and would appear to contain a paradox. In any case the formula that twice two make four is the factor which, of all others, he cannot stomach; nor do *I* look upon it in any other light than as an abomination, since it is a formula which wears an impertinent air as, meeting you on the road, it sets its arms akimbo, and spits straight in your face. True, I agree that, in its way, it is well enough; yet I also beg leave to say (if I must apportion praise all round) that the formula "Twice two make five" is not without its attractions.

Why, then, are you so absolutely, so portentously, certain that one thing, and one thing only, is normal and positive—in a word, good—for mankind? Does reason never err in estimating what is advantageous? May it not be that man occasionally loves something besides prosperity? May it not be that he also loves *adversity?* And may not adversity be as good for him as is happiness? Certainly there are times when man *does* love adversity, and love it passionately; so do not resort to history for your justification, but, rather, put the question to *yourselves*, if you are men, and have had any experience of life. For my part, I look upon undivided love of prosperity as something almost indecent; for to cause an occasional catastrophe, come weal come woe, seems to me a very pleasant thing to do. Yet I am not altogether for adversity, any more than I am altogether for prosperity; what I most stand for is my personal freewill, and for what it can do for me when I feel in the right mood to use it. I know that adversity is not thought acceptable in vaudeville plays, and that in the Palace of Crystal* it would be a thing quite unthinkable, for the reason that, since adversity connotes a denial and a doubt, no edifice of the kind could exist wherein a doubt was harboured. Nevertheless, I feel certain that man never wholly rejects adversity (in the sense of chaos and disruption of his schemes); for adversity is the mainspring of self-realisation. When beginning these letters I said that, in my opinion, self-realisation is, for man, a supreme misfortune; yet I am sure that he loves it dearly, and that he would not exchange it for any other sort of delight. For example, adversity is immeasurably superior to the formula that twice two make four; for if the latter were ever to be found, what would there remain for us to do or to realise? All that there would remain for us to do would be to

---

* A Russian expression for the millennium.

muzzle our five senses, and to relapse into a state of perpetual contemplation. The same result (namely, that there might remain nothing for us to do) might arise from self-realisation; yet in that case one could at least give oneself an occasional castigation, and revivify oneself. This might be a retrograde course to take, yet at least it would be better than nothing.   (DOSTOEVSKY, *Letters from the Underworld*.) [9]

What do we mean by "principles of civil liberties and human rights"? We cannot go far in that inquiry until we have achieved some notion of what we mean by Liberty; and that has always proved a hard concept to define. The natural, though naive, opinion is that it means no more than that each individual shall be allowed to pursue his own desires without let or hindrance; and that, although it is true that this is practically impossible, still it does remain the goal, approach to which measures our success. Why, then, is not a beehive or an anthill a perfect example of a free society? Surely you have been a curious and amused watcher beside one of these.

In and out of their crowded pueblo the denizens pass in great number, each bent upon his own urgent mission, quite oblivious of all the rest except as he must bend his path to avoid them. It is a scene of strenuous, purposeful endeavor in which each appears to be, and no doubt in fact is, accomplishing his own purpose; and yet he is at the same time accomplishing the purpose of the group as a whole. As I have gazed at it, the sentence from the Collect of the Episcopal prayer-book has come to me: "Whose service is perfect freedom."

Why is it, then, that we so positively rebel against the hive and the hill as a specimen of a free society? Why is it that such prototypes of totalitarianisms arouse our deepest hostility? Unhappily it is not because they cannot be realized, or at least because they cannot be approached, for a substantial period. Who can be sure that such appalling forecasts as Aldous Huxley's "Brave New World" or Orwell's "1984" are not prophetic? Indeed, there have often been near approaches to such an order.

Germany at the end of 1940 was probably not far removed from one, and who of us knows that there are not countless persons today living within the boundaries of Russia and perhaps of China who are not willing partners, accepting as their personal aspirations the official definitions of the good, the true and the beautiful? Indeed, there have been, and still are, in our own United States large and powerful groups who, if we are to judge their purposes by their conduct, see treason in all dissidence and would welcome an era in which all of us should think, feel and live in consonance with duly prescribed patterns.

Human nature is malleable, especially if you can indoctrinate the disciple with indefectible principles before anyone else reaches him. (I fancy that the Janissaries were as fervent Mohammedans as the authentic Turks.) Indeed, we hear from those who are entitled to an opinion that at times the abject confessions made in Russia by victims who know that they are already marked for slaughter are not wrung from them by torture or threats against their families. Rather, they come from partisans, so obsessed with the faith that when they are told that the occasion calls for scapegoats and that they have been selected, recognize and assent to the propriety of the demand and cooperate in its satisfaction. It is as though, when the right time comes, the drones agreed to their extinction in the interest of the hive.

Nor need we be surprised that men so often embrace almost any doctrines, if they are proclaimed with a voice of absolute assurance. In a universe that we do not understand, but with which we must in one way or another somehow manage to deal, and aware of the conflicting desires that clamorously beset us, between which we must choose and which we must therefore manage to weigh, we turn in our bewilderment to those who tell us that they have found a path out of the thickets and possess the scales by which to appraise our needs.

Over and over again such prophets succeed in converting us to unquestioning acceptance; there is scarcely a monstrous belief that has not had its day and its passionate adherents, so eager are we for safe footholds in our dubious course. How certain is any one of us that he, too, might not be content to follow any fantastic creed, if he was satisfied that nothing would ever wake him from the dream? And, indeed, if there were nothing to wake him, how should he distinguish its articles from the authentic dictates of verity?

Remember, too, that it is by no means clear that we are happier in the faith we do profess than we should be under the spell of an orthodoxy that was safe against all heresy. Cruel and savage as orthodoxies have always proved to be, the faithful seem able to convince themselves that the heretics, as they continue to crop up, get nothing worse than their due, and to rest with an easy conscience.

In any event, my thesis is that the best answer to such systems is not so much in their immoral quality—immoral though they be—as in the fact that they are inherently unstable, because they are at war with our only trustworthy way of living in accord with the facts. For I submit that it is only by trial and error, by insistent scrutiny and by readiness to re-examine presently accredited conclusions that we have risen, so far as in fact we have risen, from our brutish ancestors, and I believe that in our loyalty to these habits lies our only chance, not merely of progress, but even of survival.

They were not indeed a part of our aboriginal endowment: Man, as he emerged, was not prodigally equipped to master the infinite diversity of his environment. Obviously, enough of us did manage to get through; but it has been a statistical survival, for the individual's native powers of adjustment are by no means enough for his personal safety any more than are those of other creatures. The precipitate of our experience is far from absolute verity, and our exasperated resentment at all dissent is a sure index of our doubts. Take, for instance, our constant recourse to the word, "subversive," as a touchstone of impermissible deviation from accepted canons.

All discussion, all debate, all dissidence tends to question and in consequence to upset existing convictions: that is precisely its purpose and its justification. He is, indeed, a "subversive" who disputes those precepts that I most treasure and seeks to persuade me to substitute his own. He may have no shadow of desire to resort to anything but persuasion; he may be of those to whom any forcible sanction of conformity is anathema; yet it remains true that he is trying to bring about my apostasy, and I hate him just in proportion as I fear his success.

Contrast this protective resentment with the assumption that lies at the base of our whole system that the best chance for truth to emerge is a fair field for all ideas. Nothing, I submit, more completely betrays our latent disloyalty to this premise, to all that we pretend to believe, than the increasingly common resort to this and other question-begging words. Their imprecision comforts us by enabling us to suppress arguments that disturb our complacency and yet to continue to congratulate ourselves on keeping the faith as we have received it from the Founding Fathers.

Heretics have been hateful from the beginning of recorded time; they have been ostracized, exiled, tortured, maimed and butchered; but it has generally proved impossible to smother them, and when it has not, the society that has succeeded has always declined. Façades of authority, however imposing, do not survive after it has appeared that they rest upon the sands of human conjecture and compromise.

And so, if I am to say what are "the principles of civil liberties and human rights," I answer that they lie in habits, customs—conventions, if you will—that tolerate dissent and can live without irrefragable certainties; that are ready to overhaul existing assumptions; that recognize that we never see save through a glass, darkly, and that at long last we shall succeed only so far as we continue to undertake "the intolerable labor of thought"—that most distasteful of all our activities.

If such a habit and such a temper pervade a society, it will not need institutions to protect its "civil liberties and human rights"; so far as they do not, I venture to doubt how far anything else can protect them:

whether it be Bills of Rights, or courts that must in the name of interpretation read their meaning into them.

This may seem to you a bleak and cheerless conclusion, too alien to our nature to be practical. "We must live from day to day"—you will say—"to live is to act, and to act is to choose and decide. How can we carry on at all without some principles, some patterns to meet the conflicts in which each day involves us?" Indeed, we cannot, nor am I suggesting that we should try; but I *am* suggesting that it makes a vital difference—*the* vital difference—whether we deem our principles and our patterns to be eternal verities, rather than the best postulates so far attainable.

Was it not Holmes who said: "The highest courage is to stake everything on a premise that you know tomorrow's evidence may disprove"? "Ah"—you will reply—"there's the rub. That may be the highest courage, but how many have it? You are hopelessly wrong if you assume the general prevalence of such a virtue; ordinary men must be given more than conjectures if they are to face grave dangers."

But do you really believe that? Do you not see about you every day and everywhere the precise opposite? Not alone on the battlefield but in the forest, the desert and the plain; in the mountains, at sea, on the playing field, even in the laboratory and the factory—yes (do not laugh), at the card table and the racetrack—men are forever putting it "upon the touch to win or lose it all." Without some smack of uncertainty and danger, to most of us the world would be a tepid, pallid show.

Surely, like me, you have all felt something of this when you have looked on those pathetic attempts to depict in paint or stone the delights of Paradise. I own that the torments of hell never fail to horrify me; not even the glee of the demons in charge is an adequate relief, though the artist has generally been successful in giving a veracious impression of the gusto with which they discharge their duties.

But when I turn to the Congregation of the Blessed, I cannot avoid a sense of anticlimax; strive as I may, the social atmosphere seems a bit forced; and I recall those very irreverent verses of Lowes Dickinson:

> *Burning at first no doubt would be worse,*
> *But time the impression would soften,*
> *While those who are bored with praising the Lord,*
> *Would be more bored with praising him often.*

By some happy fortuity man is a projector, a designer, a builder, a craftsman; it is among his most dependable joys to impose upon the flux that passes before him some mark of himself, aware though he always must be of the odds against him. His reward is not so much in the work as in its making; not so much in the prize as in the race. We may win when we lose, if we have done what we can; for by so doing we have made real at least some part of that finished product in whose fabrication we are most concerned—ourselves.

And if at the end some friendly critic shall pass by and say, "My friend, how good a job do you really think you have made of it all?" we can answer, "I know as well as you that it is not of high quality, but I did put into it whatever I had, and that was the game I started out to play."

It is still in the lap of the gods whether a society can succeed, based on "civil liberties and human rights," conceived as I have tried to describe them; but of one thing at least we may be sure: the alternatives that have so far appeared have been immeasurably worse, and so, whatever the outcome, I submit to you that we must press along. Borrowing from Epictetus, let us say to ourselves: "Since we are men we will play the part of a Man," and how can I better end than by recalling to you the concluding passage of "Prometheus Unbound"?

> *To suffer woes which hope thinks infinite:*
> *To forgive wrongs darker than death or night;*
> *To defy Power, which seems omnipotent*
> *To love, and bear; to hope till Hope creates*
> *From its own wreck the thing it contemplates;*
> *Neither to change, nor falter, nor repent;*
> *This, like thy glory, Titan, is to be*
> *Good, great and joyous, beautiful and free;*
> *This is alone Life, Joy, Empire and Victory.*
> (LEARNED HAND, "A Plea for the Freedom of Dissent.") [10]

The main ideas concerning the aims of man suggested in these passages can be summarized as follows: man cares more for the process of attaining goals than for the goals themselves; the achievement of one goal serves principally as a jumping-off place for the pursuit of the next; man wants continuous betterment as he anticipates the future; man will deliberately imperil his comfort; man's motivation is a struggle between opposing forces—the desire for preserving a safe, secure, predictable world and the dread of completely achieving it; and finally, man is always dissatisfied, what he wants is inexpressible and unattainable.

Some of the statements in the preceding passages seem flatly to contradict the theory of human motivation based on the concept of homeostasis. Some of them seem to say that what man seeks is not equilibrium but constant disequilibrium, not constancy and stability but change, not simply the satisfaction of needs but the constant emergence of new purposes which establish new goals in a never-ending succession.

In order to act decisively we tend to assume that the significances we have experienced are certainties, not probabilities. In order to live, we must act. In order to act with some degree of confidence, we must have some constancy and stability of environment. Yet by the very nature of things we are faced with change and novelty and are forced to modify our assumptions if we do not wish to experience continuous surprise, frustration, and disappointment. The alternative seems to be a withdrawal from living, a refusal to act, dreaming of the past, merely vegetating. Thus, normal living seems to involve two apparently opposing forces: one designed to preserve what is, the other designed to change what is; one designed to provide some certainty, constancy, and stability in our world; the other designed to enable us to experience change, novelty, development, and emergence. From this point of view, man's psychological tensions would seem to be products of his strivings rather than their initiators or "causes." A passage from Dewey cited in chapter I said that "the conjunction of problematic and determinate characters in nature renders every existence, as well as every idea and human act, an experiment in fact, even though not in design."

VALUE-QUALITIES OF EXPERIENCE

With these ideas as a background, the construction of an intrinsically reasonable theory to account for human striving, for the on-goingness of human behavior, seems within the realm of possibility.

First, however, a few points should be clarified. It is often said that man eats and drinks because one of his goals is the preservation of his biological organism. This may seem logically correct, but it is not the whole story. Most civilized behavior cannot be adequately explained in terms of its ulterior consequences. From the first-person point of view, it is doubtful that the goal of preserving the organism exists as one looks over a menu, orders his lunch, and eats it. Why, then, does the individual periodically eat and drink? Are the objects—steak, potatoes, tomatoes, lettuce, bread, butter, and strawberries—goals, as such? Does an individual seek these for their own sake? Not entirely. We eat steak or strawberries partly to gain nourishment, but partly to enjoy a quality of experience.

The same characteristically human desire seems to permeate less elemental behavior. For example, why does a man want to become president of a university? Is that position, that title, his goal? It is more probable that performing the duties of the position brings to this individual certain qualities of experience which he prizes.

To say that man seeks qualities of experience rather than the satisfaction of basic needs may seem to be splitting hairs, but the differentiation is crucial if we are to have what seems to us a valid and adequate account of human striving.

For human beings seem to have the capacity to sense *qualitative* differences in experience. Our satisfactions and dissatisfactions are characterized by different value-qualities. The value-quality of a present experience is sensed in terms of value-standards registered through previous transactions of living. On the basis of our acquired hierarchy of values, we judge the worthwhileness of our present experiences and characterize them as thrilling, boring, delightful, disappointing, threatening and the like.

What we mean by differences in the value-quality of experience can be made clear by a few illustrations. A value-quality of a relatively low order pervades experience when we eat any food available if we are very hungry; a richer, higher-order value-quality pervades experience when we eat tastefully prepared food in the company of congenial companions. We feel a richness of experience when our efforts to help a person in need are received with genuine gratitude. There is a deep satisfaction from any creative activity in which we experience new meanings or insights, or see that our own efforts have produced something that we judge to be good or worthwhile. We all have moments, sometimes referred to as religious experiences, when our experience is permeated by a value-quality which can scarcely be communicated. On the other hand, we sense negative value-qualities of disillusionment, disappointment, or sadness when things go wrong. We may become angry, resentful, or jealous if we feel we are being deprived of the goods or opportunities we feel we deserve. The following excerpts describe or refer to value-qualities of experience that are so rich and subtle they almost defy description.

But the great understander of these mysterious ebbs and flows is Tolstoi. They throb all through his novels. In his *War and Peace*, the hero, Peter, is supposed to be the richest man in the Russian empire. During the French invasion he is taken prisoner, and dragged through much of the retreat. Cold, vermin, hunger, and every form of misery assail him, the result being a revelation to him of the real scale of life's values. "Here only, and for the first time, he appreciated, because he was deprived of it, the happiness of eating when he was hungry, of drinking when he was thirsty, of sleeping when he was sleepy, and of talking when he felt the desire to exchange some words. . . . Later in life he always recurred with joy to this month of captivity, and never failed to speak with enthusiasm of the powerful and ineffaceable sensations, and especially of the moral calm which he had experienced at this epoch. When at daybreak, on the morrow of his imprisonment, he saw [I abridge here Tolstoi's description] the mountains with their wooded slopes disappearing in the grayish mist; when he felt the cool breeze caress him; when he saw the light drive away the vapors, and the sun rise majestically behind the clouds and cupolas, and the crosses, the dew, the distance, the river, sparkle in the splendid, cheerful rays— his heart overflowed with emotion. This emotion kept continually with him and increased a hundred-fold as the difficulties of his situation grew graver. . . . He learnt that man is meant for happiness, and that this happiness is in him, in the satisfaction of the daily needs of existence, and that unhappiness is the fatal result, not of our need, but of our abundance. . . . When calm reigned in the camp, and the embers paled, and little by little went out, the full moon had reached the zenith. The woods and the fields roundabout lay clearly visible; and, beyond the inundation of light which filled them, the view plunged into the limitless horizon. Then Peter cast his eyes upon the firmament, filled at that hour with myriads of stars. 'All that is mine,' he thought. 'All that is in me, is me! And that is what they think they have taken prisoner! That is what they have shut up in a cabin!' So he smiled and turned in to sleep among his comrades." *

The occasion and the experience, then, are nothing. It all depends on the capacity of the soul to be grasped, to have its life-currents absorbed by what is given. "Crossing a bare common," says Emerson, "in

* *La Guerre de la paix*, 1884, vol. iii, pp. 268, 275, 316.

snow puddles, at twilight, under a clouded sky, without having in my thoughts any occurrence of special good fortune, I have enjoyed a perfect exhilaration. I am glad to the brink of fear."

(WILLIAM JAMES, "On a Certain Blindness in Human Beings.") [11]

The sophisticated philosophies of the East are even more abstract, subtle, and given to the splitting of unsubstantial hairs than those of the West, but the emotional basis of the oldest and richest Oriental religion—Hinduism—is perfectly accessible to the Western mind—more accessible, it sometimes seemed to me, than certain Christian moods.

Reduced to its crudest terms, the underlying mood of Hinduism is one of joyous acceptance of the universe—the mood exploited in American advertising by manufacturers of super-vitaminized breakfast foods or nonirritant shaving creams, and in American literature by the worst and greatest of our poets, Walt Whitman. It is the mood which makes a man sing in his bathtub, thump his chest in front of an open window, remember to kiss his wife when he leaves for the office, and to say good morning to the office boy when he arrives there; the mood which turns the seedy tramp into a joyous adventurer, stomping lustily along the highroad of life and burbling uncouth ejaculations of comradeship in half a dozen languages as he goes.

There is nothing esoteric or incomprehensible about this mood. Nearly everyone has experienced it sometime during his life. For myself, I recognized that it was this which increasingly shed a morning light over my Asiatic adventure and the whole landscape of Asia to which I had hitherto been so chilly indifferent. Never before had these feelings been so intense, so prolonged, and so frequently recurrent, but I had experienced them from time to time since my childhood.

Moreover, once the connection between this euphoric state and the mystic ecstacies in which Indian religious history abounds is recognized, mysticism no longer seems something completely remote from normal human experience, at least not the kind of mysticism which may be described as the Whitmanesque mood at its highest pitch. Such mystic experiences, I suspect, are a great deal more common than they are thought to be. I have never considered myself, nor been considered by my friends, as a mystic type, yet several times during my life the feeling of the blessedness and perfection of creation has been so intense that any effort to express it verbally resulted in the kind of incoherent babble which is the official language of mysticism.

What is startling and at first incomprehensible to the Western mind is to find India, most tragic and horror-ridden of all lands under the sun,

tainted with the curse of what James called "healthy-mindedness." It is
a paradox but it is a fact. Despite cholera, communalism, caste, and
colonialism; despite starvation, superstition, and delusion, the people of
India have glad morning temperaments. They cannot, for the most part,
be happy but their misery is interlit with flashes of pure joyousness.
They cannot be optimistic but they are often blissfully acceptant.

(EDMOND TAYLOR, *Richer by Asia.*) [12]

When a piece of sculpture or a musical composition produces an emotion that one feels to be higher, purer, truer than ordinary life, such
a work must correspond to a certain spiritual reality.

(*The Maxims of Marcel Proust.*) [13]

If I could only live at the pitch that is near madness
When everything is as it was in my childhood
Violent, vivid, and of infinite possibility:
That the sun and the moon broke over my head.

Then I cast time out of the trees and fields,
Then I stood immaculate in the Ego;
Then I eyed the world with all delight,
Reality was the perfection of my sight.

And time has big handles on the hands,
Fields and trees a way of being themselves.
I saw battalions of the race of mankind
Standing stolid, demanding a moral answer.

I gave the moral answer and I died
And into a realm of complexity came
Where nothing is possible but necessity
And the truth wailing there like a red babe.

(RICHARD EBERHART, "If I Could Only Live at the Pitch
That Is Near Madness.") [14]

And I have felt
A presence that disturbs me with the joy
Of elevated thoughts; a sense sublime,
Of something far more deeply interfused,
Whose dwelling is the light of setting suns,
And the round ocean and the living air,

And the blue sky, and in the mind of man;
A motion and a spirit, that impels
All thinking things, all objects of all thought,
And rolls through all things.
> (WILLIAM WORDSWORTH, "Lines Composed
> a Few Miles above Tintern Abbey.") [15]

VALUE-QUALITIES AND MOTIVATION

Purpose, then, may be thought of as an intention to experience a consequence—consequence being defined as value-satisfaction. The coming-into-existence of an anticipated and desired value-quality of experience may be regarded as the fulfillment of a purpose.

On the basis of the significances we experience, we are constantly guessing that certain things we do will give us the value-qualities of experience we hope for. We try to repeat many types of activities because they show high promise of recapturing or maintaining certain qualities of experience that have already proved satisfying. Likewise we try to avoid those transactions which we believe will lead to a high degree of negative value-quality, *unless* these occasions are perceived as steppingstones to eventual enhancement of the positive value-qualities of experience. Purposing, then, involves predicting what behavings will lead to value-satisfactions. It involves making choices among the probable value-satisfactions that may follow alternative courses of action we might initiate.

A phenomenon sometimes called value-adaptation should be mentioned here. Many times an experienced activity or object which at first is permeated with high positive or negative value-quality tends to become "neutral" with repetition. Habitual activity may become monotonous and boring; what thrilled us as a youth may "leave us cold" as an adult. Goals once achieved may soon come to be taken for granted. However, familiarity and repetition do not always breed indifference or contempt. The consequence of repeated behavings with respect to perceived objects and persons depends on whether or not they help us carry out our purposes and thereby experience the value-qualities we seek.

We are by no means implying that the value-satisfactions we have experienced are thrown overboard for the sake of novelty and the new satisfactions that may be ours if we undertake new activities. As indicated earlier, the process of living seems to involve both an attempt to preserve the sources and conditions of proven satisfactions so they can be repeated, and, at the same time, an attempt to use them as springboards for new undertakings that we feel hold the possibility of enhancing experience.

MULTIPLICITY OF PURPOSES

Obviously we seldom, if ever, do anything just for the sake of doing it. We do what we do either because of the value-satisfactions we experience in the doing, or because the accomplishment of one purpose will, we hope, be a step toward the fulfillment of further purposes or aims which we expect will bring still greater satisfactions. Thus, a multiplicity of purposes, establishing sub-goals in relation to achievements in the more distant future, is operative in most occasions of living. It is sometimes assumed, however, that a single purpose or a single chain of purposes sustains activity in some area of one's living. The following passage, written by a man of wide experience, indicates that this is questionable.

In the broad sense that no business can escape its balance sheet, it is true that the economic or money motive governs the administration of business. Nevertheless my observation in several different well-managed businesses convinces me that business decisions are constantly being made that are not based upon economic motives. This is something that business men seldom admit, and of which they are frequently unaware. Prestige, competitive reputation, social philosophy, social standing, philanthropic interests, combativeness, love of intrigue, dislike of friction, technical interest, Napoleonic dreams, love of accomplishing useful things, desire for regard of employees, love of publicity, fear of publicity—a long catalogue of non-economic motives actually condition the management of business, and nothing but the balance sheet keeps these non-economic motives from running wild. Yet without all these incentives I think most business would be a lifeless failure. There is not enough vitality in dollars to keep business running on any such scale as we experience it, nor are the things which can be directly purchased with money an adequate incentive.

The business man can't admit this. He seems to think he would lose caste. He feels it necessary to take a "hard-boiled" attitude. He must do everything efficiently and "not the way politicians do them." Or he fears the bankers might think him soft. (I have found them just like the rest of us but they won't admit it either.) Part of this is professional pose. Some of it is the reaction to the unpleasant things that responsibility imposes—a sort of self-protective psychology. But if you will stop taking the business man at his word and quietly watch him when he is off guard, you will find he is taking care of poor old John who couldn't be placed anywhere else, that he is risking both profit and failure rather than cut wages, that he continues an unprofitable venture on nothing but hope rather than throw his men out of work. Much of this is unsound. It would be better if economic motives did operate more effectively, but the point is that it is impossible to get to the root of personnel relations or understand labor troubles or successes on the unrealistic assumption that economic motives exclusively govern. They merely limit and guide. They control more in some cases or some businesses than others.[16]

VALUE-STANDARDS AND ASPIRATIONS

Value-qualities and what is sensed as an increment of value-quality are, of course, unique and relative to the individual. There can be no absolute standard upon which increments of value-quality are based for all individuals. Value-standards are a product of each individual's unique life history. What any person believes will bring forth an enriched experience depends almost entirely on what his present value-standards are, but irrespective of one's group identifications it seems to be characteristic of man to strive *within* those groups to better his status in his own eyes and in the eyes of others who share his standards. The frequently quoted passage from William James in the next group of selections is illustrative of this point. The final two selections of the group portray widely differing patterns of living with accompanying differences in experienced value-standards and levels of aspiration for future value-satisfactions.

With most objects of desire, physical nature restricts our choice to but one of many represented goods, and even so it is here. I am often confronted by the necessity of standing by one of my empirical selves and relinquishing the rest. Not that I would not, if I could, be both handsome and fat and well dressed, and a great athlete, and make a million a year, be a wit, a *bon-vivant*, and a lady-killer, as well as a philosopher; a philanthropist, statesman, warrior, and African explorer, as well as a "tone-poet" and saint. But the thing is simply impossible. The millionaire's work would run counter to the saint's; the *bon-vivant* and the philanthropist would trip each other up; the philosopher and the lady-killer could not well keep house in the same tenement of clay. Such different characters may conceivably at the outset of life be alike *possible* to a man. But to make any one of them actual, the rest must more or less be suppressed. So the seeker of his truest, strongest, deepest self must review the list carefully, and pick out the one on which to stake his salvation. All other selves thereupon become unreal, but the fortunes of this self are real. Its failures are real failures, its triumphs real triumphs, carrying shame and gladness with them. This is as strong an example as there is of that selective industry of the mind on which I insisted some pages back. . . . Our thought, incessantly deciding, among many things of a kind, which ones for it shall be realities, here chooses one of many possible selves or characters, and forthwith reckons it no shame to fail in any of those not adopted expressly as its own.

I, who for the time have staked my all on being a psychologist, am mortified if others know much more psychology than I. But I am contented to wallow in the grossest ignorance of Greek. My deficiencies there give me no sense of personal humiliation at all. Had I "pretensions" to be a linguist, it would have been just the reverse. So we have the paradox of a man shamed to death because he is only the second pugilist or the second oarsman in the world. That he is able to beat the whole population of the globe minus one is nothing; he has "pitted" himself to beat that one; and as long as he doesn't do that nothing else counts. He is to his own regard as if he were not, indeed he *is* not.

Yonder puny fellow, however, whom every one can beat, suffers no chagrin about it, for he has long ago abandoned the attempt to "carry that line," as the merchants say, of self at all. With no attempt there can be no failure; with no failure no humiliation. So our self-feeling in this world depends entirely on what we *back* ourselves to be and do. It is determined by the ratio of our actualities to our supposed potentialities; a fraction of which our pretensions are the denominator and the numerator our success: thus, Self-esteem $= \dfrac{\text{Success}}{\text{Pretensions}}$. Such a fraction my be increased as well by diminishing the denominator as by increasing the numerator.* To give up pretensions is as blessed a relief

---

* Cf. Carlyle: *Sartor Resartus*, "The Everlasting Yea." "I tell thee, blockhead, it all comes of thy vanity; of what thou fanciest those same deserts of thine to be. Fancy that thou deservest to be hanged (as is most likely), thou wilt feel it happiness to be only shot: fancy that thou deservest to be hanged in a hair halter, it will be luxury to die in hemp. . . . What act of legislature was there that *thou* shouldst be happy? A little while ago thou hadst no right to *be* at all." Etc., etc.

as to get them gratified; and where disappointment is incessant and the struggle unending, this is what men will always do. The history of evangelical theology, with its conviction of sin, its self-despair, and its abandonment of salvation by works, is the deepest of possible examples, but we meet others in every walk of life. There is the strangest lightness about the heart when one's nothingness in a particular line is once accepted in good faith. *All* is not bitterness in the lot of the lover sent away by the final inexorable "No." Many Bostonians, *crede experto* (and inhabitants of other cities, too, I fear), would be happier women and men to-day, if they could once for all abandon the notion of keeping up a Musical Self, and without shame let people hear them call a symphony a nuisance. How pleasant is the day when we give up striving to be young,—or slender! Thank God! we say, *those* illusions are gone. Everything added to the Self is a burden as well as a pride. A certain man who lost every penny during our civil war went and actually rolled in the dust, saying he had not felt so free and happy since he was born.

Once more, then, our self-feeling is in our power. As Carlyle says: "Make thy claim of wages a zero, then hast thou the world under thy feet. Well did the wisest of our time write, it is only with *renunciation* that life, properly speaking, can be said to begin."

Neither threats nor pleadings can move a man unless they touch some one of his potential or actual selves. Only thus can we, as a rule, get a "purchase" on another's will. The first care of diplomatists and monarchs and all who wish to rule or influence is, accordingly, to find out their victim's strongest principle of self-regard, so as to make that the fulcrum of all appeals. But if a man has given up those things which are subject to foreign fate, and ceased to regard them as parts of himself at all, we are well-nigh powerless over him. The Stoic receipt for contentment was to dispossess yourself in advance of all that was out of your own power,—then fortune's shocks might rain down unfelt. Epictetus exhorts us, by thus narrowing and at the same time solidifying our Self to make it invulnerable: "I must die; well, but must I die groaning too? I will speak what appears to be right, and if the despot says, then I will put you to death, I will reply, 'When did I ever tell you that I was immortal? You will do your part and I mine; it is yours to kill and mine to die intrepid; yours to banish, mine to depart untroubled.' How do we act in a voyage? We choose the pilot, the sailors, the hour. Afterwards comes a storm. What have I to care for? My part is performed. This matter belongs to the pilot. But the ship is sinking; what then have I to do? That which alone I can do—submit to being drowned without fear, without clamor or accusing of God, but as one who knows that what is born must likewise die."

A tolerably unanimous opinion ranges the different selves of which a man may be "seized and possessed," and the consequent different orders of his self-regard, in an *hierarchical scale, with the bodily Self at the bottom, the spiritual Self at top, and the extracorporeal material selves and the various social selves between.* Our merely natural self-seeking would lead us to aggrandize all these selves; we give up deliberately only those among them which we find we cannot keep. Our unselfishness is thus apt to be a "virtue of necessity"; and it is not without all show of reason that cynics quote the fable of the fox and the grapes in describing our progress therein. But this is the moral education of the race; and if we agree in the result that on the whole the selves we can keep are the intrinsically best, we need not complain of being led to the knowledge of their superior worth in such a tortuous way.

Of course this is not the only way in which we learn to subordinate our lower selves to our higher. A direct ethical judgment unquestionably also plays its part, and last, not least, we apply to our own persons judgments originally called forth by the acts of others. It is one of the strangest laws of our nature that many things which we are well satisfied with in ourselves disgust us when seen in others. With another man's bodily "hoggishness" hardly anyone has any sympathy;—almost as little with his cupidity, his social vanity and eagerness, his jealousy, his despotism, and his pride. Left absolutely to myself I should probably allow all these spontaneous tendencies to luxuriate in me unchecked, and it would be long before I formed a distinct notion of the order of their subordination. But having constantly to pass judgment on my associates, I come ere long to see, as Herr Horwicz says, my own lusts in the mirror of the lusts of others, and to *think* about them in a very different way from that in which I simply *feel*. Of course, the moral generalities which from childhood have been instilled into me accelerate enormously the advent of this reflective judgment on myself.

So it comes to pass that, as aforesaid, men have arranged the various selves which they may seek in an hierarchical scale according to their worth. A certain amount of bodily selfishness is required as a basis for all the other selves. But too much sensuality is despised, or at best condoned on account of the other qualities of the individual. The wider material selves are regarded as higher than the immediate body. He is esteemed a poor creature who is unable to forego a little meat and drink and warmth and sleep for the sake of getting on in the world. The social self as a whole, again, ranks higher than the material self as a whole. We must care more for our honor, our friends, our human ties, than for a sound skin or wealth. And the spiritual self is so supremely precious that, rather than lose it, a man ought to be willing to give up friends and good fame, and property, and life itself.

In each kind of self, material, social, and spiritual, men distinguish between the immediate and actual, and the remote and potential, between the narrower and the wider view, to the detriment of the former and advantage of the latter. One must forego a present bodily enjoyment for the sake of one's general health; one must abandon the dollar in the hand for the sake of the hundred dollars to come; one must make an enemy of his present interlocutor if thereby one makes friends of a more valued circle; one must go without learning and grace, and wit, the better to compass one's soul's salvation.

Of all these wider, more potential selves, *the potential social self* is the most interesting, by reason of certain apparent paradoxes to which it leads in conduct, and by reason of its connection with our moral and religious life. When for motives of honor and conscience I brave the condemnation of my own family, club, and "set"; when, as a protestant, I turn catholic; as a catholic, freethinker; as a "regular practitioner," homeopath, or what not, I am always inwardly strengthened in my course and steeled against the loss of my actual social self by the thought of other and better *possible* social judges than those whose verdict goes against me now. The ideal social self which I thus seek in appealing to their decision may be very remote: it may be represented as barely possible. I may not hope for its realization during my lifetime; I may even expect the future generations, which would approve me if they knew me, to know nothing about me when I am dead and gone. Yet still the emotion that beckons me on is indubitably the pursuit of an ideal social self, of a self that is at least *worthy* of approving recognition by the highest *possible* judging companion, if such companion there be.* This self is the true, the intimate, the ultimate, the permanent Me which I seek. This judge is God, the Absolute Mind, the "Great Companion." We hear, in these days of scientific enlightenment, a great deal of discussion about the efficacy of prayer; and many reasons are given us why we should not pray, whilst others are given us why we should. But in all this very little is said of the reason why we *do* pray, which is simply that we cannot *help* praying. It seems probable that, in spite of all that "science" may do to the contrary, men will continue to pray to the end of time, unless their mental nature changes in a manner which nothing we know should lead us to expect. The impulse

---

* It must be observed that the qualities of the Self thus ideally constituted are all qualities approved by my actual fellows in the first instance; and that my reason for now appealing from their verdict to that of the ideal judge lies in some outward peculiarity of the immediate case. What once was admired in me as courage has now become in the eyes of men "impertinence"; what was fortitude is obstinacy; what was fidelity is now fanaticism. The ideal judge alone, I now believe, can read my qualities, my willingnesses, my powers, for what they truly are. My fellows, misled by interest and prejudice, have gone astray.

to pray is a necessary consequence of the fact that whilst the innermost of the empirical selves of a man is a Self of the *social* sort, it yet can find its only adequate *Socius* in an ideal world.

(WILLIAM JAMES, *The Principles of Psychology.*) [17]

> Those who would take over the earth
> And shape it to their will
> Never, I notice, succeed.
> The earth is like a vessel so sacred
> That at the mere approach of the profane
> It is marred
> And when they reach out their fingers it is gone.
> For a time in the world some force themselves ahead
> And some are left behind,
> For a time in the world some make a great noise
> And some are held silent,
> For a time in the world some are puffed fat
> And some are kept hungry,
> For a time in the world some push aboard
> And some are tipped out:
> At no time in the world will a man who is sane
> Over-reach himself,
> Over-spend himself,
> Over-rate himself.

(LAOTZU, *The Way of Life.*) [18]

In their great days Newporters themselves were by no means averse to using figures. "A man who has a million dollars," old John Jacob Astor once told Julia Ward Howe, "is as well off as if he were rich." Other Newporters also talked in equally round numbers—Newport's "newspaper dollars," they were called. "We are not rich," Mrs. Stuyvesant Fish used to say. "We have only a few million." Maude Parker recalls that one Newport hostess barred from her dinner table people who had less than *five* million dollars; another hostess barred people whose cottage, furnished, cost less than a million. Mrs. O. H. P. Belmont was, of course, on safe ground. Her "Marble House" cost $2,000,000 to build and $9,000,000 to furnish. The Pembroke Joneses used to say that they set aside $300,000 at the beginning of each Newport season for "extra entertainment." In a similar manner, Mrs. Henry Clews, grand-niece of Dolly Madison and reputed to be Newport's best-dressed lady of her era, declared that each summer she set aside $10,000 for "mistakes in her clothes." Richard Lounsbery recalls that a single Newport ball cost $200,000—in the days, of course, when not only dollars were dollars but also when balls were balls.

Dinners were dinners, too. Both Mrs. Ogden Mills and Mrs. Elbridge Gerry used to boast that they could give a dinner for a hundred without calling in extra help. There were hand-painted individual place cards at every place and between every two guests there was an elaborate French menu in front and a powdered-haired, knee-breeched, liveried English footman behind. Ten-course meals were eaten off solid gold services. At one dinner a stream flowed down the middle of the table in which "vivid fish swam pleasantly"; at another there was a cage in the center of the table filled with parrots of "singular hues and utterances." At still another the center of the table was covered with sand; at each place was a small sterling silver pail and a matching shovel. At a given signal half a hundred guests dug frantically into the sand in front of them for their favors—thousands of dollars' worth of rubies, sapphires, emeralds and diamonds. Ordinarily, however, the pace was leisurely. The late Mrs. Maude Howe Elliott recalls a dinner at the cottage of George Wales. "We were at the table," she said, "three mortal hours."

When such dinners palled, Newporters took strong measures. At the most memorable dinner in the resort's history Newport Society was introduced to Prince del Drago from Corsica. The Prince was ersatz—a monkey attired in full evening dress. Second only to this famous "Monkey Dinner" was the so-called "Dogs' Dinner." In this, a regular Newport dinner table was taken off its foundations and placed on a veranda —on trestles about a foot high. A hundred dogs participated, most of them in fancy dress; the menu was stewed liver and rice, fricassee of bones and shredded dog biscuit.

At human fancy dress affairs Newport costumes were the height of invention. At one costume ball Philadelphia's Henry Carter and his wife arrived and explained their costume to the announcing footman at the entrance of the ballroom. Carter, a small man, was dressed as Henry IV; his wife, a large woman, represented a Norman peasant. "Henry the Fourth," shouted the footman, "and an enormous pheasant."

Grand Duke Boris, brother-in-law of Czar Nicholas II, compared pre-income tax Newport and pre-revolution Russia. "I have never dreamed of such luxury as I have seen at Newport," he said. "We have nothing to equal it in Russia." Costume balls and ten-course dinners were not the only way Newport had of showing this luxury. Philadelphia's Fairman Rogers, author of the authoritative manual of coaching, was particularly grand; he personally landscaped his estate by throwing down a magnificent Persian rug on his lawn and ordering his army of gardeners to follow its colors and patterns in exact detail. At "Bois Doré" Harrisburg's William Fahnestock hung from his trees artificial fruits which were made, like the faucets in his bathroom, of fourteen-carat gold. On the Arthur Curtiss James place in Sunrise Valley there was a complete Swiss village. There were half a hundred beautifully kept-up farm buildings and a complete roster of animals, each eulogized by a pictorial signboard in verse. In the James piggery each pig had his own individual yard and sty.

Newport built few swimming pools because its lush era antedated them; nonetheless, the resort posted many achievements in sports. Pierre Lorillard achieved what construction men at the time believed was impossible when he built a pier over the reefs in front of "The Breakers" and was thus enabled to bring his enormous yacht *Rhoda* right up to his front door. On the other hand, Philadelphia's Mrs. Richard Cadwalader could not bring her 408-foot *Savarona* even into Newport's harbor, or indeed into any port in this country. Mrs. Cadwalader refused to pay the duty involved, and her yacht, largest in the world, was reduced to ports abroad. It was fitted with antique rugs and tapestries, gold-plated bathroom fixtures, and a full-sized pipe organ. T. Suffern Tailer built the country's most elaborate private golf course. His "Ocean Links," as it was called, reproduced the most famous individual holes of all the world's most famous courses. Newport's horse-and-buggy days were unequaled anywhere. Several Newporters had as many as twenty different kinds of carriages in their stables and in the old Alfred Gwynne Vanderbilt stables the horses' names were inscribed in gold name plates. O. H. P. Belmont could not bear to have his horses under another roof; the ground floor of "Belcourt" was an all stable affair. Here, in stalls designed by Richard Hunt, with a tasteful barracks for a battery of grooms alongside, the Belmont horses had a change of equipment morning, afternoon and evening. For the night they were bedded down on pure white linen sheets with the Belmont crest embroidered on them. Above the stables, in the salon of "Belcourt," Belmont kept two stuffed horses, old favorites of his, which were mounted by stuffed riders in chain armor.

What any other social resort had, Newport had also and more besides. If Lenox's Mrs. Edwards Spencer kept a pig as a pet in her parlor, Newport's Mrs. John King Van Rensselaer recalls seeing a Newport dowager drive down Bellevue Avenue with a pig seated in her victoria beside her and a monkey on each shoulder. If at Saratoga a President of the United States, Martin Van Buren, was snubbed by Mrs. DeWitt Clinton, at Newport President Chester A. Arthur was snubbed not only by resorters but also by footmen; on the steps of the Newport Casino he was reduced to calling for his own carriage. If Bar Harbor's Joseph Pulitzer imported the entire New York Symphony Orchestra to play for himself and his guests, Newport's Mrs. Cornelius Vanderbilt Jr., thought nothing, in 1902, of closing for two days a New York hit show of that era, *The Wild Rose,* and having the entire company transported for a private performance at "Beaulieu." Even as late as the depression era the resort was in a class by itself. The late Atwater Kent was perhaps the country's greatest latter-day party-giver. His affairs cut a swath through the societies of Bar Harbor, Palm Beach, Southampton and, finally, in his last days, Hollywood itself. But even at his best party weight—which consisted of three orchestras and some three thousand guests—Kent was not up to Newport. Bar Harbor's Mrs. John DeWitt Peltz recalls that after watching Kent for several seasons at the Maine resort she had the pleasure of going down to Newport and attending several functions there. Returning to Bar Harbor, she was asked to describe them. "Why," she said, "they made At Kent look like pot luck!"

In Newport's Golden Age Newporters even went to church in a memorable manner. The box pews of old Trinity were upholstered in the same colors as the liveries of the worshipers, with the Hon. Edwin Morgan's pew taking first honors. In the rear of this, which was known as the Morgan Parlor Car and was sumptuously swathed in crimson damask, were two large armchairs. These were for Mr. and Mrs. Morgan. In front were a trio of tastefully tapestried and well-oiled swivel chairs —these, of course, for the Morgan children who, when affected by the tedium of worship, could twist and turn to their hearts' content.

It is not surprising that from such pews Newporters faced the hereafter, with its uncertain standard of living, with some alarm. Old John Jacob Astor was particularly concerned about his future life. One day, to his faithful coachman, William, he put the fateful question. "William," he said, "where do you expect to go when you die?" The answer was hardly calculated to settle John Jacob's mind.

"Why, sir," replied William, "I have always expected to go where the other people go."   (CLEVELAND AMORY, *The Last Resorts.*) [19]

"As much sand and gravel as they is about here, you wouldn't hardly think nothing would grow. But it does. Every house down here, they's a spot for a garden near it if them that lives in it ain't too trifling to put it in. We have plenty of corn and 'taters and cucumbers and tomatoes in season. We shares with them that ain't got any if they's been down on their luck. I has flowers, too. Them seeds over there in the drying box is every one of them flower seeds. I save them from one year to the next."

Fan Flanigan sat against one of the crooked sapling poles which supported the driftwood joists of the porch. She was a small wizened woman, brown, gnarled, with thin gray hair. A washed-out shapeless house dress had not been pulled low enough to hide her large bony feet.

"It's all right here," she said, "and I like it pretty fair as long as the river don't start acting up. We don't have no rent to pay, jest sort of squat here betwixt the railroad tracks and the water and build our places out of what we can git off the dump and the wood we can ketch floating down the river. Me and Mammy been here sence nineteen and thirty-two, that hard old year."

She puckered her eyes against the strong sunlight and glanced over the thirteen stilt-set shanties which straggled along the banks of the Tennessee River between the approaches to two of Knoxville's bridges. Most of them faced the railroad tracks where strings of coal cars and empty boxcars stood. Beyond the tracks was a high deeply eroded embankment crisscrossed by foot paths and littered with rusty cans, bottles, and other rubbish.

"You kind of grow to like this place," said Fan. "You'd like any place, though, if you live in it long enough, I reckon. A rich man up to Knoxville give this whole strip betwixt the bridges for poor folks to build they houses on. Them that come first taken the pick of what they was here. Ma done that. She come right after Pop died. We use to live in that biggest house over there. My brother-in-law lives there now. Him and Sis had sech a flock of children you couldn't stretch a leg without tromping on one. So me and Mammy moved out. This one room here we has is fair size and plenty for us. Mammy owns that brother-in-law house. She don't own a stick of this one.

"When you git your claim that rich man don't care what you make your house of. But they's one thing about it, the outside, I mean the roof, is got to be tin. That's the law. No way to put out a fire in Shanty Town. So it's tin roofs here or you can't put up a house."

An old woman appeared at the door. She wore a broad-brimmed man's hat, full skirted brown calico dress, and a sweater with the elbows out. Toothless and stooped, she was as wrinkled as a dried apple. Without a word she walked to the far end of the porch, dragged the wooden box near the edge back to the wall. She pulled the hat down over her eyes as she settled on the box for a sitting nap.

Fan jerked her head toward the old woman. "It sure looks to me like my uncle might know Mammy likes to drap down for a nap now and then the same as anybody. He's got a broke back-leg and can't work none. He lives on 'tother side of the house and he gits lonesome and comes around here and sets and sets and talks and then gits hisself settled on Mammy's bed. It always musses up the bed having him drap down on it. Don't you think Mammy looks awful old? She ain't, really. Jest about seventy. I guess me and her both looks more age than we is. That's the way it is when you can't keep no meat to your bones. You jest shrivel up like a simlin hit by the drouth. Folks is always thinking I'm past the age I says I am. I don't keer, though. Gals that's always studying about they looks want to fool some man into marrying them. I'm forty-seven years old and I ain't never been married. And Lord a-living! I don't want to be! I ain't hardly strong enough to live single.

"I may look bullhide strong, but I ain't. Mammy can outwork me two to one. My lands, she works out in that garden from sun-up till night come without stopping for more than a spitting spell. She's plumb stone deef. Couldn't hear you if you's to beller it right down her ear. But she knows every word I say when she can look at me talk. Every word. No matter, she's company for me and I hope the good Lord sees fit to let her live to be a hundred. She is got an old age pension and gits eleven dollars a month. It's what we live on. Besides that, we git supplies off the relief, stuff out of the garden when a drouth or a rise don't hit it.

"But Great Day! When the river rises they's no chance for a garden then. High water will drown a garden right to death. And we do git high water here off and on and the water kivers the whole place. This house is sot bout as high as any of them—ain't but one sot much higher. But you can't git away from high water. Git yourself, maybe, but not your house. The boy that's building that high one there has got hisself a city wife. He figures he's smarter than the rest around here and he's perching his house a foot or two higher. Well, that bride ain't going to be no drier than the rest of us when the river rises up and starts flooding. Day of Judgment! She's going to be wetted down and muddified like anybody else.

"Oh, I tell you I've seen that old river come up. And the gov'ment never sent us no notice of what the water was going to do. We jest set and see it come up. See it and know what we's in for. When it begins to git in the houses, we take and move everything up on the bank across the railroad tracks, and we camp there all on top of each other. Well, city folks come trotting up there gitting under our feets. Coming with soup kettles and kivers and half of them wouldn't no more set foot in your house low water times than nothing at all. I ought not to say a word against them and I know it. I 'preciates what they does. But it's mighty hard for them that's had it easy all they lives to know what 'tis to be poor.

"They's always one saying to another, 'Do you suppose them people's got little enough sense to go back to them shacks when the river goes down?' And that's jest the little sense we've got—to come back to where we got a spot for a garden and a house we've built to live in without putting out rent money when you ain't got money for eats, much less rent. Yes Lord, we'll always go back to Shanty Town till the river rises some day and forgits to go down.

"But, mercy on my soul, it's a mess when the waters run off! You got to take and rake and scrape mud off of everything. Half of what you got is plumb ruined. Oh well, when you been through it time and time again, you can git things in some sort of housekeeping shape before you know it. Then you can start pulling over the garden and seeing what ain't washed up for good. And see if there's no flowers left where you's worked nussing them like babies.

"I has right pretty flowers in the summer time. Nothing left now but that old hanging basket of moss and them mole beans. Castor beans, some calls them. They's supposed to keep a mole from rooting up your ground. No more round here I ever seen, but them beans stands the worst hot weather. They's something green to have around. My nephew trimmed them stalks up that way. He says they looks just like palmettos —them's things that grow down in Florida State. The carnival my nephew works for shows in Florida most of the time. He's a show-hand for it. When they lay off for winter, he comes back here with us. I jest count the year around till the time he's to come. He's my favorite nephew, the only one I've got.

"Mammy's a heap of company but Darcy ain't never one too many for me. He's always good to me and Ma. Gives us money now and then. He carries all the water we use and he gits the driftwood floating in the river. Brings it right to us for stove woods. They's lots men around here picks up money from selling driftwood. Darcy could, but he jest gives it to us like it ain't worth nothing. It's hard for him to git to before somebody else snatches it. I've seen men fight till they drop over whose to git a few driftwood planks. Folks around here have to make out jest every way they can. At times they has right smart luck fishing and you can always sell fresh fish. But then they make you have a license to fish and you got to pay for it. Leastways, men do. Womern don't, so at times they take womern along in the boats when they go fishing. And the Law can't say nothing, not a dadblamed word, if it don't know who made the catch.

"Womern is a big help to men more ways than one. Stretching a little money to go a long way and fixing up men's homes for them. I wish you could see that fern Jack Long's wife got off the undertaker. He had it left over from a funeral. It's so pretty. I just like to go up there and set a spell to look at it all I want to. And Jack's got as much sense as she has about gitting the best that's to be got. He was a regular carpenter before hard times drug him down here to live. When it come to setting up his house, he know'd how. Got good lumber for doing it, too. The way he done it was to go down there to Henley Street where they's building the bridge. He picked up every stick of the wood they throwed away. Got enough for everything but the walls and ceiling. That didn't stump Jack none. He jest went over to a dump heap in South Knoxville, and there he run into jest what he wanted. It was a lot of emptied out sheet-iron barrels. First he knocked the tops and bottoms out. He split the barrels open down the sides and flattened them out for the walls and roof. Right in that same dump he picked up two hundred paint buckets. They's supposed to be empty, but he scooped out about two gallons of paint. It was a plenty for spreading over his house. The colors ain't the same, but that don't matter. It's paint. See over there how he kind of worked the different kinds into stripes and wherly cues? Makes a right pretty sight, don't it? Well, then he tooled and nailed some great big split cardboard boxes for the inside walls and pasted paper over that. Then he tinned the top, for the roof has got to be tin down here in Shanty Town.

"Good Lord! Look who's headed this way! Poor Mrs. Rosson!"

A thin women dressed in black, with a white apron tied around her waist, was hurrying along the beaten foot path in front of the row of shanties. Her fingers nervously picked at her apron as she came.

"Most of the folks in Shanty Town is kin to each other," Fan said. "Mrs. Rosson is the onliest one ain't got a speck of kin around here. She's a widow womern. She ain't like the rest down here, noway. Low class and poor. When she come, all she had left was three or four dollars. Some of the men folks built a house for her from leavings and pick ups. She's scared most of the time. She lives to herself and jest always scared something is going to happen. She's been worse ever since that man tried to kill hisself jumping off the far bridge yonder. I seen him drap. I was setting right here and looking toward the river when he jumped. It didn't kill him right off. But I heard since that he's died."

The woman had reached the yard of Fan's shanty.

"Come on up and set a spell, Mrs. Rosson," Fan invited pleasantly.

The woman made no move toward the porch.

Fan said in a low voice, "She's got it in her head that the wind is going to blow that feller up out of the river. She thinks the wind troubles his sperit. Well, that body, it ain't here, I've told her time and again that Pleas Newman pulled that feller out of the river. He was as live as I am when I seen them carry him off. Pleas never did git a red cent for doing it, neither. Well, one thing he didn't need the money like most around here does. Pleas had a plenty. He bootlegged. Got his liquor from boats that come up and down the river. He was doing so well when he got killed. Making good money. His nephew up and shot him. Fairda never would have killed his Uncle Pleas if he'd been at hisself. Never in this world!"

Mrs. Rosson stood silently, staring at the river.

"It was jest the four of them living in a old houseboat up the river. Pleas, his little gal of about eleven, Fairda, and the woman who done they housekeeping. All of them was drinking the night of the shooting, except the little gal. I knowed Fairda never would shot Pleas unless he'd been crazy drunk. And that mean woman living with first one and the other of the two jest about egged him on. She's a whore. If ever was one she's it. Poor folks ain't got no chance to head the Law to the right one. No chance at all. If they had, I'd hike myself right up to court and tell them folks the straight of it. Git her burned to a crisp in the chair, instead of Fairda."

Mrs. Rosson turned away from the river. She walked to the foot of the steps and stood looking up. She spoke in a faint and worried voice.

"It's wavy today, Fan. The river's awful wavy, Fan. And the wind's up."

She did not wait for Fan to reply. Turning, she walked back in the direction she had come.

"She's gone to lock herself in," said Fan. "That's the way she does. Closes up everthing tight about the house. Well, I've got the best pot of soup back there on the stove. I had Mrs. Rosson in my head when I throwed it together this morning. She's going git a good hot dip or two of it if I has to bust down the door to git it to her. I won't have to, though. She'll let me in. I'll tote it to her in a little tin bucket with a top to it. I keeps it for toting things fit to eat to them that's sick or hungry. When she gits some of that nice, warm soup in her stummick, maybe it'll get that wind out of her head."

(DELLA YOE and JENNETTE EDWARDS, "Till the River Rises.") [20]

THE TENSION BETWEEN FORM AND FLOW

Every human transaction has both some degree of familiarity, constancy, and predictability, and also some degree of novelty. Two apparently diverse motivational tendencies struggle with each other in the process of living. One operates to preserve some form, some certainty on the basis of which we may act with confidence and with some degree of satisfaction. This form, the present world as we know it, may serve however as a springboard from which we can move into the future in seeking higher qualities of value-satisfaction. Human beings, it would seem, seek order within change, and change within order, form within flow and flow within form—a functional continuity in the process of living.

Obviously, there are enormous individual differences in the precise way these two forces work together in individual patterns of living. It is possible to rear children so that the safety-security motive tends to dominate the desire for new experience. It is likewise possible for some to develop a highly adventurous way of life, an almost chaotic instability with an unceasing demand for change. While most of us in one way or another are constantly forced to choose between security and some sort of emergent development, if human beings have no feeling of security, they seem of necessity to seek it before "development" makes sense as a reality and an alternative choice.

For this reason, man's decisions and judgments about behaving in the future are almost inevitably tinged with both hope and fear. Testing assumptions in new situations, building new assumptions, changing one's vocation or "way of life" is always a gamble; there is always the possibility of meeting frustration and disappointment, but there is also the possibility of achieving a richer, deeper level of satisfaction in living. "Speculation, when cramped by certainties, is eased of its wonder and its warmth," observes James Thurber. Mistakes may serve as steppingstones to more adequate and inclusive assumptions, and it would seem that a sense of personal development toward a more satisfying maturity can come about only if we overcome the difficulties of acting effectively in ever-emerging situations. This always involves a process of predicting in the face of uncertainty and acting on the basis of faith.

In his book *Of Men and Mountains,* Supreme Court Justice William O. Douglas tells how he had to hitch rides on freight trains to get himself from the Yakima Valley in the State of Washington to the Columbia Law School in New York. As a moving freight train was going through the Chicago freight yards, Douglas was forced by a brakeman to jump off. He was scratched and bruised, had only a few dollars to his name, was hungry, tired, and homesick. He reports his thoughts as follows:

Most of my friends and all the roots I had in life were in the Yakima Valley. There would be a job and a home awaiting me, and fishing trips and mountain climbs. . . . It was a friendly place, not hard and cruel like these freight yards. . . . I would be content and happy there.

Then why this compulsion to leave the valley? Why this drive, this impulse to leave the scenes I loved? To reach for unknown stars, to seek adventure, to abandon the convenience of home? And what of pride? What would I say if I returned? That I didn't have the guts to work my way east, to work my way through law school, to live the hard way? [21]

We can agree with Whitehead that "the ultimate motive power, alike in science, in morality, and in religion, is the sense of value, the sense of importance. It takes the various forms of wonder, of curiosity, of reverence, or worship, of tumultuous desire for merging personality in something beyond itself. This sense of value imposes on life incredible labours, and apart from it life sinks back into the passivity of its lower types." [22]

It is man's purposing and valuing that most characterize his living and that give it its greatest creativity. Each moment of awareness may be conceptualized as reflecting both determinations from the past *and creativity,* the basic thrust of freedom into the future with its own unique possibilities unknown in the present. Horace Kallen has said that "Choosing and trusting are of the inwardness of our humanity. They enter and compound in the formation of every next event, making its existence a human value, propitious or menacing, or both." [23]

✿　✿　✿

In the following chapter, we specify and illustrate some of the contributions which the unique, participating individual makes to the concrete situation. We shall be concerned with those essential factors (such as assumptions, attitudes, and habits) which we tend to think of as belonging to the person rather than to the environment, but which obviously have no independent existence apart from the total context of the full organism-environment situation. With this reminder to the reader of the necessary arbitrariness of our procedures and classifications, we next abstract and discuss the role of certain "personal" factors within the process of living.

4

Man Assuming[*]

> "When I say a thing is true, I
> mean that I cannot help believ-
> ing it . . . truth is the system
> of my limitations."
> —OLIVER WENDELL HOLMES

The ground rules of transactional inquiry allow us to abstract
any aspect of a process of living, for provisional description and
investigation, so long as what we abstract is later considered with
respect to the full transactional situation. We turn, therefore, to a
consideration of what the functioning individual contributes to a
concrete transaction of living.

In previous chapters we generally designated as "externality" all
aspects of the situation other than the person himself. Although
impingements of physical energies on the organism and the pattern
of physiological excitation play an essential role in a human transaction, we will not be directly and immediately concerned with
them in this chapter. These factors may be thought of as establishing possibilities within which the processes contributed by the individual determine what particular psychological events shall occur.

The human being is not a passive, neutral recipient of meaningful messages transmitted directly from the outside to its receptors.
Nor is a person's behaving directly controlled by external forces.
Rather, the individual himself is an active, creative participant in
all aspects of the transactions which constitute living.

In specifying certain processes which the functioning person
contributes to the situations he encounters, we are not postulating

* Notes to this chapter begin on p. 332.

specific physiological processes. When we say, for example, that assumptions, beliefs, attitudes and prejudices are or may be present in a transaction, we are referring to psychological concepts, not physiological processes. This is not to deny that such terms name what we may hope can some day be described in the physiologist's language. But in the present state of knowledge, observation of the influence of these processes is best made in terms of psychological variables. If the reader prefers to think of assumptions in physiological terms—as learned and established patterns of neuro-muscular activity or as a functional state of the organism—no great harm will be done. But we feel that it is useful and necessary to make a distinction between physiological and psychological inquiry, and to emphasize the desirability of employing psychological concepts for psychological inquiry.

A fundamental postulate for psychology is that an individual is somehow affected by his own functioning. Just how and where a person is modified by his own functioning may be a matter of speculation. But that there *is* an effect seems undeniable. Present functioning is obviously influenced by past functioning and, in turn, will influence future functioning. In general, we refer to the accumulated and organized effects of the past as the person's past experience or memory. This merely affirms that the past has been "registered" in some way that enables it to influence the present in the on-going process of living.

St. Augustine had a keen appreciation of the importance of past experience in stocking "the belly of the mind":

. . . this very memory itself is mind (for when we give a thing in charge, to be kept in memory, we say, "See that you keep it in mind"; and when we forget, we say, "It did not come to my mind," and "It slipped my mind," calling the memory itself the mind); this being so, how is it that when with joy I remember my past sorrow, the mind hath joy, the memory hath sorrow; the mind upon the joyfulness which is in it, is joyful, yet the memory upon the sadness which is in it, is not sad? Does the memory perchance not belong to the mind? Who will say so? The memory then is, as it were, the belly of the mind, and joy and sadness, like sweet and bitter food; which, when committed to the memory, are as it were, passed into the belly, where they may be stowed, but cannot taste. Ridiculous it is to imagine these to be alike; and yet are they not utterly unlike. . . .

Great is the power of memory, a fearful thing, O my God, a deep and boundless manifoldness; and this thing is the mind, and this am I myself. What am I then, O my God? What nature am I? A life various and manifold, and exceeding immense. Behold in the plains, and caves, and caverns of my memory, innumerable and innumerably full of innumerable kinds of things, either through images, as all bodies; or by actual presence, as the arts; or by certain notions or impressions, as the affections of the mind, which, even when the mind doth not feel, the memory retaineth, while yet whatsoever is in the memory is also in the mind—over all these do I run, I fly; I dive on this side and on that, as far as I can, and there is no end. So great is the force of memory, so great the force of life, even in the mortal life of man. [1]

These registered effects of the past are in a sense carried with a person all the time—but in *potential* form. It is inconceivable that all of the registered effects of the past should be relevant to a present, concrete transaction. If, for example, a person has, as we say, an anti-class X prejudice, this prejudice is operative only when some member of class X or some symbol of class X exists in awareness for the prejudiced individual. Where is the prejudice when it is not present? It is absent, non-existent but potential. It is not then what we have called an "essential factor," because it apparently does not participate in and therefore makes no difference in the transaction we are studying at the moment. Yet it is available if and when an appropriate occasion is encountered and its potential significance is relevant.

This raises the problem of how, among all the potentialities registered, only those appropriate to the occasion are "raised" to an operating level. And this is a good point at which to admit our ignorance. If the perceiving of another human being as a member of class X (a significance) depends upon an assumption or prejudice and if the coming into existence of the prejudice depends upon the perceiving, which comes first? The chicken or the egg?

It would seem reasonable to suppose that these aspects arise and develop together in mutual interdependence with neither serving as cause or effect. No relationships are determined uniquely in advance of a specific transaction. The particular assumptions which play a role in a particular transaction will depend upon the unique past of the participating individual, upon the particular pattern of physiological excitation, and on psychological variables, such as purposes. The organism functions selectively in terms of the total organism-environment situation at the moment. The problem of which comes first, which is cause and which effect, arises only if the external and internal processes are regarded as two separate, *inter*acting (rather than *trans*acting) sets of factors. The so-called personal contributions discussed in this chapter are best regarded as abstracted and conceptualized aspects of an event which inquiry finds taking place, but which owe their existence and function to all other interdependent aspects of the full transactional situation.

ASSUMPTIONS

Assumptions may be conceived as weighted averages of the registered effects of previous transactions. They are potential until they enter into a present concrete transaction. The net result of our previous transactions is that we construct for ourselves an organized and interrelated pattern of assumptions which give continuity and significance to perceiving and serve as guides and bases for future behaving. Each specific transaction of living involves the participation of and reflects the presence of certain patterns of assumptions.

We build up assumptions about things or objects, about individuals and groups, about institutions and ideologies, about nations and organizations, about cause-and-effect relationships, about the value-qualities of experience we believe will follow certain actions, and so forth. It should not be inferred that the individual is always aware of the participation of assumptions as functional variables in his perceiving and behaving. What an individual is aware of comes about through a process in which the organism takes account of many more aspects of the transaction than the individual realizes. Many of our assumptions are "subconscious." We may accept the world as we experience it as inherently given, without any recognition on our part that it is influenced by our unique past history. We may become aware of some of our assumptions only if we experience repeated disillusionment, frustrations, surprises, and disappointments as we strive to achieve our purposes.

Our assumptions generally have an implicit future reference. We assume that the sun will rise tomorrow; that if we touch a hot wire we will get a shock; that one event will be followed by another which is, to some extent, predictable. This future reference of our assumptions provides sequential significances and constitutes what might be called our world of expectancies. The role of this aspect of our assumptive world in the transactions of living will be discussed and illustrated later in the chapter. We are using the term assumption here, then, as a generic term to include knowledge, beliefs, attitudes, stereotypes, prejudices, superstitions, and other effects of past experience that can be conceptualized. The following excerpts point to the extent to which the characteristics of our psychological world are a function of both the registered past and the anticipated future.

THE SCOTTY WHO KNEW TOO MUCH*
By James Thurber

Several summers ago there was a Scotty who went to the country for a visit. He decided that all the farm dogs were cowards, because they were afraid of a certain animal that had a white stripe down its back. "You are a pussy-cat and I can lick you," the Scotty said to the farm dog who lived in the house where the Scotty was visiting. "I can lick the little animal with the white stripe, too. Show him to me." "Don't you want to ask any questions about him?" said the farm dog. "Naw," said the Scotty. "*You* ask the questions."

So the farm dog took the Scotty into the woods and showed him the white-striped animal and the Scotty closed in on him, growling and slashing. It was all over in a moment and the Scotty lay on his back. When he came to, the farm dog said, "What happened?" "He threw vitriol," said the Scotty, "but he never laid a glove on me."

A few days later the farm dog told the Scotty there was another animal all the farm dogs were afraid of. "Lead me to him," said the Scotty. "I can lick anything that doesn't wear horseshoes." "Don't you want to ask any questions about him?" said the farm dog. "Naw," said the Scotty. "Just show me where he hangs out." So the farm dog led him to a place in the woods and pointed out the little animal when he came along. "A clown," said the Scotty, "a pushover," and he closed in, leading with his left and exhibiting some mighty fancy footwork. In less than a second the Scotty was flat on his back, and when he woke up the farm dog was pulling quills out of him. "What happened?" said

* Reprinted by permission of the author; copyright 1939 The New Yorker Magazine, Inc.

the farm dog. "He pulled a knife on me," said the Scotty, "but at least I have learned how you fight out here in the country, and now I am going to beat *you* up." So he closed in on the farm dog, holding his nose with one front paw to ward off the vitriol and covering his eyes with the other front paw to keep out the knives. The Scotty couldn't see his opponent and he couldn't smell his opponent and he was so badly beaten that he had to be taken back to the city and put in a nursing home.

Moral: It is better to ask some of the questions than to know all the answers. [2]

In a part of a forest was a ram, separated from his flock. In the armor of his great fleece and horns, he roamed the wood, a tough customer.

Now one day a lion in that forest, who had a retinue of all kinds of animals, encountered him. At this unprecedented sight, since the wool so bristled in every direction as to conceal the body, the lion's heart was troubled and invaded by fear. "Surely, he is more powerful than I am," thought he. "That is why he wanders here so fearlessly." And the lion edged away.

But on a later day the lion saw the same ram cropping grass on the forest floor, and he thought: "What! The fellow nibbles grass! His strength must be in relation to his diet." So he made a quick spring and killed the ram. (*The Panchatantra.*) [3]

A dog, used to eating eggs, saw an Oyster; and opening his mouth to its widest extent, swallowed it down with the utmost relish, supposing it to be an egg. Soon afterwards suffering great pain in his stomach, he said, "I deserve all this torment, for my folly in thinking that everything round must be an egg."

They who act without sufficient thought, will often fall into unsuspected danger. (*Aesop's Fables.*) [4]

> O me! what eyes hath Love put in my head,
> Which have no correspondence with true sight;
> Or, if they have, where is my judgment fled,
> That censures falsely what they see aright?
> If that be fair whereon my false eyes dote,
> What means the world to say it is not so?
> If it be not, then love doth well denote
> Love's eye is not so true as all men's: no,

How can it? O! how can Love's eye be true,
That is so vex'd with watching and with tears?
No marvel then, though I mistake my view:
The sun itself sees not till heaven clears.
    O cunning Love! with tears thou keep'st me blind,
    Lest eyes well-seeing thy foul faults should find.
                        (WILLIAM SHAKESPEARE, "Sonnet 148.") [5]

I should say the defendants have done just that for which they are indicted. If I might agree to their conviction without creating a precedent, I cheerfully would do so. I can see in their teachings nothing but humbug, untainted by any trace of truth. But that does not dispose of the constitutional question whether misrepresentation of religious experience or belief is prosecutable; it rather emphasizes the danger of such prosecutions.

The Ballard family claimed miraculous communication with the spirit world and supernatural power to heal the sick. They were brought to trial for mail fraud on an indictment which charged that their representations were false and that they "well knew" they were false. The trial judge, obviously troubled, ruled that the court could not try whether the statements were untrue, but could inquire whether the defendants knew them to be untrue; and, if so, they could be convicted.

I find it difficult to reconcile this conclusion with our traditional religious freedom.

In the first place, as a matter of either practice or philosophy I do not see how we can separate an issue as to what is believed from considerations as to what is believable. The most convincing proof that one believes his statements is to show that they have been true in his experience. Likewise, that one knowingly falsified is best proved by showing that what he said happened never did happen. How can the Government prove these persons knew something to be false which it cannot prove to be false? If we try religious sincerity severed from religious verity, we isolate the dispute from the very considerations which in common experience provide its most reliable answer.

In the second place, any inquiry into intellectual honesty in religion raises profound psychological problems. William James, who wrote on these matters as a scientist, reminds us that it is not theology and ceremonies which keep religion going. Its vitality is in the religious experiences of many people. "If you ask what these experiences are, they are conversations with the unseen, voices and visions, responses to prayer, changes of heart, deliverances from fear, inflowings of help, assurances of support, whenever certain persons set their own internal attitude in certain appropriate ways." If religious liberty includes, as it must, the right to communicate such experiences to others, it seems to me an impossible task for juries to separate fancied ones from real ones, dreams from happenings, and hallucinations from true clairvoyance. Such experiences, like some tones and colors, have existence for one, but none at all for another. They cannot be verified to the minds of those whose field of consciousness does not include religious insight. When one comes to trial which turns on any aspect of religious belief or representation, unbelievers among his judges are likely not to understand and are almost certain not to believe him.

And then I do not know what degree of skepticism or disbelief in a religious representation amounts to actionable fraud. James points out that 'Faith means belief in something concerning which doubt is theoretically possible.' Belief in what one may demonstrate to the senses is not faith. All schools of religious thought make enormous assumptions, generally on the basis of revelations authenticated by some sign or miracle. The appeal in such matters is to a very different plane of credulity than is invoked by representations of secular fact in commerce. Some who profess belief in the Bible read literally what others read as allegory or metaphor, as they read Aesop's fables. Religious symbolism is even used by some with the same mental reservations one has in teaching of Santa Claus or Uncle Sam or Easter bunnies or dispassionate judges. It is hard in matters so mystical to say how literally one is bound to believe the doctrine he teaches and even more difficult to say how far it is reliance upon a teacher's literal belief which induces followers to give him the money.

There appear to be persons—let us hope not many—who find refreshment and courage in the teachings of the "I Am" cult. If the members of the sect get comfort from the celestial guidance of their "Saint Germain," however doubtful it seems to me, it is hard to say that they do not get what they pay for. Scores of sects flourish in this country by teaching what to me are queer notions. It is plain that there is wide variety in American religious taste. The Ballards are not alone in catering to it with a pretty dubious product.

The chief wrong which false prophets do to their following is not financial. The collections aggregate a tempting total, but individual payments are not ruinous. I doubt if the vigilance of the law is equal to making money stick by overcredulous people. But the real harm is on the mental and spiritual plane. There are those who hunger and thirst after higher values which they feel wanting in their humdrum lives.

They live in mental confusion or moral anarchy and seek vaguely for truth and beauty and moral support. When they are deluded and then disillusioned, cynicism and confusion follow. The wrong of these things, as I see it, is not in the money the victims part with half so much as in the mental and spiritual poison they get. But that is precisely the thing the Constitution put beyond the reach of the prosecutor, for the price of freedom of religion or of speech or of the press is that we must put up with, and even pay for, a good deal of rubbish.

Prosecutions of this character easily could degenerate into religious persecution. I do not doubt that religious leaders may be convicted of fraud for making false representations on matters other than faith or experience, as for example if one represents that funds are being used to construct a church when in fact they are being used for personal purposes. But that is not this case, which reaches into wholly dangerous ground. When does less than full belief in a professed credo become actionable fraud if one is soliciting gifts or legacies? Such inquiries may discomfort orthodox as well as unconventional religious teachers, for even the most regular of them are sometimes accused of taking their orthodoxy with a grain of salt.

I would dismiss the indictment and have done with this business of judicially examining other people's faiths.

(MR. JUSTICE JACKSON, *United States v. Ballard*.) [6]

When I say that a thing is true, I mean that I cannot help believing it. I am stating an experience as to which there is no choice. But as there are many things that I cannot help doing that the universe can, I do not venture to assume that my inabilities in the way of thought are inabilities of the universe. I therefore define the truth as the system of my limitations, and leave absolute truth for those who are better equipped. With absolute truth I leave absolute ideals of conduct equally on one side.

But although one believes in what commonly, with some equivocation, is called necessity; that phenomena always are found to stand in quantitatively fixed relations to earlier phenomena; it does not follow that without such absolute ideals we have nothing to do but to sit still and let time run over us. As I wrote many years ago, the mode in which the inevitable comes to pass is through effort. Consciously or unconsciously we all strive to make the kind of world that we like. And although with Spinoza we may regard criticism of the past as futile, there is every reason for doing all that we can to make a future such as we desire.

(OLIVER WENDELL HOLMES, *Collected Legal Papers*.) [7]

KNOWLEDGE, OPINION, ATTITUDE

It seems worthwhile to subdivide assumptions into knowledges, opinions, and attitudes. And it may also be useful to give special consideration to different so-called types of assumptions such as superstitions, delusions, prejudices, and stereotypes. While distinctions of this sort are quite arbitrary, they are in line with common-sense usage.

Assumptions called "knowledges" and "opinions" may be differentiated principally on the basis of whether or not, from the first-person point of view, the assumption has been tested and verified satisfactorily. An assumption may be called a "knowledge" if, from the standpoint of the individual, it has been subjected to proof and has been found to be true. Thus, an individual may know that striking the keys of a piano will produce sounds; that an unsupported object will fall; that a tennis ball will bounce; and that there is no person named Santa Claus who comes down the chimney. An individual may also know that labor unions are infiltrated with American Communist conspirators; that other people are plotting his destruction; and that stepping on cracks in the sidewalk will bring bad luck. As the saying goes: "It ain't what folks don't know that makes 'em so damned ignorant; it's the things they know that ain't so." Nonetheless, what an individual "knows" has been proved to his own satisfaction, no matter how the proof has been derived. It has been found true in his own experience. Knowledge is characterized by a high degree of surety and certainty.

An opinion, on the other hand, is still to be verified. It is, for the individual, still only within the limits of possibility. There may be difficulties in subjecting the assumption to testing. This is the reason why many assumptions which refer to the more distant future are classified as opinions. One may have an opinion concerning who the next president will be or whether or not our radar screen is fully effective. But these assumptions can be tested only in the undisclosed future. A respondent over ninety years old who was once asked on a public opinion poll if he believed in life after death said, "I don't know now, but I'll damn soon find out."

What is knowledge for one person may be opinion for another.

The criteria by which we classify a particular assumption for a particular individual are internal to the psychological reality-world of that individual. It is also evident that the participation of these different assumptions will be reflected differently in the transaction of the moment—that is, will influence experiencing-behaving differentially.

Our "attitudes" may be thought of as a phase or aspect of some assumptions. It is an aspect of assumptions which refers especially to the value-quality of experience—an assumption concerning what positive or negative value-qualities of experience will arise in the course of transacting with certain objects, persons, groups, institutions, or concepts. To put it differently, an attitude is that aspect of an assumption which gives evaluative significances to anything within the psychological world of the individual. It provides predictions or probabilities as to what value-qualities will arise in association with some aspect of the individual's psychological world. An attitude, however, never stands alone. It is an aspect of an assumption which in its other aspects is also classifiable as a knowledge or opinion. The word "attitude" refers to a subject-object relationship of an affective nature and is reflected both in awareness and in behaving.

We have repeatedly made a distinction between what is revealed by phenomenal (first-person) analysis and what is revealed through experimentation. For example, phenomenal analysis tells us that a perceived object is "out there" in the external world existing in its own right with certain inherent properties. But it can be demonstrated beyond doubt that the functioning organism contributes to the "existence" of this perceived object and that the perceived object is only a "best bet." Similarly, knowledges, opinions, and attitudes are, as phenomena, aspects of the self, not of the external environment, but neither are they entirely independent of that environment. From the transactional perspective, phenomena which appear to be inherently given as distinct entities are seen as a pattern of interdependent aspects united in a single event. The functional role of various aspects of the event are not immediately given as phenomena. A table *when seen* across the room is not immediately given in awareness as a probability, or as a prognostic directive for action; an attitude *as experienced* is not a prediction as to what value-qualities will come forth from transacting with the "object" of the attitude.

If you say, "I dislike that cat," and we take the word "dislike" as the verbal expression of an attitude, it would seem that the attitude is yours and the cat is "out there." This is correct. However, it is obvious that your attitude could not exist without some knowledge or opinion concerning the cat, which attributes certain properties to the cat. These attributed properties are interdependently related to the attitude. Furthermore, both the attributed properties and the attitude are dependent upon impingements and physiological excitation. The attitude and the cat exist in union. You are probably seeing quite a different cat than that seen by a small girl who may be standing beside you. The word "attitude," like other concepts used in psychology, can be most misleading if it is thought of—as it usually is—as being a state of mind directed toward some stimulus. There is a most important difference between the more orthodox notion of a person having "an attitude toward" something, with its implication of merely reacting to something, and the transactional notion that a person experiences something in a certain way because of the pattern of assumptions he brings to a situation, which help to determine what the situation will seem to him to be. While such a differentiation may at first seem trivial, we believe it is basic for an understanding of behavior, especially of man's social behavior.

One other point: What we have named knowledges, opinions, and attitudes are intellectualized assumptions; that is, assumptions of which the individual is aware. Perhaps a good generic term for all intellectualized assumptions would be "belief." In addition to beliefs there are, of course, those non-intellectualized assumptions of which the individual is unaware but which may play a crucial role in structuring his psychological world.

SUPERSTITIONS, DELUSIONS, PREJUDICES, AND STEREOTYPES

From what has already been said, it should be evident that our tendency to label certain assumptions as superstitions, delusions, prejudices, and stereotypes stems from adopting an external, third-person point of view. When an assumption is examined from the inside, from the first-person point of view, it is seen as consistent and true, as founded on perceived facts. Superstitions and delusions may be regarded as false assumptions in terms of some external evidence: they may fail to meet the criteria of consensual validation. But they may be completely valid and of immediate functional significance in terms of internal criteria used by the individual. There is necessarily an intimate relationship between man's beliefs and his perceived facts.

All beliefs to some degree involve prejudice or prejudgment, since it is impossible to get all the facts to carry on transactions with some object or class of objects in every conceivable context an infinite number of times. The term "prejudice," however, is used more specifically to refer to beliefs that place some "object" at an advantage or disadvantage. From a functional point of view, prejudice furnishes predictions as to what value-qualities will arise in the course of transacting with the "object."

A "stereotype" usually refers to a fixed belief which tends to be common to the reality-worlds of many individuals, which is based on very sparse evidence and which is resistant to change because of some function it serves. If the majority of people in the United States believe that college professors are absent-minded, impractical idealists, this belief can be classified as a stereotype. Stereotypes are oversimplified assumptions rigidly held yet neither so intensely believed nor so emotionally-loaded as prejudices.

No new psychological principles need be formulated in order to understand superstitions, delusions, prejudices, and stereotypes. But such beliefs are of special importance for the social psychologist and to any layman (who may also be a psychologist) concerned with public or international affairs which are, after all, ultimately rooted in the reality-worlds of individual people.

Some selections in the next group illustrate the nature of certain attitudes and prejudices and how they manifest themselves in concrete situations; others indicate some of the factors involved in the development of certain beliefs and attitudes, or describe techniques for instilling certain attitudes.

As far back as I can remember I was saddened by the amount of misery I saw in the world around me. Youth's unqualified *joie de vivre* I never really knew, and I believe that to be the case with many children, even though they appear outwardly merry and quite free from care.

One thing that specially saddened me was that the unfortunate animals had to suffer so much pain and misery. The sight of an old limping horse, tugged forward by one man while another kept beating it with a stick to get it to the knacker's yard at Colmar, haunted me for weeks.

It was quite incomprehensible to me—this was before I began going to school—why in my evening prayers I should pray for human beings only. So when my mother had prayed with me and had kissed me good-night, I used to add silently a prayer that I had composed myself for all living creatures. It ran thus: "O, heavenly Father, protect and bless all things that have breath; guard them from all evil, and let them sleep in peace."

A deep impression was made on me by something which happened during my seventh or eighth year. Henry Bräsch and I had with strips of india-rubber made ourselves catapults, with which we could shoot small stones. It was spring and the end of Lent, when one morning Henry said to me, "Come along, let's go on to the Rebberg and shoot some birds." This was to me a terrible proposal, but I did not venture to refuse for fear he should laugh at me. We got close to a tree which was still without any leaves, and on which the birds were singing beautifully to greet the morning, without showing the least fear of us. Then stooping like a Red Indian hunter, my companion put a bullet in the leather of his catapult and took aim. In obedience to his nod of command, I did the same, though with terrible twinges of conscience, vowing to myself that I would shoot directly he did. At that very moment the church bells began to ring, mingling their music with the songs of the birds and the sunshine. It was the Warning-bell, which began half an hour before the regular peal-ringing, and for me it was a voice from heaven. I shooed the birds away, so that they flew where they were safe from my companion's catapult, and then I fled home. And ever since then, when the Passiontide bells ring out to the leafless trees and the sunshine, I reflect with a rush of grateful emotion how on that day their music drove deep into my heart the commandment: "Thou shalt not kill."

From that day onward I took courage to emancipate myself from the fear of men, and whenever my inner convictions were at stake I let other people's opinions weigh less with me than they had done previously. I tried also to unlearn my former dread of being laughed at by my school-fellows. This early influence upon me of the commandment not to kill or torture other creatures is the great experience of my childhood and youth. By the side of that all others are insignificant.

While I was still going to the village school we had a dog with a light brown coat, named Phylax. Like many others of his kind, he could not endure a uniform, and always went for the postman. I was, therefore, commissioned to keep him in order whenever the postman came, for he was inclined to bite, and had already been guilty of the crime of attacking a policeman. I therefore used to take a switch and drive him into a corner of the yard, and keep him there till the postman had gone. What a feeling of pride it gave me to stand, like a wild beast tamer, before him while he barked and showed his teeth, and to control him with blows of the switch whenever he tried to break out of the corner! But this feeling of pride did not last. When, later in the day, we sat side by side as friends, I blamed myself for having struck him; I knew that I could keep him back from the postman if I held him by his collar and stroked him. But when the fatal hour came round again I yielded once more to the pleasurable intoxication of being a wild beast tamer!

During the holidays I was allowed to act as driver for our next door neighbour. His chestnut horse was old and asthmatic, and was not allowed to trot much, but in my pride of drivership I let myself again and again be seduced into whipping him into a trot, even though I knew and felt that he was tired. The pride of sitting behind a trotting horse infatuated me, and the man let me go on in order not to spoil my pleasure. But what was the end of the pleasure? When we got home and I noticed during the unharnessing what I had not looked at in the same way when I was in the cart, viz. how the poor animal's flanks were working, what good was it to me to look into his tired eyes and silently ask him to forgive me?

On another occasion—it was while I was at the Gymnasium, and at home for the Christmas holidays—I was driving a sledge when neighbour Löscher's dog, which was known to be vicious, ran yelping out of the house and sprang at the horse's head. I thought I was fully justified in trying to sting him up well with the whip, although it was evident that he only ran at the sledge in play. But my aim was too good; the lash caught him in the eye, and he rolled howling in the snow. His cries of pain haunted me; I could not get them out of my ears for weeks.

I have twice gone fishing with rod and line just because other boys asked me to, but this sport was soon made impossible for me by the treatment of the worms that were put on the hook for bait, and the wrenching of the mouths of the fishes that were caught. I gave it up, and even found courage enough to dissuade other boys from going.

(ALBERT SCHWEITZER, *Memoirs of Childhood and Youth*.) [8]

I remember how, when we were returning home from the Okhta along the banks of the Neva, I was first told about Vladimir Ilyich's brother,

Alexander. He was a member of the Narodnaya Volya, and took part in the attempt on the life of Alexander III in 1886. He perished at the hands of the Tsar's hangmen before he had even come of age. He was very fond of Alexander. They had many common tastes, and both of them liked to remain alone for long periods in order to concentrate. They usually lived together, at one time in a special part of the house. And when any of their numerous boy or girl cousins called, the brothers had a favourite phrase: "Oblige us with your absence." Both brothers were tenacious workers, and both were of revolutionary dispositions. But the difference in age probably made itself felt. For Alexander Ilyich did not tell Vladimir about everything.

Vladimir Ilyich told me of his brother's activity as a naturalist. The last summer that he came home, he had been preparing a dissertation on worms and was working all the time at the microscope. In order to get as much light as possible, he rose at daybreak and immediately set to work. "No, my brother won't make a revolutionary, I thought then," Vladimir Ilyich recounted; "a revolutionary cannot devote so much time to the study of worms." He soon saw how he was mistaken.

The fate of his brother undoubtedly profoundly influenced Vladimir Ilyich. What in addition played an important part was the fact that by this time Vladimir Ilyich had already begun to think independently on many subjects, and had already come to his own decision as to the necessity of revolutionary struggle.

Had it been otherwise, probably his brother's fate would only have caused him profound grief, or at the most awakened in him the resolve and aspiration to follow his brother's footsteps. In these circumstances his brother's fate whetted his brain, brought out in him an unusual sobriety of thought, the capacity to look truth straight in the face, not for one moment to be carried away by phrases or illusions. It developed in him an extremely honest approach to all problems.

(NADEZHDA K. KRUPSKAYA, *Memories of Lenin.*) [9]

The following selection is an excerpt from a translation of an approved textbook used in teacher training in Soviet Russia:

Pupils must come to know that in our Soviet country the interests of the people are inseparable from the interests of their government. The source of Soviet patriotism is found in the fact that the people themselves under the leadership of the Communist Party have built their own life, and in the further fact that our rich and beautiful land only now, under Soviet power, is genuinely open to the workers. And the natural attachment to the native country is strengthened by pride in one's socialist Motherland, in the Bolshevik Party, in the leader of the workers of the entire world—Comrade Stalin. It is a great honor to any individual to be a citizen of and to defend such a fatherland.

Pupils must become acquainted with the great past of our Motherland which fills the workers of our country with pride. Lenin in his work on *The National Pride of the Great Russians* wrote: "Is the feeling of national pride alien to us, Great Russians, conscious proletarians? Certainly not! We love our language and our Motherland, we work tirelessly to raise her toiling masses, nine-tenths of her population, to the conscious life of democrats and socialists. It grieves us to see and feel to what violence, oppression, and ridicule the czarist executioners, noblemen, and capitalists subject our beautiful Motherland. We are proud of the fact that this violence evokes opposition out of our midst, out of the midst of the Great Russians, that the Great Russians produced Radizhchev, the Decembrists, and the revolutionary intelligentsia of the seventies, that the Great Russian working class created in 1905 a powerful revolutionary party of the masses. . . ." *

In the history of our country the Great Russian people occupy a special place. The history of this people is the history of its heroic struggle for independence and freedom against innumerable enemies—against invaders and conquerors. In 1242 the Great Russian people defeated the Teutonic knights. In 1613 they shattered and destroyed the Polish attackers. In 1709 they destroyed the Swedish invaders. In 1812 they destroyed the army of the conqueror of Europe—Napoleon I. Collaborating with and leading other peoples of our country, the Russian people carried on a heroic and victorious struggle against the violence and mockery of the boyars and the czars, the landlords and the capitalists.

Under the harsh conditions of tyranny and violence the Russian people have created an extraordinary culture. In the fields of science and art they have exhibited astonishing power, creating in spite of the difficult conditions of monarchical oppression, a magnificent literature, remarkable paintings, and original music, enjoyed by the whole world. "Sealed were the lips of the people, tied were the wings of the spirit, but its heart gave birth to tens of great artists of word, sound, color." (Gorky.) The Russian classics focus attention squarely on the struggle for the freedom of mankind and show their power, above all, in their identification with the people.

The Russian people are rightfully proud of the names of Lomonossov, Radizhchev, Pestel, Rileev, Pushkin, Lermontov, Gogol, Herzen, Chernishevsky, Dobroliubov, Nekrasov, Saltikov-Shchedrin, Tolstoy, Gorky,

* Lenin, *Works,* Vol. XVIII, p. 81.

and others. The Russian culture unquestionably has had a significant influence on the development of the foremost world cultures.

That great patriot of our Motherland, I. V. Stalin, speaking with contempt of the fascist cannibals, reveals the role and significance of the Russian nation: "And these people devoid of conscience and honor, people with the morality of animals, have the insolence to invoke the destruction of the Great Russian nation, the nation of Plekhanov and Lenin, Belinsky and Chernishevsky, Pushkin and Tolstoy, Glinka and Tschaikovsky, Gorky and Chekov, Sechenov and Pavlov, Repin and Surikov, Suvorov and Kutuzov!" *

In his speech in the Kremlin on May 24, 1945, in honor of the commanding troops of the Red Army, Comrade Stalin characterized the Russian people as "the most remarkable of all the nations entering into the composition of the Soviet Union." The Russian people, in the words of Comrade Stalin, "merit general recognition in the Great Patriotic War as the leading power among all the peoples of our country . . . they have a clear mind, steadfast character, and endurance."

V. G. Belinsky in the "almanac of 1840" wrote: "We envy our grandchildren and great-grandchildren who are destined to see Russia in 1940 standing at the head of the civilized world, giving laws to science and art, and receiving reverent tribute from all enlightened humanity." These remarkable words have been fulfilled.

The Russian working class, in the struggle for the building of a new socialist society, has stood at the head of and has led the entire people. We are filled with a feeling of national pride because the Russian nation created this revolutionary class and proved itself capable of giving to mankind the great models of the struggle for freedom and for socialism. The numerous peoples of the Soviet Union were liberated from national oppression, from the oppression of landlords and capitalists, through the direct aid of the Russian proletariat. The services of the Russian people are exceptionally great, not only to the peoples of the Soviet Union, but also to all mankind. The Soviet Union by its example inspires the workers of the entire world for the struggle against exploiters and ravishers. The history of the Russian people proves to all mankind their political wisdom, their military valor, and their genius.

These facts from the past of our heroic people must be skillfully presented to the pupils in order to awaken in them a feeling of just pride in everything progressive and revolutionary which has so enriched the history of our country.

At the same time it is the task of the teacher and the school to reveal to the pupils everything loathsome and hideous committed by the ruling

* Stalin, *The Great Patriotic War of the Soviet Union,* 1944, p. 28.

classes of czarist Russia, to show them the oppression, the bondage, and the injustice suffered by the workers in pre-October Russia. The best people of our country carried on the most resolute struggle against monarchy, landlords, and capitalists.

All of this, to be sure, must be presented imaginatively and emotionally. And then the pupils will understand why we must strengthen, cherish, protect, and love our socialist Motherland—why we must hate oppression and exploitation.

The pupils of the Soviet school must realize that the feeling of Soviet patriotism is saturated with irreconcilable hatred toward the enemies of socialist society.

Hatred gives birth to class revolutionary vigilance and creates a feeling of irreconcilability toward the class enemy; the weakening of such vigilance undermines the cause of the socialist revolution. It is necessary to learn, not only to hate the enemy, but also to struggle with him, in time to unmask him, and finally, if he does not surrender, to destroy him.

Through materials dealing with the Great Patriotic War one must show the pupils the international significance of our struggle with the German robbers. We proved to be the only power capable, not only of halting the dark surge of fascism, but also of inflicting on it a decisive and fatal defeat. At the Twenty-Fourth Anniversary of the Great October Socialist Revolution Comrade Stalin, turning to the army, said: "The whole world looks upon you as the power capable of destroying the pillaging regiments of the German robbers. The enslaved peoples of Europe who have fallen under the yoke of the German robbers look upon you as their saviors. A great liberating mission falls to your lot. Be worthy of this mission! The war which you conduct is a war of liberation, a war of justice." * Here with remarkable clarity is revealed the union of the interests of our Motherland with the interests of the workers of the entire world.   (GEORGE S. COUNTS and NUCIA P. LODGE [trans.], *I Want to Be Like Stalin.*) [10]

An extraordinary, semipolitical, social gathering which I once attended in New Delhi brought out in sharp relief the difference between some of these Indian political attitudes and our own. It was a rather large but casual buffet supper at the leading Indian club, organized, as far as I could gather, by a group of women in order to give some of the wartime Americans in Delhi a favorable view of Indian life.

There were about a dozen other Americans, mostly from the house on Man Singh road where I lived myself, two elderly, civilian Britishers, and an almost incredibly heterogeneous collection of Indians. The domi-

* *Ibid.,* pp. 36–37.

nant note was Congress and Hindu, but there was a good sprinkling of
Moslems, several Communists or socialist revolutionaries, one or two
Parsees, and a quite large representation of "official" Indians—those who
continued to hold office under the British and were consequently de-
nounced as traitors or collaborationists by the extreme nationalists.

Such politically mixed company can be seen at large gatherings in
Washington or any Western capital and mayhem seldom results, even
in times of political tension, but they are not quite the same kind of
gathering this one was. Though it was fairly large, it was not a rigidly
social function, and an air of informality was carefully maintained.
Furthermore, it had a definite cultural, if not political, intent; it was in
a sense deliberate propaganda.

The hostesses had evidently contrived this buffet in order to show
their foreign guests that, however much Indians might disagree among
themselves on political questions, they were members of a united nation.
This underlying purpose must have been explained in advance to the
Indian guests and they had not only accepted but were playing the roles
expected of them.

If some isolationist hostess in Washington in the days of bitter controversy before Pearl Harbor had tried to assemble a group of repre-
sentative isolationists and interventionists of various sects in a social
gathering of this sort in order to show a group of visiting Latin Americans that we were basically united despite our differences, she would
have encountered considerable difficulty. If she had invited me I would
have refused, on the ground that I did not want to give any foreigners
the impression that I was basically united with isolationists.

Knowing the bitterness of partisan feeling that divided many of these
Indians—the basic Hindu-Moslem antagonism, the venomous feud between the Congress members and the Communists, who were at that
time vociferously supporting the British war effort, the contempt of all
the revolutionaries for the "officials"—it seemed to me remarkable that
they were there at all. Far more remarkable was the way they behaved
toward one another.

There was no constraint, very little merely social chitchat and apparently no effort to avoid conversational thin ice. The talk was largely
political throughout the evening. Courteously but emphatically the
Indians, both among themselves and in front of the foreigners, expressed
their contradictory opinions about the issues of the day. Perhaps the
most amazing thing about them was that they seemed to listen to Indians
of conflicting belief, actually listen to the arguments of adversaries, not
just keep silent in order to give the adversary his inning.

Most of these Indians seemed to be old friends, which explained the lack of constraint or rancor in their intercourse, but what was not explained was how they had happened to remain friends despite their differences. It is true that the most extreme shades of Congress opinion were represented by women, the men being in jail at that time, but the female of the species is seldom less fanatical than the male, and we had with us as the main attraction of the evening one of the leading political firebrands of India, Mrs. Sarojini Naidu, distinguished poetess, one-time president of the All-India Congress, also one-time jailbird.

Mrs. Naidu, a rich exuberant personality, a deep-bosomed and deep-minded Indian version of the clubwoman type, was then at large on probation, being forbidden to make speeches or to carry on any political activity. At a signal from one of the hostesses she rose and made us a little speech, a witty, barbed, and yet good-humored one, explaining that she was not making a speech because she was forbidden to make them. Her remarks, with evident self-enjoyment, were directed mainly at the two Britishers. Then she read us one of her poems, a melodious and effective bit of verse expressing the age-old pan-religious ideal of India by subtly blending and orchestrating the street-noises of world's religions, the bells of Christendom, the muezzin's cry from Islam's minaret, the chants of Jewish rabbi and Buddhist monk, the religious songs of Hinduism.

It was an apt and convincing pointing of the evening's lesson, I thought. The courtesy, the broad tolerance, the respect for sincerely opposed opinion, which these Indians of conflicting political faiths manifested in their behavior toward one another, had ancient cultural and religious roots. Throughout the ages the "thousand waving arms" of Hindu pantheism had welcomed adherents of the most diverse belief and observance. From a theological point of view it seemed difficult to consider the Kali-worshipers, who sacrifice living animals to the Goddess of Death and eat meat, the Vaishnavites, whose worship of Vishnu as a personal and ethical deity is closely akin to Christianity, and the Brahma-worshipers whose God is an abstract, impersonal, all-embracing theistic principle, as members of the same religion. Yet to the Hindus these three cults are not even different sects but specialized branches of Hinduism in the sense that the various monastic orders are specialized branches of Catholicism.

Even those outside the pale of Hinduism had never seemed wholly creatures of the outer darkness to the Indian mind. Since the Moslem invasions, and despite the secular strife they engendered, the theological liberalism of Hinduism had actually increased, there had been a reaching-out toward Islam, a definite effort to appreciate the values of Islam, and this had tempered the fierce Moslem intolerance, created at least the beginnings of an Indian, not just a Hindu, tolerance. This tolerance, in its purest Hindu form, was not mere passive toleration of alien belief; far more remarkable than the fact that Hinduism has never persecuted heretics or unbelievers, is the fact that the most devout Hindus have always considered it a duty of the mind to listen respectfully to their arguments.

How far this tolerance applies to the modern political religions was illustrated by the next item on the evening's program. A clamor arose for another poetess to be heard from, and when the poetess, Miss Mumtaz Shanawas, a young woman with the vivid, black-eyed Persian type of beauty, seemed reluctant to be heard after greatness, Mrs. Naidu took the lead in urging her, with many expressions of familiar endearment.

The younger woman, I gathered, was both a close personal friend and a literary disciple of Mrs. Naidu. Under the latter's indulgent but not patronizing eye, while across the room her wealthy, conservative Moslem parents beamed with tender pride, Miss Shanawas recited several vigorously talented verses filled with the woes and battle-cries of the Indian proletariat, for poetry happened to be only her hobby—she was an ardent and active member of the Indian Communist Party. When she had finished, Mrs. Naidu led the warm burst of applause from the whole room and then embraced her.

Considering that Miss Shanawas' poetry, despite its literary merits, was straight Marxist propaganda, that her political comrades were supporting the alien government which kept Mrs. Naidu's in jail—and not just supporting the British but viciously attacking Congress as well—this seemed to me quite an interesting performance. If, in the black autumn of 1939, I had been called upon to hear a young Communist poet recite verses denouncing the imperialist war which the Soviet-Nazi nonaggression pact had done so much to make inevitable, I doubt very much that I could have achieved the mellowness of Mrs. Naidu's attitude. Yet she was no confused liberal, no compromiser, no appeaser, as the British had long since learned.

Indians—at least the Hindus—I decided, were more successful than we are at dissociating their feelings about a human being from their feelings about his ideas. More than that, they had a different feeling about ideas, about political truth. Again, it seemed to me, this attitude stemmed from their religious traditions.

Hinduism, unlike Christianity (or Marxism) is not a religion of revealed truth but of truths—truths which by their very plurality are suggestive guide-posts to the discovery of God rather than unbreakable rules for salvation. Men are pilgrims and each man in his own age must find his own way to God. An individual pilgrim may feel that his path is the best for himself—or even for all men—but, if he is a Hindu, he is not disturbed when others take different paths, because what is important to him is not the path but the ultimate goal. Faith, to the Hindu, seems to mean an intense longing and constant striving for religious fulfillment rather than any kind of systematic belief; there is a definite feeling that the intensity of the longing is a much greater factor in religious success than the rightness of the belief.

(EDMOND TAYLOR, *Richer by Asia.*) [11]

PURPOSES, ASSUMPTIONS, PERCEIVING

In any one occasion of living, we tend to be most aware of those aspects of the environment which have a bearing on our purposes at a given time. The familiar phenomenon called "selective sleep" is of interest in this connection. The mother of a young baby may, for example, sleep through a thunderstorm but awaken at the slightest whimper from the baby; the coast guard may sleep soundly while the foghorn blows, but wake up the instant the foghorn stops because of some mechanical failure. The reader can supply many other illustrations from his own experience of the interrelationships existing among purposes, assumptions, and awareness.

Our range of awareness may vary on different occasions from a single object to a multiplicity of objects and their interrelationships, depending upon the particular purposes contributing to the transaction of the moment. An artist may be aware only of the color of an object at a given time, while the awareness of a fire watcher atop a mountain may include a broad sweep of the surrounding territory. Generally, we are not aware of advertisements for products wholly irrelevant to our purposes; at least, after leafing through a magazine we do not recall having seen them, although we must have glanced at them in order to avoid them and to see what we do remember having seen. Without some knowledge of an individual's assumptive world and of his purposes at the moment it is utterly impossible to predict accurately the significances he is aware of merely from a knowledge of what is potentially available in the environment.

HABITS

When our actions confirm the hypotheses provided by our perceptions, the experienced significances tend to become constancies and the actions, we say, tend to become habits. Actions that have proved their adaptive value generally recede almost completely from awareness except when they operate at the wrong time or under the wrong circumstances, and thus lead to surprise or frustration. For example, one morning a friend of ours was in a special hurry to get to work. So, thinking he would save time, he got dressed while waiting for the tub to fill up with water for his morning bath! But usually by definition habits operate with high reliability and tend constantly to confirm certain aspects of our expectancies. They may not be accompanied by high-order value-qualities of experience. But they do provide a constancy and consistency in many important phases of our experiencing-doing which we appreciate especially when we are away from our usual environment and cannot effectively utilize the habits we have built up and which take care of so many of the routines of life for us. After talking with Charlie Goldman, the man who trained Rocky Marciano, former heavyweight champion, a reporter wrote, "It is his greatest regret that he didn't get Marciano when Marciano was in about the second grade of public school. 'He would have learned to do things right without thinking,' Mr. Goldman says. 'Then all he would have to think about is what he wanted to do.'" [12]

EXPECTANCIES

We turn now to consider a bit more what we have called "expectancies." Every experience of the present, in addition to being rooted in the past, also includes an anticipated future. Purposive activity has a future reference; we can check our perceptual significances only by comparing significances experienced now with significances experienced as we act to carry out our purposes. The physiologist Lillie has written that "directiveness is a universal character of living organisms; and, if we may judge from our immediate experience, it always includes some element of anticipation and subjective aim, involving future reference; these are characteristic features of the psychical. The psychical is foreseeing and integrative in its essential nature; it tends to finish or round off an uncompleted experience. To recognize this property as having its special importance in the living organism is not to ignore or undervalue the stable physical conditions which also form an indispensable part of the vital organization. In the psychophysical system which is the organism, factors of both kinds are to be regarded as equally important and as always supplementing one another in the total activity of the system." [13]

It is because of expectancy that we are able to give a reasonable account of illusions, surprises, and disappointments, as well as of hopes and fears, joys and sorrows. We experience surprise (or perhaps shock or disappointment) when something is perceived which lies outside our immediate expectancies or when we experience a significance different from that based on our expectancy. For one who does not know about "bouncing putty," his expectancy is upset the first time he drops it on a hard surface. Some people are surprised when they discover that an eminent surgeon turns out to be a woman, when a renowned scientist or statesman turns out to be a Negro, when a small town clerk can answer the $64,000 question on a quiz program.

Depending on the particular circumstances, we experience anger, fear, joy, humor, or some other emotion when we experience something for which our assumptions and expectancies have not fully prepared us.

Here are some examples. We experience *anxiety* when we feel that our expectancies and assumptions are not reliable enough to serve as guides for action or for predicting the outcome of what is to us an important event in the future. To live without anxiety we must have a high degree of certainty that our actions will further our purposes. When we feel very unsure that we can cope with an unexpectedly encountered situation or that we can act effectively, we experience *fear*. And if we encounter a situation in which some behavior on our part seems absolutely essential for survival and if we have no assumptions that seem to provide guides for appropriate action, we may experience *panic*. Millions of Americans were panic-stricken on Halloween night in 1938, for example, when they heard a broadcast purporting to describe an invasion by Martians from whom there appeared to be no escape. [14] Some of the conditions and the nature of panic are amusingly illustrated in James Thurber's account of the day the people of Columbus, Ohio, believed the dam had broken.

THE DAY THE DAM BROKE*
By James Thurber

My memories of what my family and I went through during the 1913 flood in Ohio I would gladly forget. And yet neither the hardships we endured nor the turmoil and confusion we experienced can alter my feeling toward my native state and city. I am having a fine time now and wish Columbus were here, but if anyone ever wished a city was in hell it was during that frightful and perilous afternoon in 1913 when the dam broke, or, to be more exact, when everybody in town thought that the dam broke. We were both ennobled and demoralized by the experience. Grandfather especially rose to magnificent heights which can never lose their splendor for me, even though his reactions to the flood were based upon a profound misconception: namely, that Nathan Bedford Forrest's cavalry was the menace we were called upon to face. The only possible means of escape for us was to flee the house, a step which grandfather sternly forbade, brandishing his old army saber in his hand. "Let the sons —— —— come!" he roared. Meanwhile hundreds of people were streaming by our house in wild panic, screaming "Go east! Go east!" We had to stun grandfather with the ironing board. Impeded as we were by the inert form of the old gentleman—he was taller than six feet and weighed almost a hundred and seventy pounds— we were passed, in the first half-mile, by practically everybody else in the city. Had grandfather not come to, at the corner of Parsons Avenue and Town Street, we would unquestionably have been overtaken and engulfed by the roaring waters—that is, if there had *been* any roaring waters. Later, when the panic had died down and people had gone rather sheepishly back to their homes and their offices, minimizing the distances they had run and offering various reasons for running, city engineers pointed out that even if the dam had broken, the water level would not have risen more than two additional inches in the West Side. The West Side was, at the time of the dam scare, under thirty feet of water—as, indeed, were all Ohio river towns during the great spring floods of twenty years ago. The East Side (where we lived and where all the running occurred) had never been in any danger at all. Only a rise of some ninety-five feet could have caused the flood waters to flow over High Street—the thoroughfare that divided the east side of town from the west—and engulf the East Side.

The fact that we were all as safe as kittens under a cookstove did not, however, assuage in the least the despair and the grotesque desperation which seized upon the residents of the East Side when the cry spread like a grass fire that the dam had given way. Some of the most dignified, staid, cynical, and clear-thinking men in town abandoned their wives, stenographers, homes, and offices and ran east. There are few alarms in the world more terrifying than "The dam has broken!" There are few persons capable of stopping to reason when that clarion cry strikes upon their ears, even persons who live in towns no nearer than five hundred miles to a dam.

The Columbus, Ohio, broken-dam rumor began, as I recall it, about noon of March 12, 1913. High Street, the main canyon of trade, was loud with the placid hum of business and the buzzing of placid business-men arguing, computing, wheedling, offering, refusing, compromising. Darius Conningway, one of the foremost corporation lawyers in the Middle-West, was telling the Public Utilities Commission in the language of Julius Caesar that they might as well try to move the Northern star as to move him. Other men were making their little boasts and their little gestures. Suddenly somebody began to run. It may be that he had simply remembered, all of a moment, an engagement to meet his wife, for which he was now frightfully late. Whatever it was, he ran east on Broad Street (probably toward the Maramor Restaurant, a favorite place for a man to meet his wife). Somebody else began to run, perhaps a newsboy in high spirits. Another man, a portly gentleman of affairs, broke into a trot. Inside of ten minutes, everybody on High Street, from the Union Depot to the Courthouse was running. A loud mumble gradually crystallized into the dread word "dam." "The dam has broke!" The fear was put into words by a little old lady in an electric, or by a traffic cop, or by a small boy: nobody knows who, nor does it now really matter. Two thousand people were abruptly in full flight. "Go east!," was the cry that arose—east away from the river, east to safety. "Go east! Go east! Go east!"

Black streams of people flowed eastward down all the streets leading in that direction; these streams, whose headwaters were in the drygoods stores, office buildings, harness shops, movie theaters, were fed by trickles of housewives, children, cripples, servants, dogs and cats, slipping out of the houses past which the main streams flowed, shouting and screaming. People ran out leaving fires burning and food cooking and doors wide open. I remember, however, that my mother turned out all the fires and that she took with her a dozen eggs and two loaves of bread. It was her plan to make Memorial Hall, just two blocks away, and take refuge somewhere in the top of it, in one of the dusty rooms where war veterans met and where old battle flags and stage scenery were stored. But the seething throngs, shouting "Go east!" drew her along and the rest of us with her. When grandfather regained full consciousness, at Parsons Avenue, he turned upon the retreating mob like a vengeful prophet and exhorted the men to form ranks and stand off the Rebel dogs, but at length he, too, got the idea that the dam had broken and, roaring "Go east!" in his powerful voice, he caught up in one arm a small child and in the other a slight clerkish man of perhaps forty-two and we slowly began to gain on those ahead of us.

A scattering of firemen, policemen, and army officers in dress uniform —there had been a review at Fort Hayes, in the northern part of town— added color to the surging billows of people. "Go east!" cried a little child in a piping voice, as she ran past a porch on which drowsed a lieutenant-colonel of infantry. Used to quick decisions, trained to immediate obedience, the officer bounded off the porch and, running at full tilt, soon passed the child, bawling "Go east!" The two of them emptied rapidly the houses of the little street they were on. "What is it? What is it?" demanded a fat, waddling man who intercepted the colonel. The officer dropped behind and asked the little child what it was. "The dam has broke!" gasped the girl. "The dam has broke!" roared the colonel. "Go east! Go east! Go east!" He was soon leading, with the exhausted child in his arms, a fleeing company of three hundred persons who had gathered around him from living-rooms, shops, garages, backyards, and basements.

Nobody has ever been able to compute with any exactness how many people took part in the great rout of 1913, for the panic, which extended from the Winslow Bottling Works in the south end to Clintonville, six miles north, ended as abruptly as it began and the bobtail and ragtag and velvet-gowned groups of refugees melted away and slunk home, leaving the streets peaceful and deserted. The shouting, weeping, tangled evacuation of the city lasted not more than two hours in all. Some few people got as far east as Reynoldsburg, twelve miles away; fifty or more reached the Country Club, eight miles away; most of the others gave up, exhausted, or climbed trees in Franklin Park, four miles

out. Order was restored and fear dispelled finally by means of militia-
men riding about in motor lorries bawling through megaphones: "The
dam has *not* broken!" At first this tended only to add to the confusion
and increase the panic, for many stampeders thought the soldiers were
bellowing "The dam has *now* broken!," thus setting an official seal of
authentication on the calamity.

All the time, the sun shone quietly and there was nowhere any sign
of oncoming waters. A visitor in an airplane, looking down on the strag-
gling, agitated masses of people below, would have been hard put to it
to divine a reason for the phenomenon. It must have inspired, in such
an observer, a peculiar kind of terror, like the sight of the *Marie Celeste,*
abandoned at sea, its galley fires peacefully burning, its tranquil decks
bright in the sunlight.

An aunt of mine, Aunt Edith Taylor, was in a movie theater on High
Street when, over and above the sound of the piano in the pit (a W. S.
Hart picture was being shown), there rose the steadily increasing tromp
of running feet. Persistent shouts rose above the tromping. An elderly
man, sitting near my aunt, mumbled something, got out of his seat, and
went up the aisle at a dogtrot. This started everybody. In an instant the
audience was jamming the aisles. "Fire!" shouted a woman who always
expected to be burned up in a theater; but now the shouts outside were
louder and coherent. "The dam has broke!" cried somebody. "Go east!"
screamed a small woman in front of my aunt. And east they went, pushing and shoving and clawing, knocking women and children down,
emerging finally into the street, torn and sprawling. Inside the theater,
Bill Hart was calmly calling some desperado's bluff and the brave girl
at the piano played "Row! Row! Row!" loudly and then "In My Harem."
Outside, men were streaming across the Statehouse yard, others were
climbing trees, a woman managed to get up onto the "These Are My
Jewels" statue, whose bronze figures of Sherman, Stanton, Grant, and
Sheridan watched with cold unconcern the going to pieces of the capital
city.

"I ran south to State Street, east on State to Third, south on Third
to Town, and out east on Town," my Aunt Edith has written me. "A
tall spare woman with grim eyes and a determined chin ran past me
down the middle of the street. I was still uncertain as to what was the
matter, in spite of all the shouting. I drew up alongside the woman
with some effort, for although she was in her late fifties, she had a
beautiful easy running form and seemed to be in excellent condition.
'What is it?' I puffed. She gave me a quick glance and then looked
ahead again, stepping up her pace a trifle. 'Don't ask me, ask God!' she
said.

"When I reached Grant Avenue, I was so spent that Dr. H. R. Mallory —you remember Dr. Mallory, the man with the white beard who looks like Robert Browning?—well, Dr. Mallory, whom I had drawn away from at the corner of Fifth and Town, passed me. 'It's got us!' he shouted, and I felt sure that whatever it was *did* have us, for you know what conviction Dr. Mallory's statements always carried. I didn't know at the time what he meant, but I found out later. There was a boy behind him on roller-skates, and Dr. Mallory mistook the swishing of the skates for the sound of rushing water. He eventually reached the Columbus School for Girls, at the corner of Parsons Avenue and Town Street, where he collapsed, expecting the cold frothing waters of the Scioto to sweep him into oblivion. The boy on the skates swirled past him and Dr. Mallory realized for the first time what he had been running from. Looking back up the street, he could see no signs of water, but nevertheless, after resting a few minutes, he jogged on east again. He caught up with me at Ohio Avenue, where we rested together. I should say that about seven hundred people passed us. A funny thing was that all of them were on foot. Nobody seems to have had the courage to stop and start his car; but as I remember it, all cars had to be cranked in those days, which is probably the reason."

The next day, the city went about its business as if nothing had happened, but there was no joking. It was two years or more before you dared treat the breaking of the dam lightly. And even now, twenty years after, there are a few persons, like Dr. Mallory, who will shut up like a clam if you mention the Afternoon of the Great Run.[15]

We experience *joy* when, in a continuing situation in which our expectancies have been ambiguous and when the outcome may be either disastrous or highly advantageous, the situation resolves itself in our favor. When, for example, a member of our family undergoes a dangerous operation which may restore health, the period of waiting for the outcome is filled with both hope and anxiety. If our hope is fulfilled, we experience an intense joy; and if our worst expectancies are confirmed, we suffer a deep sorrow.

We become *suggestible* when we are unsure of our assumptions and expectancies or when we have no guides for action which appear to be relevant. In these cases we actively seek the advice and suggestions of others. Mass movements, the initiation and spread of rumors, and the effectiveness of propaganda, can be understood in great measure in terms of the development and function of assumptions.

We experience *disappointment* when an expectancy that positive value-qualities of experience will be forthcoming in a certain situation turns out to be wrong. If we experience much less than the expected level of positive value-quality, or if we experience the situation as neutral, we suffer disappointment.

In a culture where money is essential for security, the assumption commonly develops that high-level satisfactions depend upon experiences associated with objects which money provides—a nice house, a late-model automobile, a television set. Exclusive devotion to such an assumption, however, provides no opportunity to experience value-qualities obtainable through intellectual or aesthetic pursuits, or through some variety of creative activity. The first of the following group of selections is an excerpt from a legend by Tolstoy and concerns a Russian peasant named Pakhóm, who assumed that the value-qualities to be obtained from living were proportional to his wealth as measured by the standards of his group. The other selections also negate the view that happiness is closely associated with material possessions.

Thus Pakhóm lived for three years. He rented land, and sowed wheat. The years were good, and the wheat grew well, and he had some money laid by. He could live and live, but it appeared tiresome to Pakhóm to buy new land from people each year, and to have to fuss about the land: where there was any good land the peasants would swoop down on it and take it all up, and unless he was quick in getting it, he would not have any land to sow in. And in the third year he rented with a merchant a pasture on shares, and they ploughed it all up, but the peasants from whom they rented it went to court about it, and all their work was lost. "If it were all my land," he thought, "I should not bow to any one, and there would be no worry."

Pakhóm began to inquire where he could buy land in perpetuity, and he found a peasant who would sell. The peasant had bought five hundred desyatínas, but he had lost money, and now wanted to sell the land cheap. Pakhóm began to bargain with him. He bargained and bargained, and finally got it for fifteen hundred roubles, half of it on time. They had almost settled the matter, when a transient merchant stopped at his farm to get something to eat. They drank tea, and started to talk. The merchant told him that he had come from the far-off country of the Bashkirs. There, he said, he had bought about five thousand desyatínas from the Bashkirs, and for this he had to pay only one thousand roubles. Pakhóm began to question him. The merchant told him all about it.

"All I had to do," he said, "was to gain over the old men. I gave in presents about one hundred roubles' worth of cloaks and rugs, and a caddy of tea, and filled up with wine those who would drink. I gave twenty kopeks per desyatína." He showed the deed. "The land," he said, "lies along a river, and it is all a prairie."

Pakhóm began to question him all about it.

"You can't walk around the land in a year," he said, "and it all belongs to the Bashkirs. And the people have no sense, just like sheep. You can get it almost for nothing."

"Well," thought Pakhóm, "why do I want to buy five hundred desyatínas for one thousand roubles, and take a debt on my neck? There I can get rich for one thousand roubles."

Pakhóm inquired how to get there, and as soon as he saw the merchant off he got ready to go. He left his house to his wife, and took his hired help, and went with him. They travelled to the city, bought a caddy of tea, presents, and wine, just as the merchant had said. They travelled and travelled, until they had five hundred versts behind them. On the seventh day they came to the Bashkir roaming-grounds. Everything was as the merchant had said. They all live in the steppe, above the river, in felt tents. They themselves neither plough nor eat bread, but the cattle and horses run in droves in the steppe. Back of the tents the colts are tied, and twice a day they drive the mares there, and milk them, and make kumys of the milk. The women churn the kumys and make cheese, and all the men do is to drink kumys and tea, eat mutton, and play a pipe. They look sleek and merry, and they celebrate the whole summer. The people are all ignorant, and know no Russian, but they are kind.

As soon as they saw Pakhóm, they came out of their tents, and surrounded the guest. There was an interpreter there. Pakhóm told him that he had come to see about some land. The Bashkirs were happy, and they took Pakhóm by his arms, and led him to a nice tent, seated him on rugs, placed down pillows under him, sat around him in a circle, and began to treat him to tea and to kumys. They killed a sheep, and filled him with mutton. Pakhóm fetched the presents from the tarantás, and began to distribute them to the Bashkirs. Pakhóm gave the presents to the Bashkirs, and distributed the tea among them. The Bashkirs were happy. They prattled among themselves, and then told the interpreter to translate.

"They command me to tell you," said the interpreter, "that they like you, and that it is our custom to give our guests every pleasure, and to return presents. You have given us presents; now tell us what you like us to give you of our things."

"What I like," said Pakhóm, "most of all, here, is your land. Where I live," he said, "the land is crowded and worn out by ploughing, but you have much and good land. I have never seen such before."

The interpreter translated. The Bashkirs talked among themselves. Pakhóm did not understand what they were saying, but he saw that they were merry, shouting and laughing. Then they grew silent, and looked at Pakhóm, but the interpreter said:

"They command me to tell you that for the good which you have done them they are glad to give you as much land as you want. You have just to point to it, and it is yours."

Then they talked again, and disputed among themselves. Pakhóm asked what they were disputing, and the interpreter said:

"Some say that they must ask the elder about the land, and that they cannot do it without him. But others say that they can do it without him."

The Bashkirs went on disputing, when suddenly a man in a fox cap came in. They all grew silent and got up, and the interpreter said:

"This is their elder."

Pakhóm immediately took out the best cloak and five pounds of tea, and took this to the elder. The elder received the presents, and sat down in the place of honour. The Bashkirs began at once to talk to him. The elder listened and listened to them, and shook his head to them, for them to keep quiet. Then he began to speak in Russian to Pakhóm.

"Well, you may have it," he said. "Take it wherever you like. There is a great deal of land here."

"How can I take as much as I want?" thought Pakhóm. "I must get some statement, or else they will say that it is mine, and then they will take it away from me."

"Thank you," he said, "for your kind words. You have a great deal of land, but I want only a small part of it. How shall I know which is mine? I must measure it off, and get a statement of some kind. For God disposes of life and of death. You good people give it to me, but your children may come and take it away."

"You are right," said the elder, "we shall give you a statement."

Then Pakhóm said:

"I have heard that a merchant came to see you. You made a present of some land and gave him a deed: I ought to get one myself."

The elder understood it all.

"That is all possible," he said. "We have a scribe, and we will go to town, and affix our seals."

"And what will the price be?" asked Pakhóm.

"We have but one price: one thousand roubles a day."

Pakhóm did not understand him.

"What kind of a measure is a day? How many desyatínas are there in it?"

"We cannot figure it out," he said. "We sell by the day; as much as you can walk over in one day is yours, and a day's price is one thousand roubles."

Pakhóm was surprised.

"But in one day you can walk around a great deal of land," he said.

The elder laughed.

"It is all yours," he said. "But there is just one condition: if you do not come back in one day to the place from which you start, your money is lost."

"But how can I mark off what I walk over?" asked Pakhóm.

"We shall stand on the spot which you will choose, and you will start on the circuit: take with you a spade, and wherever necessary, in the corners, dig a hole, and pile up some turf, and we shall later make a furrow with a plough from hole to hole. Make any circuit you please, but by sundown you must come back to the spot from which you have started. Whatever ground you cover is yours."

Pakhóm was happy. They decided to go out early in the morning. They talked awhile, drank more kumys, ate some mutton, and had tea again; it was getting dark. They bedded Pakhóm on feather beds, and then the Bashkirs went away. They promised to meet him at daybreak, and to go out to the spot before the sun was up.

Pakhóm lay down on the feather bed and could not sleep: he was thinking all the time of the land.

"I will slice off a mighty tract," he thought. "I can walk about fifty versts in one day. The day is long now; in fifty versts there will be a lot of land. The worst I will sell, or let to the peasants, and the best I will keep, and I will settle on myself. I will buy me two ox-teams and will hire two more hands; I will plough up about fifty desyatínas, and on the rest I will let the cattle roam."

Pakhóm could not fall asleep all night. It was only before daybreak that he forgot himself. The moment he became unconscious, he had a dream. He saw himself lying in the same tent, and some one on the outside was roaring with laughter. He wanted to see who was laughing there, and he thought he went out of the tent, and saw the same Bashkir sitting before the tent, holding his belly with both his hands and swaying in his laughter. He went up to him and said: "What are you laughing about?" And it seemed to him that it was not the Bashkir, but the merchant who had stopped at his house and had told him all about the land. And he asked the merchant: "How long have you been here?" But it was no longer the merchant; it was the peasant that long ago had come from the lower country. And Pakhóm saw that it was not the peasant, but the devil himself with horns and hoofs: he was sitting, and laughing, and before him lay a man, in his bare feet, and in a shirt and trousers. And Pakhóm took a closer look to see who the man was. And he saw that it was a dead man,—himself. Pakhóm was frightened, and awoke. "A man will dream anything," he said, as he awoke. He looked around through the open door, and day was breaking, and it was getting light.

"I must wake the people now," he thought, "it is time to start."

Pakhóm got up, woke his labourer in the tarantás, ordered him to hitch up, and went himself to wake the Bashkirs.

"It is time to go out to lay off the land," he said.

The Bashkirs got up, and gathered together, and the elder arrived. The Bashkirs began again to drink kumys and wanted to treat Pakhóm to tea, but he would not wait so long.

"If we are to go, let us go," he said. "It is time."

The Bashkirs came together, and some went on horseback, and others in tarantáses, and they started. Pakhóm went with his labourer in his little tarantás, taking a spade with them. They arrived in the steppe just as it was dawning. They rode up a mound, called "shikhan" in the Bashkir language. They got out of their tarantáses and dismounted from their horses, and gathered in a circle. The elder walked over to Pakhóm, and pointed with his hand.

"Everything you see," he said, "is ours. Choose whatever you please."

Pakhóm's eyes were burning: it was all prairie land, as smooth as the palm of the hand and as black as the poppy, and wherever there was a hollow there were different kinds of grass, breast-high.

The elder took off his fox cap and put it on the ground.

"This will be the goal," he said. "From here you will start, and here you will come back. Whatever you circle about will be yours."

Pakhóm took out the money, put it on the cap, and pulled off his caftan, and so was left in his sleeveless coat. He pulled his girdle tighter over his belly, drew up his trousers, put a wallet with bread in his bosom, tied a can of water to his belt, pulled up his boot-legs, took the spade from his labourer, and got ready to go. He thought for awhile in what direction to start,—it was nice everywhere. He thought: "It makes no difference. I will go eastward." He turned his face toward the sun, stretched himself, and waited for the sun to peep out. He thought: "I must not waste time in vain. It is easier to walk while it is fresh." The moment the sun just glistened over the edge, Pakhóm threw the spade over his shoulder and started over the steppe.

Pakhóm walked neither leisurely, nor fast. He walked about a verst; he stopped, dug a hole, and put some turf in a heap, so as to make the sign clearer. He went on. He was getting limbered up, and he increased his step. After walking a distance, he dug another hole.

Pakhóm looked around. The shikhan could easily be seen in the sunshine, and the people were standing there, and the tires on the wheels of the tarantáses glistened. Pakhóm guessed that he had walked five versts. He was getting warm, so he took off his coat, threw it over his shoulder, and marched on. It grew warm. He looked at the sun. It was time to think of breakfast.

"I have walked the distance of a ploughing," thought Pakhóm, "and there are four of them in a day,—it is too early yet to turn. I must just take off my boots."

He sat down, pulled off his boots, stuck them in his girdle, and started off again. It was easy to walk now. He thought: "I will walk another five versts, then I will turn to the left. The land is so fine, it is a pity to leave it out." The farther he went, the nicer it was. He went straight ahead. He turned back to look: the shikhan was barely visible, and the people looked like black ants, and something could barely be seen glistening in the sun.

"Well," thought Pakhóm, "I have walked enough in this direction. I must turn in. I am hot, too: I must take a drink."

He stopped, dug a large hole, piled up the turf, untied the can, took a drink, and bent sharply to the left. He walked on and on, and the grass was high, and he felt hot.

Pakhóm was beginning to grow tired; he looked at the sun, and saw that it was exactly noon.

"Well," he thought, "I must take a rest."

Pakhóm stopped and sat down. He ate a piece of bread and drank some water, but did not lie down: he was afraid he might fall asleep. After sitting awhile he started off again. At first the walking was easy. The lunch gave him new strength. It grew very hot, and he felt sleepy;

but he kept walking, thinking that he would have to suffer but a little while, and would have to live long.

He walked quite a distance in this direction. He was on the point of turning, when, behold, he came upon a wet hollow; it was a pity to lose this. He thought that flax would do well there. He walked on straight. He took in the hollow, then dug a hole beyond it, and turned around the second corner. Pakhóm looked back at the shikhan; it was mist-covered from the heat, quivering in the air, and through the haze he could barely see the people.

"Well," thought Pakhóm, "I have taken two long sides. I must make this one shorter."

He started on his third side, and began to increase his speed. He looked at the sun, and it was already near the middle of the afternoon, but he had made only two versts on the third side. To the goal it was still fifteen versts.

"Yes," he thought, "though it is going to be a crooked estate, I must walk in a straight line. I must not take in too much,—as it is I have a great deal."

Pakhóm quickly dug a hole, and turned straight toward the shikhan.

Pakhóm walked straight toward the shikhan, and it was getting hard. He was thirsty, and he had cut and hurt his feet, and he began to totter. He wanted to rest, but he could not, for he would not get back by sundown. The sun did not wait, and kept going down and down.

"Oh," he said, "I hope I have not made a mistake and taken in too much. What if I do not get back in time?"

He looked ahead of him at the shikhan and up at the sun; it was still far to the shikhan, and the sun was not far from the horizon.

Pakhóm walked, and it was hard for him, but he kept increasing his gait. He walked and walked, and it was far still, so he began to trot. He threw away his coat, his boots, and the can; he threw away his cap, but held on to the spade to lean on it.

"Oh," he thought, "I have made a mistake and have ruined the whole affair. I shall not get back before sundown."

And terror took his breath away. He ran, and his shirt and trousers stuck to his body from perspiration, and his mouth was dry. In his breast it was as though bellows were being pumped, and in his heart there was a hammering, and his legs gave way under him. Pakhóm felt badly: he was afraid he might die from too much straining.

He was afraid he might die, but he did not dare to stop.

"I have run so much," he thought, "so how can I stop now? They will only call me a fool."

He ran and ran, and was getting near, and could hear the Bashkirs screaming and shouting to him, but their noise made him still more excited. He ran with all his might, and the sun was getting near the edge: it was lost in the mist, and looked as red as blood. It was just beginning to go down. The sun was nearly gone, but it was no longer far to the goal. He saw the people waving their hands at him from the shikhan, and encouraging him. He saw the fox cap on the ground and the money on top of it; and he saw the elder sitting on the ground, holding his hands over his belly. And Pakhóm recalled his dream.

"There is a lot of land," he thought, "but will God grant me to live on it? Oh, I have ruined myself," he thought. "I shall not reach the spot."

Pakhóm looked at the sun, and it was down to the ground,—a part of it was down, and only an arch was standing out from the horizon. Pakhóm made a last effort and bent forward with his whole body: his legs hardly moved fast enough to keep him from falling. He ran up to the shikhan, when suddenly it grew dark. He looked around, and the sun was down. He groaned.

"My labour is lost," he thought.

He wanted to stop, but he heard the Bashkirs shouting to him, and then he recalled that here below it seemed to him that the sun was down, but that on the shikhan it was not yet down. Pakhóm made a last effort, and ran up the shikhan. On the shikhan it was still light. He ran up, and saw the cap. In front of the cap sat the elder, laughing and holding his hands on his belly. Pakhóm recalled the dream. He groaned, and his legs gave way, and he fell forward, and his hands touched the cap.

"You are a fine fellow!" cried the elder. "You have come into a lot of land."

Pakhóm's labourer ran up, wishing to raise him, but blood was flowing from his mouth, and he was dead.

The Bashkirs clicked their tongues, pitying him.

The labourer picked up the spade, and dug a grave for Pakhóm, as much as he measured from his feet to his head,—three arshíns,—and buried him in it.   (TOLSTOY, "How Much Land a Man Needs.") [16]

I asked professors who teach the meaning of life to tell me what is happiness.
And I went to famous executives who boss the work of thousands of men.
They all shook their heads and gave me a smile as though I was trying to fool with them.
And then one Sunday afternoon I wandered out along the Desplaines river

And I saw a crowd of Hungarians under the trees with their women
and children and a keg of beer and an accordion.

(CARL SANDBURG, "Happiness.") [17]

In certain remote corners of the Old World you may still sometimes
stumble upon a small district that seems to have been forgotten amid
the general tumult, and to have remained stationary while everything
around it was in motion. The inhabitants, for the most part, are extremely
ignorant and poor; they take no part in the business of the country and
are frequently oppressed by the government, yet their countenances
are generally placid and their spirits light.

In America I saw the freest and most enlightened men placed in
the happiest circumstances that the world affords; it seemed to me as
if a cloud habitually hung upon their brow, and I thought them serious
and almost sad, even in their pleasures.

The chief reason for this contrast is that the former do not think of the
ills they endure, while the latter are forever brooding over advantages
they do not possess. It is strange to see with what feverish ardor the
Americans pursue their own welfare, and to watch the vague dread
that constantly torments them lest they should not have chosen the
shortest path which may lead to it.

A native of the United States clings to this world's goods as if he were
certain never to die; and he is so hasty in grasping at all within his
reach that one would suppose he was constantly afraid of not living long
enough to enjoy them. He clutches everything, he holds nothing fast, but
soon loosens his grasp to pursue fresh gratifications.

In the United States a man builds a house in which to spend his old
age, and he sells it before the roof is on; he plants a garden and lets
it just as the trees are coming into bearing; he brings a field into tillage
and leaves other men to gather the crops; he embraces a profession and
gives it up; he settles in a place, which he soon afterwards leaves to
carry his changeable longings elsewhere. If his private affairs leave
him any leisure, he instantly plunges into the vortex of politics; and if
at the end of a year of unremitting labor he finds he has a few days'
vacation, his eager curiosity whirls him over the vast extent of the
United States, and he will travel fifteen hundred miles in a few days to
shake off his happiness. Death at length overtakes him, but it is before
he is weary of his bootless chase of that complete felicity which forever
escapes him.

At first sight there is something surprising in this strange unrest of so
many happy men, restless in the midst of abundance. The spectacle

itself, however, is as old as the world; the novelty is to see a whole people furnish an exemplification of it.

Their taste for physical gratifications must be regarded as the original source of that secret disquietude which the actions of the Americans betray and of that inconstancy of which they daily afford fresh examples. He who has set his heart exclusively upon the pursuit of worldly welfare is always in a hurry, for he has but a limited time at his disposal to reach, to grasp, and to enjoy it. The recollection of the shortness of life is a constant spur to him. Besides the good things that he possesses, he every instant fancies a thousand others that death will prevent him from trying if he does not try them soon. This thought fills him with anxiety, fear, and regret and keeps his mind in ceaseless trepidations, which leads him perpetually to change his plans and his abode.

If in addition to the taste for physical well-being a social condition be added in which neither laws nor customs retain any person in his place, there is a great additional stimulant to this restlessness of temper. Men will then be seen continually to change their track for fear of missing the shortest cut to happiness.

It may readily be conceived that if men passionately bent upon physical gratifications desire eagerly, they are also easily discouraged; as their ultimate object is to enjoy, the means to reach that object must be prompt and easy or the trouble of acquiring the gratification would be greater than the gratification itself. Their prevailing frame of mind, then, is at once ardent and relaxed, violent and enervated. Death is often less dreaded by them than perseverance in continuous efforts to one end.

The equality of conditions leads by a still straighter road to several of the effects that I have here described. When all the privileges of birth and fortune are abolished, when all professions are accessible to all, and a man's own energies may place him at the top of any one of them, an easy and unbounded career seems open to his ambition and he will readily persuade himself that he is born to no common destinies. But this is an erroneous notion, which is corrected by daily experience. The same equality that allows every citizen to conceive these lofty hopes renders all the citizens less able to realize them; it circumscribes their powers on every side, while it gives freer scope to their desires. Not only are they themselves powerless, but they are met at every step by immense obstacles, which they did not at first perceive. They have swept away the privileges of some of their fellow creatures which stood in their way, but they have opened the door to universal competition; the barrier has changed its shape rather than its position. When men are nearly alike and all follow the same track, it is very difficult for any one individual to walk quickly and cleave a way through the dense throng that surrounds and presses on him. This constant strife between the inclination springing from the equality of condition and the means it supplies to satisfy them harasses and wearies the mind.

It is possible to conceive of men arrived at a degree of freedom that should completely content them; they would then enjoy their independence without anxiety and without impatience. But men will never establish any equality with which they can be contented. Whatever efforts a people may make, they will never succeed in reducing all the conditions of society to a perfect level; and even if they unhappily attained that absolute and complete equality of position, the inequality of minds would still remain, which, coming directly from the hand of God, will forever escape the laws of man. However democratic, then, the social state and the political constitution of a people may be, it is certain that every member of the community will always find out several points about him which overlook his own position; and we may foresee that his looks will be doggedly fixed in that direction. When inequality of conditions is the common law of society, the most marked inequalities do not strike the eye; when everything is nearly on the same level, the slightest are marked enough to hurt it. Hence the desire of equality always becomes more insatiable in proportion as equality is more complete.

Among democratic nations, men easily attain a certain equality of condition, but they can never attain as much as they desire. It perpetually retires from before them, yet without hiding itself from their sight, and in retiring draws them on. At every moment they think they are about to grasp it; it escapes at every moment from their hold. They are near enough to see its charms, but too far off to enjoy them; and before they have fully tasted its delights, they die.

(ALEXIS DE TOCQUEVILLE, *Democracy in America*.) [18]

ASSUMPTIONS, FRUSTRATIONS, LEARNING

Since the future can never be fully predicted, and since some degree of change and novelty is constantly encountered in living, illusions, surprises, frustrations, and disappointments will never be wholly eliminated. These experiences provide us with challenges, with opportunities for better understanding through increasing the adequacy and inclusiveness of our assumptions. And our assumptions are likely to change only insofar as we find through our own experience or through experience we can share that our present assumptions cannot serve further as a basis for effective action.

Intellectual knowledge alone is usually by no means sufficient to change attitudes. We may still cling to attitudes we know are "wrong" if we feel that they are helpful in carrying forward some deeply rooted purpose. We return to a discussion of the function of mistakes, frustrations, and disappointments in the following chapter. Here we are only making note of their relationship to expectancies.

Learning is a process through which an individual develops assumptions which give significance to the world around him as he strives to fulfill his purposes. After numerous investigations and observations, F. C. Bartlett wrote that every human cognitive reaction can be properly understood as "an effort after *meaning*. Certain of the tendencies which the subject brings with him into the situation with which he is called upon to deal are utilized so as to make his reaction the 'easiest,' or the least disagreeable, or the quickest and least obstructed that is at the time possible. When we try to discover how this is done we find that always it is by an effort to connect what is given with something else. Thus, the immediately present 'stands for' something not immediately present, and 'meaning,' in a psychological sense, has its origin." [19]

The learning process can be seen at work in everyday life when we observe the behavior of infants and children as they go about the task of testing the environment and discovering what will be useful to them. When an infant is hungry he will regard anything that touches his mouth as a possible source of satisfaction. But he soon learns that mother's breast or a bottle is more likely to be significant in achieving his purpose. Through manipulating objects, trying to put them into his mouth, the child learns something about the size of various objects. Mother's voice will become significant very early as it becomes part of an event which includes the satisfaction of needs.

By the end of the first year of life the infant has some notion of what is "me," and his psychological world becomes increasingly differentiated into the "I" and the "not-I." The child, likewise, gradually senses his relations to others, his position in the family, the customs and folkways he must observe in order to be a good boy or girl. He learns what objects, people, and groups are significant to him in achieving the measure of satisfaction which he seeks.

With the onset of puberty the child must modify his assumptive world. He must learn to play a masculine or feminine role, including the development of new significances for members of the opposite sex. Most young people experience some insecurity and anxiety as they make alterations in the reality-world they had perceived before puberty. Parents are perceived differently, old loyalties are transformed, and for a time frustration, surprise, and disappointment occur frequently as the individual is treated sometimes as an adult and sometimes as a child.

Just as we develop assumptions and expectancies concerning the normal size, shape, and other characteristics of objects, so we develop expectancies concerning the roles played by others and are surprised, disillusioned, or disappointed when these expectancies are upset. The next selections illustrate some of the effects of expectancies upon perceiving.

There seemed to be a greater air of release in Shanghai than in Japan. The quiet orderliness of Tokyo streets was replaced by scenes of confusion and a more uninhibited atmosphere altogether. It was impossible to pay a pedicab driver without a brief drama of shouts and recriminations in front of the inevitable audience of interested spectators. On any street there was a mock fight in progress with foreigners or with other Chinese. All this embarrassed Clare dreadfully. She found the open screaming and discussion of money as difficult and uncomfortable as most Westerners do. She never understood the fun of bargaining or the economic necessity that forces you to overcharge a stranger if you can get away with it.

"But, Clare," I used to say, feeling that this was much more like India and our way of doing things, "they seem to be a nation of actors, the audience has fun, the kids in the streets enjoy it, and it's not really a waste of time because no one is in that much of a hurry here."

"I don't see why they can't *fix* their prices," Clare would say indignantly.

"Well, clearly, as long as there are people like you who would rather pay up than be embarrassed in public, it's worth their while *not* to."

The city was so crowded with refugees from the north that people slept, lived, cooked and played on the streets. Occasionally we saw a body lying at the edge of the sidewalk, either too ill to move or else dead. "How appalling," Clare would say, or, "How callous—they just walk by." The first time she saw it, she was furious. The body lay against a bank building on one of the main streets of Shanghai. Clare rushed into the bank and found a teller who spoke English.

"There's a woman outside your bank," she said, "I think she's dead. Dead on the *street*, and nobody seems to notice. Can't you do something . . . *call* someone?"

The teller looked up with startled eyes. "But if they live on the street, where are they to die except the street?"

In Asia life is not a carefully protected thing, and death is not shocking. It is the one certainty.

Another thing that puzzled Clare was the curious reversal in China of the position of man and his machines. Coming from a country in which human labor is the expensive commodity, and the product of the machine is not—the hand-embroidered handkerchief costs more than the machine-made one—she was continually surprised that you could buy a hand-made cigarette case, say, more cheaply than the machine-turned one. Of the three modes of transport in Shanghai, the taxi, the pedicab, and the hand-drawn ricksha, the cheapest was the ricksha although it needed the greatest expenditure of human labor.

"In New York," she said, "you pay the world to go around Central Park in a hansom cab, instead of a taxi, and even that is pulled by a horse, not a man."　　　　　(SANTHA RAMA RAU, *East of Home.*) [20]

It seems to me that they are building staircases steeper than they used to. The risers are higher, or there are more of them, or something. Maybe this is because it is so much further today from the first floor to the second floor but I've noticed it is getting harder to make two steps at a time any more. Nowadays it is all I can do to make one at a time.

Another thing I've noticed is the small print they're using lately. Newspapers are getting farther and farther away when I hold them and I have to squint to make them out. The other day I had to back half way out of a telephone booth in order to read the number on the coin box. It is obviously ridiculous to suggest that a person my age needs glasses but the only other way I can find out what's going on is to have somebody read aloud to me and that's not too satisfactory because people speak in such a low voice these days that I can't hear them very well.

Everything is farther away than it used to be. It's twice the distance from my house to the station now and they've added a fair-sized hill that I never noticed before. The trains leave sooner too. I've given up running for them because they start faster these days when I try to catch them.

You can't depend on the time tables any more and it's no use asking the conductor. I ask him a dozen times a trip if the next station is where I get off and he always says it isn't. How can you trust a conductor like that? Usually I gather my bundles and put on my hat and coat and stand in the aisle a couple of stops away, just to make sure I don't go past my destination. Sometimes I make doubly sure by getting off at the station ahead.

A lot of other things are different lately. Barbers no longer hold up a mirror behind me when they're finished, so I can see the back of my head, and my wife has been taking care of tickets lately when we go to the theatre. They don't put the same materials in clothes any more either. I've noticed that all my suits have a tendency to shrink, especially in certain places such as around the waist or in the seat of the pants and the laces they put in shoes nowadays are much harder to reach.

Even the weather is changing. It's getting colder in winter, and the summers are hotter than they used to be. I'd go away, if it wasn't so far. Snow is heavier when I try to shovel it and I have to put on rubbers whenever I go out, because rain today is wetter than the rain we used to get. Drafts are more severe too. It must be the way they build windows now.

People are changing too. For one thing, they're growing younger than they used to be when I was their age. I went back recently to an alumni reunion at the college I graduated from in 1943—that is, 1933, I mean 1923—and I was shocked to see the mere tots they're admitting as students these days. The average age of the freshman class couldn't have been more than seven. They seem to be more polite than in my time, though; several undergraduates called me, "Sir," and one of them asked me if he could help me across the street. . . .

(COREY FORD, "How to Guess Your Age.") [21]

Hope is a tattered flag and a dream out of time.
Hope is a heartspun word, the rainbow, the shadblow in white,
The evening star inviolable over the coal mines,
The shimmer of northern lights across a bitter winter night,
The blue hills beyond the smoke of the steel works,
The birds who go on singing to their mates in peace, war, peace,

The ten-cent crocus bulb blooming in a used-car salesroom,
The horseshoe over the door, the luckpiece in the pocket,
The kiss and the comforting laugh and resolve—
Hope is an echo, hope ties itself yonder, yonder.

The spring grass showing itself where least expected,
The rolling fluff of white clouds on a changeable sky,
The broadcast of strings from Japan, bells from Moscow,
Of the voice of the prime minister of Sweden carried
Across the sea in behalf of a world family of nations
And children singing chorals of the Christ child
And Bach being broadcast from Bethlehem, Pennsylvania
And tall skyscrapers practically empty of tenants
And the hands of strong men groping for handholds
And the Salvation Army singing God loves us. . . .

(CARL SANDBURG, *The People, Yes*.) [22]

In this chapter we have detached the functioning person from the total person-environment situation and have tried to indicate some of the processes by means of which an individual contributes to the meaning and impact of psychological events. We have seen that the registered effects of past transactions are brought forward through time and serve as essential variables in present transactions. We have noted that these processes give meaning and significance to living and serve the function of supplying predictions on the basis of which we act in striving to maintain the world as we assume it to be or as we transform it when we sense its possibilities for the future. But the processes we have named assumptions—knowledges, opinions, attitudes, delusions, prejudices, and expectancies—are not independently existing entities. They become "realities" only in concrete transactions, only as they exist in their interdependent relationship with other aspects of the full organism-environmental event.

Even though every perceiving is a creation, and no perceiving discloses with absolute certainty what will occur if and when one acts, one *must* act in order to go on living. Despite surprises, mistakes, and frustrations, one must believe and act *as if* probable events were certainties. At the same time we must always be ready to modify our assumptions. For whether we realize it or not or whether we like it or not, every act alters our assumptive world to a greater or lesser degree for better or for worse.

Unique human beings always find themselves in the midst of a unique "here-and-now" occasion, faced with uncertainties, probabilities, and alternatives related to the past, present, and future. By "here" and "now" we do not refer to a point in geographical space or a moment of Greenwich Mean Time, but to that space and time encompassed by the individual's psychological world as determined by his purposes and expectancies.

In the next chapter we examine the individual in the midst of and as an aspect of an on-going situation. This means a consideration of such aspects of a transaction as choosing, the various modes of inquiry and decision-making, the sense of individual responsibility, frustrations and mistakes, and action. As is the case with all other aspects so far discussed, these aspects are significant in the process of living because of the function they serve in their interdependent relationship with all the other aspects of the on-going process.

5

Man Choosing [*]

THE DETERMINISM-INDETERMINISM ISSUE

If you had piled before you all that has been written on the question of whether or not man has some degree of freedom and control over his own living, you would be faced with many large volumes indeed. This question has intrigued men and women for centuries and they have expressed their opinions in magnificent abundance.

In a discussion of the problem of causation in modern science in one of the reading selections which follows, Schrödinger points out that the methods of pure reasoning allow us either to derive chance from law or law from chance. One may take the position that undetermined chance is primary and is not further explicable. From this point of view, law arises only statistically in mass phenomena, because of the co-operation of myriads of chances. On the other hand, one may take the position that the compulsion of law is primary and not further explicable. From this point of view chance is seen as the co-operation of innumerable partial causes all of which cannot be simultaneously known. Schrödinger reminds us that there

[*] Notes to this chapter begin on p. 333.

is scarcely any possibility of putting this issue to experimental test.

The person who adopts a deterministic position holds that if all the antecedent and concomitant conditions related to a given event, including human events, were fully and simultaneously known, it would then be seen that the event in question, and no other event, could occur. If this combination of conditions occurred again and were known, the event could be predicted. Stated this way, it is immediately obvious that such an hypothesis is untestable. For how could one know when he had all the information needed, when he had exhausted every possible case? How could one ascertain and measure simultaneously all the relevant variables? Would not the very intrusion of the experimenter, the very process of measurement, modify the events from what they otherwise would have been? Even though these limitations are recognized as existing now, the determinist may still believe that it may someday be possible to demonstrate the existence of rigid causality throughout the natural order.

The indeterminist, on the other hand, may defend the position that every human being knows by direct experience that he participates in the selection of his own experience, directs his own behavior, foresees its effects, experiences a sense of responsibility, and that this evidence of a basic human freedom is incontestable. He might further argue that the concept of guilt found in nearly all cultures and legal systems—as well as the experience of guilt nearly all "normal" individuals have at times—is evidence for the fact of personal choice with its accompanying sense of personal freedom and responsibility.

Before we follow this issue further and attempt to resolve it, let's see what a few scientists as well as a few non-scientists have had to say about it.

In human freedom in the philosophical sense I am definitely a disbeliever. Everybody acts not only under external compulsion but also in accordance with inner necessity. Schopenhauer's saying, "a man can do what he wants, but not want what he wants," has been an inspiration to me since my youth up, and a continual consolation and unfailing well-spring of patience in the face of the hardships of life, my own and others. This feeling mercifully not only mitigates the sense of responsibility which so easily becomes paralysing, but it also prevents us from

taking ourselves and other people too seriously; it conduces to a view
of life in which humour, above all, has its due place.

(ALBERT EINSTEIN, *The World as I See It.*) [1]

> ". . . the world is blind;
> And thou in truth comest from it. Ye, who live,
> Do so each cause refer to heaven above,
> E'en as its motion, of necessity,
> Drew with it all that moves. If this were so,
> Free choice in you were none; nor justice would
> There should be joy for virtue, woe for ill.
> Your movements have their primal bent from heaven;
> Not all: yet said I all; what then ensues?
> Light have ye still to follow evil or good,
> And of the will free power, which, if it stand
> Firm and unwearied in Heaven's first assay,
> Conquers at last, so it be cherished well,
> Triumphant over all. To mightier force,
> To better nature subject, ye abide
> Free, not constrained by that which forms in you
> The reasoning mind uninfluenced of the stars.
> If then the present race of mankind err,
> Seek in yourselves the cause, and find it there. . . ."

(DANTE, *Divine Comedy.*) [2]

What bearing has all this—the indeterminism of modern physics—
upon the problem of human freedom, so hotly debated from century
to century by churchmen and philosophers alike? Some will answer "the
closest," others that it has "none at all." When Spinoza declared that a
stone thrown into the air, if it possessed consciousness would suppose
itself to fall to the ground of its own free will, how did he know this?
He did not know it. He merely made the assertion. He desired to dis-
credit and deride the notion of human freedom. How does the matter
stand to-day? Exactly as it did, save in a single but important particular.
If physics cannot account for the activities within the atom, still less can
it account for the activities of the organism. If determinism be set aside
as unproven in the realm of nature, where evidence for it appeared
overwhelming, where is warrant for it to be found in the more difficult
region of the soul? If it be discarded in physics, it can hardly in the
absence of evidence be adduced to buttress determinism in psychology,
where it is in opposition the most flagrant to the universal, never-

questioned conviction of the natural man. Denials of human freedom will no longer serve, save to betray the naked prejudice which gave the dogma birth. Something more will now be required of its adherents than pious opinion. The foundations of the doctrine have been undermined. The onus of proof lies with the determinists, for their cherished fancy has, one fears, and in the house of its quondam friends, received its death-wound.

And one may, perhaps, be allowed the hope that we have heard the last of this tiresome and unprofitable controversy, this spider's web of dialectic, and are permitted a return to common sense. The strictest determinists act as if they possessed the freedom they deny, and cling to it in practice as the pivot of human intercourse. And what is the point of asking men to mend their ways, and live better lives, if you at the same time insist that they are tethered animals, and all they do, or can do has been fore-ordained since the beginning of the world? Or will you issue to them a metaphysical manual which explains that, none the less, for all their actions they are responsible? We must continue to believe that the soul or self is not a piece upon the chessboard of time, moved as a wheel or lever is moved. Our thoughts are our own, mine mine, yours yours, and if our thoughts, then also our acts. The soul stands for itself, and is in its own nature a purposive mover, however limited and conditioned a factor in the origination and passage of events. The individual self, the finite centre of impulse is, as Nietzsche held, both determined and free, limited by the presence of the other individuals, in itself free and creative. It is related of Diogenes that when he heard arguments against motion his manner of refutation was not by means of words. He contented himself by doing what had been declared impossible—moving by walking away. In this workaday world there is at times something to be said for this fashion of refutation.

(W. MACNEILE DIXON, *The Human Situation*.) [3]

This process of correcting one world-outlook by the others, this moderation of those specialistic attitudes, which left to themselves are so often apt to be extreme if not fanatical, has results in all spheres of life. The successful application of quantitative, physico-chemical, deterministic modes of explanation to psychological events, would not necessarily lead us to imagine ourselves mere marionettes at the mercy of the ceaseless play of the atoms and obeying only the laws of chance. That it would do so has been, perhaps, a popular belief. It would be an interesting occupation to trace the reverberations of the mechanistic theory of life in the affairs of Law, raising, as it would naturally tend to do, the difficult question of responsibility. But in truth the value and applicability of scientific fictions is irrelevant in philosophy no less than in practical life; and whatever mechanism can explain, nothing is diminished from our conviction of its abstraction and one-sidedness.

Another point of some importance arises here. The attempt has been made in the past to place both the spiritual part and the mechanical part actually in external things, and to call one the method of the other. This equation of the two hemispheres of events was what Lotze tried to do; having said that mechanism was universal and at the same time secondary, he placed the mechanical and the non-mechanical in objectivity, and endeavoured to show—as I think, unsuccessfully—how they intertwined with one another there. In the case of the imaginary discovery which we are discussing, the line that could be taken would be to assert that the chemical brain condition played an integral rôle in the coming-to-be of poetic inspiration. This is the argument with which St. Joan, in Bernard Shaw's play, silenced Robert de Baudricourt.

JOAN: I hear voices telling me what to do. They come from God.
ROBERT: They come from your imagination.
JOAN: Of course. That is how the messages of God come to us.
POULENGEY: Checkmate!

But this is not a satisfactory answer, for Robert had a judgment of validity in mind. Such a position involves too great a mixture of spiritual and material processes, or rather, too much interweaving of philosophical and scientific arguments. The modern Lucretius has admitted a great deal, but he does insist that the atoms be left to themselves in their own sphere of description. Only one fiction should be allowed to hold the floor at one time. Both sorts of description, the mechanical and the non-mechanical, are essentially subjective, and they cannot be both projected at the same moment into external nature. It is better to acquiesce in an apparent contradiction, since time may remove it, rather than to rest in a confused solution, since time will certainly destroy it.

Thus Lucretius and I expect that, in the future, bio-chemical experimentation, including under that head all the bio-physics and bio-mathematics of the future, will reveal, strange though it may seem, the cerebral mechanisms associated with mental states. These states themselves, as far as science is concerned, must remain epiphenomena, side-issues, shadows, and their conative aspects illusions, since behaviour will be physico-chemically interpreted and even politics expressed, perhaps, in the terminology of the tropism. But for philosophy these states will have a real significance, for, in one way regarded, the whole universe of science is itself a great abstract construction produced by the activity of mind, and its results are far from having any metaphysical importance. We shall rest content with them as far as they go, and, correcting them with the wisdom gained in other realms of experience, set them in their proper place in the mosaic of our world.

Thus to the neo-mechanist, as such, the problem of the relation between body and mind is unanswerable, because to ask it implies that the words we use for dealing with each half represent something real. This they do not, for mechanistic and non-mechanistic alike are simply fictions. He is concerned to push mechanistic explanations as far as they will go, and he believes that they will go every inch of the way; but, to continue the metaphor, he does not for a moment suppose they cover the whole width of the road. Body and mind, like determinism and freedom, only appear as separate because we dissect them in thought; in themselves they are indissolubly one. Both kinds of descriptions being partial, distorted, and the offspring of the same creator, to try to employ both at the same time is to forget Joseph Glanvill's Aristotelian antagonist, who in 1668 objected to the wearing of spectacles on the ground that with two pairs superimposed, you saw worse than with one. The ingenious explanations of psycho-physical interaction due to Boussinesq, Clerk-Maxwell and others, and well reviewed by Lotka, are therefore little more than a fascinating pastime, for they rest on the belief that both sides of the equation have a real existence. It is like matching ghost with ghost in a shadowy wrestling match.

(JOSEPH NEEDHAM, *The Sceptical Biologist*.) [4]

After reading these passages, the reader may feel a bit confused and a little weary of the problem of determinism-indeterminism. He may feel that he is asked to grapple with a pseudo-problem, an unnecessary dichotomy. A brief consideration of some related matters may open the door to a resolution of the difficulties.

First of all, as human beings we should be aware of our intellectual limitations, of the limitations of our thinking processes. Like it or not, we, as human beings, are inescapably contributors to what we observe and think. This imposes a system of limitations. In discussing the imperfectibility of human reasoning and conceptualizing, P. W. Bridgman has made it clear that "many of the well-known paradoxes of logic arise when a system tries to deal with itself. A stock example is the ostensibly complete map of the city in which the map itself is located. If the map is complete, it must contain a map of itself; that is, the map must have a map of the map, and this in turn demands a map of the map of the map, and you are off on a chase that has no end. Within the last few years, a theorem with regard to such a system has been proved, a theorem which has been hailed among logicians as a truly epoch-making discovery in logic. This theorem was enunciated by Godel. . . . In very crude language, the theorem states that no logical system can ever prove that it itself is a perfect system in the sense that it may not contain concealed self-contradictions. . . . This means that the human intelligence can never be sure of itself; it is not a tool capable of unlimited perfectibility, as is so often fondly imagined. All we can ever say is that, up to the present, we have found no inconsistencies where we have looked." [5]

Any conclusions which have been reached or which may be reached concerning causality and freedom are clearly limited by human perspectives. Absolute certainty, it would appear, must forever remain to some degree unattained and unattainable.

In its most general sense, freedom might be defined as the human capacity for choosing among possibilities of achievement combined with the capacity for action related to the choosing. This interpretation of freedom need not conflict with theories of determinism which stress the role of the past in human behavior. Such determinism usually looks backward for a retrospective analysis of human behavior. Freedom, on the other hand, looks ahead for a prospective evaluation of human achievement. Men as diverse as Aquinas and Dewey have suggested that freedom is akin to self-determinism. This interpretation of freedom, however, does not imply a miracle subject to no law. Freedom has its limitations and its orders.

Perhaps a great deal of our difficulty in resolving the determinism-indeterminism issue is due to (1) a tendency to think of events as necessarily happening *to* something or *to* someone; and (2) a tendency to separate past, present and future in our conceptualizing.

It is admittedly difficult to think of happenings not as happenings to concrete things, but as themselves the concrete "realities." If, in our thinking, we separate man and environment, stimulus and response, knower and known, process and content, form and flow, we are likely to adopt an interactional model which demands enduring individuals or substances *to* which events occur in a wholly determined and uncreative manner. But this common notion that happenings must happen *to* something may at best be only a convenient (and misleading) way of thinking and talking.

If, in harmony with much twentieth-century scientific and philosophical thinking, we postulate process, change, and diversity as the all-pervading realities, then persons or things can be viewed only as certain abstracted stabilities in the flux of events. What we abstract as you, as a human being, is on-going functional process (not persisting substance) with a *partial repetitiveness* of form and *partial novelty* of form. Whatever is compounded of old and new must necessarily be new. If, in thought, one stops the on-going process and examines an event, this abstracted event would bear the same relation to human reality as a "still" of a movie would bear to the moving figures in action on the screen. And it would be as ambiguously reliable as any "still" is in pointing to what is to follow.

What do we mean by the psychological present, and its relation to past and future? What is the matrix [6] of a present situation in which psychological events occur?

If it is necessary to take into account the on-going purposes of the perceiver and the predictive function of perceiving, it follows that the psychological present must include more than a frozen moment of time. The "here and now" of a perceived object must include, for example, its significance in sequential situations that would follow if we acted on that object in carrying forward a purpose.

In a very real sense, then, any frozen psychological moment would contain within it the past, the present, and the future. But moments cannot be frozen, and past, present, and future are only convenient abstractions. In the midst of on-going process, the established form of the past meets the undetermined of the present in a continually emerging creative synthesis. Laotzu said: "The is is the was of what shall be." And St. Augustine was very clear that the psychological "now" includes both a push from the past as well as those psychological events encompassed within one's present purposes and expectancies:

I ask, Father, I affirm not: O God, rule and guide me. "Who will tell me that there are not three times (as we learned when boys, and taught boys), past, present, and future; but present only, because those two are not? Or are they also; and when from future it becometh present, doth

it come out of some secret place; and so, when retiring, from present it
becometh past? For where did they, who foretold things to come, see
them, if as yet they be not? For that which is not, cannot be seen. And
they who relate things past, could not relate them, if in mind they did
not discern them, and if they were not, they could no way be discerned.
Things then past and to come, are." . . .

What now is clear and plain is, that neither things to come nor past
are. Nor is it properly said, "there be three times, past, present, and to
come": yet perchance it might be properly said, "there be three times;
a present of things past, a present of things present, and a present of
things future." For these three do exist in some sort, in the soul, but
otherwhere do I not see them; present of things past, memory; present
of things present, sight; present of things future, expectation. If thus
we be permitted to speak, I see three times, and I confess there are
three. Let it be said too, "there be three times, past, present, and to
come": in our incorrect way. See, I object not, nor gainsay, nor find
fault, if what is so said be but understood, that neither what is to be,
now is, nor what is past. For but few things are there, which we speak
properly, most things improperly; still the things intended are understood. [7]

Each psychological event, then, arises in part both from the
determinations from its own past and from creativity, which is the
basic thrust of freedom into the future, with its own unique and
undisclosed possibilities in the present. In man's resolute search
for reliable knowledge, he has discovered some regularity, predictability, and constancy in his world. In his science he has been
and continues to be concerned with uncovering the conditions
under which something is what it is. Man has discovered that if
something is so, then something else will occur with such and such
probability. Science does not say that the second something *must*
occur, and furthermore, science does not say that any given set of
conditions *must* come into being. But to admit the half-truth of
determinism need not rob us of our conviction that we participate
creatively in our own advance. As human beings we can still, within
limits, ask the question: "What do I choose to become?"

In his search for reliable predictions, man has never fully succeeded. He has discovered also a basic indeterminism (even though
it may stem from a methodological limitation), a seemingly open-
ended future while he is in the midst of a situation participating in

the on-goingness of human living. Thus, determinism and freedom can be viewed as necessary and complementary explanatory concepts, useful in accounting for certain aspects of the on-going events which constitute human being and human becoming. Such appears to us the proper resolution of the causality-freedom question.

Now the process of choosing can be brought into sharper focus for psychological scrutiny.

THE PROCESS OF CHOOSING

All of us, as human beings, have a conviction that in many occasions of living we are faced with alternatives, with the problem of arriving at a decision to do one thing rather than another. We sense that our choice is our own, that we and we alone are really responsible for whatever results from what we do. It is probably safe to say that if ever there is really only one thing to do, there is no uncertainty, no problem, and no hesitation. If we hesitate to act, it is because we suspect that there are other possibilities. The area within which choice is possible may be very restricted, but some choice is nearly always possible.

What, then, is choosing? In what kinds of situation does choosing occur? Here are some concrete cases in which choosing seems to be involved. Some of the latter selections in the following group illustrate the nature of, differences between, and interrelationship of, what we will shortly discuss as how-to-do and what-for decisions. The reader may want to refer back to these selections after reading the textual material which follows them.

> Two roads diverged in a yellow wood,
> And sorry I could not travel both
> And be one traveler, long I stood
> And looked down one as far as I could
> To where it bent in the undergrowth;
>
> Then took the other, as just as fair,
> And having perhaps the better claim,
> Because it was grassy and wanted wear;
> Though as for that the passing there
> Had worn them really about the same,

And both that morning equally lay
In leaves no step had trodden black.
Oh, I kept the first for another day!
Yet knowing how way leads on to way,
I doubted if I should ever come back.

I shall be telling this with a sigh
Somewhere ages and ages hence:
Two roads diverged in a wood, and I—
I took the one less traveled by,
And that has made all the difference.

(ROBERT FROST, "The Road Not Taken.") [8]

It is true that convictions can best be supported with experience and clear thinking. On this point one must agree unreservedly with the extreme rationalist. The weak point of his conception is, however, this, that those convictions which are necessary and determinant for our conduct and judgments, cannot be found solely along this solid scientific way.

For the scientific method can teach us nothing else beyond how facts are related to, and conditioned by, each other. The aspiration toward such objective knowledge belongs to the highest of which man is capable, and you will certainly not suspect me of wishing to belittle the achievements and the heroic efforts of man in this sphere. Yet it is equally clear that knowledge of what *is* does not open the door directly to what *should be*. One can have the clearest and most complete knowledge of what *is*, and yet not be able to deduct from what should be the *goal* of our human aspirations. Objective knowledge provides us with powerful instruments for the achievements of certain ends, but the ultimate goal itself and the longing to reach it must come from another source. And it is hardly necessary to argue for the view that our existence and our activity acquire meaning only by the setting up of such a goal and of corresponding values. The knowledge of truth as such is wonderful, but it is so little capable of acting as a guide that it cannot prove even the justification and the value of the aspiration towards that very knowledge of truth. Here we face, therefore, the limits of the purely rational conception of our existence.

(ALBERT EINSTEIN, *Out of My Later Years.*) [9]

Gifts had been bestowed on me before when I returned to India in 1899, but this time the farewell was overwhelming. The gifts of course included things in gold and silver, but there were articles of costly diamond as well.

What right had I to accept all these gifts? Accepting them, how could I persuade myself that I was serving the community without remuneration? All the gifts, excepting a few from my clients, were purely for my service to the community, and I could make no difference between my clients and co-workers; for the clients also helped me in my public work.

One of the gifts was a gold necklace worth fifty guineas, meant for my wife. But even that gift was given because of my public work, and so it could not be separated from the rest.

The evening I was presented with the bulk of these things I had a sleepless night. I walked up and down my room deeply agitated, but could find no solution. It was difficult for me to forego gifts worth hundreds, it was more difficult to keep them.

And even if I could keep them, what about my children? What about my wife? They were being trained to a life of service and to an understanding that service was its own reward.

I had no costly ornaments in the house. We had been fast simplifying our life. How then could we afford to have gold watches? How could we afford to wear gold chains and diamond rings? Even then I was exhorting people to conquer the infatuation for jewellery. What was I now to do with the jewellery that had come upon me?

I decided that I could not keep these things. I drafted a letter, creating a trust of them in favour of the community and appointing Parsi Rustomji and others trustees. In the morning I held a consultation with my wife and children and finally got rid of the heavy incubus.

I knew that I should have some difficulty in persuading my wife, and I was sure that I should have none so far as the children were concerned. So I decided to constitute them my attorneys.

The children readily agreed to my proposal. 'We do not need these costly presents, we must return them to the community, and should we ever need them, we could easily purchase them,' they said.

I was delighted. 'Then you will plead with mother, won't you?' I asked them.

'Certainly,' said they. 'That is our business. She does not need to wear the ornaments. She would want to keep them for us, and if we don't want them, why should she not agree to part with them?'

But it was easier said than done.

'You may not need them,' said my wife. 'Your children may not need them. Cajoled they will dance to your tune. I can understand your not permitting me to wear them. But what about my daughters-in-law? They will be sure to need them. And who knows what will happen tomorrow? I would be the last person to part with gifts so lovingly given.'

And thus the torrent of argument went on, reinforced, in the end, by tears. But the children were adamant. And I was unmoved.

I mildly put in: 'The children have yet to get married. We do not want to see them married young. When they are grown up, they can take care of themselves. And surely we shall not have, for our sons, brides who are fond of ornaments. And if after all, we need to provide them with ornaments, I am there. You will ask me then.'

'Ask you? I know you by this time. You deprived me of my ornaments, you would not leave me in peace with them. Fancy you offering to get ornaments for the daughters-in-law! You who are trying to make *sadhus* of my boys from today! No, the ornaments will not be returned. And pray what right have you to my necklace?'

'But,' I rejoined, 'is the necklace given you for your service or for my service?'

'I agree. But service rendered by you is as good as rendered by me. I have toiled and moiled for you day and night. Is that no service? You forced all and sundry on me, making me weep bitter tears, and I slaved for them!'

These were pointed thrusts, and some of them went home. But I was determined to return the ornaments. I somehow succeeded in extorting a consent from her. The gifts received in 1896 and 1901 were all returned. A trust-deed was prepared, and they were deposited with a bank, to be used for the service of the community, according to my wishes or to those of the trustees.

Often, when I was in need of funds for public purposes, and felt that I must draw upon the trust, I have been able to raise the requisite amount, leaving the trust money intact. The fund is still there, being operated upon in times of need, and it has regularly accumulated.

I have never since regretted the step, and as the years have gone by, my wife has also seen its wisdom. It has saved us from many temptations.

I am definitely of opinion that a public worker should accept no costly gifts. (*Gandhi's Autobiography.*) [10]

In the work of the doctor, the still, small, inner voice of conscience is always cropping up with doubts, accusations and promptings. A patient comes to you suffering from a condition so clear-cut that any advanced medical student could outline the treatment at once. Yet at the back of your mind you are uneasy. You have a strange "hunch." You decide to abandon safe routine methods and embark on a course that appears hazardous and almost unjustifiable. Such was my experience in the case of the railwayman's arm.

One Saturday morning the hospital called. A bad accident case had come in—a man with a smashed arm. Could I come at once?

The house surgeon was waiting for me. "One of the worst cases I've seen; arm caught between the buffers of two freight cars," he said grimly. "Immediate amputation, I think."

Jim, the patient, worked in the railway yards, and he was also a semiprofessional wrestler. "Good thing," remarked the house surgeon. "He's as strong as a horse, and that should help to pull him through."

The man's right arm had been crushed to pulp. There were multiple fractures. There had been profuse bleeding and the patient was only semiconscious.

The only sensible procedure was amputation. Any attempt at reconstruction would be foolhardy, courting danger of sepsis and gangrene; prolonged operative treatment would increase the already heavy shock to an intolerable degree.

Everything was made ready and the anesthetist was about to proceed when for some reason I looked at the patient. He was too weak to speak, but his eyes were eloquent. They were pleading with me—a trusting, imploring look. Was he appealing to me to save his life? He need not worry about that. Then suddenly I realized that he wanted me to save his arm. I was sure of it—though how I knew it I could not say. Yet, with those multiple injuries, a limb with no skin, from which masses of muscle had been torn—the idea was ridiculous. I turned away, about to sign to the anesthetist to proceed.

What followed was one of the most curious experiences I have ever had. It was as though a second self within me were arguing, disputing my honesty, accusing me of accepting the idea of amputation merely because I was too lazy to think about a fantastic alternative.

It would be criminal, I told myself, to expose the patient to further dangers, to depart from the principle that the first consideration in an emergency is to save life. Nonetheless, the look in the man's eyes said clearly and forcefully: "Take what risks you like. I would rather be dead than have only one arm. Please—please don't amputate."

The anesthetist was getting impatient now; the puzzled house surgeon was looking at me. I set my jaw. "I shall not amputate," I said.

The house surgeon expostulated, telling me what I already knew. Instead of an amputation lasting for perhaps half an hour, I was about to subject this unhappy man to three hours or more of shock while I carried out an operation that, if he survived it, might well have to be followed by the amputation it sought to avoid. What I proposed to do was utterly unconventional, almost revolutionary. But I was certain that it was right.

The patient was put under anesthesia and I began. First, the whole of the limb had to be thoroughly cleansed. The tattered skin, tendons and muscle had to be trimmed and made as normal as possible. All muscle tissue had to be reduced to about two thirds of its former bulk. This took 60 long minutes, and the main part of the operation had not yet begun.

The next problem was to find skin. So large an area could not be left uncovered without virtually condemning the patient to gangrene and death. Four thin strips of skin, each perhaps ten inches long by four inches wide, were cut from the patient's abdomen. This exposed area, with its undamaged tissues, would heal with little danger.

These four strips were then used to form a sort of sleeve. Before it could be stitched on, however, the broken bones had to be set. One of them had been broken into three pieces, so that the center portion tended to slip away; as its edges had been badly chipped, the ends had to be cut and molded to fit properly. But at last this was done; the skin-graft sleeve was firmly attached and the operation was over.

By the time the arm was encased in plaster of Paris, the patient was more dead than alive. The anesthetist was looking grave; he had been hard put to maintain the man's respiration and heart. I glanced at my watch. Three and a half hours. As I watched the patient being wheeled away I began to wonder if perhaps I had been guilty of a grave error. The risks I had taken appalled me more and more as I reconsidered them.

For ten days the patient was barely kept alive by blood transfusions. He remained comatose and unresponsive, until at last there seemed nothing to do but wait for the end. And then, with dramatic suddenness, Jim recovered consciousness. More than that, awaking from his coma in the early morning, he demanded a substantial breakfast. From that moment his general recovery was steady if not spectacular.

One phase of the fight had been won. But anything might be happening beneath that cumbrous mass of plaster—infection, gangrene, a defective skin graft. I longed to break the cast apart to see for myself.

It was 45 days after the operation that the "unveiling" took place, 45 days of hopes and fears. By this time the case had acquired a certain fame—or notoriety—and many members of the hospital staff found excuses to be present. I broke the cast and stripped away the oiled gauze beneath. There followed one of the most grateful sounds I have ever heard, a great communal sigh of happy surprise. For the bones had been joined successfully and the whole area had healed beautifully.

Considering the amount of muscle that had been removed from the arm, I did not expect that its movement would ever be normal. But Jim was determined. He submitted regularly and patiently to treatment by the physiotherapists. Eighteen months after his accident he was able to resume his old work.

One day he and his wife came to see me; there were tears in her eyes. "It was wonderful, Doctor—a miracle. You sent him back to me just as he was."

"But to do it," I said, "I had to subject your husband to risks that were beyond all justification. If he had died on the table, you might have cursed me for attempting the impossible—and you would have been right."

Jim smiled grimly and shook his head. "No, sir. That's where you're wrong. I know why you did what you did," he said; and I glanced at him in amazement.

"Yes," he went on. "You remember the way you looked at me just before they started to give me the gas? I don't often pray, sir, but I did then, as hard as I knew how. I asked God to tell you not to amputate my arm, but do anything else even if it meant I'd die. I could never work with one arm—never! And God was good to me, sir. He told you what to do—and you did it."

(GEORGE SAVA, *A Surgeon Remembers*.) [11]

HUMPHREY: Later on to-night

When they've all gone small into their beauty-sleep
I'll procure the key and come to your cell. Is that
Agreeable?
JENNET: Is it so to you?
Aren't you building your castles in foul air?
HUMPHREY: Foul? No; it's give and take, the basis
Of all understanding.
JENNET: You mean you give me a choice:
To sleep with you, or to-morrow to sleep with my fathers.
And if I value the gift of life,
Which, dear heaven, I do, I can scarcely refuse.
HUMPHREY: Isn't that sense?
JENNET: Admirable sense.
Oh, why, why am I not sensible?
Oddly enough, I hesitate. Can I
So dislike being cornered by a young lecher
That I should rather die? That would be

The maniac pitch of pride. Indeed, it might
Even be sin. Can I believe my ears?
I seem to be considering heaven. And heaven,
From this angle, seems considerable.
HUMPHREY: Now, please, we're not going to confuse the soul and the
  body.
This, speaking bodily, is merely an exchange
Of compliments.
JENNET: And surely throwing away
  My life for the sake of pride would seem to heaven
  A bodily blasphemy, a suicide?
HUMPHREY: Even if heaven were interested. Or even
  If you cared for heaven. Am I unattractive to you?
JENNET: Except that you have the manners of a sparrowhawk,
  With less reason, no, you are not. But even so
  I no more run to your arms than I wish to run
  To death. I ask myself why. Surely I'm not
  Mesmerized by some snake of chastity?
HUMPHREY: This isn't the time—
JENNET: Don't speak, contemptible boy,
  I'll tell you: I am not. We have
  To look elsewhere—for instance, into my heart
  Where recently I heard begin
  A bell of longing which calls no one to church.
  But need that, ringing anyway in vain,
  Drown the milkmaid singing in my blood
  And freeze into the tolling of my knell?
  That would be pretty, indeed, but unproductive.
  No, it's not that.
HUMPHREY: Jennet, before they come
  And interrupt us—
JENNET: I am interested
  In my feelings. I seem to wish to have some importance
  In the play of time. If not,
  Then sad was my mother's pain, sad my breath,
  Sad the articulation of my bones,
  Sad, sad my alacritous web of nerves,
  Woefully, woefully sad my wondering brain,
  To be shaped and sharpened into such tendrils
  Of anticipation, to feed the swamp of space.
  What is deep, as love is deep, I'll have
  Deeply. What is good, as love is good,

I'll have well. Then if time and space
Have any purpose, I shall belong to it.
If not, if all is a pretty fiction
To distract the cherubim and seraphim
Who so continually do cry, the least
I can do is to fill the curled shell of the world
With human deep-sea sound, and hold it to
The ear of God, until he has appetite
To taste our salt sorrow on his lips.
And so you see it might be better to die.
Though, on the other hand, I admit it might
Be immensely foolish.

(CHRISTOPHER FRY, *The Lady's Not for Burning.*) [12]

A father sees a son nearing manhood.
What shall he tell that son?
"Life is hard; be steel; be a rock."
And this might stand him for the storms
and serve him for humdrum and monotony
and guide him amid sudden betrayals
and tighten him for slack moments.
"Life is a soft loam; be gentle; go easy."
And this too might serve him.
Brutes have been gentled where lashes failed.
The growth of a frail flower in a path up
has sometimes shattered and split a rock.
A tough will counts. So does desire.
So does a rich soft wanting.
Without rich wanting nothing arrives.
Tell him too much money has killed men
and left them dead years before burial:
the quest of lucre beyond a few easy needs
has twisted good enough men
sometimes into dry thwarted worms.
Tell him time as a stuff can be wasted.
Tell him to be a fool every so often
and to have no shame over having been a fool
yet learning something out of every folly
hoping to repeat none of the cheap follies
thus arriving at intimate understanding
of a world numbering many fools.
Tell him to be alone often and get at himself

and above all tell himself no lies about himself
whatever the white lies and protective fronts
he may use amongst other people.
Tell him solitude is creative if he is strong
and the final decisions are made in silent rooms.
Tell him to be different from other people
if it comes natural and easy being different.
Let him have lazy days seeking his deeper motives.
Let him seek deep for where he is a born natural.
   Then he may understand Shakespeare
   and the Wright brothers, Pasteur, Pavlov,
   Michael Faraday and free imaginations
bringing changes into a world resenting change.
     He will be lonely enough
     to have time for the work
     he knows as his own.
(CARL SANDBURG, *The People, Yes.*) [13]

O LORD GOD, in whose hands are the wills and affections of men, kindle in my mind holy desires, and repress sinful and corrupt imaginations; enable me to love thy commandments, and to desire thy promises; let me, by thy protection and influence, so pass through things temporal, as finally not to lose the things eternal; and among the hopes and fears, the pleasures and sorrows, the dangers and deliverances, and all the changes of this life, let my heart be surely fixed, by the help of thy Holy Spirit, on the everlasting fruition of thy presence, where true joys are to be found. Grant, O Lord, these petitions. Forgive, O merciful Lord, whatever I have done contrary to thy laws. Give me such a sense of my wickedness as may produce true contrition and effectual repentance, so that when I shall be called into another state, I may be received among the sinners to whom sorrow and reformation have obtained pardon, for Jesus Christ's sake. Amen.
(*Doctor Johnson's Prayers.*) [14]

There seems to be something common to all choice situations: two or more lines of action exist in awareness not only as possible, but also as desirable and as mutually exclusive. When we become aware of such alternatives, we experience tugs in different directions, an uncertainty which calls for study of the situation and then for decision. The instant the anticipated consequences of one line of action emerge from the process of decision-making as imperative, the choosing and the problem dissolve. It does not follow, however, that the rejected alternatives may not continue to haunt our memories and imagination.

For our purpose here, we need to make a distinction only between two types of choices or decision-making processes. When, in a problem situation, we ask ourselves: "What shall I do?" we *may* really be asking: "*How* should I perform a particular task, how achieve a particular goal already existing?" On the other hand, the question "What shall I do?" *may* mean "*Why* should I do a particular thing? Which of several goals is worth striving for? Which of two or more possible courses of action is right and good?"

A "how-to-do" difficulty is encountered when we are not sure of the way to achieve a desired goal. Suppose, for example, you have decided to refinish an old piece of furniture and you want to achieve a particular dull finish which you have never attempted before. In this situation you may seek the advice of a carpenter friend or an old cabinet-maker, get a book from the library on refinishing antique furniture, or consult the local paint and varnish dealer. In this case you know what goal you want to achieve, but you don't know how to achieve it. The problem is one of means, not ends.

On the other hand, a problem of the "what-for" or "why" type involves reaching a decision concerning the goal for which to strive. The issue is not one of facts but of values. Suppose, for example, that a junior executive in a company discovers the president of the company in a serious misconduct. Suppose, further, that the president has offered a promotion and very substantial increase in salary if the junior executive will keep the matter a secret. What shall the young man do? He wants to do what he feels is his duty through exposure of a violation of law. He also wants the promotion and salary increase. Both alternatives appear desirable—but are mutually exclusive. There is no problem of how to accomplish either the exposure or the secrecy, but the young man must reach a decision concerning *why* he should act one way or the other.

It should be made clear at the outset that these types of decision-making interpenetrate one another. It would be false to assume that processes of decision-making are of two mutually exclusive types—those involving only intellectual, logical thinking in the search for "how-to-do" solutions, and those involving only non-rational feelings and hunches in the search for "what-for" solutions. W. H. Roberts, for example, reminds us that:

. . . Actually reason is very rarely, if ever, pure. Impulse is seldom totally blind. We are creatures of more or less intelligent impulses and more or less emotionally befuddled intelligence. "Pure reason" and "blind impulse" are ideal limits of abstraction from the real business of living. They are like those useful, indeed indispensable, fictions that serve as the elements of geometry—points of no size at all, lines with no breadth, planes without thickness. Or we might compare them to the asymptotes of a hyperbola, which the curve—in this case life itself—approaches continually but never quite reaches.[15]

Despite the interpenetration of rational and non-rational factors in decision-making, it is nevertheless useful to recognize that some decisions emerge from a process predominantly intellectual or rational while other decisions emerge from a process which is predominantly, but not wholly, non-rational. We may focus our attention momentarily on one of these aspects as long as we realize we are failing to see everything at once.

Modern scientific inquiry is an outstanding example of the process arising from encountering a "how-to-do" difficulty. The role of so-called "pure" science is essentially that of extending man's awareness of heretofore unrecognized sequential phenomena of nature, while applied science extends the range and reliability of man's sequential behavior, his "how-to-do" solutions, through the creation of artifacts. Because of man's intellectual capacities, his capacity to manipulate symbols, and to create abstractions, he may attack a "how-to-do" problem through a process generally called rational or intellectual inquiry. It should be remembered, however, that scientific inquiry itself would not proceed at all, that scientists could not be impartially analytical about their inquiries without the value-judgments which precede and undergird their scientific endeavors.

The half-truth of irrationalism protects us against a distorted and sentimental view of rationality, and it is well that it has been stated so vigorously and so often in the last decades. One half of this half-truth is the affirmation of the existence and the importance of non-rational factors in the make-up of the human self—the menagerie of drives, passions, hates, joys, hopes, insights and anxieties which we are.

To be rational is simply to accept ideas and ideals after critical reflection, after a careful consideration of what would follow from the acceptance of a given idea or ideal. A rational person is a reasoning person, one who advances by pushing out before him the antennae of signs, exploring the terrain of self and surrounding world before committing himself on how to act or how henceforth to be. To renounce rationality in the sense of reasoning is to renounce the making of oneself, to reject one's humanness.

It does not follow that a rational person is or should be always reasoning. For it is the urgency of life in some precarious situation that motivates thinking, controls it, terminates it. To attempt to think endlessly would be to end oneself and thinking. Thought is an agency in the construction of life, and life is lived in an insistent present. Ideas are teased into being in strange and devious ways, by relaxation and receptivity as often as by athletic inference. Once in being they may be elaborated, brought into relation with other ideas, their consequences traced, the evidence for their truth scrutinized. But the pressure of a present urgency always motivates and terminates this process. Even as thinker the self must continually accept or reject the ideas it entertains, favoring one to another, committing itself to belief on the basis of a given amount of evidence. It is the whole self that thinks, and the problems of the self are temporal and not timeless. Decisions must be made or thinking itself becomes vacuous, without eventuation, uneventful.

Ideals differ from ideas precisely in the fact that we now prefer what is signified. This increment of preference stems from the urgencies of the self as it is at the moment. The act of acceptance of one ideal rather than another may be for a while delayed. The presumed consequences for oneself and for other selves may be considered. The self may stall, hesitate, vacillate. But its urgencies are insistent, and it must extend the hand of acceptance to one possible alternative rather than to others. Reasoning airs preferences, holds before the self alternative possibilities of liking and disliking, and in the process the self transforms itself and its allegiances. Even Aristotle admitted that the good is what is *preferred* after deliberation. *The act of preference remains, and to prefer is more than to reason.* To live is to be for some things and against others. Neutrality is a moment in which preferences are being formed. The only persistently neutral self is a dead self. [16]

When we recognize that the process of decision-making is diversified, many-sided, and complexly human, we are not likely to make the mistake of assuming that choosing is either a wholly rational, intellectual process or, on the other hand, a wholly non-rational, feeling process. Our decision-making achieves its unity through the interdependencies and compenetrations of both processes.

Nevertheless, it is worthwhile and necessary to talk about a process which eventuates in what can be called a value-judgment.

When we try to decide why we should pursue one goal rather than others, the process of inquiry is distinguishable from the processes involved in inquiries designed to overcome procedural difficulties. This process is often referred to by words or phrases such as meditation, communion with one's self, and the like. In value-inquiry we are seeking standards of rightness, goodness, beauty, and decency (to name but a few) which may serve as prognoses of the probable value-satisfactions we will experience through following a particular course of action. The weighing process involves consideration of our duties, loyalties, and responsibilities. It involves our conscience, and our ethical and religious principles and convictions. Most of the selections in the preceding group of readings illustrate, at least in part, the nature of a value-judgment.

Christ and Gandhi are often singled out as examples of individuals who were trying to act on the basis of value-judgments emerging from their value-inquiry. Although most of us do not go to the top of a mountain to meditate, or indulge in days of silence or prolonged fasts, we do want to be alone at times to mull things over, to take stock of our living. By insulating ourselves from immediate "here-and-now" conditions and the pressures of everyday, routine activities, we may become more sensitive to standards and values that, in a sense, are not bounded by considerations of space and time. We thus allow our deeper feelings and our higher values the best possible chance to be weighed in the decision-making process. This contributing condition to the process of value-judgment has been dramatically symbolized by Herman Melville in his account of Father Mapple's pulpit:

I had not been seated very long ere a man of a certain venerable robustness entered; immediately as the storm-pelted door flew back upon admitting him, a quick regardful eyeing of him by all the congregation, sufficiently attested that this fine old man was the chaplain. Yes, it was the famous Father Mapple, so called by the whalemen, among whom he was a very great favorite. He had been a sailor and a harpooneer in his youth, but for many years past had dedicated his life to the ministry. At the time I now write of, Father Mapple was in the hardy winter of a healthy old age, that sort of old age which seems merging into a second flowering youth, for among all the fissures of his wrinkles, there shone certain mild gleams of a newly developing bloom —the spring verdure peeping forth even beneath February's snow. No one having previously heard his history, could for the first time behold Father Mapple without the utmost interest, because there were certain engrafted clerical peculiarities about him, imputable to that adventurous maritime life he had led. When he entered I observed that he carried no umbrella, and certainly had not come in his carriage, for his tarpaulin hat ran down with melting sleet, and his great pilot cloth jacket seemed almost to drag him to the floor with the weight of the water it had absorbed. However, hat and coat and overshoes were one by one removed, and hung up in a little space in an adjacent corner; when, arrayed in a decent suit, he quietly approached the pulpit.

Like most old fashioned pulpits, it was a very lofty one, and since a regular stairs to such a height would, by its long angle with the floor, seriously contract the already small area of the chapel, the architect, it seemed, had acted upon the hint of Father Mapple, and finished the pulpit without a stairs, substituting a perpendicular side ladder, like those used in mounting a ship from a boat at sea. The wife of a whaling captain had provided the chapel with a handsome pair of red worsted man-ropes for this ladder, which, being itself nicely headed, and stained with a mahogany color, the whole contrivance, considering what manner of chapel it was, seemed by no means in bad taste. Halting for an instant at the foot of the ladder, and with both hands grasping the ornamental knobs of the man-ropes, Father Mapple cast a look upwards, and then with a truly sailor-like but still reverential dexterity, hand over hand, mounted the steps as if ascending the main-top of his vessel.

The perpendicular parts of this side ladder, as is usually the case with swinging ones, were of cloth-covered rope, only the rounds were of wood, so that at every step there was a joint. At my first glimpse of the pulpit, it had not escaped me that however convenient for a ship, these joints in the present instance seemed unnecessary. For I was not prepared to see Father Mapple after gaining the height, slowly turn round, and stooping over the pulpit, deliberately drag up the ladder step by step, till the whole was deposited within, leaving him impregnable in his little Quebec.

I pondered some time without fully comprehending the reason for this. Father Mapple enjoyed such a wide reputation for sincerity and sanctity, that I could not suspect him of courting notoriety by any mere tricks of the stage. No, thought I, there must be some sober reason for this thing; furthermore, it must symbolize something unseen. Can it be, then, that by that act of physical isolation, he signifies his spiritual withdrawal for the time, from all outward worldly ties and connexions? Yes, for replenished with the meat and wine of the word, to the faithful man of God, this pulpit, I see, is a self-containing stronghold—a lofty Ehrenbreitstein, with a perennial well of water within the walls.

(HERMAN MELVILLE, *Moby Dick.*) [17]

In the weighing of factors to reach a value-judgment, intellectual or logical processes may bring into the process more and more factors to be considered. But these must exist in a context of feeling and value-processes if the judgment is to predict with high reliability the satisfyingness which will emerge from the carrying forward of the chosen purpose. For it is evident that rational inquiry alone cannot give the answers to questions of why and what for, to the question of what the goals of human living should be.

Value-judgments, then, supply our most reliable guides to action in new, emerging situations. It must be remembered, however, that the range within which a person can make effective value-judgments is often very limited. It is limited by the extent of his relevant past experience and by the reliability of the assumptions which play a role in the process. "Intuition" will serve as a reliable guide only when it is based upon past experience and upon a sharpened sensitivity to deep ethical feelings in which reason is supported by conscience and conscience is informed by reason.

How good your value-judgments will turn out to be in terms of predicting the effectiveness and satisfyingness of action based upon them can best be sensed in terms of the value-quality you experience in the process of arriving at the judgment. The richer the quality you experience, the more probable that action based on your judgment will bring greater satisfaction in living. No matter how your actions may be judged by others, unless you yourself experience a satisfaction and enrichment through them, they are not successful for you. This does not, of course, justify a purely selfish morality. Because of the reciprocal influences of the purposes of one individual on those of another, actions will prove effective and deeply satisfying only when the purposes of other individuals are included and weighed in the decision-making process.

A danger arises in using value-judgments as guides to action because of the difficulty in knowing whether the quality we experience in arriving at a decision is simply a deeply-rooted biogenic emotion or a more subtle, all-pervading value-quality of experience arising from conscience, the ethical and religious assumptions that are aspects of our total self. Not that emotions are evil or that action based on emotion is necessarily wrong, but our most profound problems, our most fundamental decisions in living, seem to demand taking into account subtle feelings emanating from the very core of our whole being. These feelings need to be differentiated from what the psychologist generally calls emotions. Modern psychology faces a methodological challenge in finding ways to explore man's feelings, in understanding the role that the ineffable value-qualities of experience play in our choosing and purposing, and in all behaving not governed by reflexes or simple homeostatic principles.

While the Western world does seem to be ahead in what we like to call "technological know-how," some peoples in the East may be ahead in inquiry concerning motives and directional insights. However, it is probably fair to say that people in the East have traditionally sought their answers in contemplating or pursuing abstractions without bringing them to life through action in concrete situations. However, Gandhi showed what could be done by a leader who was able to devise a strategy of action directed by and consistent with a great moral principle. The following gives us an example of his policy of non-violence:

Just before his arrest, Gandhi had drafted a letter to the Viceroy announcing his intention, "God willing," to raid the Dharasana Salt Works with some companions. God, apparently, was not willing, but the companions proceeded to effect the plan. Mrs. Sorojini Naidu, the poet, led twenty-five hundred Volunteers to the site 150 miles north of Bombay and, after morning prayers, warned them that they would be beaten "but," she said, "you must not resist; you must not even raise a hand to ward off a blow."

Webb Miller, the well-known correspondent of the United Press who died in England during the Second World War, was on the scene and described the proceedings. Manilal Gandhi moved forward at the head of the marchers and approached the great salt pans which were surrounded by ditches and barbed wire and guarded by four hundred Surat policemen under the command of six British officers. "In complete silence the Gandhi men drew up and halted a hundred yards from the stockade. A picked column advanced from the crowd, waded the ditches, and approached the barbed-wire stockade." The police officers ordered them to retreat. They continued to advance. "Suddenly," Webb Miller reported, "at a word of command, scores of native policemen rushed upon the advancing marchers and rained blows on their heads with their steel-shod lathis. Not one of the marchers even raised an arm to fend off the blows. They went down like ten-pins. From where I stood I heard the sickening whack of the clubs on unprotected skulls. The waiting crowd of marchers groaned and sucked in their breath in sympathetic pain at every blow. Those struck down fell sprawling, unconscious or writhing with fractured skulls or broken shoulders. . . . The survivors, without breaking ranks, silently and doggedly marched on until struck down." When the first column was laid low, another advanced. "Although everyone knew," Webb Miller wrote, "that within a few minutes he would be beaten down, perhaps killed, I could detect no signs of wavering or fear. They marched steadily, with heads up, without the encouragement of music or cheering or any possibility that they might escape serious injury or death. The police rushed out and methodically and mechanically beat down the second column. There was no fight, no struggle; the marchers simply walked forward till struck down."

Another group of twenty-five advanced and sat down. "The police," Webb Miller testifies, "commenced savagely kicking the seated men in the abdomen and testicles." Another column advanced and sat down. Enraged, the police dragged them by their arms and feet and threw them into the ditches. "One was dragged to a ditch where I stood," Miller wrote, "the splash of his body doused me with muddy water. Another policeman dragged a Gandhi man to the ditch, threw him in, and belabored him over the head with his lathi. Hour after hour stretcher-bearers carried back a stream of inert, bleeding bodies."

A British officer approached Mrs. Naidu, touched her arm, and said, "Sarojini Naidu, you are under arrest." She shook off his hand. "I'll come," she declared, "but don't touch me." Manilal was also arrested.

"By eleven [in the morning]," Webb Miller continued, "the heat had reached 116 and the activities of the Gandhi volunteers subsided." He went to the temporary hospital and counted 320 injured, many of them still unconscious, others in agony from the body and head blows. Two men had died. The same scenes were repeated for several days.

India was now free. Technically, legally, nothing had changed. India was still a British colony. Tagore explained the difference. "Those who live in England, far away from the East," he told the *Manchester Guardian* of May 17, 1930, "have now got to realize that Europe has completely lost her former moral prestige in Asia. She is no longer regarded as the champion throughout the world of fair dealing and the exponent of high principle, but as the upholder of Western race supremacy and the exploiter of those outside her own borders.

"For Europe this is, in actual fact, a great moral defeat that has happened. Even though Asia is still physically weak and unable to protect herself from aggression where her vital interests are menaced, nevertheless she can now afford to look down on Europe where before she looked up." He attributed the achievement in India to Mahatma Gandhi.

Gandhi did two things in 1930: he made the British people aware that they were cruelly subjugating India, and he gave Indians the conviction that they could, by lifting their heads and straightening their spines, lift the yoke from their shoulders. After that, it was inevitable that Britain should some day refuse to rule India and that India should some day refuse to be ruled.

The British beat the Indians with batons and rifle butts. The Indians neither cringed nor complained nor retreated. That made England powerless and India invincible.

(LOUIS FISCHER, *The Life of Mahatma Gandhi.*) [18]

THE ROLE OF INADEQUACIES

In much of the business of living, the processes of perceiving, purposing, and behaving may go along more or less smoothly with very little surprise, frustration, or disappointment. If our reality-world is to be sustained, there must be a preponderance of relatively successful occasions in which one's prognoses, when tested in action, bring an anticipated degree of satisfaction, even though what may be anticipated as satisfying by some people might be thought of as misery by others. Otherwise, confidence and self-esteem tend to sink to a low ebb.

At the same time it seems obvious that if there is to be any emergence and flow from already established form, a person must sense some inadequacy of the reality-world he has perceived until now. This inadequacy he experiences in terms of some problem, frustration, obstacle, illusion, surprise, shock, mistake, failure, disappointment, or the like. These always arise as aspects of a particular occasion of living. The recognition and admission of obstacles, mistakes, and failures allows for the possibility of change and growth. These mistakes and failures can be either on the level of doing (how-to-do) or of valuing (what-for).

There is, of course, a great difference between admitting one's own inadequacies and blaming oneself. In admitting mistakes, we are only recognizing the inadequacies in the prognoses furnished by the assumptions and expectancies which played a role in making the situation what it was. In blaming ourselves or others, we tend to "freeze" our assumptive world, not recognizing its functional role in supplying predictive probabilities to test through action. As a consequence, instead of the humility generated by admitted inadequacies, we may experience marked inferiority, self-pity or a sense of guilt.

Recognition of mistakes and failures provides an opportunity to try to become aware of just where the inadequacy is in our total pattern of assumptions. Is it on the perceptual, the sequential, or the evaluatory level? Many times an individual assigns the wrong cause to his failure. Mistakes which are accepted as challenges and opportunities invite inquiry and provide opportunity for growth and emergence. Genuine success in living must raise new problems, provide bases for emergence to higher levels of value-quality in living. A sense of living successfully therefore does not consist merely in accomplishing purposes; it must also include the recognition of inadequacies and mistakes and the use of one's capacity for choice to attain more precise and inclusive assumptions and "higher" standards of value. Only in this way can we more or less continuously participate in the creation of a "reality" which will more effectively further our basic motivations as human beings.

It should be clear, therefore, that the opportunity for choice and learning exists when one senses an inadequacy of some aspect of his reality-world through inability to achieve some purpose. If the individual can become aware that there are other possible perceptions, other prognoses of sequential phenomena, other standards of value which might provide a more adequate prognosis for successful action, he may weigh the relative reliability of alternative prognoses for action and exercise choice. The nature of the choice which faces him will vary, of course, with the nature of the experience that resulted in the sensed inadequacy.

The following passages suggest the extent to which there is general recognition of this potential value of frustrations, inadequacies, and mistakes in the development of human living to its highest levels.

> The sword gathers rust for want of use.
> So man's will loses its brilliancy
> When not engaged in vigorously forging its
>   way against obstacles.
>   (*The Wisdom of Wu Ming Fu.*) [19]

Almost immediately after the Ahmedabad meeting I went to Nadiad. It was here that I first used the expression "Himalayan miscalculation" which obtained such a wide currency afterwards. Even at Ahmedabad I had begun to have a dim perception of my mistake. But when I reached Nadiad and saw the actual state of things there and heard reports about a large number of people from Kheda district having been arrested, it suddenly dawned upon me that I had committed a grave error in calling upon the people in the Kheda district and elsewhere to launch upon civil disobedience prematurely, as it now seemed to me. I was addressing a public meeting. My confession brought down upon me no small amount of ridicule. But I have never regretted having made that confession. For I have always held that it is only when one sees one's own mistakes with a convex lens, and does just the reverse in the case of others, that one is able to arrive at a just relative estimate of the two. I further believe that a scrupulous and conscientious observance of this rule is necessary for one who wants to be a Satyagrahi.
                    (*Gandhi's Autobiography.*) [20]

I want to get to the point when I shall be able to say quite simply, and without affectation, that the two great turning points in my life were when my father sent me to Oxford, and when society sent me to prison. I will not say that prison is the best thing that could have happened to me; for that phrase would savour of too great bitterness towards myself. I would sooner say, or hear it said of me, that I was so typical a child of my age, that in my perversity, and for that perversity's sake, I turned the good things of my life to evil, and the evil things of my life to good.

What is said, however, by myself or by others, matters little. The important thing, the thing that lies before me, the thing that I have to do, if the brief remainder of my days is not to be maimed, marred, and incomplete, is to absorb into my nature all that has been done to me,

to make it part of me, to accept it without complaint, fear, or re-
luctance. The supreme vice is shallowness. Whatever is realised is right.

When first I was put into prison some people advised me to try and
forget who I was. It was ruinous advice. It is only by realising what I
am that I have found comfort of any kind. Now I am advised by others
to try on my release to forget that I have ever been in a prison at all.
I know that would be equally fatal. It would mean that I would always
be haunted by an intolerable sense of disgrace, and that those things
that are meant for me as much as for anybody else—the beauty of the
sun and moon, the pageant of the seasons, the music of daybreak and
the silence of great nights, the rain falling through the leaves, or the
dew creeping over the grass and making it silver—would all be tainted
for me, and lose their healing power and their power of communicating
joy. To regret one's own experiences is to arrest one's own development.
To deny one's own experiences is to put a lie into the lips of one's own
life. It is no less than a denial of the soul.

For just as the body absorbs things of all kinds, things common and
unclean no less than those that the priest or a vision has cleansed, and
converts them into swiftness or strength, into the play of beautiful
muscles and the moulding of fair flesh, into the curves and colours of
the hair, the lips, the eye; so the soul in its turn has its nutritive functions also, and can transform into noble moods of thought and passions
of high import what in itself is base, cruel, and degrading; nay, more,
may find in these its most august modes of assertion, and can often
reveal itself most perfectly through what was intended to desecrate or
destroy. (Oscar Wilde, *De Profundis.*) [21]

These are the times that try men's souls. The summer soldier and the
sunshine patriot will in this crisis shrink from the service of his country;
but he that stands it NOW, deserves the love and thanks of man and
woman. Tyranny, like hell, is not easily conquered; yet we have this
consolation with us, that the harder the conflict, the more glorious the
triumph. What we obtain too cheap, we esteem too lightly; 'tis dearness
only that gives everything its value. Heaven knows how to set a proper
price upon its goods; and it would be strange indeed, if so celestial
an article as FREEDOM should not be highly rated.
(Thomas Paine, *The Selected Work of Tom Paine.*) [22]

Lord, we pray not for tranquility, nor that our tribulations may cease;
we pray for Thy Spirit and Thy Love, that Thou grant us strength
and grace to overcome adversity; through Jesus Christ. Amen.
(Girolamo Savonarola.) [23]

As already indicated, our failure to achieve a purpose may lie in a faulty prognosis furnished by perception (a mountain may be perceived as much closer than it "is"); in a faulty prognosis of sequential phenomena (we may misjudge the effect of our action upon some other person); in a faulty prognosis based upon inappropriate standards of value (a man who successfully fulfills his purpose of making a lot of money may find in later life that his living is empty, devoid of deep satisfaction). There are also innumerable other types of situations in which one may become aware of mistakes. But whatever the reason for the inadequacy, a correct diagnosis of the basis for the incorrect prognosis revealed through action is obviously necessary if we are to work out new hypotheses, and submit them to test through further action with renewed confidence in the emergence of a more satisfying quality in the on-going process of living.

It also seems evident that much of education in our modern push-button Western world is concerned with "how-to-do's" which can be acquired by instruction with a minimum experience of inadequacies, frustrations, or failures. To a degree this is right and proper: it is important that every individual should be capable of making use of modern tools and gadgets as means of accomplishing purposes. However, it is clear that education limited to *how* to accomplish purposes leaves out of consideration the necessity of training and development in the capacity to make value-choices between alternative purposes.

It thus appears that a crucial problem for education is to devise methods for teaching people how to improve value-judgments which, in turn, will increase the probability of having a richer quality of experience. By and large, it is only in the area of extra-curricular activity or in some added special program associated with the formal educational process that most students today are given the opportunity to exercise and develop their capacity to make value-judgments. In general, it is only in such situations that the developing individual must deal with issues that are both personal and important to him, issues that can only be resolved by some value-judgment on the basis of which he must act with consequences to him which modify, for better or for worse, his capacity to make value-judgments in the future.

The widespread interest and participation in recreational sports appears to stem from the desire to experience the satisfactions associated with sequences of prognoses, partial success and partial failure, revision of prognoses, and with testing new prognoses through new action. If a sport becomes too highly mechanized, if push-buttons and mechanical artifacts replace human co-ordination and judgment, then the sport soon loses its zest.

INTELLECTUAL KNOWLEDGE AND WISDOM

As we have seen, intellectual inquiry and its resulting concepts, theories, and abstractions play an indispensable role in man's understanding of himself and his world. It is equally evident that knowledge acquired through purely symbolic means, knowledge which has not been tested in the crucible of everyday activity, is limited in its predictive value. A person can have no real wisdom in a field in which he has had no concrete, firsthand experience, a type of learning sometimes referred to as "gut-learning." For wisdom involves acting on value-judgments which have been distilled out of the failures, choices, and refinements which are inevitably met in real-life situations. A story has been reported of a Kentucky resident who was asked, on his one-hundredth birthday: "How does it happen you're so wise?" The old man answered: "Because I've got good judgment. My good judgment comes from experience and experience—well, that comes from poor judgment."

Thus a distinguished professor of political science who decides to seek public office may be defeated by a far less-educated practical politician unless and until he has tested the points contained in his lecture notes in the rough-and-tumble of politics. Likewise, a young physician, even though he may have had a brilliant academic record in medical school, may not be a trustworthy physician or surgeon until he has tested his theoretical knowledge through concrete action with individual patients in the sick-room and in the operating room. Successful, rewarding, enriching, purposeful action requires experience and practice, failure and profit therefrom, whether one is a teacher, cook, soldier, farmer, carpenter, or salesman.

In the entrance hall of one of the buildings at the University of Delhi there is the following quotation from Tagore: "A teacher can never truly teach unless he is still learning himself. A lamp can never light another lamp unless it continues to burn its own flame. The teacher who has come to the end of his subject, who has no living traffic with his knowledge but merely repeats his lesson to his students can only load their minds; he cannot quicken them. Truth not only must inform but also must inspire; if the inspiration dies out and the information only accumulates, then truth loses its infinity. The greater part of our learning in the schools has been waste because for most of our teachers their subjects are like dead specimens of once living things with which they have a learned acquaintance but no communication of life and love."

In the dedication of one of his books, Chester Barnard wrote: "To my father—at a crisis in my youth he taught me the wisdom of choice: To try and fail is at least to learn; to fail to try is to suffer the inestimable loss of what might have been." [24]

The following excerpts point to some of the differences between intellectual, theoretical knowledge and practical wisdom, and illustrate the role of action in testing and altering assumptions in the development of greater wisdom.

WISDOM

What is wisdom?
It is not merely knowledge,
But the application of knowledge to the guidance of
  the individual in his relations with the Universe.
                    (*The Wisdom of Wu Ming Fu.*) [25]

Now I see the secret of the making of the best persons,
It is to grow in the open air and to eat and sleep with the earth.

Here a great personal deed has room,
(Such a deed seizes upon the hearts of the whole race of men,
Its effusion of strength and will overwhelms law and mocks all authority
  and all argument against it).

Here is the test of wisdom,
Wisdom is not finally tested in schools,
Wisdom cannot be pass'd from one having it to another not having it,
Wisdom is of the soul, is not susceptible of proof, is its own proof,
Applies to all stages and objects and qualities and is content,
Is the certainty of reality and immortality of things, and the excellence
  of things;
Something there is in the float of the sight of things that provokes it
  out of the soul.

Now I re-examine philosophies and religions,
They may prove well in lecture-rooms, yet not prove at all under the
  spacious clouds and along the landscape and flowing currents.
Here is realisation,
Here is a man tallied—he realises here what he has in him,
The past, the future, majesty, love—if they are vacant of you, you are
  vacant of them.

(WALT WHITMAN, "Song of the Open Road.") [26]

Good words, my son, come easily, when he
That speaks is wise, and speaks but for the right.
Else come they never! Swift are thine, and bright
As though with thought, yet have no thought at all.

(EURIPIDES, *The Bacchae*.) [27]

The generous youths who came to manhood between 1820 and 1830, while this deadly era was maturing, seem to have undergone a revulsion against the world almost before touching it; at least two of them suffered, revolted, and condemned, while still boys sitting on benches in school, and came forth advancing upon this old society like gladiators. The activity of William Lloyd Garrison, the man of action, preceded by several years that of Emerson, who is his prophet. Both of them were parts of one revolution. One of Emerson's articles of faith was that a man's thoughts spring from his actions rather than his actions from his thoughts, and possibly the same thing holds good for society at large. Perhaps all truths, whether moral or economic, must be worked out in real life before they are discovered by the student, and it was therefore necessary that Garrison should be evolved earlier than Emerson.   (JOHN JAY CHAPMAN, *Emerson and Other Essays*.) [28]

Gandhi's two years and eight months in England came at a formative phase of his life and must have shaped his personality. But their influence was probably less than normal. For Gandhi was not the student type; he did not learn essential things by studying. He was the doer, and he grew and gained knowledge through action. Books, people, and conditions affected him. But the real Gandhi, the Gandhi of history, did not emerge, did not even hint of his existence in the years of schooling and study. Perhaps it is unfair to expect too much of the frail provincial Indian transplanted to metropolitan London at the green age of eighteen. Yet the contrast between the mediocre, unimpressive, handicapped, floundering M. K. Gandhi, attorney-at-law, who left England in 1891, and the Mahatma leader of millions is so great as to suggest that until public service tapped his enormous reserves of intuition, will power, energy, and self-confidence, his true personality lay dormant. To be sure, he fed it unconsciously; his loyalty to the vow of no meat, no wine, no women, was a youthful exercise in will and devotion which later flowered into a way of life. But only when it was touched by the magic wand of action in South Africa did the personality of Gandhi burgeon. In *Young India* of September 4, 1924, he said his college days were before the time "when . . . I began life."

Gandhi advanced to greatness by doing. The *Gita*, Hinduism's holy scripture, therefore became Gandhi's gospel, for it glorifies action.

(Louis Fischer, *The Life of Mahatma Gandhi.*) [29]

. . . neither by abstaining from action, doth man attain tranquility. . . .

Perform, therefore, all prescribed deeds . . . for to do is better than not to do, . . .

By work the great attained bliss.

All men are bound together by their deeds. This is the law of life; thou also must perform thy task.

Whatsoever the superior person doeth, others also do, what he setteth forth by his behavior, that, all men follow. He then who leadeth the excellent life giveth by his deeds example to those about him. By acts alone, excellence is demonstrated to others.

(*The Bhagavad-Gita,* translated by D. G. Mukerji.) [30]

Now we return briefly to the matter of individual responsibility mentioned in the early sections of this chapter. There are occasions when human beings may experience a deep conflict between what they feel is their duty as a human being and what they feel is their duty in some special role they have in life, whether it be that of public official, teacher, banker, labor-leader, or military officer. There are other situations in which a person may feel no responsibility for the consequences of his acts if these were ordered by superiors and a person feels he has been caught in a web of circumstances over which he has no control. Choice may seem to be absent, yet action which conflicts with human and ethical values may seem to be demanded. The nature of this type of situation is strikingly illustrated in the following passage:

The heat in the large third-class car, that had been exposed to the rays of the sun all day and was now crowded, was so oppressive that

Nekhlúdof did not enter it, but remained outside on the platform. Even here, however, no air was stirring, and Nekhlúdof breathed freely only when the cars had passed the houses and he began to feel the breeze. "Yes, they were murdered," and he repeated to himself the words he had used when talking with his sister. And among the various impressions of the day his imagination pictured the handsome face of the second convict who had died,—its smiling lips, its severe brow, and the small, well-shaped ear on the side of the shaven bluish skull. And the most appalling part of all this was that the man was murdered, and no one knew who did the deed. But there could be no question about the fact, the man had undoubtedly been killed. He was led out with the others, by the order of Máslennikof. Máslennikof had probably given the usual order, had signed his name with its stupid flourish to a formal paper with a printed heading, and of course will not consider himself responsible. Still less blame could be attributed to the careful prison doctor who examined the convicts. He did his duty punctiliously,—he separated the feeble ones and could not be expected to know that the throng would be led out so late in the day or that its ranks would be so crowded, neither could he have foreseen the terrific heat. The Inspector? . . . but he had only obeyed his order to send off a certain number of exiles and convicts of both sexes on a given day. Neither could the officer of the convoy be blamed, for his duty consisted in receiving a certain number and in sending off a certain number. He had led them according to the usual regulations and surely could not have expected that such robust-looking men as the two whom Nekhlúdof had seen, would have succumbed and died in consequence of the heat and fatigue. No one was to blame, and yet the men were dead, killed by those who could not really be blamed for their death.

"And all this," said Nekhlúdof to himself, "comes from the fact that all these governors, inspectors, police officers, and policemen are convinced that there are conditions in life when a man owes no duty to his fellow-man. Every one of these men, Máslennikof, the Inspector, the soldiers of the convoy, if they had not been governors, inspectors, and officers, would have hesitated twenty times before sending men and women off in such a crowded throng and in such heat; they would have paused twenty times on the way if they had seen that a man was growing faint, or was gasping for breath; they would have separated him from the others, would have allowed him to rest in the shade, would have given him water, and then if anything had happened, they would have pitied him. But they did nothing of the sort; they even prevented others from giving aid, only because they took no account whatever of the men before them, or of their own responsibilities towards them.

They magnified their office and its requirements to the disadvantage of their duties to mankind. This is the sum and substance of the matter," thought Nekhlúdof. "If a man were to admit that there could be anything of more importance than the love one owes his fellow-man, even for a single hour, or in any single instance, he might commit any conceivable crime that a man could commit and yet consider himself innocent."

Nekhlúdof was so absorbed in his thoughts that he had not noticed the change in the weather. The sun was hidden behind a low-hanging ragged cloud, and a compact light-gray cloud was advancing from the west. He could see the rain far away in the distance across the fields and the forest, coming in slanting, driving streaks. The air was saturated with moisture. Now and then the cloud was rent with a flash of lightning, and the rattling of the train intermingled more and more frequently with the crashes of thunder. The cloud drew nearer and nearer and the slanting rain-drops, driven by the wind, fell on the platform of the car and on Nekhlúdof's coat. He crossed to the opposite side, and inhaling the fresh moisture and the fragrance of growing wheat rising from the parched fields, he gazed at the fleeting gardens, groves, and fields of ripening yellow rye, at the green strips of oats and the black furrows between the rows of dark green potatoes in bloom. The fields looked as if they had been varnished. As all green things were more vivid in color, so were the yellows and the blacks.

"More, more!" cried Nekhlúdof, rejoicing at the sight of the reviving fields, the flower and the kitchen gardens.

But the violent rain did not last long. The cloud had partly spent itself and partly passed over, and only the last fine drops were falling gently on the moistened ground. The sun reappeared, everything glistened, and the low curve of a brilliant rainbow, with a conspicuous violet stripe, broken at one end, illumined the eastern horizon.

"What was I thinking about?" Nekhlúdof asked himself when all these changes in nature had passed and the train was speeding through a cutting between two high banks. "Oh, yes, I remember, I was thinking that all these men, the Inspector, the convoy, and the others, are by nature kind and gentle. Being officials has made them cruel."

He remembered Máslennikof's indifference when he told him what was going on in the prison, the Inspector's severity, the harshness of the officer of the convoy when he refused places on the carts to those who asked for them, and paid no heed to the woman on the train who was in child-labor. Evidently the reason why all these people were so invulnerable, so impenetrable to feelings of compassion, was simply due to the fact that they were officials. As officials they were no more receptive of the sensations of compassion than this paved earth is of the rain from heaven! he thought, as he gazed at the embankment of the cut,—paved with multi-colored stones, down which the rainwater streamed, instead of soaking into the earth. "It may be necessary to pave the cut, but it is a melancholy thought that so much soil must be deprived of its productiveness, for it might be yielding grain, grass, shrubs, and trees, like those that grow above it. And it is the same among men," he thought; "it is possible that the governors, inspectors, policemen may be needed, but it is terrible to see men who have lost the attribute that differentiates them from the beasts—love and pity for each other.

"The whole matter may be summed up thus," he went on: "these men accept as a law that which is not a law, and do not accept that which is the eternal, immutable and unchangeable law that God Himself has written in the hearts of men. That is the reason why I am so unhappy in their presence," he thought. "I am simply afraid of them. And they are indeed terrible. More terrible than brigands. After all a brigand might be susceptible to pity, but these men are incapable of it. They are insured against pity, as these stones are against vegetation, and that's what makes them so terrible. Men call Pugatchóf and Rázin terrible. But these men are a thousand times more dreadful," he went on thinking. "If a psychological problem were to be propounded: what can be done to make the men of the present—Christians, humanitarians, or simply kind-hearted men—insensible to the crimes they are committing, there could be but one solution, namely, make them all governors, inspectors, officers, policemen, etc., which means, in the first place, that they must be convinced of the existence of a business called 'Government Service,' which allows men to be treated like immaterial objects, thereby excluding all fraternal relationship with them, and in the second place that the members of this Government Service should be united in such a way that the responsibility for their dealings with men could never fall on any individual member. Otherwise it would be simply out of the question for human beings to countenance in these days such terrible deeds as those, for example, that I have witnessed to-day. The fact is, that men think that their fellow-beings may be treated without love, but no such conditions exist. Immaterial objects may be dealt with in that fashion; one may chop trees, make bricks, and hammer iron without love. But human beings cannot be treated without love,—just as bees cannot be handled without care. Such is the nature of the bee. If one handles a bee without care, he will injure both the bee and himself. It is just the same with men. And this cannot be otherwise, because mutual love is the fundamental law of human life. It is true that a man cannot compel himself to love as he can compel himself to work, but that does not imply that men may be treated without love, especially if something is required from them. If one feels no love for men, let him be quiet about it," thought Nekhlúdof, now talking to himself, "let him busy himself with objects, or even with himself alone, with anything he pleases,—only not with men. As it is only possible to eat without injury when one is hungry, so men can be handled to advantage only when one loves them. But if a man just allows himself to deal with men without love, as for instance you yourself dealt yesterday with your brother-in-law, there are no limits to the suffering and cruelty which you might be capable of inflicting on others, an example of which I witnessed to-day; nor limits to the suffering you would bring to yourself, and this also have I experienced in my own life. Yes, that is true," thought Nekhlúdof. "Everything is all right now," he repeated to himself, experiencing the double delight of the refreshing coolness after intense heat and the assurance of having come to a clear understanding of a question that had long interested him.

(TOLSTOY, *Resurrection.*) [31]

IMPORTANCE AND FUNCTION OF ACTION

When we think of the consequences of our actions, we usually think of their effects upon other things or upon other people. We may forget that our actions always have consequences for us. Often this is their most important result. The effects of all our actions are registered at least in some subtle way and affect what we do later and how we do it.

Changes in the way we look at things or in our ways of thinking seem to come about only as a result of our own action or our sharing the action of others as it goes along. For example, a person may know intellectually all about the shape of the distorted room described in chapter II, but will still see it as cubical. The optimum conditions under which he learns to see the room as it "really is," are conditions involving testing the shape of the room with action —in this instance, touching various parts of the room with a long stick or trying to throw tennis balls at certain points in the room. After a person gets adept at this and can act in the room without being fooled, then he sees it distorted. He will also learn to see the distortion if he only watches another person using the stick or throwing the balls. He apparently sees how the other person fails through doing what he himself would do. So he, too, learns his assumptions were wrong through action which he vicariously shares.

New ideas and abstractions are made meaningful and become real to us only if we are able to put them to use in our own lives and experience some satisfactions from having done so. The great prophets and political innovators have always known this.

It is for this reason that we generally feel it is safer to rely on assumptions built up through our own previous action than on some new intellectual knowledge which contradicts our beliefs. Except in critical situations, we generally will not accept suggestions from others because we have not ourselves tested their reliability through experiencing their consequences. Even though old assumptions mislead us, we may still cling to them if we do not feel sufficiently thwarted or frustrated in carrying out our purposes. Deep-seated assumptions generally change only after repeated or unusually impressive demonstration that they are inadequate in providing the quality of satisfactions we use as our standard of success.

The speed and consistency of our judgments and actions reflect how sure we are of the existing significances and how confident we are that we can act successfully in terms of these significances. It is commonplace to observe that no matter how much deliberation has preceded an act, it is the whole person that acts, and that intellectual analysis at the time of action may interfere with its smooth performance. This point is illustrated by Chester Barnard: "A friend of mine, a man of high intellectual attainments, of scientific training, and having conspicuously an incisive, logical type of mind, once said to me as we were playing golf: 'Barnard, there is a place for brains in golf, but they must be used before you start the swing. If they are used during the action, it is invariably ruined.' " [32] And Robert Bridges seems to have expressed a similar observation when he wrote:

All terrestrial Life, in all functions and motions, operateth thru' alliance of living entities disparate in their structure but logically correlated in action under some final cause. Suchlike co-ordinations may be acquired in man with reason'd purpose consciently, as when a learner on viol or flute diligently traineth his hand to the intricat fingering of the stops and strings; or may be innate, as the spontaneous flight of birds; or antenatal and altogether inconscient, as the food-organs, call'd vegetativ because such cellular connivance is the life of plants.

The main co-ordinations whereon life hangeth were ever automatous, and such states when acquired tend to become self-working as they are perfected, dropping out of our ken: the proverb truly spake *Habit is second nature*, and 'twil function best without superintendence, for the least brain-wave or timid rippling of self-consciousness can rob the bodily movements of their nativ grace. . . . [33]

Only rarely, if ever, in any concrete situation do all the significances involved in the decision-making process confirm and supplement one another in perfect fashion. We experience the extent of the disharmony among them as assurance or lack of assurance. We can extend the scope of the situations in which we can act with a high degree of confidence only as we increase the inclusiveness of our assumptions. However, we must remember that new contingencies are introduced in each transaction of living. No matter how much confidence we feel that our decision on which we are about to act is right, it is still only a probability. The most difficult decisions we have to make are those about which we feel unsure but which we feel compelled to make anyway.

Thus, behaving plays several different roles in the on-going process of living. It is only through action that our experiential world takes on significance; it is only through action in conjunction with awareness that we acquire beliefs and assumptions; and it is only through action that we are able to check the reliability of our perceptions and our "how-to-do" and "what-for" decisions.

6

Man and Fellow Man^{*}

> "There's always something
> one's ignorant of
> About anyone, however well
> one knows them;
> And that may be something of
> the greatest importance."
>
> —T. S. ELIOT

INDIVIDUAL AND COMMUNITY

No one can be human unless he is an active participant in a social environment. And to be human has a multitude of social consequences. Once we have passed through the stage of infancy practically all of our thought and behavior is in some way affected by the psychological presence of other people or by codes or symbols created by them. Even when we are quite alone, our behavior and our thoughts reflect our social learning.

While these obvious facts sometimes have been forgotten by the professional psychologist, they are seldom forgotten by any keen observer of the process of living. In this chapter we can do little more than indicate briefly some of the fascinating psychological consequences of man's dependence upon man.

Just as we need to learn ways of perceiving inanimate objects so there will be maximum correspondence between what we *assume* to be "out there" and what we *discover* to be "out there" after we test our assumptions by action, so too must we learn how to per-

---

* Notes to this chapter begin on p. 335.

ceive other people. If we do not, then our behavior with others will have little chance of accomplishing the purposes intended.

When perception does involve other people, among other new and different things added is the fact that other people have purposes of their own. So if we are to build up useful assumptions concerning the properties and characteristics of people, we must attribute some reliable significances to their purposes. Only if we do this will our perception of others turn out to be a good guide in predicting both the short- and long-range consequences of social behavior on us and on those with whom we deal.

Since individual purposes vary so much with developmental age, with cultural and subcultural influences, and with the specific situation in which an individual is operating, our perception of others' purposes is often unsure and can easily be wrong. Yet if our social life is to be anything but a series of shocks, surprises, frustrations, and disappointments, we must create for ourselves certain *social* constancies, just as we create *object*-constancies in the inanimate world. We must be able to guess with some degree of accuracy what an individual's role is, how his role will be affected by different situations, how he is likely to act toward us if we do this or that. This also assumes that we acquire our own sense of *self*-constancy against which we judge the constancy and variability of others.

As some of the following readings indicate, it seems unlikely that we shall ever be able to understand any other human being or group of human beings completely. Samuel Johnson once made a remark to the effect that each one of us knows something worse about himself than he can be sure of in others. Most of us are much more surprised by the behavior of others than we are by our own behavior.

It would seem that the best way to get the most complete understanding possible of other people is to participate with them in situations that are new both to them and to us. Only in such participation can we see the full play of their value-judgments, compare the weighing they give different cues to the weighing we give those same cues. The way a person acts in a relatively new situation demonstrates the extent to which various cultural norms and abstractions are put into operation in concrete situations, revealing the value-emphases made and demonstrating what ingenuity the individual can muster in the "how-to-do's" of accomplishment.

The following selections are divided into two groups, the first of which emphasizes man's dependence upon his fellow man. The second group is concerned with the difficulties and potential rewards of social perception, of understanding the reality-worlds of other persons.

In former days, when all a man's limbs did not work together as amicably as they do now, but each had a will and a way of its own, the Members generally began to find fault with the Belly for spending an idle luxurious life, while they were wholly occupied in laboring for its support, and ministering to its wants and pleasures; so they entered into a conspiracy to cut off its supplies for the future. The Hands were no longer to carry food to the Mouth, nor the Mouth to receive the food, nor the Teeth to chew it. They had not long persisted in this course of starving the Belly into subjection, ere they all began, one by one, to fail and flag, and the whole body to pine away. Then the Members were convinced that the Belly also, cumbersome and useless as it seemed, had an important function of its own; that they could no more do without it than it could do without them; and that if they would have the constitution of the body in a healthy state, they must work together, each in his proper sphere, for the common good of all.

(Aesop's Fables.) [1]

Somebody has to make the tubs and pails.
Not yet do the tubs and pails grow on trees
    and all you do is pick 'em.
For tubs and pails we go first to the timber cruisers, to the loggers,
    hewers, sawyers, choppers, peelers, pilers, saw filers, skid greasers, slip
    tenders, teamsters, lumber shovers, tallymen, planers, bandsawmen,
    circular-saw-men, hoopers, matchers, nailers, painters, truckmen,
    packers, haulers,
For the sake of a tub or a pail to you.

And for the sake of a jack-knife in your pocket,
    or a scissors on your table,
The dynamite works get into production and deliver to the miners
    who blast, the mule drivers, engineers and firemen on the dinkies, the
    pumpmen, the rope riders, the sinkers and sorters, the carpenters,
    electricians and repairmen, the foremen and straw-bosses,

They get out the ore and send it to the smelters, the converters where
   by the hands and craft of furnace crushers and hot blast handlers,
   ladlers, puddlers, the drag-out man, the hook-up man, the chipper,
   the spannerman, the shearsman, the squeezer,
There is steel for the molders, the cutlers, buffers, finishers, forgers,
   grinders, polishers, temperers—
This for the sake of a jack-knife to your pocket or a shears on your table.

These are the people, with flaws and failings, with patience, sacrifice,
   devotion, the people.
The people is a farmer, a tenant and a share-cropper, a plowman, a
   plow-grinder and a choreman, a churner, a chicken-picker and a
   combine driver, a threshing crew and an old settlers' picnic, a cream-
   ery co-operative, or a line of men on wagons selling tomatoes or
   sugar-beets on contract to a cannery, a refinery,
The people is a tall freight-handler and a tough longshoreman, a greasy
   fireman and a gambling oil-well shooter with a driller and tooler
   ready, a groping miner going underground with a headlamp, an
   engineer and a fireman with an eye for semaphores, a seaman, deck-
   hand, pilot at the wheel in fog and stars.
The people? A weaver of steel-and-concrete floors and walls fifty floors
   up, a blue-print designer, an expert calculator and accountant, a
   carpenter with an eye for joists and elbows, a bricklayer with an ear
   for the pling of a trowel, a pile-driver crew pounding down the
   pier-posts.
The people? Harness bulls and narcotic dicks, multigraph girls and soda-
   jerkers, hat girls, bat boys, sports writers, ghost writers, popcorn and
   peanut squads, flatfeet, scavengers, mugs saying "Aw go button your
   nose," squirts hollering "Aw go kiss yourself outa dis game intuh
   anuddah," dead-heads, hops, cappers, come-ons, tin horns, small
   timers, the night club outfits helping the soup-and-fish who have to do
   something between midnight and bedtime.
The people? A puddler in the flaring splinters of newmade steel, a milk-
   wagon-driver getting the once-over from a milk inspector, a sand-hog
   with "the bends," a pack-rat, a snow-queen, janitors, jockeys, white
   collar lads, pearl divers, peddlers, bundlestiffs, pants pressers, cleaners
   and dyers, lice and rat exterminators.
So many forgotten, so many never remembered at all, yet there are
   well-diggers, school-teachers, window washers who unless buckled
   proper dance on air and go down down, coal heavers, roundhouse
   wipers, hostlers, sweepers, samplers, weighers, sackers, carvers, bloom
   chippers, kiln burners, cooks, bakers, beekeepers, goat raisers, goat

hay growers, slag-rollers, melters, solderers, track greasers, jiggermen,
snow-plow drivers, clamdiggers, stoolpigeons, the buck private, the
gob, the leatherneck, the cop—
In uniform, in white collars, in overalls, in denim and gingham, a number on an assembly line, a name on a polling list, a postoffice address,
a crime and sports page reader, a movie goer and radio listener, a
stock-market sucker, a sure thing for slick gamblers, a union man or
non-union, a job holder or a job hunter,
Always either employed, disemployed, unemployed and employable or
unemployable, a world series fan, a home buyer on a shoestring,
a down-and-out or a game fighter who will die fighting.
The people is the grand canyon of humanity
and many many miles across.
The people is pandora's box, humpty dumpty, a clock of doom and an
avalanche when it turns loose.
The people rest on land and weather, on time and the changing winds.
The people have come far and can look back and say,
"We will go farther yet."
The people is a plucked goose and a shorn sheep of legalized fraud
And the people is one of those mountain slopes holding a volcano
of retribution,
Slow in all things, slow in its gathered wrath, slow in its onward heave,
Slow in its asking: "Where are we now? what time is it?"
(CARL SANDBURG, *The People, Yes.*) [2]

If I face a human being as my *Thou,* and say the primary word
I-Thou to him, he is not a thing among things, and does not consist of
things.

This human being is not *He* or *She,* bounded from every other *He* and
She, a specific point in space and time within the net of the world; nor
is he a nature able to be experienced and described, a loose bundle of
named qualities. But with no neighbour, and whole in himself, he is
Thou and fills the heavens. This does not mean that nothing exists except
himself. But all else lives in *his* light.

Just as the melody is not made up of notes nor the verse of words nor
the statue of lines, but they must be tugged and dragged till their unity
has been scattered into these many pieces, so with the man to whom I
say *Thou.* I can take out from him the colour of his hair, or of his
speech, or of his goodness. I must continually do this. But each time I do
it he ceases to be *Thou.*

And just as prayer is not in time but time in prayer, sacrifice not in
space but space in sacrifice, and to reverse the relation is to abolish the

reality, so with the man to whom I say *Thou*. I do not meet with him at some time and place or other. I can set him in a particular time and place; I must continually do it: but I set only a *He* or a *She*, that is an *It*, no longer my *Thou*.

So long as the heaven of *Thou* is spread out over me the winds of causality cower at my heels, and the whirlpool of fate stays its course.

I do not experience the man to whom I say *Thou*. But I take my stand in relation to him, in the sanctity of the primary word. Only when I step out of it do I experience him once more. In the act of experience *Thou* is far away.

Even if the man to whom I say *Thou* is not aware of it in the midst of his experience, yet relation may exist. For *Thou* is more than *It* realises. No deception penetrates here; here is the cradle of the Real Life.

(MARTIN BUBER, *I and Thou*.) [3]

. . . Americans of all ages, all conditions, and all dispositions constantly form associations. They have not only commercial and manufacturing companies, in which all take part, but associations of a thousand other kinds, religious, moral, serious, futile, general or restricted, enormous or diminutive. The Americans make associations to give entertainments, to found seminaries, to build inns, to construct churches, to diffuse books, to send missionaries to the antipodes; in this manner they found hospitals, prisons, and schools. If it is proposed to inculcate some truth or to foster some feeling by the encouragement of a great example, they form a society. Wherever at the head of some new undertaking you see the government in France, or a man of rank in England, in the United States you will be sure to find an association.

I met with several kinds of associations in America of which I confess I had no previous notion; and I have often admired the extreme skill with which the inhabitants of the United States succeed in proposing a common object for the exertions of a great many men and in inducing them voluntarily to pursue it. . . .

Thus the most democratic country on the face of the earth is that in which men have, in our time, carried to the highest perfection the art of pursuing in common the object of their common desires and have applied this new science to the greatest number of purposes. Is this the result of accident, or is there in reality any necessary connection between the principle of association and that of equality?

Aristocratic communities always contain, among a multitude of persons who by themselves are powerless, a small number of powerful and wealthy citizens, each of whom can achieve great undertakings single-handed. In aristocratic societies men do not need to combine in order to act, because they are strongly held together. Every wealthy and powerful citizen constitutes the head of a permanent and compulsory association, composed of all those who are dependent upon him or whom he makes subservient to the execution of his designs.

Among democratic nations, on the contrary, all the citizens are independent and feeble; they can do hardly anything by themselves, and none of them can oblige his fellow men to lend him their assistance. They all, therefore, become powerless if they do not learn voluntarily to help one another. If men living in democratic countries had no right and no inclination to associate for political purposes, their independence would be in great jeopardy, but they might long preserve their wealth and their cultivation; whereas if they never acquired the habit of forming associations in ordinary life, civilization itself would be endangered. A people among whom individuals lost the power of achieving great things single-handed, without acquiring the means of producing them by united exertions, would soon relapse into barbarism.

Unhappily, the same social condition that renders associations so necessary to democratic nations renders their formation more difficult among those nations than among all others. When several members of an aristocracy agree to combine, they easily succeed in doing so; as each of them brings great strength to the partnership, the number of its members may be very limited; and when the members of an association are limited in number, they may easily become mutually acquainted, understand each other, and establish fixed regulations. The same opportunities do not occur among democratic nations, where the associated members must always be very numerous for their association to have any power. . . .

Feelings and opinions are recruited, the heart is enlarged, and the human mind is developed only by the reciprocal influence of men upon one another. . . .

As soon as several of the inhabitants of the United States have taken up an opinion or a feeling which they wish to promote in the world, they look out for mutual assistance; and as soon as they have found one another out, they combine. From that moment they are no longer isolated men, but a power seen from afar, whose actions serve for an example and whose language is listened to. The first time I heard in the United States that a hundred thousand men had bound themselves publicly to abstain from spirituous liquors, it appeared to me more like a joke than a serious engagement, and I did not at once perceive why these temperate citizens could not content themselves with drinking water by their own firesides. I at last understood that these hundred thousand Americans, alarmed by the progress of drunkenness around them, had made up their minds to patronize temperance. They acted in just the same way as a man of high rank who should dress very plainly in order to inspire the humbler orders with a contempt of luxury. It is probable that if these hundred thousand men had lived in France, each of them would singly have memorialized the government to watch the public houses all over the kingdom.

Nothing, in my opinion, is more deserving of our attention than the intellectual and moral associations of America. The political and industrial associations of that country strike us forcibly; but the others elude our observation, or if we discover them, we understand them imperfectly because we have hardly ever seen anything of the kind. It must be acknowledged, however, that they are as necessary to the American people as the former, and perhaps more so. In democratic countries the science of association is the mother of science; the progress of all the rest depends upon the progress it has made.

Among the laws that rule human societies there is one which seems to be more precise and clear than all others. If men are to remain civilized or to become so, the art of associating together must grow and improve in the same ratio in which the equality of conditions is increased.   (ALEXIS DE TOCQUEVILLE, *Democracy in America*.) [4]

In the critical World War II year of 1944 a vast "I Am an American Day" ceremony was held in Central Park, New York City, on May 21. Many thousands of people were present, including a large number of new citizens. Learned Hand's brief address was so eloquent and so moving that the text immediately became the object of wide demand. It was quickly printed and reprinted and also put into anthologies. The impact was so great that the speaker was invited to address a similar gathering the next year.

We have gathered here to affirm a faith, a faith in a common purpose, a common conviction, a common devotion. Some of us have chosen America as the land of our adoption; the rest have come from those who did the same. For this reason we have some right to consider ourselves a picked group, a group of those who had the courage to break from the past and brave the dangers and the loneliness of a strange land. What was the object that nerved us, or those who went before us, to this choice? We sought liberty; freedom from oppression, freedom from want, freedom to be ourselves. This we then sought; this we now believe that we are by way of winning. What do we mean when we say that first of all we seek liberty? I often wonder whether we do not rest our hopes too much upon constitutions, upon laws, and upon courts. These are false hopes; believe me, these are false hopes. Liberty lies in the hearts of men and women; when it dies there, no constitution, no law, no court can save it; no constitution, no law, no court can even do much to help it. While it lies there it needs no constitution, no law, no court to save it. And what is this liberty which must lie in the hearts of men and women? It is not the ruthless, the unbridled will; it is not freedom to do as one likes. That is the denial of liberty, and leads straight to its overthrow. A society in which men recognize no check upon their freedom soon becomes a society where freedom is the possession of only a savage few; as we have learned to our sorrow.

What then is the spirit of liberty? I cannot define it; I can only tell you my own faith. The spirit of liberty is the spirit which is not too sure that it is right; the spirit of liberty is the spirit which seeks to understand the minds of other men and women; the spirit of liberty is the spirit which weighs their interests alongside its own without bias; the spirit of liberty remembers that not even a sparrow falls to earth unheeded; the spirit of liberty is the spirit of Him who, near two thousand years ago, taught mankind that lesson it has never learned, but has never quite forgotten;* that there may be a kingdom where the least shall be heard and considered side by side with the greatest. And now in that spirit, that spirit of an America which has never been, and which may never be; nay, which never will be except as the conscience and courage of Americans create it; yet in the spirit of that America which lies hidden in some form in the aspirations of us all; in the spirit of that America for which our young men are at this moment fighting and dying; in that spirit of liberty and of America I ask you to rise and with me pledge our faith in the glorious destiny of our beloved country. (LEARNED HAND, *The Spirit of Liberty*.) [5]

Though I speak with the tongues of men and of angels, and have not charity, I am become as sounding brass, or a tinkling cymbal.

And though I have the gift of prophecy, and understand all mysteries, and all knowledge; and though I have all faith, so that I could remove mountains, and have not charity, I am nothing.

And though I bestow all my goods to feed the poor, and though I give my body to be burned, and have not charity, it profiteth me nothing.

---

* This clause was taken in substance from the following clause in H. G. Wells's *The Outline of History* (volume II, page 632, George Newnes, Ltd., London): ". . . whose pitiless and difficult doctrine of self-abandonment and self-forgetfulness we can neither disregard nor yet bring ourselves to obey." L. H.

Charity suffereth long, and is kind; charity envieth not; charity vaunteth not itself, is not puffed up,

Doth not behave itself unseemly, seeketh not her own, is not easily provoked, thinketh no evil;

Rejoiceth not in iniquity, but rejoiceth in the truth;

Beareth all things, believeth all things, hopeth all things, endureth all things.

Charity never faileth: but whether there be prophecies, they shall fail; whether there be tongues, they shall cease; whether there be knowledge, it shall vanish away.

For we know in part, and we prophesy in part.

But when that which is perfect is come, then that which is in part shall be done away.

When I was a child, I spake as a child, I understood as a child, I thought as a child: but when I became a man, I put away childish things.

For now we see through a glass, darkly; but then face to face: now I know in part; but then shall I know even as also I am known.

And now abideth faith, hope, charity, these three; but the greatest of these is charity.   (*I Corinthians, 13.*) [6]

LAUDISI: Excuse me, what can you find out? What can we really know about other people—who they are—what they are—what they are doing, and why they are doing it?

SIGNORA SIRELLI: How can we know? Why not? By asking, of course! You tell me what you know, and I tell you what I know.

LAUDISI: In that case, madam, you ought to be the best informed person in the world. Why, your husband knows more about what others are doing than any other man—or woman, for that matter—in this neighborhood.

SIRELLI [*deprecating but pleased*]: Oh I say, I say . . .

SIGNORA SIRELLI [*to her husband*]: No dear, he's right, he's right. [*Then turning to* AMALIA.] The real truth, Amalia, is this: for all my husband says he knows, I never manage to keep posted on anything!

SIRELLI: And no wonder! The trouble is—that woman never trusts me! The moment I tell her something she is convinced it is not *quite* as I say. Then, sooner or later, she claims that it *can't* be as I say. And at last she is certain it is the exact opposite of what I say!

SIGNORA SIRELLI: Well, you ought to hear all he tells me!

LAUDISI [*laughing aloud*]: May I speak, madam? Let me answer your husband. My dear Sirelli, how do you expect your wife to be satisfied with things as you explain them to her, if you, as is natural, represent them as they seem to you?

SIGNORA SIRELLI: And that means—as they cannot possibly be!

LAUDISI: Why no, Signora, now you are wrong. From your husband's point of view things are, I assure you, exactly as he represents them.

SIRELLI: As they are in reality!

SIGNORA SIRELLI: Not at all! You are always wrong.

SIRELLI: No, not a bit of it! It is you who are always wrong. I am always right.

LAUDISI: The fact is that neither of you is wrong. May I explain? I will prove it to you. Now here you are, you, Sirelli, and Signora Sirelli, your wife, there; and here I am. You see me, don't you?

SIRELLI: Well . . . er . . . yes.

LAUDISI: Do you see me, or do you not?

SIRELLI: Oh, I'll bite! Of course I see you.

LAUDISI: So you see me! But that's not enough. Come here!

SIRELLI [*smiling, he obeys, but with a puzzled expression on his face as though he fails to understand what* LAUDISI *is driving at*]: Well, here I am!

LAUDISI: Yes! Now take a better look at me . . . Touch me! That's it—that's it! Now you are touching me, are you not? And you see me! You're sure you see me?

SIRELLI: Why, I should say . . .

LAUDISI: Yes, but the point is, you're sure! Of course you're sure! Now if you please, Signora Sirelli, you come here—or rather . . . no . . . [*Gallantly.*] it is my place to come to you! [*He goes over to* SIGNORA SIRELLI *and kneels chivalrously on one knee.*] You see me, do you not, madam? Now that hand of yours . . . touch me! A pretty hand, on my word! [*He pats her hand.*]

SIRELLI: Easy! Easy!

LAUDISI: Never mind your husband, madam! Now, you have touched me, have you not? And you see me? And you are absolutely sure about me, are you not? Well now, madam, I beg of you; do not tell your husband, nor my sister, nor my niece, nor Signora Cini here, what you think of me; because, if you were to do that, they would all tell you that you are completely wrong. But, you see, you are really right; because I am really what you take me to be; though, my dear madam, that does not prevent me from also being really what your husband, my sister, my niece, and Signora Cini take me to be—because they also are absolutely right!

SIGNORA SIRELLI: In other words you are a different person for each of us.

LAUDISI: Of course I'm a different person! And you, madam, pretty as you are, aren't you a different person, too?

SIGNORA SIRELLI [*hastily*]: No siree! I assure you, as far as I'm concerned, I'm always the same always, yesterday, today, and forever!

LAUDISI: Ah, but so am I, from my point of view, believe me! And, I would say that you are all mistaken unless you see me as I see myself; but that would be an inexcusable presumption on my part—as it would be on yours, my dear madam!

SIRELLI: And what has all this rigmarole got to do with it, may I ask?

LAUDISI: What has it got to do with it? Why . . . I find all you people here at your wits' ends trying to find out who and what other people are; just as though other people had to be this, or that, and nothing else.

SIGNORA SIRELLI: All you are saying is that we can never find out the truth! A dreadful idea!

SIGNORA CINI: I give up! I give up! If we can't believe even what we see with our eyes and feel with our fingers . . .

LAUDISI: But you must understand, madam! All I'm saying is that you should show some respect for what other people see and feel, even though it be the exact opposite of what you see and feel.

SIGNORA SIRELLI: The way to answer you is to refuse to talk with you. See, I turn my back on you! You're driving me mad!

(LUIGI PIRANDELLO, *It Is So!* [*If You Think So*].) [7]

. . . But then, even in the most insignificant details of our daily life, none of us can be said to constitute a material whole, which is identical for everyone, and need only be turned up like a page in an account-book or the record of a will; our social personality is created by the thoughts of other people. Even the simple act which we describe as "seeing some one we know" is, to some extent, an intellectual process. We pack the physical outline of the creature we see with all the ideas we have already formed about him, and in the complete picture of him which we compose in our minds those ideas have certainly the principal place.   (MARCEL PROUST, *Swann's Way.*) [8]

At first, men are hard to know. But everyone thinks that he is able to know men. Therefore when one looks at men by comparison with oneself, they may be considered knowable. But when we see men examining other men, we may conclude that knowledge is not obtained. Why? Because a man can know the goodness that is like his own, but he may lose beauty which is of a different kind. How shall we know that this is so?

The man of sublime behavior, with uprightness as his rule, when he is looking at all the abilities, may recognize the constants of human nature and behavior, but he will be suspicious of the deceitfulness of strategy.

The legalist has conformity to a standard as his rule. Therefore he is able to recognize the standards by which squareness and uprightness are compared, but cannot value the strategy of transformation.

The strategist has the thinking of plans as his rule. Therefore he is able to achieve the wonders of strategy, but cannot recognize the goodness of obeying the law.

The man of instrumental ability has the doing of things as his rule. Therefore he is able to recognize the working of a plan, but he cannot see the origins of institutions.

The astute man has innate ingenuity as his rule. Therefore he is able to recognize the versatility of strategy and cleverness, but cannot value the constancy of doctrine.

The practical man has the desire of achievement as his rule. Therefore he is able to recognize the achievement of progress, but cannot understand the transforming power of virtue.

The critic has watchfulness and investigation as his rule. Therefore he is able to recognize the illumination of reprimanding, but cannot be contented with the variations of masterfulness.

The man of words has analysis as his rule. Therefore he is able to recognize the advantage of quick retort, but cannot understand the beauty of rhetoric.

So all these men contradict one another, and no one is willing to admit that the others are right. When they are dealing with their own kind, they will understand one another at the first meeting. When they are dealing with a different kind (of man) from themselves, they cannot comprehend one another, although they may be together for a long time.

(The *Jen Wu Chih* of Liu Shao.) [9]

> A sound man is good at salvage,
> At seeing that nothing is lost.
> Having what is called insight,
> A good man, before he can help a bad man,
> Finds in himself the matter with the bad man.
> And whichever teacher
> Discounts the lesson
> Is as far off the road as the other,
> Whatever else he may know
> That is the heart of it.

(LAOTZU, *The Way of Life*.) [10]

A sound man's heart is not shut within itself
But is open to other people's hearts:
I find good people good,
And I find bad people good
If I am good enough;
I trust men of their word,
And I trust liars
If I am true enough;
I feel the heart-beats of others
Above my own
If I am enough of a father,
Enough of a son.

(Laotzu, *ibid.*) [11]

In social living a wide variety of different types of purposes can be potentially involved. We can, for example, use other people without any more concern than is absolutely necessary for their own welfare; or we can merely interact with them impersonally, as we do in many of the more routine contacts of daily living. Or we can participate with others, taking their purposes into account as we fulfill our own purposes, trying to be thoughtful or considerate, in this way obtaining a different quality of experience from our social life than we do merely by reacting to others or using them. The importance of caring and sharing in our relations with others has been simply and beautifully expressed by Laotzu:

Everyone says that my way of life is the way of a simpleton.
Being largely the way of a simpleton is what makes it worth while.
If it were not the way of a simpleton
It would long ago have been worthless,
These possessions of a simpleton being the three I choose
And cherish:
To care,
To be fair,
To be humble.
When a man cares he is unafraid,
When he is fair he leaves enough for others,
When he is humble he can grow;
Whereas if, like men of today, he be bold without caring,
Self-indulgent without sharing,
Self-important without shame,

He is dead.
The invincible shield
Of caring
Is a weapon from the sky
Against being dead. [12]

Any perceptive person knows, consciously or unconsciously, that the most rewarding and valued experiences he has in life are those in which other people are involved, where experience is shared. If we hear some exceedingly good personal news, we want to tell someone in our family or a close friend about it; if the news is shocking or sad, we feel relieved if appropriate other people are also told what happened. In both cases we are trying to broaden the base of a shared reality. We get more of a feeling that we are living as human beings should live when the environment within which we participate includes other human beings with purposes and values similar or complementary to our own.

The consequences of an inability to share grief with others is poignantly illustrated in the following story by Chekov:

It is twilight. A thick wet snow is slowly twirling around the newly lighted street-lamps, and lying in soft thin layers on the roofs, the horses' backs, people's shoulders and hats. The cabdriver, Iona Potapov, is quite white, and looks like a phantom; he is bent double as far as a human body can bend double; he is seated on his box, and never makes a move. If a whole snowdrift fell on him, it seems as if he would not find it necessary to shake it off. His little horse is also quite white, and remains motionless; its immobility, its angularity, and its straight wooden-looking legs, even close by give it the appearance of a ginger-bread horse worth a kopeck. It is, no doubt, plunged in deep thought. If you were snatched from the plough, from your usual grey surroundings, and were thrown into this slough full of monstrous lights, unceasing noise and hurrying people, you too would find it difficult not to think.

Iona and his little horse have not moved from their place for a long time. They left their yard before dinner, and, up to now, not a "fare." The evening mist is descending over the town, the white lights of the lamps are replacing brighter rays, and the hubbub of the street is getting louder. "Cabby, for Viborg way!" suddenly hears Iona. "Cabby!"

Iona jumps, and through his snow-covered eyelashes, sees an officer in a greatcoat, with his hood over his head.

"Viborg way!" the officer repeats. "Are you asleep, eh? Viborg way!"

With a nod of assent Iona picks up the reins, in consequence of which layers of snow slip off the horse's back and neck. The officer seats himself in the sleigh, the cab-driver smacks his lips to encourage his horse, stretches out his neck like a swan, sits up, and, more from habit than necessity, brandishes his whip. The little horse also stretches his neck, bends his wooden-looking legs, and makes a move undecidedly.

"What are you doing, were-wolf!" is the exclamation Iona hears, from the dark mass moving to and fro as soon as they started.

"Where the devil are you going? To the r-r-right!"

"You do not know how to drive. Keep to the right!" calls the officer angrily.

A coachman from a private carriage swears at him; a passer-by, who has run across the road and rubbed his shoulder against the horse's nose, looks at him furiously as he sweeps the snow from his sleeve. Iona shifts about on his seat as if he were on needles, moves his elbows as if he were trying to keep his equilibrium, and gapes about like someone suffocating, and who does not understand why and wherefore he is there.

"What scoundrels they all are!" jokes the officer; "one would think they had all entered into an agreement to jostle you or fall under your horse."

Iona looks round at the officer, and moves his lips. He evidently wants to say something but the only sound that issues is a snuffle.

"What?" asks the officer.

Iona twists his mouth into a smile, and with an effort says hoarsely: "My son, barin, died this week."

"Hm! What did he die of?"

Iona turns with his whole body towards his fare, and says:

"And who knows! They say high fever. He was three days in hospital, and then died. . . . God's will be done."

"Turn round! The devil!" sounded from the darkness. "Have you popped off, old doggie, eh? Use your eyes!"

"Go on, go on," said the officer, "otherwise we shall not get there by to-morrow. Hurry a bit!"

The cab-driver again stretches his neck, sits up, and, with a bad grace, brandishes his whip. Several times again he turns to look at his fare, but the latter had closed his eyes, and apparently is not disposed to listen. Having deposited the officer in the Viborg, he stops by the tavern, doubles himself up on his seat, and again remains motionless, while the snow once more begins to cover him and his horse. An hour, and another. . . . Then, along the footpath, with a squeak of galoshes, and quarrelling, came three young men, two of them tall and lanky, the third one short and hump-backed.

"Cabby, to the Police Bridge!" in a cracked voice calls the hump-back. "The three of us for two griveniks!" (20 kopecks.)

Iona picks up his reins, and smacks his lips. Two griveniks is not a fair price, but he does not mind if it is a rouble or five kopecks—to him it is all the same now, so long as they are wayfarers. The young men, jostling each other and using bad language, approach the sleigh, and all three at once try to get on to the seat; then begins a discussion which two shall sit and who shall be the one to stand. After wrangling, abusing each other, and much petulance, it was at last decided that the hump-back should stand, as he was the smallest.

"Now then, hurry up!" says the hump-back in a twanging voice, as he takes his place, and breathes in Iona's neck. "Old furry. Here, mate, what a cap you have got, there is not a worse one to be found in all Petersburg! . . ."

"Hi-hi, hi-hi," giggles Iona. "Such a . . ."

"Now you, 'such a,' hurry up, are you going the whole way at this pace? Are you? . . . Do you want it in the neck?"

"My head feels like bursting," says one of the lanky ones. "Last night at the Donkmasovs, Vaska and I drank the whole of four bottles of cognac."

"I don't understand what you lie for," said the other lanky one angrily; "you lie like a brute."

"God strike me, it's the truth!"

"It's as much a truth as that a louse coughs!"

"Hi, hi," grins Iona, "what gay young gentlemen!"

"Pshaw, go to the devil!" indignantly says the hump-back.

"Are you going to get on or not, you old pest. Is that the way to drive? Use the whip a bit! Go on, devil, go on, give it him well!"

Iona feels at his back the little man wriggling, and the tremble in his voice. He listens to the insults hurled at him, sees the people, and little by little the feeling of loneliness leaves him. The hump-back goes on swearing until he gets mixed up in some elaborate six-foot oath, or chokes with coughing. The lankies begin to talk about a certain Nadejda Petrovna. Iona looks round at them several times; he waits for a temporary silence, then, turning round again, he murmurs:

"My son—died this week."

"We must all die," sighed the hump-back, wiping his lips after an attack of coughing. "Now, hurry up, hurry up! Gentlemen, I really cannot go any farther like this! When will he get us there?"

"Well, just you stimulate him a little in the neck!"

"You old pest, do you hear, I'll bone your neck for you! If one treated the like of you with ceremony one would have to go on foot! Do you hear, old serpent Gorinytch! Or do you not care a spit?"

Iona hears rather than feels the blows they deal him.

"Hi, hi," he laughs. "They are gay young gentlemen, God bless 'em!"

"Cabby, are you married?" asks a lanky one.

"I? Hi, hi, gay young gentlemen! Now I have only a wife: the moist ground . . . Hi, ho, ho . . . that is to say, the grave! My son has died, and I am alive. . . . A wonderful thing, death mistook the door . . . instead of coming to me, it went to my son. . . ."

Iona turns round to tell them how his son died, but at this moment the hump-back, giving a little sigh, announces, "Thank God, they have at last reached their destination," and Iona watches them disappear through the dark entrance. Once more he is alone, and again surrounded by silence. . . . His grief, which had abated for a short while, returns and rends his heart with greater force. With an anxious and a hurried look, he searches among the crowds passing on either side of the street to find if there is just one person who will listen to him. But the crowds hurry by without noticing him or his trouble. Yet it is such an immense, illimitable grief. Should his heart break and the grief pour out, it would flow over the whole earth it seems, and yet, no one sees it. It has managed to conceal itself in such an insignificant shell that no one can see it even by day and with a light.

Iona sees a hall-porter with some sacking, and decides to talk to him.

"Friend, what sort of time is it?" he asks.

"Past nine. What are you standing here for? Move on."

Iona moves on a few steps, doubles himself up, and abandons himself to his grief. He sees it is useless to turn to people for help. In less than five minutes he straightens himself, holds up his head as if he felt some sharp pain, and gives a tug at the reins: he can bear it no longer, "The stables," he thinks, and the little horse, as if he understood, starts off at a trot.

About an hour and a half later Iona is seated by a large dirty stove. Around the stove, on the floor, on the benches, people are snoring; the air is thick and suffocatingly hot. Iona looks at the sleepers, scratches himself, and regrets having returned so early.

"I have not even earned my fodder," he thinks. "That's what's my trouble. A man who knows his job, who has had enough to eat, and his horse too, can always sleep peacefully."

A young cab-driver in one of the corners half gets up, grunts sleepily, and stretches towards a bucket of water.

"Do you want a drink?" Iona asks him.

"Don't I want a drink!"

"That's so? Your good health! But, listen, mate—you know, my son is dead. . . . Did you hear? This week, in hospital. . . . It's a long story."

Iona looks to see what effect his words have, but sees none—the young man has hidden his face, and is fast asleep again. The old man sighs, and scratches his head. Just as much as the young man wanted to drink, the old man wanted to talk. It will soon be a week since his son died, and he has not been able to speak about it properly to anyone. One must tell it slowly and carefully; how his son fell ill, how he suffered, what he said before he died, how he died. One must describe every detail of the funeral, and the journey to the hospital to fetch the defunct's clothes. His daughter Anissia remained in the village—one must talk about her too. Was it nothing he had to tell? Surely the listener would gasp and sigh, and sympathise with him? It is better, too, to talk to women; although they are stupid, two words are enough to make them sob.

"I'll go and look at my horse," thinks Iona; "there's always time to sleep. No fear of that!"

He puts on his coat, and goes to the stables to his horse; he thinks of the corn, the hay, the weather. When he is alone, he dare not think of his son; he could speak about him to anyone, but to think of him, and picture him to himself, is unbearably painful.

"Are you tucking in?" Iona asks his horse, looking at his bright eyes; "go on, tuck in, though we've not earned our corn, we can eat hay. Yes! I am too old to drive—my son could have, not I. He was a first-rate cab-driver. If only he had lived!"

Iona is silent for a moment, then continues:

"That's how it is, my old horse. There's no more Kuzma Ionitch. He has left us to live, and he went off pop. Now let's say, you had a foal, you were that foal's mother, and suddenly, let's say, that foal went and left you to live after him. It would be sad, wouldn't it?"

The little horse munches, listens, and breathes over his master's hand. . . .

Iona's feelings are too much for him, and he tells the little horse the whole story.   (Anton Chekov, "To Whom Shall I Tell My Grief?") [13]

Man's capacity to share the joys and sorrows of others is, as we have said earlier, largely derived by experiencing the consequences of his actions, actions which for man as a human being so frequently involve other people. Thus the consequences of our actions are judged in terms of their effects on others as they are transmitted to us and others, in turn, judge the consequences of their actions in terms of their effect on us. A mutual feed-back process is involved, but it is much more than the feed-back operation the scientist talks about with respect to machines and computers. For the human being also experiences a value-satisfaction in the process of doing. The point is explicitly recognized in the *Bhagavad-Gita,* as shown by the following brief excerpts:

Thy task is not concerned with the fruits of thine act. Let not reward be the motive of thy deed; neither become wedded to inaction.

Those who work for reward are lost. . . . Acts tainted by desire are inferior to work done with a mind indifferent to result.

The wise should perform tasks without attachment, yet with as much ardor as the foolish who are bound up in the results of their deeds—thus to the world shall they set example.

No living being can exist without action, but he who relinquisheth the desire for the reward may be called a free man. [14]

Often, irrespective of any communicable effects our actions may have on others, the process of acting the way we do is its own reward or punishment; we may be the only ones in the world who know we have done certain good deeds or who know we have sinned. Anyone who is sensitive to his own feelings will have noticed how much personal satisfaction he himself gets even from some little act of kindness, helpfulness, or love shown someone else.

It is the quality and the significance of the participation we have with others that makes our life so much what it is. Since we seek to participate with people whose values are more or less congenial to our own, we are often led far beyond our own neighborhood in time or space. Our participation with others may involve writers, thinkers, builders, prophets, artists, or musicians who have lived many years ago in distant lands. And in a day and age when many people travel so much from place to place, or work at jobs that may provide little opportunity for personal participation, there is a particular craving for a consistent and meaningful social life which will in turn give the individual a sense of his own constancy.

It is characteristic of man that he wants to be appreciated, that he wants to feel needed. In reporting on a conference he once held with representatives of an organization of relief recipients, Chester Barnard points out that "it is important for you to know that men often cannot talk about what they most want even when they are conscious of it. They could not say either to me or even to each other 'I am starving to be recognized as a man, as a citizen, as a part of the community.' To do so would itself destroy self-respect and would be futile as well." [15] If a person feels needed and if he senses appreciation from others, then he can develop and sustain a sense of his own worth. The following observation by the naturalist and dog lover, Konrad Lorentz, rings true for this reason:

Let us . . . not lie to ourselves that we need the dog as a protection for our house. We *do* need him, but not as a watch-dog. I, at least in dreary foreign towns, have certainly stood in need of my dog's company and I have derived, from the mere fact of his existence, a great sense of inward security, such as one finds in a childhood memory or in the prospect of the scenery of one's own home country, for me the Blue Danube, for you the White Cliffs of Dover. In the almost film-like flitting-by of modern life, a man needs something to tell him, from time to time, that he is still himself, and nothing can give him this assurance in so comforting a manner as the "four feet trotting behind." [16]

THE TIES THAT BIND

In the process of participation we develop attachments to and affections for certain individuals, neighborhoods, types of social behavior, and even certain inanimate objects. We refer to these attachments, affections, or identifications as loyalties. They hold our social organism together just as the forces within an atom hold together its various constituent but interdependent parts. [17]

We build up these loyalties because we discover from our own experience that certain individuals, neighborhoods, or forms of behavior help us in one way or another carry out our own purposes, either protecting us from threats to the satisfactions we have enjoyed up to now, or holding out the promise of repeated or new satisfactions. The pattern of loyalties we develop provides a major part of our reality-world. And the consistency of our loyalties is reflected as a consistency we feel within us. Furthermore, while this pattern of loyalties helps provide us with a consistent form for living effectively, it also provides us with a take-off for flow, for change and development. This is reflected, for example, in Kenneth Grahame's description of the feelings of Mole after his return to his old home in the beloved children's book, *The Wind in the Willows.*

The weary Mole also was glad to turn in without delay, and soon had his head on his pillow, in great joy and contentment. But ere he closed his eyes he let them wander round his old room, mellow in the glow of the firelight that played or rested on familiar and friendly things which had long been unconsciously a part of him, and now smilingly received him back, without rancour. He was now in just the frame of mind that the tactful Rat had quietly worked to bring about in him. He saw clearly how plain and simple—how narrow, even—it all was; but clearly, too, how much it all meant to him, and the special value of some such anchorage in one's existence. He did not at all want to abandon the new life and its splendid spaces, to turn his back on sun and air and all they offered him and creep home and stay there; the upper world was all too strong, it called to him still, even down there, and he knew he must return to the larger stage. But it was good to think he had this to come back to, this place which was all his own, these things which were so glad to see him again and could always be counted upon for the same simple welcome. [18]

Incidentally, we should note in passing that familiarity in and of itself does not always create fond memory for something we want to return to or re-examine. Nor does it inevitably breed contempt. We mention this point here because, as we shall see later when we discuss the problem of social change, the psychological consequences of familiarity—that is, of repeated participation in situations that involve the same objects or persons—depend upon whether or not those objects or persons help us satisfy our immediate or long-range purposes. We try to perpetuate those loyalties which will give us repeated value-satisfactions or which will further enrich our experience in some way. And we slough off those loyalties that have outworn their usefulness because of changed situations and changed purposes.

Loyalties are mutual when there is a recognition by all participants involved in a situation of their interdependency in fulfilling their individual purposes. And it would appear that if loyalties are to be enduring, this fulfillment of purposes must involve mutual development and flow, not simply ceaseless routine.

The satisfaction our loyalties provide is apparently a satisfaction that guarantees a certain constancy and predictability and yet provides a context for growth and change. If friendships are to endure, they must necessarily involve a high degree of aid in carrying forward the basic purposes of each party. Many of our friendships, such as those of early childhood or those formed during a short vacation, may prove transient indeed because the purposes which brought us together originally have dissolved as we have changed and gone about our various diverse activities.

The highest loyalty is, of course, what we call love: love of another person, love of a group, a nation or an ideal. The experience of love refers to a condition where the welfare and happiness of another individual are a necessary condition for our own welfare or happiness and, ideally, where our welfare and happiness are a necessary condition for his satisfaction. We "lose" ourselves in others; we dedicate ourselves to some cause which has brought us a sense of the worthwhileness of living.

The following selections deal with the nature of loyalties and love and with some of the other topics discussed so far.

Certitude is not the test of certainty. We have been cock-sure of many things that were not so. If I may quote myself again, property, friendship, and truth have a common root in time. One can not be wrenched from the rocky crevices into which one has grown for many years without feeling that one is attacked in one's life. What we most love and revere generally is determined by early associations. I love granite rocks and barberry bushes, no doubt because with them were my earliest joys that reach back through the past eternity of my life. But while one's experience thus makes certain preferences dogmatic for oneself, recognition of how they came to be so leaves one able to see that others, poor souls, may be equally dogmatic about something else. And this again means scepticism. Not that one's belief or love does not remain. Not that we would not fight and die for it if important—we all, whether we know it or not, are fighting to make the kind of a world that we should like—but that we have learned to recognize that others will fight and die to make a different world, with equal sincerity or belief. Deep-seated preferences can not be argued about—you can not argue a man into liking a glass of beer—and therefore, when differences are sufficiently far reaching, we try to kill the other man rather than let him have his way. But that is perfectly consistent with admitting that, so far as appears, his grounds are just as good as ours.

(OLIVER WENDELL HOLMES, *Collected Legal Papers*.) [19]

While men in combat outfits kid each other around, they have a sort of family complex about it. No outsiders may join. Anybody who does a dangerous job in this war has his own particular kind of kidding among his own friends, and sometimes it doesn't even sound like kidding. Bomber crews and paratroopers and infantry squads are about the same in that respect. If a stranger comes up to a group of them when they are bulling, they ignore him. If he takes it upon himself to laugh at something funny they have said, they freeze their expressions, turn slowly around, stare at him until his stature has shrunk to about four inches and he slinks away, and then they go back to their kidding again.

It's like a group of prosperous businessmen telling a risqué joke and then glaring at the waiter who joins in the guffaws. Combat people are an exclusive set, and if they want to be that way, it is their privilege. They certainly earn it. New men in outfits have to work their way in slowly, but they are eventually accepted. Sometimes they have to change some of their ways of living. An introvert or a recluse is not going to last long in combat without friends, so he learns to come out of his shell. Once he has "arrived" he is pretty proud of his clique, and he in turn is chilly toward outsiders.

That's why, during some of the worst periods in Italy, many guys who had a chance to hang around a town for a few days after being discharged from a hospital where they had recovered from wounds, with nobody the wiser, didn't take advantage of it. They weren't eager to get back up and get in the war, by any means, and many of them did hang around a few days. But those who did hang around didn't feel exactly right about it, and those who went right back did it for a very simple reason—not because they felt that their presence was going to make a lot of difference in the big scheme of the war, and not to uphold the traditions of the umpteenth regiment. A lot of guys don't know the name of their regimental commander. They went back because they knew their companies were very shorthanded, and they were sure that if somebody else in their own squad or section were in their own shoes, and the situation were reversed, those friends would come back to make the load lighter on *them*.   (BILL MAULDIN, *Up Front.*) [20]

> Give all to love;
> Obey thy heart;
> Friends, kindred, days,
> Estate, good-fame,
> Plans, credit and the Muse,—
> Nothing refuse.
>
> 'Tis a brave master;
> Let it have scope:
> Follow it utterly
> Hope beyond hope:
> High and more high

It dives into noon,
With wing unspent,
Untold intent;
But it is a god,
Knows its own path
And the outlets of the sky.

It was never for the mean;
It requireth courage stout.
Souls above doubt,
Valor unbending,
It will reward,—
They shall return
More than they were,
And ever ascending.

Leave all for love;
Yet, hear me, yet,
One word more thy heart behoved,
One pulse more of firm endeavor,—
Keep thee to-day
To-morrow, forever,
Free as an Arab
Of thy beloved.

Cling with life to the maid;
But when the surprise
First vague shadow of surmise
Flits across her bosom young,
Of a joy apart from thee,
Free be she, fancy-free;
Nor thou detain her vesture's hem,
Nor the palest rose she flung
From her summer diadem.

Though thou loved her as thyself,
As a self of purer clay,
Though her parting dims the day,
Stealing grace from all alive;
Heartily know,
When half-gods go,
The gods arrive.
        (RALPH WALDO EMERSON, "Give All to Love.") [21]

Music I heard with you was more than music,
And bread I broke with you was more than bread;
Now that I am without you, all is desolate;
All that was once so beautiful is dead.

Your hands once touched this table and this silver,
And I have seen your fingers hold this glass.
These things do not remember you, belovèd,—
And yet your touch upon them will not pass.

For it was in my heart you moved among them,
And blessed them with your hands and with your eyes;
And in my heart they will remember always,—
They knew you once, O beautiful and wise.

(CONRAD AIKEN, "Music I Heard with You.") [22]

Dull sublunary lovers love
    (Whose soule is sense) cannot admit
Absence, because it doth remove
    Those things which elemented it.

But we by a love, so much refin'd,
    That our selves know not what it is,
Inter-assured of the mind,
    Care lesse, eyes, lips, and hands to misse.

Our two soules therefore, which are one,
    Though I must goe, endure not yet
A breach, but an expansion,
    Like gold to aiery thinnesse beate.

(JOHN DONNE, "A Valediction: Forbidding Mourning.") [23]

NINA: . . . What use is my life to me or anyone? But I must make it of use—by giving it! [*Fiercely*] I must learn to give myself, do you hear—give and give until I can make that gift of myself for a man's happiness without scruple, without fear, without joy except in his joy! When I've accomplished this I'll have found myself, I'll know how to start in living my own life again!

(EUGENE O'NEILL, *Strange Interlude.*) [24]

And a youth said, Speak to us of Friendship.
And he answered, saying:
Your friend is your needs answered.

He is your field which you sow with love and reap with thanksgiving.
And he is your board and your fireside.
For you come to him with your hunger, and you seek him for peace.

When your friend speaks his mind you fear not the "nay" in your
own mind, nor do you withhold the "ay."
And when he is silent your heart ceases not to listen to his heart;
For without words, in friendship, all thoughts, all desires, all expec-
tations are born and shared, with joy that is unacclaimed.
When you part from your friend, you grieve not;
For that which you love most in him may be clearer in his absence,
as the mountain to the climber is clearer from the plain.
And let there be no purpose in friendship save the deepening of the
spirit.
For love that seeks aught but the disclosure of its own mystery is not
love but a net cast forth: and only the unprofitable is caught.

And let your best be for your friend.
If he must know the ebb of your tide, let him know its flood also.
For what is your friend that you should seek him with hours to kill?
Seek him always with hours to live.
For it is his to fill your need, but not your emptiness.
And in the sweetness of friendship let there be laughter, and sharing
of pleasures.
For in the dew of little things the heart finds its morning and is re-
freshed.   (KAHLIL GIBRAN, *The Prophet*.) [25]

GROUPS

By the time an individual reaches adulthood, he has become a
member of various groups—his family, his tribe, his team, his labor
union, his business associates or army group, etc. In addition, he has
identified himself with broad classifications of people whose standards have become his: a sex group, a religious group, a national
group and so forth. These membership and reference group identifications define a person's role.

The norms and standards developed by an individual give some
measure of order, predictability, and consistency to his psychological world, as do all assumptions and expectancies. The standards of
the group provide a repeatability we can more or less count on,
just as the built-in standards of man-made artifacts provide repeatability that makes these artifacts useful and reliable. A person

makes judgments concerning himself and others in terms of these norms and standards.

For most of us it is generally within some membership or reference group identification that we try to enhance the value-quality of our experience by achieving the standards set or valued by the group. Our behavior reflects the role we assume we are playing and which others in the group expect us to play. We maintain or enhance our status both in our own eyes and in the eyes of others insofar as we behave within the framework or according to the rules of the group within which our transactions of living occur. And all of us seek some recognizable signs that our participation has been effective in building, maintaining, or strengthening the loyalties that bind us to other people and that bind them to us. If this happens, and if those we respect or love in turn appear to us to respect or to love us, then we experience a sense of belongingness, of security, of deep satisfaction and pride. If the reverse happens, we begin to feel insecure, isolated, depressed, outcast, and ashamed.

The groups with which we have identified expect us to conform to the role we have assumed. Emily Dickinson expressed the pressure for conformity when she wrote,

> Much madness is divinest sense
> To a discerning eye;
> Much sense the starkest madness.
> 'Tis the majority
> In this, as all, prevails.
> Assent, and you are sane;
> Demur,—you're straightaway dangerous,
> And handled with a chain. [26]

Almost all of the important characteristics of a true group, as well as the conditions under which a group tends to dissolve, are portrayed in the following excerpt from *The Adventures of Huckleberry Finn*. And the passage from William Manning, written in the year 1798, clearly recognizes the binding force of common interests.

"Now, we'll start this band of robbers and call it Tom Sawyer's Gang. Everybody that wants to join has got to take an oath, and write his name in blood."

Everybody was willing. So Tom got out a sheet of paper that he had wrote the oath on, and read it. It swore every boy to stick to the band, and never tell any of the secrets; and if anybody done anything to any boy in the band, whichever boy was ordered to kill that person and his family must do it, and he mustn't eat and he mustn't sleep till he had killed them and hacked a cross in their breasts, which was the sign of the band. And nobody that didn't belong to the band could use that mark, and if he did he must be sued; and if he done it again he must be killed. And if anybody that belonged to the band told the secrets, he must have his throat cut, and then have his carcass burnt up and the ashes scattered all around, and his name blotted off the list with blood and never mentioned again by the gang, but have a curse put on it and be forgot forever.

Everybody said it was a real beautiful oath, and asked Tom if he got it out of his own head. He said some of it, but the rest was out of pirate-books and robber-books, and every gang that was high-toned had it.

Some thought it would be good to kill the *families* of boys that told the secrets. Tom said it was a good idea, so he took a pencil and wrote it in. Then Ben Rogers says:

"Here's Huck Finn, he hain't got no family; what you going to do 'bout him?"

"Well, hain't he got a father?" says Tom Sawyer.

"Yes, he's got a father, but you can't never find him these days. He used to lay drunk with the hogs in the tanyard, but he hain't been seen in these parts for a year or more."

They talked it over, and they was going to rule me out, because they said every boy must have a family or somebody to kill, or else it wouldn't be fair and square for the others. Well, nobody could think of anything to do—everybody was stumped, and set still. I was most ready to cry; but all at once I thought of a way, and so I offered them Miss Watson—they could kill her. Everybody said:

"Oh, she'll do. That's all right. Huck can come in."

Then they all stuck a pin in their fingers to get blood to sign with, and I made my mark on the paper.

"Now," says Ben Rogers, "what's the line of business of this Gang?"

"Nothing only robbery and murder," Tom said.

"But who are we going to rob?—houses, or cattle, or—"

"Stuff! stealing cattle and such things ain't robbery; it's burglary," says Tom Sawyer. "We ain't burglars. That ain't no sort of style. We are highwaymen. We stop stages and carriages on the road, with masks on, and kill the people and take their watches and money."

"Must we always kill the people?"

"Oh, certainly. It's best. Some authorities think different, but mostly it's considered best to kill them—except some that you bring to the cave here, and keep them till they're ransomed."

"Ransomed? What's that?"

"I don't know. But that's what they do. I've seen it in books; and so of course that's what we've got to do."

"But how can we do it if we don't know what it is?"

"Why, blame it all, we've *got* to do it. Don't I tell you it's in the books? Do you want to go to doing different from what's in the books, and get things all muddled up?"

"Oh, that's all very fine to *say*, Tom Sawyer, but how in the nation are these fellows going to be ransomed if we don't know how to do it to them?—that's the thing I want to get at. Now, what do you *reckon* it is?"

"Well, I don't know. But per'aps if we keep them till they're ransomed, it means that we keep them till they're dead."

"Now, that's something *like*.—That'll answer. Why couldn't you said that before? We'll keep them till they're ransomed to death; and a bothersome lot they'll be, too—eating up everything, and always trying to get loose."

"How you talk, Ben Rogers. How can they get loose when there's a guard over them, ready to shoot them down if they move a peg?"

"A guard! Well, that *is* good. So somebody's got to set up all night and never get any sleep, just so as to watch them. I think that's foolishness. Why can't a body take a club and ransom them as soon as they get here?"

"Because it ain't in the books so—that's why. Now, Ben Rogers, do you want to do things regular, or don't you?—that's the idea. Don't you reckon that the people that made the books knows what's the correct thing to do? Do you reckon *you* can learn 'em anything? Not by a good deal. No, sir, we'll just go on and ransom them in the regular way."

"All right. I don't mind; but I say it's a fool way, anyhow. Say, do we kill the women, too?"

"Well, Ben Rogers, if I was as ignorant as you I wouldn't let on. Kill the women? No; nobody ever saw anything in the books like that. You fetch them to the cave, and you're always as polite as pie to them; and by and by they fall in love with you, and never want to go home any more."

"Well, if that's the way I'm agreed, but I don't take no stock in it. Mighty soon we'll have the cave so cluttered up with women, and fellows waiting to be ransomed, that there won't be no place for the robbers. But go ahead, I ain't got nothing to say."

Little Tommy Barnes was asleep by now, and when they waked him up he was scared, and cried, and said he wanted to go home to his ma, and didn't want to be a robber any more.

So they all made fun of him, and called him cry-baby, and that made him mad, and he said he would go straight and tell all the secrets. But Tom give him five cents to keep quiet, and said we would all go home and meet next week, and rob somebody and kill some people.

Ben Rogers said he couldn't get out much, only Sundays, and so he wanted to begin next Sunday; but all the boys said it would be wicked to do it on Sunday, and that settled the thing. They agreed to get together and fix a day as soon as they could, and then we elected Tom Sawyer first captain and Joe Harper second captain of the Gang, and so started home. . . .

We played robber now and then about a month, and then I resigned. All the boys did. We hadn't robbed nobody, hadn't killed any people, but only just pretended. We used to hop out of the woods and go charging down on hog-drivers and women in carts taking garden stuff to market, but we never hived any of them. Tom Sawyer called the hogs "ingots," and he called the turnips and stuff "julery," and we would go to the cave and powwow over what we had done, and how many people we had killed and marked. But I couldn't see no profit in it. One time Tom sent a boy to run about town with a blazing stick, which he called a slogan (which was the sign for the Gang to get together), and then he said he had got secret news by his spies that next day a whole parcel of Spanish merchants and rich A-rabs was going to camp in Cave Hollow with two hundred elephants, and six hundred camels, and over a thousand "sumter" mules, all loaded down with di'monds, and they didn't have only a guard of four hundred soldiers, and so we would lay in ambuscade, as he called it, and kill the lot and scoop the things. He said we must slick up our swords and guns, and get ready. He never could go after even a turnip-cart but he must have the swords and guns all scoured up for it, though they was only lath and broomsticks, and you might scour at them till you rotted, and then they warn't worth a mouthful of ashes more than what they was before. I didn't believe we could lick such a crowd of Spaniards and A-rabs, but I wanted to see the camels and elephants, so I was on hand next day, Saturday, in the ambuscade; and when we got the word we rushed out of the woods and down the hill. But there warn't no Spaniards and A-rabs, and there warn't no camels nor no elephants. It warn't anything but a Sunday-school picnic, and only a primer class at that. We busted it up, and chased the children up the hollow; but we never got anything but some doughnuts and jam, though Ben Rogers got a rag doll, and

Joe Harper got a hymn-book and a tract; and then the teacher charged in, and made us drop everything and cut. I didn't see no di'monds, and I told Tom Sawyer so. He said there was loads of them there, anyway, and he said there was A-rabs there, too, and elephants and things. I said, why couldn't we see them, then? He said if I warn't so ignorant, but had read a book called *Don Quixote*, I would know without asking. He said it was all done by enchantment. He said there was hundreds of soldiers there, and elephants and treasure, and so on, but he had enemies which he called magicians, and they had turned the whole thing into an infant Sunday-school, just out of spite. I said, all right; then the thing for us to do was to go for the magicians. Tom Sawyer said I was a numbskull.

"Why," said he, "a magician could call up a lot of genies, and they would hash you up like nothing before you could say Jack Robinson. They are as tall as a tree and as big around as a church."

"Well," I says, "s'pose we got some genies to help *us*—can't we lick the other crowd then?"

"How you going to get them?"

"I don't know. How do *they* get them?"

"Why, they rub an old tin lamp or an iron ring, and then the genies come tearing in, with the thunder and lightning a-ripping around and the smoke a-rolling, and everything they're told to do they up and do it. They don't think nothing of pulling a shot-tower up by the roots, and belting a Sunday-school superintendent over the head with it—or any other man."

"Who makes them tear around so?"

"Why, whoever rubs the lamp or the ring. They belong to whoever rubs the lamp or the ring, and they've got to do whatever he says. If he tells them to build a palace forty miles long out of di'monds, and fill it full of chewing-gum, or whatever you want, and fetch an emperor's daughter from China, for you to marry, they've got to do it—and they've got to do it before sun-up next morning, too. And more: they've got to waltz that palace around over the country wherever you want it, you understand."

"Well," says I, "I think they are a pack of flatheads for not keeping the palace themselves 'stead of fooling them away like that. And what's more—if I was one of them I would see a man in Jericho before I would drop my business and come to him for the rubbing of an old tin lamp."

"How you talk, Huck Finn. Why, you'd *have* to come when he rubbed it, whether you wanted to or not."

"What! and I as high as a tree and as big as a church? All right,

then; I *would* come; but I lay I'd make that man climb the highest tree
there was in the country."

"Shucks, it ain't no use to talk to you, Huck Finn. You don't seem to
know anything, somehow—perfect saphead."

I thought all this over for two or three days, and then I reckoned
I would see if there was anything in it. I got an old tin lamp and an
iron ring, and went out in the woods and rubbed and rubbed till I
sweat like an Injun, calculating to build a palace and sell it; but it
warn't no use, none of the genies come. So then I judged that all that
stuff was only just one of Tom Sawyer's lies. I reckoned he believed
in the A-rabs and the elephants, but as for me I think different. It had
all the marks of a Sunday-school.

(MARK TWAIN, *Huckleberry Finn.*) 27

In the swet of thy face shall thou git thy bread untill thou return to
the ground, is the erivarsable sentance of Heaven on Man for his rebellion. To be sentanced to hard Labour dureing life is very unplesent to
humane Nature. Their is a grate avartion to it purceivable in all men—
yet it is absolutely nesecary that a large majority of the world should
labour, or we could not subsist. For Labour is the soul parrant of all
property—the land yealdeth nothing without it, & their is no food,
clothing, shelter, vessel, or any nesecary of life but what costs Labour &
is generally esteemed valuable according to the Labour it costs. Therefore no person can posess property without labouring, unless he git it by
force or craft, fraud or fortun out of the earnings of others.

But from the grate veriety of capacietyes strength & abilityes of men,
their always was, & always will be, a very unequel distribution of property in the world. Many are so rich that they can live without Labour.
Also the marchent, phisition, lawyer & divine, the philosipher and
school master, the Juditial & Executive Officers, & many others who
could honestly git a living without bodily labours. As all these professions require a considerable expence of time & property to qualify themselves therefor, & as no person after this qualifying himselfe & making
a pick on a profession by which he meens to live, can desire to have it
dishonourable or unproductive, so all these professions naturally unite
in their skems to make their callings as honourable & lucrative as pos-
sable. Also as ease & rest from Labour are reaconed amongue the gratest pleasures of Life, pursued by all with the gratest avidity & when
attained at once creates a sense of superiority & as pride & ostentation
are natural to the humain harte, these ordirs of men generally asotiate
together and look down with two much contempt on those that labour.

On the other hand the Labourer being contious that it is Labour that seports the hole, & that the more there is that live without Labour & the higher they live or the grater their salleryes & fees are, so much the harder he must work, or the shorter he must live, this makes the Labourer watch the other with a jelous eye & often has reason to complain of real impositions. . . .

In a free government the few, finding their scheems & vues of interest borne down by the many, to gain the power they cant constitutionally obtain, Always indevour to git it by cunning & corruption, contious at the same time that userpation when once began the safty of the userper consists ondly in grasping the hole. To efect this no cost nor pains is spared, but they first unite their plans & scheems by asotiations, conventions, & coraspondances with each other. The Marchents asotiate by themselves, the Phitisians by themselves, the Ministers by themselves, the Juditial & Executive Officers are by their professions often called together & know each others minds, & all letirary men & the over grown rich, that can live without labouring, can spare time for consultation. All being bound together by common interest, which is the stronges bond of union, join in their secret coraspondance to counter act the interests of the many & pick their pockets, which is efected ondly for want of the meens of knowledg amongue them.

(WILLIAM MANNING, *The Key of Libberty.*) [28]

We frequently see people who use group-membership as an escape from all important decisions, and who thereby lose their individuality and creativeness. They may tend to accept as right and proper whatever the group feels is right and proper and, since each group is limited in the area of life that is its major concern, such people join a number of groups as they seek group decisions or group confirmation of their judgments in nearly all areas of life. In contrast to the "joiners" is the innovator, the creator, the pioneer, one who dreams and creates the "impossible." Hence he is outside any group norms in the area of his creativity. He feels cramped by "belonging," feels pulled down to a common denominator, slowed up, held back. While he often pays for his freedom by occasional feelings of profound loneliness, he much prefers this to the irritation or even agony he knows he would feel if he compromised with his own unique visions.

Trust thyself! In the following selections Emerson, Einstein, and Amiel emphasize the importance of self-reliance, of maintaining one's individuality, freedom, and creativeness within the larger context of one's community.

I read the other day some verses written by an eminent painter which were original and not conventional. The soul always hears an admonition in such lines, let the subject be what it may. The sentiment they instil is of more value than any thought they may contain. To believe your own thought, to believe that what is true for you in your private heart is true for all men—that is genius. Speak your latent conviction, and it shall be the universal sense; for the inmost in due time becomes the outmost, and our first thought is rendered back to us by the trumpets of the Last Judgment. Familiar as the voice of the mind is to each, the highest merit we ascribe to Moses, Plato and Milton is that they set at naught books and traditions, and spoke not what men, but what *they* thought. A man should learn to detect and watch that gleam of light which flashes across his mind from within, more than the lustre of the firmament of bards and sages. Yet he dismisses without notice his thought, because it is his. In every work of genius we recognize our own rejected thoughts; they come back to us with a certain alienated majesty. Great works of art have no more affecting lesson for us than this. They teach us to abide by our spontaneous impression with good-humored inflexibility then most when the whole cry of voices is on the other side. Else to-morrow a stranger will say with masterly good sense precisely what we have thought and felt all the time, and we shall be forced to take with shame our own opinion from another.

There is a time in every man's education when he arrives at the conviction that envy is ignorance; that imitation is suicide; that he must take himself for better for worse as his portion; that though the wide universe is full of good, no kernel of nourishing corn can come to him but through his toil bestowed on that plot of ground which is given to him to till. The power which resides in him is new in nature, and none but he knows what that is which he can do, nor does he know until he has tried. Not for nothing one face, one character, one fact, makes much impression on him, and another none. This sculpture in the memory is not without preëstablished harmony. The eye was placed where one ray should fall, that it might testify of that particular ray. We but half express ourselves, and are ashamed of that divine idea which each of us represents. It may be safely trusted as proportionate and of good issues, so it be faithfully imparted, but God will not have his work made manifest by cowards. A man is relieved and gay when he has put his heart into his work and done his best; but what he has said or done otherwise shall give him no peace. It is a deliverance which does not deliver. In the attempt his genius deserts him; no muse befriends; no invention, no hope.

Trust thyself; every heart vibrates to that iron string. Accept the place the divine providence has found for you, the society of your contemporaries, the connection of events. Great men have always done so, and confided themselves childlike to the genius of their age, betraying their perception that the absolutely trustworthy was seated at their heart, working through their hands, predominating in all their being. And we are now men, and must accept in the highest mind the same transcendent destiny; and not minors and invalids in a protected corner, not cowards fleeing before a revolution, but guides, redeemers and benefactors, obeying the Almighty effort and advancing on Chaos and the Dark. . . .

What I must do is all that concerns me, not what the people think. This rule, equally arduous in actual and in intellectual life, may serve for the whole distinction between greatness and meanness. It is the harder because you will always find those who think they know what is your duty better than you know it. It is easy in the world to live after the world's opinion; it is easy in solitude to live after our own; but the great man is he who in the midst of the crowd keeps with perfect sweetness the independence of solitude. . . .

For nonconformity the world whips you with its displeasure. And therefore a man must know how to estimate a sour face. The bystanders look askance on him in the public street or in the friend's parlor. If this aversion had its origin in contempt and resistance like his own he might well go home with a sad countenance; but the sour faces of the multitude, like their sweet faces, have no deep cause, but are put on and off as the wind blows and a newspaper directs. Yet is the discontent of the multitude more formidable than that of the senate and the college. It is easy enough for a firm man who knows the world to brook the rage of the cultivated classes. Their rage is decorous and prudent, for they are timid, as being very vulnerable themselves. But when to their feminine rage the indignation of the people is added, when the ignorant and the poor are aroused, when the unintelligent brute force that lies at the bottom of society is made to growl and mow, it needs the habit of magnanimity and religion to treat it godlike as a trifle of no concernment.

The other terror that scares us from self-trust is our consistency; a reverence for our past act or word because the eyes of others have no other data for computing our orbit than our past acts, and we are loth to disappoint them. . . .

. . . A foolish consistency is the hobgoblin of little minds, adored by little statesmen and philosophers and divines. With consistency a great soul has simply nothing to do. He may as well concern himself with his shadow on the wall. Speak what you think now in hard words and to-morrow speak what to-morrow thinks in hard words again, though it contradict every thing you said to-day.—"Ah, so you shall be sure to be misunderstood."—Is it so bad then to be misunderstood? Pythagoras was misunderstood, and Socrates, and Jesus, and Luther, and Copernicus, and Galileo, and Newton, and every pure and wise spirit that ever took flesh. To be great is to be misunderstood.

(RALPH WALDO EMERSON, "Self-Reliance.") [29]

When we survey our lives and endeavours, we soon observe that almost the whole of our actions and desires are bound up with the existence of other human beings. We see that our whole nature resembles that of the social animals. We eat food that others have grown, wear clothes that others have made, live in houses that others have built. The greater part of our knowledge and beliefs has been communicated to us by other people through the medium of a language which others have created. Without language our mental capacities would be poor indeed, comparable to those of the higher animals; we have, therefore, to admit that we owe our principal advantage over the beasts to the fact of living in human society. The individual, if left alone from birth, would remain primitive and beast-like in his thoughts and feelings to a degree that we can hardly conceive. The individual is what he is and has the significance that he has not so much in virtue of his individuality, but rather as a member of a great human society, which directs his material and spiritual existence from the cradle to the grave.

A man's value to the community depends primarily on how far his feelings, thoughts, and actions are directed towards promoting the good of his fellows. We call him good or bad according to how he stands in this matter. It looks at first sight as if our estimate of a man depended entirely on his social qualities.

And yet such an attitude would be wrong. It is clear that all the valuable things, material, spiritual, and moral, which we receive from society can be traced back through countless generations to certain creative individuals. The use of fire, the cultivation of edible plants, the steam engine—each was discovered by one man.

Only the individual can think, and thereby create new values for society, nay, even set up new moral standards to which the life of the community conforms. Without creative personalities able to think and judge independently, the upward development of society is as un-thinkable as the development of the individual personality without the nourishing soil of the community.

The health of society thus depends quite as much on the independ-ence of the individuals composing it as on their close political cohesion.

(ALBERT EINSTEIN, *The World as I See It.*) [30]

June 17, 1852.—Every despotism has a specially keen and hostile instinct for whatever keeps up human dignity, and independence. And it is curious to see scientific and realist teaching used everywhere as a means of stifling all freedom of investigation as addressed to moral questions under a dead weight of facts. Materialism is the auxiliary doctrine of every tyranny, whether of the one or of the masses. To crush what is spiritual, moral, human so to speak, in man, by specializ-ing him; to form mere wheels of the great social machine, instead of perfect individuals; to make society and not conscience the center of life, to enslave the soul to things, to de-personalize man, this is the dom-inant drift of our epoch. Everywhere you may see a tendency to substi-tute the laws of dead matter (number, mass) for the laws of the moral nature (persuasion, adhesion, faith), equality, the principle of medi-ocrity, becoming a dogma; unity aimed at through uniformity; numbers doing duty for argument; negative liberty, which has no law *in itself*, and recognizes no limit except in force, everywhere taking the place of positive liberty, which means action guided by an inner law and curbed by a moral authority. Socialism *versus* individualism: this is how Vinet put the dilemma. I should say rather that it is only the eternal antagonism between letter and spirit, between form and matter, between the outward and the inward, appearance and reality, which is always present in every conception and in all ideas.

Materialism coarsens and petrifies everything; makes everything vul-gar and every truth false. And there is a religious and political ma-terialism which spoils all that it touches, liberty, equality, individuality. So that there are two ways of understanding democracy. . . .

What is threatened to-day is moral liberty, conscience, respect for the soul, the very nobility of man. To defend the soul, its interests, its rights, its dignity, is the most pressing duty for whoever sees the danger. What the writer, the teacher, the pastor, the philosopher, has to do, is to de-fend humanity in man. Man! the true man, the ideal man! Such should be their motto, their rallying cry. War to all that debases, diminishes, hinders, and degrades him; protection for all that fortifies, ennobles, and raises him. The test of every religious, political, or educational system, is the man which it forms. If a system injures the intelligence it is bad. If it injures the character it is vicious. If it injures the conscience it is criminal. (*Amiel's Journal.*) [31]

Fortunately, man has the capacity to imagine, and thus can enlarge the role he plays or the status he has if only for a few fleeting and tenuous moments. We see how absorbing and exciting it is for children to "be" a cowboy, an engineer, a doctor, a nurse. It is likely that even many "normal" adults have their secret moments of role-playing. Certainly through our reading of biographies, explorations, and history we can vicariously participate in the lives of other real people. Novels, the drama, the movies, and television enable us to identify ourselves with characters who are strange and wonderful or who are what we would like to be, and to play roles for a few carefree hours that are impossible for us to sustain in our own space-time worlds in which the limitations imposed on our actions bring our free-wheeling fantasies to a quick stop. The role of fantasy in the life of an "average" man is portrayed in the story about Walter Mitty.

THE SECRET LIFE OF WALTER MITTY*
By James Thurber

"We're going through!" The Commander's voice was like thin ice breaking. He wore his full-dress uniform, with the heavily braided white cap pulled down rakishly over one cold gray eye. "We can't make it, sir. It's spoiling for a hurricane, if you ask me." "I'm not asking you, Lieutenant Berg," said the Commander. "Throw on the power lights! Rev her up to 8,500! We're going through!" The pounding of the cylinders increased: tapocketa-pocketa-pocketa-*pocketa-pocketa*. The Commander stared at the ice forming on the pilot window. He walked over and twisted a row of complicated dials. "Switch on No. 8 auxiliary!" he shouted. "Switch on No. 8 auxiliary!" repeated Lieutenant Berg. "Full strength in No. 3 turret!" shouted the Commander. "Full strength in No. 3 turret!" The crew, bending to their various tasks in the huge, hurtling eight-engined Navy hydroplane, looked at each other and grinned. "The

Old Man'll get us through," they said to one another. "The Old Man ain't afraid of Hell!" . . .

"Not so fast! You're driving too fast!" said Mrs. Mitty. "What are you driving so fast for?"

"Hmm?" said Walter Mitty. He looked at his wife, in the seat beside him, with shocked astonishment. She seemed grossly unfamiliar, like a strange woman who had yelled at him in a crowd. "You were up to fifty-five," she said. "You know I don't like to go more than forty. You were up to fifty-five." Walter Mitty drove on toward Waterbury in silence, the roaring of the SN202 through the worst storm in twenty years of Navy flying fading in the remote, intimate airways of his mind. "You're tensed up again," said Mrs. Mitty. "It's one of your days. I wish you'd let Dr. Renshaw look you over."

Walter Mitty stopped the car in front of the building where his wife went to have her hair done. "Remember to get those overshoes while I'm having my hair done," she said. "I don't need overshoes," said Mitty. She put her mirror back into her bag. "We've been all through that," she said, getting out of the car. "You're not a young man any longer." He raced the engine a little. "Why don't you wear your gloves? Have you lost your gloves?" Walter Mitty reached in a pocket and brought out the gloves. He put them on, but after she had turned and gone into the building and he had driven on to a red light, he took them off again. "Pick it up, brother!" snapped a cop as the light changed, and Mitty hastily pulled on his gloves and lurched ahead. He drove around the streets aimlessly for a time, and then he drove past the hospital on his way to the parking lot.

. . . "It's the millionaire banker, Wellington McMillan," said the pretty nurse. "Yes?" said Walter Mitty, removing his gloves slowly. "Who has the case?" "Dr. Renshaw and Dr. Benbow, but there are two specialists here, Dr. Remington from New York and Dr. Pritchard-Mitford from London. He flew over." A door opened down a long, cool corridor and Dr. Renshaw came out. He looked distraught and haggard. "Hello, Mitty," he said. "We're having the devil's own time with McMillan, the millionaire banker and close personal friend of Roosevelt. Obstreosis of the ductal tract. Tertiary. Wish you'd take a look at him." "Glad to," said Mitty.

In the operating room there were whispered introductions: "Dr. Remington, Dr. Mitty. Dr. Pritchard-Mitford, Dr. Mitty." "I've read your book on streptothricosis," said Pritchard-Mitford, shaking hands. "A brilliant performance, sir." "Thank you," said Walter Mitty. "Didn't know you were in the States, Mitty," grumbled Remington. "Coals to Newcastle, bringing Mitford and me up here for a tertiary." "You are very kind," said Mitty. A huge, complicated machine, connected to the operating table, with many tubes and wires, began at this moment to go pocketa-pocketa-pocketa. "The new anaesthetizer is giving away!" shouted an interne. "There is no one in the East who knows how to fix it!" "Quiet, man!" said Mitty, in a low, cool voice. He sprang to the machine, which was now going pocketa-pocketa-queep-pocketa-queep. He began fingering delicately a row of glistening dials. "Give me a fountain pen!" he snapped. Someone handed him a fountain pen. He pulled a faulty piston out of the machine and inserted the pen in its place. "That will hold for ten minutes," he said. "Get on with the operation." A nurse hurried over and whispered to Renshaw, and Mitty saw the man turn pale. "Coreopsis has set in," said Renshaw nervously. "If you would take over, Mitty?" Mitty looked at him and at the craven figure of Benbow, who drank, and at the grave, uncertain faces of the two great specialists. "If you wish," he said. They slipped a white gown on him; he adjusted a mask and drew on thin gloves; nurses handed him shining . . .

"Back it up, Mac! Look out for that Buick!" Walter Mitty jammed on the brakes. "Wrong lane, Mac," said the parking-lot attendant, looking at Mitty closely. "Gee. Yeh," muttered Mitty. He began cautiously to back out of the lane marked "Exit Only." "Leave her sit there," said the attendant. "I'll put her away." Mitty got out of the car. "Hey, better leave the key." "Oh," said Mitty, handing the man the ignition key. The attendant vaulted into the car, backed it up with insolent skill, and put it where it belonged.

They're so damn cocky, thought Walter Mitty, walking along Main Street; they think they know everything. Once he had tried to take his chains off, outside New Milford, and he had got them wound around the axles. A man had had to come out in a wrecking car and unwind them, a young, grinning garageman. Since then Mrs. Mitty always made him drive to a garage to have the chains taken off. The next time, he thought, I'll wear my right arm in a sling; they won't grin at me then. I'll have my right arm in a sling and they'll see I couldn't possibly take the chains off myself. He kicked at the slush on the sidewalk. "Overshoes," he said to himself, and he began looking for a shoe store.

When he came out into the street again, with the overshoes in a box under his arm, Walter Mitty began to wonder what the other thing was his wife had told him to get. She had told him, twice before they set out from their house for Waterbury. In a way he hated these weekly trips to town—he was always getting something wrong. Kleenex, he thought, Squibb's, razor blades? No. Toothpaste, toothbrush, bicarbonate, carborundum, initiative and referendum? He gave it up. But she would remember it. "Where's the what's-its-name?" she would ask. "Don't tell me you forgot the what's-its-name." A newsboy went by shouting something about the Waterbury trial.

. . . "Perhaps this will refresh your memory." The District Attorney suddenly thrust a heavy automatic at the quiet figure on the witness stand. "Have you ever seen this before?" Walter Mitty took the gun and examined it expertly. "This is my Webley-Vickers 50.80," he said calmly. An excited buzz ran around the courtroom. The Judge rapped for order. "You are a crack shot with any sort of firearms, I believe?" said the District Attorney, insinuatingly. "Objection!" shouted Mitty's attorney. "We have shown that the defendant could not have fired the shot. We have shown that he wore his right arm in a sling on the night of the fourteenth of July." Walter Mitty raised his hand briefly and the bickering attorneys were stilled. "With any known make of gun," he said evenly, "I could have killed Gregory Fitzhurst at three hundred feet *with my left hand*." Pandemonium broke loose in the courtroom. A woman's scream rose above the bedlam and suddenly a lovely, dark-haired girl was in Walter Mitty's arms. The District Attorney struck at her savagely. Without rising from his chair, Mitty let the man have it on the point of the chin. "You miserable cur!" . . .

"Puppy biscuit," said Walter Mitty. He stopped walking and the buildings of Waterbury rose up out of the misty courtroom and surrounded him again. A woman who was passing laughed. "He said 'Puppy biscuit,'" she said to her companion. "That man said 'Puppy biscuit' to himself." Walter Mitty hurried on. He went into an A. & P., not the first one he came to but a smaller one farther up the street. "I want some biscuit for small, young dogs," he said to the clerk. "Any special brand, sir?" The greatest pistol shot in the world thought a moment. "It says 'Puppies Bark for It' on the box," said Walter Mitty.

His wife would be through at the hairdresser's in fifteen minutes, Mitty saw in looking at his watch, unless they had trouble drying it; sometimes they had trouble drying it. She didn't like to get to the hotel first; she would want him to be there waiting for her as usual. He found a big leather chair in the lobby, facing a window, and he put the overshoes and the puppy biscuit on the floor beside it. He picked up an old copy of *Liberty* and sank down into the chair. "Can Germany Conquer the World Through the Air?" Walter Mitty looked at the pictures of bombing planes and of ruined streets.

. . . "The cannonading has got the wind up in young Raleigh, sir," said the sergeant. Captain Mitty looked up at him through tousled hair. "Get him to bed," he said wearily, "with the others. I'll fly alone." "But you can't, sir," said the sergeant anxiously. "It takes two men to handle that bomber and the Archies are pounding hell out of the air. Von

Richtman's circus is between here and Saulier." "Somebody's got to get that ammunition dump," said Mitty. "I'm going over. Spot of brandy?" He poured a drink for the sergeant and one for himself. War thundered and whined around the dugout and battered at the door. There was a rending of wood and splinters flew through the room. "A bit of a near thing," said Captain Mitty carelessly. "The box barrage is closing in," said the sergeant. "We only live once, Sergeant," said Mitty, with his faint, fleeting smile. "Or do we?" He poured another brandy and tossed it off. "I never see a man could hold his brandy like you, sir," said the sergeant. "Begging your pardon, sir." Captain Mitty stood up and strapped on his huge Webley-Vickers automatic. "It's forty kilometres through hell, sir," said the sergeant. Mitty finished one last brandy. "After all," he said softly, "what isn't?" The pounding of the cannon increased; there was the rat-tat-tatting of machine guns, and from somewhere came the menacing pocketa-pocketa-pocketa of the new flame-throwers. Walter Mitty walked to the door of the dugout humming "Auprès de Ma Blonde." He turned and waved to the sergeant. "Cheerio!" he said. . . .

Something struck his shoulder. "I've been looking all over this hotel for you," said Mrs. Mitty. "Why do you have to hide in this old chair? How did you expect me to find you?" "Things close in," said Walter Mitty vaguely. "What?" Mrs. Mitty said. "Did you get the what's-its-name? The puppy biscuit? What's in that box?" "Overshoes," said Mitty. "Couldn't you have put them on in the store?" "I was thinking," said Walter Mitty. "Does it ever occur to you that I am sometimes thinking?" She looked at him. "I'm going to take your temperature when I get you home," she said.

They went out through the revolving doors that made a faintly derisive whistling sound when you pushed them. It was two blocks to the parking lot. At the drugstore on the corner she said, "Wait here for me. I forgot something. I won't be a minute." She was more than a minute. Walter Mitty lighted a cigarette. It began to rain, rain with sleet in it. He stood up against the wall of the drugstore, smoking. . . . He put his shoulders back and and his heels together. "To hell with the handkerchief," said Walter Mitty scornfully. He took one last drag on his cigarette and snapped it away. Then, with that faint, fleeting smile playing about his lips, he faced the firing squad; erect and motionless, proud and disdainful, Walter Mitty the Undefeated, inscrutable to the last. [32]

The main risk that comes from multiple group identifications and loyalties is the risk of experiencing a sense of conflict within ourselves because the standards of the groups to which we belong or refer ourselves to are themselves in conflict. Divided loyalties are a major source of indecision, uncertainty, and anxiety. The young Communist in the Soviet Union may be torn between loyalty to the Party and loyalty to his family when the Party tells him it is his duty to put Party above all else. Many people throughout the world at this stage of its development are torn between loyalty to their nation and loyalty to their class. A union worker on strike may feel disloyal to his family; a shop foreman may be torn between loyalty to his employer and loyalty to his men. There is no easy solution to many of these conflicts, and it is doubtful if many are successfully resolved by personal psychotherapy. An enduring solution, of course, can come about only when an individual is able to build up congenial and complementary loyalties. But in most parts of the world today, with their complicated and varied social structures, an integration of loyalties is not easy to bring about quickly.

Any group itself will tend to endure insofar as it can provide the possibility of genuine participation of individual members in such a way that each member can experience some satisfying consequences from his own action through participation in the group. Group morale will be high when individual members are able to play an active role in setting group standards and selecting group goals and then following through toward these goals with other members of the group. The group will disintegrate if and when it no longer serves its original functions or if the functions it once served can be provided for more easily in other ways. Thus in the United States the introduction of social security for older people dispelled many groups such as the Townsendites, originally organized to attain some benefits for the aged; gangs of delinquents disintegrate if the community takes the proper measures to fill the needs of adolescents in socially adapted ways; state or national rivalries dissolve when common purposes or common threats become sufficiently important.

MORES, CUSTOMS, RITUALS

Rituals, customs, mores, and laws enable us to share more common significances with other people more continuously and more extensively. They are prescriptions society has developed and exercised which have proved, at least to some people, to be methods of increasing the value-satisfactions of life by providing definite and repeatable behavior which has acquired value-significance. The observance of customs, rituals, and mores provides a more or less permanent link by means of which the individual can feel joined to a group, society, or ideology. Thus, in Western culture the gentleman removes his hat when he enters a house, the good Catholic tells his beads, the gang-member knows a password or a secret code, the American salutes the flag, the Zulu has his tribal dance, and so forth. Nearly all action that has a high degree of communality and patterning is in some way meaningfully related to the purposes of the participants and enables them to share a common reality. If a person feels that his bond with the group, society, or ideology is weakening and needs strengthening, he can voluntarily repeat a ritual, thus connecting himself functionally to the abstraction it refers to and making the abstraction "real."

This participation in common significance has, of course, been enormously enlarged in recent years with the development of modern techniques of mass communication, as millions of people participate in the "same" experiences concurrently. Thus there is at least the potentiality of larger social-political or religious groupings.

February 27, 1874.—Among the peoples, in whom the social gifts are the strongest, the individual fears ridicule above all things, and ridicule is the certain result of originality. No one, therefore, wishes to make a party of his own; everyone wishes to be on the side of all the world. "All the world" is the greatest of powers; it is sovereign, and calls itself *we*. *We* dress, *we* dine, *we* walk, *we* go out, *we* come in, like this, and not like that. This *we* is always right, whatever it does. The subjects of *We* are more prostrate than the slaves of the East before the Padishah. The good pleasure of the sovereign decides every appeal; his caprice is law. What *we* does or says is called custom, what it thinks is called opinion, what it believes to be beautiful or good is called fashion. Among such nations as these *we* is the brain, the conscience, the reason, the taste, and the judgment of all. The individual finds everything decided for him without his troubling about it. He is dispensed from the task of finding out anything whatever. Provided that he imitates, copies, and repeats the models furnished by *we*, he has nothing more to fear. He knows all that he need know, and has entered into salvation.

(*Amiel's Journal.*) [33]

Conspicuous consumption of valuable goods is a means of reputability to the gentleman of leisure. As wealth accumulates on his hands, his own unaided effort will not avail to sufficiently put his opulence in evidence by this method. The aid of friends and competitors is therefore brought in by resorting to the giving of valuable presents and expensive feasts and entertainments. Presents and feasts had probably another origin than that of naïve ostentation, but they acquired their utility for this purpose very early, and they have retained that character to the present; so that their utility in this respect has now long been the substantial ground on which these usages rest. Costly entertainments, such as the potlatch or the ball, are peculiarly adapted to serve this end. The competitor with whom the entertainer wishes to institute a comparison is, by this method, made to serve as a means to the end. He consumes vicariously for his host at the same time that he is a witness to the consumption of that excess of good things which his host is unable to dispose of single-handed, and he is also made to witness his host's facility in etiquette. . . .

As wealth accumulates, the leisure class develops further in function and structure, and there arises a differentiation within the class. There is a more or less elaborate system of rank and grades. This differentiation is furthered by the inheritance of wealth and the consequent inheritance of gentility. With the inheritance of gentility goes the inheritance of obligatory leisure; and gentility of a sufficient potency to entail a life of leisure may be inherited without the complement of wealth required to maintain a dignified leisure. Gentle blood may be transmitted without goods enough to afford a reputably free consumption at one's ease. Hence results a class of impecunious gentlemen of leisure, incidentally referred to already. These half-caste gentlemen of leisure fall into a system of hierarchical gradations. Those who stand near the higher and the highest grades of the wealthy leisure class, in point of birth, or in point of wealth, or both, outrank the remoter-born and the pecuniarily weaker. These lower grades, especially the impecunious, or marginal, gentlemen of leisure, affiliate themselves by a system of dependence or fealty to the great ones; by so doing they gain an increment of repute, or of the means with which to lead a life of leisure, from their patron. They become his courtiers or retainers, servants; and being fed and countenanced by their patron they are indices of his rank and vicarious consumers of his superfluous wealth. Many of these affiliated gentlemen of leisure are at the same time lesser men of substance in their own right; so that some of them are scarcely at all, others only partially, to be rated as vicarious consumers. So many of them, however, as make up the retainers and hangers-on of the patron may be classed as vicarious consumers without qualification. Many of these again, and also many of the other aristocracy of less degree, have in turn attached to their persons a more or less comprehensive group of vicarious consumers in the persons of their wives and children, their servants, retainers, etc.

Throughout this graduated scheme of vicarious leisure and vicarious consumption the rule holds that these offices must be performed in some such manner, or under some such circumstance or insignia, as shall point plainly to the master to whom this leisure or consumption pertains, and to whom therefore the resulting increment of good repute of right enures. The consumption and leisure executed by these persons for their master or patron represents an investment on his part with a view to an increase of good fame. As regards feasts and largesses this is obvious enough, and the imputation of repute to the host or patron here takes place immediately, on the ground of common notoriety. Where leisure and consumption is performed vicariously by henchmen and retainers, imputation of the resulting repute to the patron is effected by their residing near his person so that it may be plain to all men from what source they draw. As the group whose good esteem is to be secured in this way grows larger, more patent means are required to indicate the imputation of merit for the leisure performed, and to this end uniforms, badges, and liveries come into vogue. The wearing of uniforms or liveries implies a considerable degree of dependence, and may even be said to be a mark of servitude, real or ostensible. The wearers of uniforms and liveries may be roughly divided into two classes —the free and the servile, or the noble and the ignoble. The services performed by them are likewise divisible into noble and ignoble. Of course the distinction is not observed with strict consistency in practice; the less debasing of the base services and the less honorific of the noble functions are not infrequently merged in the same person. But the general distinction is not on that account to be overlooked. What may add some perplexity is the fact that this fundamental distinction between noble and ignoble, which rests on the nature of the ostensible service performed, is traversed by a secondary distinction into honorific and humiliating, resting on the rank of the person for whom the service is performed or whose livery is worn. So, those offices which are by right the proper employment of the leisure class are noble; such are government, fighting, hunting, the care of arms and accoutrements, and the like, —in short, those which may be classed as ostensibly predatory employments. On the other hand, those employments which properly fall to the industrious class are ignoble; such as handicraft or other productive labour, menial services, and the like. But a base service performed for a person of very high degree may become a very honorific office; as for instance the office of a Maid of Honour or of a Lady in Waiting to the Queen, or the King's Master of the Horse or his Keeper of the Hounds. The two offices last named suggest a principle of some general bearing. Whenever, as in these cases, the menial service in question has to do directly with the primary leisure employments of fighting and hunting, it easily acquires a reflected honorific character. In this way great honour may come to attach to an employment which in its own nature belongs to the baser sort.

In the later development of peaceable industry, the usage of employing an idle corps of uniformed men-at-arms gradually lapses. Vicarious consumption by dependents bearing the insignia of their patron or master narrows down to a corps of liveried menials. In a heightened degree, therefore, the livery comes to be a badge of servitude, or rather of servility. Something of a honorific character always attached to the livery of the armed retainer, but this honorific character disappears when the livery becomes the exclusive badge of the menial. The livery becomes obnoxious to nearly all who are required to wear it. We are yet so little removed from a state of effective slavery as still to be fully sensitive to the sting of any imputation of servility. This antipathy asserts itself even in the case of the liveries or uniforms which some corporations prescribe as the distinctive dress of their employees. In this country the aversion even goes the length of discrediting—in a mild and uncertain way—those government employments, military and civil, which require the wearing of a livery or uniform.

With the disappearance of servitude, the number of vicarious consumers attached to any one gentleman tends, on the whole, to decrease. The like is of course true, and perhaps in a still higher degree, of the number of dependents who perform vicarious leisure for him. In a general way, though not wholly nor consistently, these two groups coincide. The dependent who was first delegated for these duties was the wife, or the chief wife; and, as would be expected, in the later development of the institution, when the number of persons by whom these duties are customarily performed gradually narrows, the wife remains the last. In the higher grades of society a large volume of both these kinds of service is required; and here the wife is of course still assisted in the work by a more or less numerous corps of menials. But as we descend the social scale, the point is presently reached where the duties of vicarious leisure and consumption devolve upon the wife alone. In the communities of Western culture, this point is at present found among the lower middle class.

And here occurs a curious inversion. It is a fact of common observation that in this lower middle class there is no pretence of leisure on the part of the head of the household. Through force of circumstances it has fallen into disuse. But the middle-class wife still carries on the business of vicarious leisure, for the good name of the household and its master. In descending the social scale in any modern industrial community, the primary fact—the conspicuous leisure of the master of the household—disappears at a relatively high point. The head of the middle-class household has been reduced by economic circumstances to turn his hand to gaining a livelihood by occupations which often partake largely of the character of industry, as in the case of the ordinary business man of to-day. But the derivative fact—the vicarious leisure and consumption rendered by the wife, and the auxiliary vicarious performance of leisure by menials—remains in vogue as a conventionality which the demands of reputability will not suffer to be slighted. It is by no means an uncommon spectacle to find a man applying himself to work with the utmost assiduity, in order that his wife may in due form render for him that degree of vicarious leisure which the common sense of the time demands.

The leisure rendered by the wife in such cases is, of course, not a simple manifestation of idleness or indolence. It almost invariably occurs disguised under some form of work or household duties or social amenities, which prove on analysis to serve little or no ulterior end beyond showing that she does not and need not occupy herself with anything that is gainful or that is of substantial use. As has already been noticed under the head of manners, the greater part of the customary round of domestic cares to which the middle-class housewife gives her time and effort is of this character. Not that the results of her attention to household matters, of a decorative and mundificatory character, are not pleasing to the sense of men trained in middle-class proprieties; but the taste to which these effects of household adornment and tidiness appeal is a taste which has been formed under the selective guidance of a canon of propriety that demands just these evidences of wasted effort. The effects are pleasing to us chiefly because we have been taught to find them pleasing. There goes into these domestic duties much solicitude for a proper combination of form and colour, and for other ends that are to be classed as aesthetic in the proper sense of the term; and it is not denied that effects having some substantial aesthetic value are sometimes attained. Pretty much all that is here insisted on is that, as regards these amenities of life, the housewife's efforts are under the guidance of traditions that have been shaped by the law of conspicuously wasteful expenditure of time and substance. If beauty or comfort is achieved,—and it is a more or less fortuitous circumstance if they are,—they must be achieved by means and methods that commend themselves to the great economic law of wasted effort. The more reputable, "presentable" portion of middle-class household paraphernalia are, on the one hand, items of conspicuous consumption, and on the other hand, apparatus for putting in evidence the vicarious leisure rendered by the housewife.

The requirement of vicarious consumption at the hands of the wife continues in force even at a lower point in the pecuniary scale than the requirement of vicarious leisure. At a point below which little if any pretence of wasted effort, in ceremonial cleanness and the like, is observable, and where there is assuredly no conscious attempt at ostensible leisure, decency still requires the wife to consume some goods conspicuously for the reputability of the household and its head. So that, as the latter-day outcome of this evolution of an archaic institution, the wife, who was at the outset the drudge and chattel of the man, both in fact and in theory,—the producer of goods for him to consume,—has become the ceremonial consumer of goods which he produces. But she still quite unmistakably remains his chattel in theory; for the habitual rendering of vicarious leisure and consumption is the abiding mark of the unfree servant.

This vicarious consumption practised by the household of the middle and lower classes can not be counted as a direct expression of the leisure-class scheme of life, since the household of this pecuniary grade does not belong within the leisure class. It is rather that the leisure-class scheme of life here comes to an expression at the second remove. The leisure class stands at the head of the social structure in point of reputability; and its manner of life and its standards of worth therefore afford the norm of reputability for the community. The observance of these standards, in some degree of approximation, becomes incumbent upon all classes lower in the scale. In modern civilized communities the lines of demarcation between social classes have grown vague and transient, and wherever this happens the norm of reputability imposed by the upper class extends its coercive influence with but slight hindrance down through the social structure to the lowest strata. The result is that the members of each stratum accept as their ideal of decency the scheme of life in vogue in the next higher stratum, and bend their energies to live up to that ideal. On pain of forfeiting their good name and their self-respect in case of failure, they must conform to the accepted code, at least in appearance.

The basis on which good repute in any highly organised industrial community ultimately rests is pecuniary strength; and the means of showing pecuniary strength, and so of gaining or retaining a good name, are leisure and a conspicuous consumption of goods. Accordingly, both of these methods are in vogue as far down the scale as it remains possible; and in the lower strata in which the two methods are employed, both offices are in great part delegated to the wife and children of the household. Lower still, where any degree of leisure, even ostensible, has become impracticable for the wife, the conspicuous consumption of goods remains and is carried on by the wife and children. The man of the household also can do something in this direction, and, indeed, he commonly does; but with a still lower descent into the levels of indigence —along the margin of the slums—the man, and presently also the children, virtually cease to consume valuable goods for appearances, and the woman remains virtually the sole exponent of the household's pecuniary decency. No class of society, not even the most abjectly poor, foregoes all customary conspicuous consumption. The last items of this category of consumption are not given up except under stress of the direst necessity. Very much of squalor and discomfort will be endured before the last trinket or the last pretence of pecuniary decency is put away. There is no class and no country that has yielded so abjectly before the pressure of physical want as to deny themselves all gratification of this higher or spiritual need.

(THORSTEIN VEBLEN, *The Theory of the Leisure Class.*) [34]

COMMUNICATION

Communication is so commonplace in our experience that we are likely to overlook its complexity and wonder, forgetting that for the individual and for the human race communication has had to develop out of man's frustrations when he found he could not give and receive the messages he wanted. We notice something of this when we observe the intense efforts of a child trying in its own highly individualistic way to communicate its feelings of delight, discovery, or pain; we feel our own inability to communicate at times when some experience seems beyond words to convey.

The process of communication, like all the other abstract aspects of the process of living, develops and has its existence only because it is imbedded in the living process itself. Our very survival and the quality of our experience clearly depend upon how successfully we "give" appropriate significances to the signs which we become aware of. Obviously there would be no social life unless one individual could appreciate how and in what way his behavior was affecting another person, and could in turn somehow tell that other person of his own experiences in any participation they might have together.

The devices by means of which people communicate with each other are legion: they may be postures, bodily movements, or facial expressions; they may be sounds or silences; they may be words or ideographic symbols; they may be the mathematician's signs or the drumbeats of a Zulu warrior; they may be the signals conveyed by the code of Braille or the touch of a lover; they may be the caress of a mother or some form of punishment. Man has devised the dance, music, and the visual arts to help him share his subtler and more profound feelings. One of the readings below indicates a unique kind of communication Gandhi developed—that of fasting for days on end to let the illiterate masses of India know quickly that he had a message for them. Other selections in the following group indicate that spoken or written language is a very imperfect instrument for communication, while others point to forms of non-verbal communication.

Gandhi had been ill for months in jail. Then came the urgent appendectomy. The wound suppurated and healed slowly. Convalescence was retarded. Weeks of tense talks followed by weeks of strenuous touring wore him out. The political situation depressed him; years of work seemed to have been lost. At a conference of the All-India Congress Committee in June, when he realized how many of his associates really did not believe in non-violence, he wept in public. The steady stream of reports on Hindu-Moslem fighting and the atmosphere of bickering, hate, and gloom weighed heavily on his body and spirit. He was fifty-five. He knew that a twenty-one-day fast might be fatal. He did not want to die. There were too many unfinished tasks. He reveled in life. Suicide was religiously and physically repugnant to him. The fast was no tryst with death. It gave him no pleasure to suffer. The fast was dictated by duty to the highest cause—the universal brotherhood of man.

For Gandhi, an act had to be right and true. Then he never counted the cost to himself or even to others; in this sense, he was without mercy. Service meant sacrifice, renunciation, and detachment. You detach yourself from yourself. All that remains is duty. On September 18, 1924, Gandhi felt it his duty to fast.

Gandhi always kept his eye on his objective, and when he could not see it he kept his eye on the spot where he thought it would appear. He also had an eye for drama. He fasted in the home of a Moslem, Mohamed Ali, the younger brother of Shaukat. Mohamed Ali was a staunch Congress supporter, a champion of Hindu-Moslem friendship. But the Moslem community was moving away from him. Gandhi had said in his article that "the key to the situation lies with the Hindus," but with his heart, the senior partner of his mind, he knew that Moslems were the offenders; conditions, he said, were making the Moslem "a bully." Gandhi wished to strengthen Mohamed Ali's hand. "It is our duty," he once wrote, "to strengthen by our fasting those who hold the same ideals but are likely to weaken under pressure." For twenty-one days India's attention would be focused on the house where Gandhi lay fasting. Moslems would see that Mohandas and Mohamed were brothers. Hindus, moreover, would note that their saint had confided his life to a Moslem.

No personal benefit could come to Gandhi from the fast; on the contrary. Nor was there any element of compulsion in it. The Moslem in Calcutta or Agra, the Hindu in Amritsar or Allahabad would not be compelled to change their conduct because Gandhi was dying for Hindu-Moslem amity. They would change, if at all, because the Mahatma's great sacrifice established a spiritual bond between him and them, a kind of common wave-length, a means of communication over which he conveyed to them the importance, the necessity, the urgency, the sacredness of the cause for which he was fasting. It was his way of going out to them, of entering their hearts, of uniting himself with them.

In part, this is Eastern, Indian. The bridges of the West are made of concrete, steel, wire, words. Eastern bridges are of spirit. To communicate, the West moves or talks. The East sits, contemplates, suffers. Gandhi partook of West and East. When Western methods failed him, he used Eastern methods.

(Louis Fischer, *The Life of Mahatma Gandhi*.) [35]

We feel in one world; we think and name in another. Between the two we can set up a system of references but not fill the gap.

(*The Maxims of Marcel Proust*.) [36]

The word is a symbol and a delight which sucks up men and scenes, trees, plants, factories, and Pekinese. Then the Thing becomes the Word and back to Thing again, but warped and woven into a fantastic pattern . . .   (JOHN STEINBECK, *Cannery Row.*) [37]

"I don't know what you mean by 'glory,'" Alice said. Humpty Dumpty smiled contemptuously. "Of course you don't—till I tell you. I meant 'there's a nice knock-down argument for you'!"

"But 'glory' doesn't mean 'a nice knock-down argument,'" Alice objected.

"When *I* use a word," Humpty Dumpty said, in rather a scornful tone, "it means just what I choose it to mean—neither more nor less."

"The question is," said Alice, "whether you *can* make words mean so many different things."

"The question is," said Humpty Dumpty, "which is to be master— that's all."   (LEWIS CARROLL, *Through the Looking-Glass.*) [38]

. . . Some persons seem to think that absolute truth, in the form of rigidly stated propositions, is all that conversation admits. This is precisely as if a musician should insist on having nothing but perfect chords and simple melodies,—no diminished fifths, no flat sevenths, no flourishes, on any account. Now it is fair to say, that, just as music must have all these, so conversation must have its partial truths, its embellished truths, its exaggerated truths. It is in its higher forms an artistic product, and admits the ideal element as much as pictures or statues. One man who is a little too literal can spoil the talk of a whole tableful of men of *esprit.*—"Yes," you say, "but who wants to hear fanciful people's nonsense? Put the facts to it, and then see where it is!"—Certainly, if a man is too fond of paradox,—if he is flighty and empty,—if, instead of striking those fifths and sevenths, those harmonious discords, often so much better than the twinned octaves, in the music of thought, —if, instead of striking these, he jangles the chords, stick a fact into him like a stiletto. But remember that talking is one of the fine arts,—the noblest, the most important, and the most difficult,—and that its fluent harmonies may be spoiled by the intrusion of a single harsh note. Therefore conversation which is suggestive rather than argumentative, which lets out the most of each talker's results of thought, is commonly the pleasantest and the most profitable. It is not easy, at the best, for two persons talking together to make the most of each other's thoughts, there are so many of them. . . .

When John and Thomas, for instance, are talking together, it is natural enough that among the six there should be more or less confusion and misapprehension. . . . There are at least six personalities distinctly to be recognized as taking part in that dialogue between John and Thomas.

Three Johns.
$$\left\{\begin{array}{l} \text{1. The real John; known only to his Maker.} \\ \text{2. John's ideal John; never the real one, and} \\ \quad \text{often very unlike him.} \\ \text{3. Thomas's ideal John; never the real John,} \\ \quad \text{nor John's John, but often very unlike either.} \end{array}\right.$$

Three Thomases.
$$\left\{\begin{array}{l} \text{1. The real Thomas.} \\ \text{2. Thomas's ideal Thomas.} \\ \text{3. John's ideal Thomas.} \end{array}\right.$$

Only one of the three Johns is taxed; only one can be weighed on a platform-balance; but the other two are just as important in the conversation. Let us suppose the real John to be old, dull, and ill-looking. But as the Higher Powers have not conferred on men the gift of seeing themselves in the true light, John very possibly conceives himself to be youthful, witty, and fascinating, and talks from the point of view of this ideal. Thomas, again, believes him to be an artful rogue, we will say; therefore he *is*, so far as Thomas's attitude in the conversation is concerned, an artful rogue, though really simple and stupid. The same conditions apply to the three Thomases. It follows, that, until a man can be found who knows himself as his Maker knows him, or who sees himself as others see him, there must be at least six persons engaged in every dialogue between two. Of these, the least important, philosophically speaking, is the one that we have called the real person. No wonder two disputants often get angry, when there are six of them talking and listening all at the same time.

(OLIVER WENDELL HOLMES, *The Autocrat of the Breakfast Table.*) [39]

I wish to suggest a harmless form of entertainment. There are so few amusements that are not blameworthy!

When you go out of a morning, intending to stroll along the busy streets, fill your pockets with little inventions, costing a half-penny each —the little flat jumpingjack moved by a single piece of string, the blacksmiths hammering on their anvil, the rider and his horse whose tail is a whistle—and, at every tavern or tree you pass, pay homage with them to the poor little strangers whom you meet. You'll see their eyes widen beyond measure. At first they will not dare to take your offering; they will doubt their good fortune. Then their hands will eagerly seize the gift, and they'll run away—as a cat does when it carries off a morsel you have given it, because it has learnt to distrust human beings.

At a roadside, behind the railings of a vast garden at the end of which could be seen a pretty white country house soaked in sunlight, stood a handsome, clean little boy dressed in those country clothes that are always so attractive.

Children like this grow so handsome—as a result of luxury, freedom from care, and the accustomed spectacle of wealth—that they seem to be made of another clay than are children of moderate fortune or of poverty.

By this child's side lay on the grass a splendid toy, as clean as its owner, varnished, gilded, clad in a purple robe and covered with plumes and trinkets. But the child was paying no attention to his favourite toy; he was looking at something else.

On the other side of the railings, amongst the thistles and nettles at the road's edge, was another child, unwashed, puny, grimy, one of those pariah-brats in whom an impartial eye might discover beauty—if, like the eye of a connoisseur discovering a magnificent painting behind a coachbuilder's layer of varnish, it could clean off the revolting patina of poverty.

Through this symbolic barrier between two worlds, between the high-road and the country house, the poor child was showing the rich child the former's own toy, which the rich child was avidly examining as a rare and unknown object. This toy, which the little guttersnipe was tormenting and shaking in a cage, was a live rat! His family, to save money, no doubt, had obtained the toy from life itself.

And the two children were fraternally laughing, one to the other, with teeth of an "egalitarian" whiteness.

(CHARLES BAUDELAIRE, *My Heart Laid Bare and Other Prose Writings.*) [40]

. . . A beautiful verse is like a violin-bow drawn across the resonant fibres of our soul. It is not his own thoughts, but ours, that the Poet sets singing within us. When he tells us of a woman he loves, it is our loves and griefs he awakes entrancingly in our souls. He is an evoker of spirits. When we understand him, we are as much poets as he. We have in us, every one of us, a copy of each of our poets which no man knows of and which will perish utterly and for ever with all its variants when we shall cease to feel and know. And do you suppose we should love our lyric bards so fondly, if they spoke to us of aught else but our own selves? It is all a happy misapprehension! The best of them are sheer egoists. They are thinking of themselves all the time. It is only themselves they have put into their verses—and it is only *ourselves* we find there. . . .   (ANATOLE FRANCE, *The Garden of Epicurus.*) [41]

Language exists only when it is listened to as well as spoken. The hearer is an indispensable partner. The work of art is complete only as

it works in the experience of others than the one who created it. Thus language involves what logicians call a triadic relation. There is the speaker, the thing said, and the one spoken to. The external object, the product of art, is the connecting link between artist and audience. Even when the artist works in solitude all three terms are present. The work is there in progress, and the artist has to become vicariously the receiving audience. He can speak only as his work appeals to him as one spoken to through what he perceives. He observes and understands as a third person might note and interpret. Matisse is reported to have said: "When a painting is finished, it is like a new-born child. The artist himself must have time for understanding it." It must be lived with as a child is lived with, if we are to grasp the meaning of his being.
(JOHN DEWEY, *Art as Experience.*) [42]

All human perception is symbolic. We are able to use symbols for communication because the significance assigned to the symbol is widely agreed upon. Obviously, this is not to say that there is complete agreement concerning the meaning of all words or other symbols—far from it. But at least the word or symbol tends to map out an area of concern or a slice of human activity which is sufficiently agreed upon so that one individual can roughly predict what another individual is trying to communicate.

Nearly every word or symbol or gesture that we comprehend is a perception with a long history of its own. The words and symbols of others have significance for us only as we attribute significance to them on the basis of assumptions which we have acquired through our past transactions. The same word may and often does have different significances for different persons, or different significances for the same person in different situations.

There is obviously no inherent meaning in any word or symbol itself. The meaning is man-made. Whitehead has reminded us that "spoken language is just a series of squeaks." Symbols will have common significance insofar as people have common experiences with the words or symbols. Just as we noticed that we have a tendency to assign certain fixed characteristics to objects or things in the environment around us, so too do we tend to reify words, using them as though they were fixed and absolute, despite the fact that they are all abstractions man has devised to serve his purposes.

At best, communication can only be fragmentary and probable, not complete and certain. Words and symbols have meanings for us because of what we know or assume we know through repeated experience about the actions and intentions sequentially linked with these words and symbols. But the total reference of a word is the sum of all its potential sequential significances to all its users. Some people, such as political orators, will often deliberately use vague phrases that mean *almost nothing* or that could mean almost anything. This possibility is amusingly illustrated by the following excerpt from an address proposed by A. Parker Nevin to fit almost any occasion:

Subject: THE CRISIS
(or any other topic)

Mr. Chairman, Ladies and Gentlemen: It is indeed a great and undeserved privilege to address such an audience as I see before me. At no previous time in the history of human civilization have greater problems confronted and challenged the ingenuity of man's intellect than now. Let us look around us. What do we see on the horizon? What forces are at work? Whither are we drifting? Under what mist of clouds does the future stand obscured?

My friends, casting aside the raiment of all human speech, the crucial test for the solution of these intricate problems, to which I have just alluded, is the sheer and forceful application of those immutable laws which, down the corridors of time, have always guided the hand of man, groping, as it were, for some faint beacon-light for his hopes and aspirations. Without these great vital principles, we are but puppets, responding to whim and fancy, failing entirely to grasp the hidden meaning of it all. We must readdress ourselves to these questions which press for answer and solution. The issues cannot be avoided. There they stand. It is upon you—and you—and yes, even upon me, that the yoke of responsibility falls.

What then, is our duty? Shall we continue to drift? No! with all the emphasis of my being I hurl back the message: No! Drifting must stop. We must press onward and upward toward that ultimate goal to which all must aspire.

But I cannot conclude my remarks, dear friends, without touching, briefly, on a subject which I know is steeped in your very consciousness. I refer to that spirit that gleams from the eyes of the newborn babe; that animates the toiling masses; that sways all the hosts of humanity, past and present. Without this energizing principle all commerce, trade, and industry are hushed and will perish from this earth as surely as the crimson sunset follows the golden sunrise. Mark you, I do not seek to unduly alarm or distress the mothers and fathers, sons and daughters, gathered before me in this vast assemblage; but I would indeed be recreant to a high resolve, which I made as a youth, if I did not at this time, and in this place, and with the full realizing sense of the responsibility which I assume, publicly declare and affirm my dedication and my consecration to the eternal principles and precepts of simple, ordinary, commonplace Justice. . . . [43]

It would even be well-nigh impossible for a single individual to become aware of and to spell out all the sequential significances which any single word such as "chair" might have for him. But fortunately we can be reasonably sure that in a large number of occurrences for a large number of people certain meanings will hold. It is the function of a dictionary to report the sequential significances which are agreed upon by a large number of individuals.

But even dictionaries must be revised with new words added as others become obsolete. Change and uncertainty seem to be the inescapable lot of man if we look at him with any degree of perspective. Living is not only being but becoming. In the next chapter we turn our attention to the process of change and some of its consequences for the human situation, both individual and social.

7

Man, Society, and Change*

> "The essence of life is to be
> found in the frustration of es-
> tablished order."
>
> —A. N. WHITEHEAD

THE ONLY PERMANENCE IS CHANGE

If the world around us were not constantly changing, our assumptions and our symbols would no doubt eventually serve us
adequately enough and would not cause the trouble they do. But
ceaseless change is the rule of nature and of human nature. What
we call "permanent" has been defined by the philosopher as change
that goes on so slowly that we cannot observe it. And not only the
world around us changes; we ourselves, being part of the world,
change as the years bring about the rhythm of development determined by the genetic pattern of our species, from birth and ado-
lescence through old age to death, and as the circumstances of our
lives bring about the particular development of new capacities,
new interests, new loyalties, new aspirations, and new problems.

Even though the universe, including man, is an on-going stream
of events, continuously creative, never repeating itself exactly, we
have a tendency to think of things as fixed, as "there" to be analyzed and, once analyzed, understood forever. This tendency no
doubt helps to put us more at ease, and fosters at least occasional
complacency that brings relief and escape. As a result people often
look on change with a sense of anxiety and fear. They want things
to stay the way they are, or they try to recapture the good old

* Notes to this chapter begin on p. 337.

days. But not only is change the rule of nature and human nature; change is potentially man's chief source of hope. Change is exciting when it has a direction and it apparently has a direction *if* we are able to discover it. Change goes on relentlessly. As Lucretius put it:

> No single thing abides; but all things flow.
> Fragment to fragment clings—the things thus grow
>   Until we know and name them. By degrees
> They melt, and are no more the things we know.
>
> Globed from the atoms falling slow or swift
> I see the suns, I see the systems lift
>   Their forms; and even the systems and the suns
> Shall go back slowly to the eternal drift.
>
> Thou too, oh earth—thine empires, lands, and seas—
> Least, with thy stars, of all the galaxies,
>   Globed from the drift like these, like these thou too
> Shalt go. Thou art going, hour by hour, like these.
>
> Nothing abides. Thy seas in delicate haze
> Go off; those mooned sands forsake their place;
>   And where they are, shall other seas in turn
> Mow with their scythes of whiteness other days. [1]

Change is something we must anticipate and accept, something we must try to make serve human ends as we can. Living without change would be inconceivable and unbearable. At the same time few of us would care to go on living in the midst of ceaseless, chaotic, completely unpredictable change. Individuals who are plugged into concreteness are usually sensitive to change and the need to adapt to it. In his second inaugural address, Lincoln said, "The dogmas of the quiet past are inadequate to the stormy present. The occasion is piled high with difficulty and we must rise to the occasion. As our case is new—so we must think anew and act anew." And the need to be aware of change was expressed by Thomas à Kempis in the fifteenth century in one of his prayers:

Who can tell what a day may bring forth? Cause us, therefore, gracious God, to live every day as if it were to be our last, for that we know not but it may be such. Cause us to live so at present as we shall wish we had done when we come to die. O grant that we may not die with any guilt upon our consciences, or any known sin unrepented of, but that we may be found in Christ, Who is our only Saviour and Redeemer. Amen. [2]

We are concerned here with the problem of how to make ceaseless revisions in our reality-worlds (to accord with change) without at the same time undermining the form and security these reality-worlds provide. In this chapter we can only explore a few of the many conditions and consequences of change in human existence, and some examples of the impact of change on human relations.

INVENTIONS AND ARTIFACTS

One of man's most noticeable characteristics is his capacity to invent and to create artifacts of all kinds which help him carry out his purposes. By means of these he humanizes nature according to his own interests and designs: he creates dwelling places, tools, instruments, roads, communications, dams, irrigation systems, power plants, cities, and thousands of other artifacts and patterns of artifacts in unending procession.

From the psychological point of view, man's inventions and artifacts serve two important functions. In the first place, nearly all of them can be viewed as devices for extending the range and accuracy of man's sense organs or the range and accuracy of his muscular effort. In the former category we have such modern inventions as the radio, telescope, television, thermometer, or microscope; in the latter category, such artifacts as wheels, pumps, motors, plows, and tractors.

A second function artifacts perform is that of increasing the range and reliability of repeatable phenomena by creating devices that can be counted on to perform in relatively standardized and fixed ways. Man's long experience in breeding and domesticating animals and agricultural products are in this category as well, of course, as man's more obvious technical artifacts such as shovels, arrows, guns, ball-bearings, self-starters, baseballs, pencils, or the whole host of other objects which anyone can think of that have built-in specifications so they can be counted upon to help man perform some particular job for which they are designed.

Two important consequences of man's inventions and artifacts with respect to social change should be particularly borne in mind. First, every major invention has had the effect of modifying to some degree the standards in terms of which individuals judge the quality of living. New inventions and artifacts provide possibilities for new experiences and new aspirations for those who learn about them and who want to share in the greater efficiency, comfort, or pleasure they provide. Secondly, major inventions give rise almost invariably to new and unforeseen consequences in human relations.

It is important to stress that these latter consequences are by and large almost entirely unpredictable. One can get some idea of this unpredictability by thinking for an instant of the variety of social consequences brought about by the apparently simple artifact of the wheel. It made possible all manner of new locomotion, new machinery, new timepieces, new scientific instruments, and such a variety of artifacts that it would take hundreds of pages even to list them. The consequences of these artifacts on man's relation with man are also legion—the change in the size of social units with improved transportation; the change in the structure of the family and the social group; the change in governmental organizations possible with more rapid and easier communication; new vocational opportunities opened up by all the machinery that utilizes wheels of some variety. Another illustration, taken at random, is the microscope, with the enormous social implications it has had because of its usefulness in identifying and aiding in the control of micro-organisms (such as those responsible for malaria or yellow fever), and with the subsequent population increases with their stupendous political-geographical effects. Comparable hosts of unpredictable social consequences have followed almost every other major invention, such as the printing press, the steam engine, the cyclotron, or the jet engine.

Furthermore, each new artifact before long begins to demonstrate that many of our current ways of behaving and thinking are inappropriate and inadequate to meet the conditions brought into existence by the new discovery. Our reality-worlds, we find, require some alteration if the complicated economic, political, and social problems many major inventions create are to be satisfactorily met. The whole use of atomic energy both for peace and war is, of course, the clearest illustration in modern times of the reorientation required in thinking about our socio-economic-political structure.

The unplanned and unforeseeable effects of new inventions and discoveries on human beings and their social structures are illustrated in the following readings.

Gletkin looked at Rubashov with his usual expressionless gaze, and asked him, in his usual expressionless voice:

"Were you given a watch as a boy?"

Rubashov looked at him in astonishment. The most conspicuous trait of the Neanderthal character was its absolute humourlessness or, more exactly, its lack of frivolity.

"Don't you want to answer my question?" asked Gletkin.

"Certainly," said Rubashov, more and more astonished.

"How old were you when the watch was given you?"

"I don't quite know," said Rubashov, "eight or nine probably."

"I," said Gletkin in his usual correct voice, "was sixteen years old when I learnt that the hour was divided into minutes. In my village, when the peasants had to travel to town, they would go to the railway station at sunrise and lie down to sleep in the waiting-room until the train came, which was usually at about midday; sometimes it only came in the evening or next morning. These are the peasants who now work in our factories. For example, in my village is now the biggest steel-rail factory in the world. In the first year, the foremen would lie down to sleep between two emptyings of the blast furnace, until they were shot. In all other countries, the peasants had one or two hundred years to develop the habit of industrial precision and of the handling of machines. Here they only had ten years. If we didn't sack them and shoot them for every trifle, the whole country would come to a standstill, and the peasants would lie down to sleep in the factory yards until grass grew out of the chimneys and everything became as it was before. Last year a women's delegation came to us from Manchester in England. They were shown everything, and afterwards they wrote indignant articles, saying that the textile workers in Manchester would never stand such treatment. I have read that the cotton industry in Manchester is two hundred years old. I have also read, what the treatment of the workers there was like two hundred years ago, when it started. You,

Comrade Rubashov, have just used the same arguments as this women's delegation from Manchester. You, of course, know better than these women. So one may wonder at your using the same arguments. But then, you have something in common with them: you were given a watch as a child. . . ."   (ARTHUR KOESTLER, *Darkness at Noon*.) [3]

The mechanical works of man, invention after invention, supervene upon each other with unpredictable consequences to the life of man. They have changed him, where they prevail, from an independent farmer or herder or artisan into a dependent member of a factory organization. The division of labor which the machine enables and the factory channels has thinned him down from a man living his life into a machine tender earning his living; it has diminished his vocational need for knowledge and reduced his skill to a few simple repetitive acts. By making of those, items in the clocklike sequence of the conveyer system, it has given him a fixed station in an associative order of enforced co-operation, a co-operation required not by the understanding and decision of the men at work, not even of the managers, but by the structure of the machine and the layout of the factory which the operation of that tool determines. The associations in which this sets a man are imposed, not chosen; they are external to his awareness and kept secret from his understanding. He stands no longer as the master of his tools and materials, as an artisan or craftsman with a proper name. He stands as a factory hand with a number. He is a psychosomatic gadget attached to a gargantuan automatic instrument. He is the servant of his tools and materials. He is exclusively a producer. But though a producer, he is not permitted to know either the components of his product, nor their original nature, nor their sources, nor how they came to him, nor what they cost, nor what it costs to make them over into his product, nor who buys his product, nor at what price. This knowledge is the monopoly of management. It is private property, a patent right, a trade secret, social and economic power. By virtue of it, it is the management and not the men, it is the factory and not the factory hands that is the producer. The hands count, like the cogs of a wheel, merely as interlocking fractions of a wound-up whole. The hands are *labor*, but management is industry. And because this is the case, labor tends to be hired and fired at the will of managements. Having established no rights in their industry, laborers have no power over their own support.* It is in order to attain this power and to share in the knowledge of the whole, where they otherwise count merely as replaceable parts, that they form

* See *The Federalist*, no. 10.

the conscious free organizations of workers called trades unions, with which they strive to guide and reshape the human effects of the unconscious hierarchical organization of work called industry.

Factory organization of work has brought city organization of life. Cities multiply and grow. The modern world is so pre-eminently an urban world because it is an industrial world. Men of industrial society live together as they work together, in great multitudes, interdependently, yet emotionally and intellectually isolated and unaware. As the factory is the workplace where the mechanic works by day to earn his living, the great city has become the market place where the mechanic spends by night to live his life. The fruits of his day's labor are consumed in his night's leisure. The industrial worker, automatized in his role of producer, is therein a bondsman. But unlike the preindustrial slave or serf, he becomes a free man in his role of consumer. Whereas his forebears lived on one, modern man lives on two, for the most part, incommensurable levels. The first is essentially a means; the other is genuinely an end. He is a producer and a consumer and he produces in order to consume. But machinery has set up an unprecedented dichotomy between production and consumption. It has led to the idea of an economy of abundance in thoughts and things, in goods, services, and ideas. Contracting space and condensing time, bringing all the diverse products of all the cultures of the world within the reach of industrial men, machinery has inverted the natural and historic relationships between them. It has exalted production into the end and degraded consumption into the means. Thus it has brought on a sharp conflict between the economy of industry and the nature of man. For we are born consumers, and all our doings, our thinking, playing, eating, drinking, fighting, loving, making things, and destroying things, insofar as they are spontaneous and not compelled, are consummatory. For example, we own an instinct of workmanship, which skill and knowledge channel and express, by whose virtue every craftsman is a creative artist, and every artist a free man consuming his energies in free activities. Since even the serf and slave of preindustrial times owned a modicum of this inner freedom, the values of day-life and of night-life were not separated and opposed for him. But they are so for us. They are so for us because modern production is mass production based on the division of labor. Its morcellation into ever more numerous and separate steps creates a vacuum for the instinct of workmanship; its automatic machines replace craftsmanship by engineering and demote knowledge and skill to superfluities. At the same time they enable men to produce infinitely more. Where an economy of abundance obtains and is left free to work itself out, it does in fact reduce the hours of labor, increase the hours of leisure, and raise the standard of living beyond all precedent. But it simultaneously deepens the distinction between living and earning a living, between leisure and labor, between consumption and production. Consequent on the psychic distance which separates these modes of human activity and ensuing upon their correlative forms of association—i.e., private monopolies, state trusts, and the like—come their business cycles with their booms and busts, their *crises plethoriques,* with the familiar "starvation amid plenty." Supervening upon these come then the plans to resolve them devised by medievalists, communists, and fascists, and implemented with such tragic consequences in lands like Spain and Poland, Russia, Italy, and Germany.

(HORACE M. KALLEN, *The Liberal Spirit.*) [4]

PROPAGANDA

In contrast to the unplanned social effects of inventions and artifacts are the deliberate and systematically planned effects brought about by individuals or organizations propagandizing for some cause. In propaganda, an interested party is trying to persuade or somehow manipulate other individuals to see the significances he, the propagandist, wants them to see in the events going on around him, in certain people, objects or programs of action. By getting people to call significant what he, the propagandist, wants them to feel as significant, the propagandist hopes of course that people will then act in such a way that his own cause is promoted—whether this is merely the purchase of some advertised product or the overthrow of a social system.

The effective and skilled propagandist must have an accurate understanding of the reality-worlds of the people he deals with. He must know their loyalties, their anxieties, their hopes, their fears, and their aspirations. He must know what appeals will appear plausible to them, what needs and frustrations he can exploit and exacerbate in order to guide people along the road he wants them to follow. Hitler's master propagandist, Joseph Goebbels, said that "to see with the eyes of the masses is the whole riddle of successful propaganda."

A wide variety of principles and techniques are exploited by the skillful propagandist according to the situation confronting him.

Sometimes he will capitalize on existing symbols and attitudes, connecting the product or idea he is trying to sell to significances people already value highly; sometimes the propagandist will have to take a slower course and, through a long process of apparent "explanation" or "education" or the dissemination of "news," try to build up significances he wants people to perceive. Sometimes he will stage events which arouse public interest and pose a problem with an implied solution. Sometimes he will try to bewilder and puzzle people, break down their assumptions, try to increase their anxiety and frustration so that his "solution," when it comes along, will appear to be the answer people are looking for.

The successful propagandist is skillful in creating all kinds of devices to capture attention. He knows the enormous value of repetition. He knows that appeals must be simple and readily understood. He knows that the best appeal will fail if it is not properly timed. He knows what individuals, what symbols have prestige value and for what kinds of people. And, among other things, the skillful propagandist knows that propaganda has certain limitations, that people are likely to become sophisticated and make what is called the "propaganda discount" if the same simple tactic is used too often or too long without bringing satisfying consequences in its wake.

While we tend to associate most propaganda with individuals or causes that seem in some way anti-social, we should not forget that propaganda is "good" or "bad" depending upon the significances we ourselves attach to the cause the propagandist is trying to promote. Effective promotion for the Red Cross, for the United Nations, or for some charitable enterprise often follows well-known propaganda strategy and techniques, although of course the individual who is sincerely promoting a cause in the interests of human welfare is apt to be quickly censored if he knowingly indulges in misrepresentation and falsification.

The excerpts which follow illustrate the strategy of the successful propagandist. The first is a discussion by Hitler of techniques of persuasion and war propaganda; the other excerpt describes one of the ways in which the Russian Communists systematically use education for propaganda purposes, and is an eloquent protest against some of the effects of mass suggestion.

WAR PROPAGANDA

At the time of my attentive following of all political events, the activities of propaganda had always been of extremely great interest to me. In it I saw an instrument which just the Socialist-Marxist organizations mastered and knew how to apply with expert skill. I learned very soon that the right use of propaganda represents an art which was and remained almost entirely unknown to the *bourgeois* parties. Only the Christian-Socialist movement, especially during Lueger's time, acquired a certain virtuosity with this instrument and it owed much of its success to it.

But it was shown only during the War to what enormously important results a suitably applied propaganda may lead. Unfortunately, everything has to be studied on the other side; for the activity on our side was more than modest in this respect. However, the very failure of the entire enlightenment on the side of the Germans—a fact which was bound to stare in the face of every soldier—now caused me to occupy myself still more thoroughly with this question.

There was often more than enough time for thinking, but it was unfortunately the enemy who gave us only too good an object lesson.

For what we failed to do in this direction was made up by the enemy with really unheard-of skill and ingenious deliberation. I learned infinitely much more from the enemy's war propaganda. But time marched on without leaving an impression on the brains of those who most of all should have taken this as a lesson; partly because they deemed themselves too clever to take lessons from others, and partly because the honest will to do so was lacking.

Was there any propaganda at all on our side?

To my regret, I can only answer no. Everything that was actually undertaken in this direction was so incomplete and wrong from the very first moment that it not only did not help, but sometimes did considerable harm.

Insufficient in form its nature was psychologically wrong: this was necessarily the result of a careful examination of the German war propaganda.

It seemed that one was not quite clear about the first question, namely: Is war propaganda a means or an end?

It is a means, and therefore it has to be judged from the point of view of the end. But its form has to be properly adapted to the aim which it serves. But it is also clear that the importance of its aim can be a different one according to the point of view of the general demand and that therefore propaganda is also defined differently according to its inner value. But the aim for which the War was fought was the most sublime and the most overpowering which man is able to imagine: it was the freedom and independence of our nation, the assurance of subsistence for the future, and—the honor of the nation; something that, despite all opinions to the contrary, is still present today or rather ought to be present, as nations without honor usually lose their freedom and independence, which, in turn, corresponds only to a higher justice, as generations of scoundrels without honor do not deserve freedom. But he who wants to be a cowardly slave must not and cannot have any honor, as thus honor would become subject to general disdain within the shortest time. . . .

During the War propaganda was a means to an end, but this in turn was the German people's fight for existence; thus propaganda could therefore be looked upon only from the principles proper to it. Then the most cruel weapons were humane if they conditioned the quicker victory, and beautiful were only those methods which helped the nation to secure the dignity of its freedom.

This was the only possible attitude towards the question of war propaganda in such a fight for life or death.

Had the so-called responsible authorities made this clear to themselves, the uncertainty about the form and the application of this weapon would never have originated; for this is also only a weapon, though a frightful one, in the hand of the expert.

The second question of actually decisive importance was the following: To whom has propaganda to appeal? To the scientific intelligentsia or to the less educated masses?

It has to appeal forever and only to the masses!

Propaganda is not for the intelligentsia or for those who unfortunately call themselves by that name today, but scientific teaching. But propaganda is in its contents as far from being science as perhaps a poster is art in its presentation as such. A poster's art lies in the designer's ability to catch the masses' attention by outline and color. The poster for an art exhibition has to point only to the art of the exhibition; the more it succeeds in this, the greater therefore is the art of the poster itself. Further, the poster is to give to the masses an idea of the importance of the exhibition, but it is in no way to be a substitute for the art represented by the exhibition. Therefore, he who wants to occupy himself with art itself has really to study more than the poster; yes, for him it is by far not sufficient merely to "walk through" the exhibition. It may be expected of him that he bury himself in the individual works by thoroughly looking them over so that then he may gradually form a just opinion for himself.

The situation is a similar one with what today we call propaganda.

The task of propaganda lies not in a scientific training of the individual, but rather in directing the masses towards certain facts, events, necessities, etc., the purpose being to move their importance into the masses' field of vision.

The art now is exclusively to attack this so skillfully that a general conviction of the reality of a fact, of the necessity of an event, that something that is necessary is also right, etc., is created. But as it is not and cannot be science in itself, as its task consists of catching the masses' attention, just like that of the poster, and not in teaching one who is already scientifically experienced or is striving towards education and knowledge, its effect has always to be directed more and more towards the feeling, and only to a certain extent to so-called reason.

All propaganda has to be popular and has to adapt its spiritual level to the perception of the least intelligent of those towards whom it intends to direct itself. Therefore its spiritual level has to be screwed the lower, the greater the mass of people which one wants to attract. But if the problem involved, like the propaganda for carrying on a war, is to include an entire people in its field of action, the caution in avoiding too high spiritual assumptions cannot be too great.

The more modest, then, its scientific ballast is, and the more it exclusively considers the feelings of the masses, the more striking will be its success. This, however, is the best proof whether a particular piece of propaganda is right or wrong, and not the successful satisfaction of a few scholars or "aesthetic" languishing monkeys.

This is just the art of propaganda that it, understanding the great masses' world of ideas and feelings, finds, by a correct psychological form, the way to the attention, and further to the heart, of the great masses. That our super-clever heads never understand this proves only their mental inertia or their conceit.

But if one understands the necessity of the attitude of the attracting skill of propaganda towards the great masses, the following rule then results:

It is wrong to wish to give propaganda the versatility of perhaps scientific teaching.

The great masses' receptive ability is only very limited, their understanding is small, but their forgetfulness is great. As a consequence of these facts, all effective propaganda has to limit itself only to a very few points and to use them like slogans until even the very last man is able to imagine what is intended by such a word. As soon as one sacrifices this basic principle and tries to become versatile, the effect will fritter away, as the masses are neither able to digest the material offered nor to retain it. Thus the result is weakened and finally eliminated.

(ADOLF HITLER, *Mein Kampf.*) [5]

This brief account of the moral education of the younger generation may well be closed with an account of the presentation of the first passport to a group of boys and girls on reaching the age of sixteen. The system of internal passports, as we know, was employed in old Russia to aid the police in combating subversion and revolution. It has generally been regarded as a mark of autocracy and despotism. Abolished at the time of the revolution, it was revived when Stalin was well advanced on the road to power. And now an effort is being made to convert the passport into a thing of honor, a badge of citizenship, a credential of maturity. An entire page of the December 4, 1955, issue of *Komsomol'skaia Pravda,* the official organ of the League of Young Communists, is devoted to reporting the giving of passports to sixteen-year-olds in Ivanovo, an important industrial center. The day is declared a holiday; parents, relatives, and friends are present; some old Bolsheviks grace the occasion; and the hall is draped in flags and flowers. The major speech, delivered by F. E. Titov, First Secretary of the Provincial Committee of the Communist Party, follows:

Dear Young Friends!

Today you receive your first passport. This is a great event in your life.

A Soviet citizen!

How proudly and majestically this sounds! An honorable and responsible title. We are proud that the creator of the first socialist state in the world and its great citizen was Vladimir Ilich Lenin.

Everything that is advanced and progressive is linked with the title of Soviet citizen. Guard then the high honor of this title!

You are happy that you live in the land where the Basic Law is our Constitution, the most democratic in the world. In our country Soviet man enjoys, not only the greatest rights and civic responsibilities, but also all conditions for the realization of these rights.

Before you are bright roads. For you doors to schools, colleges, institutes, mills, and factories are wide open. Take advantage then of these great rights—study, work, harden yourselves!

Prepare yourselves to enter life. You are receiving the first passport in a heroic time, when our multi-national free people-creator selflessly struggles for the building of a Communist society. Mighty is the spectacle of this gigantic construction. In mills and in factories, on collective farms and virgin lands, in lumber mills, in institute laboratories, at the helm of the ship and the wheel of the locomotive, millions of Soviet people create their happy present and future.

Much is being built also in our Ivanovo province! Already has begun the filling of the bed of the Gorky sea, which will feed a tremendous electric station on the Volga; work on the Volga-Ivanovo canal is started, new machine-construction mills and textile factories are being erected, blocks of new homes are being built, cities are being improved.

Young friends, these deeds await your hands!

You are receiving your first passport at the time of the glorious fifty years of the first Russian revolution. Fifty years ago the older generation of the working class, your grandparents, under the leadership of Vladimir Ilich Lenin raised the banner of the struggle for a bright future. To the lot of your generation falls the joy of carrying the banner to a victorious conclusion.

So, guard, preserve and develop the glorious traditions of your people, of our great Communist Party! Herein lies the guarantee of your success.

You receive your first passport in the city of Ivanovo, in a city of glorious revolutionary tradition of the working class, about whose heroic struggle Vladimir Ilich Lenin not infrequently spoke with admiration. The working class of Ivanovo created the prototype of the Soviet power—one of the first of the Soviets of workers' deputies in Russia. The toilers of the city with their own hands transformed Ivanovo from a wretched backward city into a great industrial center. During the years of the civil and Patriotic wars Ivanovo gave thousands of heroes who selflessly defended their socialist Motherland.

Years will pass, many of you will become highly trained and distinguished workers, engineers, teachers, pilots, tankists, navigators. Perhaps life will scatter you over the wide reaches of your Motherland, but you received your first passport in Ivanovo. Be proud of it. Do not disgrace the glorious name of this revolutionary city.

The response to the Secretary of the Party was made by a girl, Ira Shaldina, under the title "I Am a Citizen of the Soviet Union: I Am

Sixteen Years Old." It suggests clearly that the occasion partook of the nature of an initiation ceremony into adult life. But let Ira speak:

I hold here in my hands my first passport. Now I am no longer a little one and everybody will treat me as a grownup. And this means that I too must from now on treat everything in life seriously, evaluate all my actions correctly, be more strict toward myself and my comrades.

With this passport I will be admitted as an equal in any mill, in any factory. There I shall be able to strengthen with my work the might of my Motherland. On reaching the age of eighteen I will go with this passport to the polling place and exercise my right of electing the organs of my government.

I am now mature and the demands made upon an adult will be made upon me everywhere—at home or in school. Heretofore, when a serious request was made to me and I was not inclined to act upon it, I usually said: "I am still a little one."

And I was left alone. What could be expected of a little one? But now, from today, I shall be unable to say to anyone: "It is too hard for me, I am a little one." The young guardsmen and the young builders of Komsomolsk-on-Amur had exactly the same passports. To them the Soviet passport and the Komsomol card were the civic conscience of the Soviet man. These people feared no difficulties, they knew no fear, and during the years of the great ordeals of their Motherland, they said they were grown up and could help their people, their country in her hour of trial.

On the first page of my passport the name of my city is given, a city of revolutionary traditions, a city of glorious textile workers; and I want to carry the esteemed labor honor of our Ivanovo through the entire great country, no matter where I may happen to live and work. Everywhere I shall proclaim with pride: "I am from Ivanovo where I first received my passport."

Sixteen years! How many times have I dreamed about this! I wanted to be sixteen faster. Not infrequently I would go to the library and ask for some interesting book, but I would receive the offending words: "You will understand nothing in this book; when you are older, then if you please, you may read it." Or in the summer, I would ask for a boat—no permission; they would say: no boats for children under sixteen. And how many times in school when we were noisy during recitation, the teacher would reprimand us: "Aren't you ashamed of yourselves to behave thus; you will soon receive your passport." But we consoled ourselves in the meantime with the thought that we were still children, and much would be forgiven us.

And at last today this carefree time of childhood is gone. Everybody will regard us now as adults, respect our opinions, and even consult us. For we are no longer children.

Today is the usual work-day, not even Sunday. But I noticed from early in the morning that the people of our city talked about today's celebration of presenting the first passport, and were making preparations for the occasion. The entire city rejoiced in this celebration, rejoiced for us, the sixteen-year-olds.

I would like to see everywhere in our province, in all other provinces and regions of our Motherland, the same celebration marking the day of presenting the first passport. Let this day serve as a good beginning, an example to all. The warm attention given us, young boys and girls, obliges us to study yet harder and to be worthy of the high honor paid us today in this hall.

Here several hundred people are gathered. And everyone present will now remember us, remember our faces and know that we are grownups. This puts great demands upon us. When I was coming here this evening I somehow forgot about the school. All of us girls talked on the way about the concert, about dances, and in general thought of nothing but the pleasant time we anticipated. But now as I hold my passport and look into the warm faces of the people, I feel ashamed for my grade of 3 in literature. This I myself admit to you honestly. I promise to correct this 3 and in the future shall try with all my strength never to receive such a mark either in school or in my work.

In a year I shall be in the tenth grade. I know from my older friends that in the tenth grade they write essays on the theme of the Soviet man, what sort of person he should be, what it means to love one's Motherland. If I should write an essay on this theme, I would certainly begin with a description of today's celebration. I would write about the concern of our Motherland for us, the sixteen-year-old ones, about what our Motherland and the entire Soviet people expect of us, about how we shall carry our first passport throughout our lives with honor.

Among the honored guests were several old Bolsheviks. They chatted with the sixteen-year-olds about life in prerevolutionary times. They related how they had "passed their youth" in stifling and damp factory buildings, in conspiratorial quarters, in jails, in *katorga*. One of them, a participant in three revolutions, addressed the youth formally. Here are a few of his remarks:

> We, old men, are happy in your happiness. It appears that our struggle was not in vain. You were born in the Soviet time, you did not experience forced labor, you did not hear the clanking of chains. We lived differently. Listen to this old document of pre-revolutionary life—a contract of the sale by a peasant of his son, a sale into slavery to a factory owner of Ivanovo, one Grachev. . . .
>
> To what desperation could capitalism lead a man if he is forced to sell his own son into slavery! . . .
>
> And so, my friends, guard with honor your Soviet passport, carry it with honor. May it ever remind you of the great rights and duties of a free Soviet citizen.

One can only wonder if these young people had ever read Lenin's castigation of the system of internal passports. In the fateful year of 1903, when he was laying the foundations of Bolshevism, he characterized as follows this instrument for controlling the movements, the behavior, and the mind of the Russian peasant:

> What does this mean, this *freedom to move from place to place?* It means that the peasant must be free to go where he pleases, to move wherever he wishes, to choose for himself the village or the town he prefers, without having to ask for permission. It means that passports must be abolished in Russia too (in foreign countries passports were abolished long ago), that no police officer, no Zemsky Nachalnik must be allowed to stop any peasant from settling down or working wherever he pleases. The Russian peasant is still the serf of the officials to such an extent that he is not free to move to a town, or free to settle in a new district. The Minister issues orders that the governors should not allow *unauthorized* settlement! The governor knows better than the peasant what place is good for the peasant! The peasant is a child who dares not move without authority! Is this not serfdom, I ask you?

Where and when in previous history has man transformed an instrument of tyranny into such a glorious symbol of freedom? Perhaps the Bolsheviks are actually changing human nature, in accordance with their boasts, and they are doing this under the banners of the sacred "cause of Lenin."

(GEORGE S. COUNTS, *The Challenge of Soviet Education.*) [6]

RESISTANCE TO CHANGE

Assumptions and beliefs tend to be self-validating and to preserve themselves so long as they serve the function for which they were intended. New experience filters through them and happenings contradictory to them tend to be screened out. If such happenings are perceived, the effect may be minimal and transitory because memory too is selective. Furthermore, because of certain assumptions or beliefs we often actively avoid exposing ourselves to contradictory data or situations, deliberately limiting our possibilities of encountering new experiences which might disturb us. We tend to read a newspaper more or less congenial to our own views; we are more likely to go hear a speaker if we think he will in some way confirm our beliefs rather than upset them. A further conservative force is, of course, social support and social pressure, a wide consensus of approval of certain patterns and assumptions from respected social groups.

So it is that our assumptions, our attitudes, our prejudices, and our beliefs tend to nourish themselves, providing through their effects upon our perceiving and behaving more or less constant confirmation of their own correctness and utility. This process is by no means a highly conscious one. It generally takes some unusual or extraordinary occurrence to make us conscious of our normal deeply rooted assumptions. Surprises, paradoxes, mistakes, and disappointments challenge the neutral world composed of the assumptions we have hitherto taken for granted.

And so people quite naturally put up some resistance to anything new that appears to them likely to threaten the form, stability, and continuity of their present reality-world, *if* this reality-world itself is quite satisfying. In the fundamentals of a way of life slow change is the general rule: an idea may appear dangerous or radical in one era, but may be readily accepted a century later. The biologist, Louis Agassiz, said that "every great scientific truth goes through three stages. First, people say it conflicts with the Bible. Next, they say it has been discovered before. Lastly, they say they have always believed it."

When we look back upon the resistances men and women have put up in the past to ideas, inventions, or discoveries that have since proven enormously beneficial, the story seems incredibly stupid. Included in the next readings is an example of the hard sledding which a relatively modern innovation had before it was accepted. Hundreds of different examples might have been included, for the documented stories of man's resistance to change are abundant indeed: how railroads were first regarded as nonsensical and how farmers, among others, protested against them because they felt the noise of the railroads would prevent their cattle from grazing and their hens from laying eggs. Even such distinguished men as Ruskin and Daniel Webster inveighed against railroads. The automobile was at first called a fanatical device, and it was even argued before the British Association for the Advancement of Science that the horseless carriage would never be widely used because the human driver "has not the advantage of the intelligence of the horse in shaping his path." The story of Robert Fulton's steamboat—"Fulton's Folly"—is familiar to every American school child. Fulton himself wrote: "Never did a single encouraging remark, a bright hope, a warm wish, cross my path." The printing press developed strong resistance, not only from calligraphers whose craft was threatened by the new device, but especially by those who foresaw some of the social consequences if the masses began to read. In 1671, the Governor of Virginia stated as his official opinion, "I thank God we have no free schools nor printing; and I hope we shall not have these hundred years. For learning has brought disobedience and heresy and sects into the world; and printing has divulged them and libels against the government. God keep us from both." So the story goes for the telegraph, the airplane, the incandescent lamp, the typewriter. Even the humble bathtub, when first introduced into the United States, was objected to as "an epicurean innovation from England designed to corrupt the democratic simplicity of the Republic"; when President Fillmore had a bathtub installed in the White House in 1851, he was promptly charged with the crime of "monarchical luxury."

The reading which follows is the detailed account by an historian of the resistance by an established institution to a new invention which had consequences for the structure of the institution itself. Although the passage is rather long, we include it because such detailed and fascinating accounts are rare.

In the early days of the last war, when armaments of all kinds were in short supply, the British, I am told, made use of a venerable field piece that had come down to them from previous generations. The honorable past of this light artillery stretched back, in fact, to the Boer War. In the days of uncertainty after the fall of France, these guns, hitched to trucks, served as useful mobile units in the coast defense. But it was felt that the rapidity of fire could be increased. A time-motion expert was, therefore, called in to suggest ways to simplify the firing procedures. He watched one of the gun crews of five men at practice in the field for some time. Puzzled by certain aspects of the procedures, he took some slow-motion pictures of the soldiers performing the loading, aiming, and firing routines.

When he ran these pictures over once or twice, he noticed something that appeared odd to him. A moment before the firing two members of the gun crew ceased all activity and came to attention for a three-second interval, extending throughout the discharge of the gun. He summoned an old colonel of artillery, showed him the pictures, and pointed out this strange behaviour. What, he asked the colonel, did it mean? The colonel, too, was puzzled. He asked to see the pictures again. "Ah," he said when the performance was over, "I have it. They are holding the horses."

This story, true or not, and I am told it is true, suggests nicely the pain with which the human being accommodates himself to changing conditions. The tendency is apparently involuntary and immediate to protect oneself against the shock of change by continuing in the presence of altered situations the familiar habits, however incongruous, of the past.

Yet, if human beings are attached to the known, to the realm of things as they are, they also, regrettably for their peace of mind, are incessantly attracted to the unknown and to things as they might be. As Ecclesiastes glumly pointed out, men persist in disordering their settled ways and beliefs by seeking out many inventions.

The point is obvious. Change has always been a constant in human affairs; today, indeed, it is one of the determining characteristics of our civilization. In our relatively shapeless social organization, the shifts from station to station are fast and easy. More important for our immediate purpose, America is fundamentally an industrial society in a time of tremendous technological development. We are thus constantly presented with new devices or new forms of power that, in their refinement and extension, continually bombard the fixed structure of our habits of mind and behaviour. Under such conditions, our salvation, or at least our peace of mind, appears to depend upon how successfully we can in the future become what has been called in an excellent phrase a completely "adaptive society."

It is interesting, in view of all this, that so little investigation, relatively, has been made of the process of change and human responses to it. Recently psychologists, sociologists and cultural anthropologists have addressed themselves to the subject with suggestive results. But we are still far from a full understanding of the process, and still farther from knowing how we can set about simplifying and assisting an individual's or a group's accommodation to new machines or new ideas.

With these things in mind, I thought it might be interesting and perhaps useful to examine historically a changing situation within a society; to see if from this examination we can discover how the new machines or ideas that introduced the changing situation developed; to see who introduces them, who resists them, what points of friction or tension in the social structure are produced by the innovation, and perhaps why they are produced and what, if anything, may be done about it. For this case study, the introduction of continuous-aim firing in the United States Navy has been selected. The system, first devised by an English officer in 1898, was introduced into our Navy in the years 1900–1902.

I have chosen to study this episode for two reasons. First, a navy is not unlike a society that has been placed under laboratory conditions. Its dimensions are severely limited; it is beautifully ordered and articulated; it is relatively isolated from random influences. For these reasons the impact of change can be clearly discerned, the resulting dislocations in the structure easily discovered and marked out. In the second place, the development of continuous-aim firing rests upon mechanical devices. It, therefore, presents for study a concrete, durable situation. It is not like many other innovating reagents—a Manichean heresy, or Marxism, or the views of Sigmund Freud—that can be shoved and hauled out of shape by contending forces or conflicting prejudices. At all times we know exactly what continuous-aim firing really is. It will be well now to describe, as briefly as possible, *what it is.*

The governing fact in gunfire at sea is that the gun is mounted on an unstable platform—a rolling ship. This constant motion obviously complicates the problem of holding a steady aim. Before 1898 this problem was solved in the following elementary fashion. A gun pointer estimated the range of the target—ordinarily about 2800 yards. He then raised the gun barrel to give the gun the elevation to carry the shell to the target at the estimated range. This was acomplished by turning a small wheel on the gun mount that operated the elevating gears. With the gun thus fixed for range, the gun pointer peered through open sights, not unlike those on a small rifle, and waited until the roll of the ship brought the sights on the target. He then pressed the firing button that discharged the gun. There were, by 1898, on some naval guns, telescope sights which naturally enlarged the image of the target for the gun pointer. But these sights were rarely used by gun pointers. They were lashed securely to the gun barrel and, recoiling with the barrel, jammed back against the unwary pointer's eye. Therefore, when used at all, they were used only to take an initial sight for purposes of estimating the range before the gun was fired.

Notice now two things about the process. First of all, the rapidity of fire was controlled by the rolling period of the ship. Pointers had to wait for the one moment in the roll when the sights were brought on the target. Notice also this: There is in every pointer what is called a "firing interval"—the time lag between his impulse to fire the gun and the translation of this impulse into the act of pressing the firing button. A pointer, because of this reaction time, could not wait to fire the gun until the exact moment when the roll of the ship brought the sights onto the target; he had to will to fire a little before, while the sights were off the target. Since the firing interval was an individual matter, varying obviously from man to man, each pointer had to estimate, from long practice, his own interval and compensate for it accordingly.

These things, together with others we need not here investigate, conspired to make gunfire at sea relatively uncertain and ineffective. The pointer, on a moving platform, estimating range and firing interval, shooting while his sight was off the target, became in a sense an individual artist.

In 1898, many of the uncertainties were removed from the process, and the position of the gun pointer radically altered, by the introduction of continuous-aim firing. The major change was that which enabled the gun pointer to keep his sight and gun barrel on the target throughout the roll of the ship. This was accomplished by altering the gear ratio in the elevating gear to permit a pointer to compensate for the roll of the vessel by rapidly elevating and depressing the gun. From this change another followed. With the possibility of maintaining the gun always on the target, the desirability of improved sights became immediately apparent. The advantages of the telescope sight, as opposed to the open sight, were for the first time fully realized. But the existing telescope sight, it will be recalled, moved with the recoil of the gun and jammed back against the eye of the gunner. To correct this, the sight was mounted on a sleeve that permitted the gun barrel to recoil through it without moving the telescope.

These two improvements—in elevating gear and sighting—eliminated the major uncertainties in gunfire at sea and greatly increased the possibilities of both accurate and rapid fire.

You must take my word for it that this changed naval gunnery from an art to a science, and that gunnery accuracy in the British and our Navy increased about 3000 per cent in six years. This doesn't mean much except to suggest a great increase in accuracy. The following comparative figures may mean a little more. In 1899 five ships of the North Atlantic Squadron fired five minutes each at a lightship hulk at the conventional range of 1600 yards. After twenty-five minutes of banging away two hits had been made on the sails of the elderly vessel. Six years later one naval gunner made 15 hits in one minute at a target 75 x 25 feet at the same range; half of them hit in a bull's eye 50 inches square.

Now with the instruments (the gun, elevating gear, and telescope), the method, and the results of continuous-aim firing in mind, let us turn to the subject of major interest: how was the idea, obviously so simple an idea, of continuous-aim firing developed; who introduced it; and what was its reception?

Introduction of an idea

The idea was the product of the fertile mind of the English officer, Admiral Sir Percy Scott. He arrived at it in this way, while, in 1898, he was the captain of H. M. S. *Scylla*. For the previous two or three years he had given much thought, independently and almost alone in the British Navy, to means of improving gunnery. One rough day, when the ship, at target practice, was pitching and rolling violently, he walked up and down the gun deck watching his gun crews. Because of the heavy weather they were making very bad scores. Scott noticed, however, that one pointer was appreciably more accurate than the rest. He watched this man with care and saw, after a time, that he was unconsciously working his elevating gear back and forth in a partially successful effort to compensate for the roll of the vessel. It flashed through Scott's mind at that moment that here was the sovereign remedy for the problems of inaccurate fire. What one man could do partially and unconsciously, perhaps all men could be trained to do consciously and completely.

Acting on this assumption, he did three things. First, in all the guns of the *Scylla*, he changed the gear ratio in the elevating gear, previously used only to set the gun in fixed position for range, so that a gunner could easily elevate and depress the gun to follow a target throughout the roll. Second, he rerigged his telescopes so that they would not be influenced by the recoil of the gun. Third, he rigged a small target at the mouth of the gun, which was moved up and down by a crank to simulate a moving target. By following this target as it moved, and firing at it with a subcalibre rifle rigged in the breech of the gun, the pointer could practice every day. Thus equipped, the ship became a training ground for gunners. Where before the good pointer was an individual artist, pointers now became trained technicians, fairly uniform in their capacity to shoot. The effect was immediately felt. Within a year the *Scylla* established records that were remarkable.

At this point I should like to stop a minute to notice several things directly related to, and involved in, the process of innovation. First, the personality of the innovator. I wish there were space to say a good deal about Admiral Sir Percy Scott. He was a wonderful man. Three small bits of evidence must suffice, however. First, he had a certain mechanical ingenuity. Second, his personal life was shot through with frustration and bitterness. There was a divorce, and a quarrel with the ambitious Lord Charles Beresford—the sounds of which, Scott liked to recall, penetrated to the last outposts of empire. Finally, he possessed, like Swift, a savage indignation directed ordinarily at the inelastic intelligence of all constituted authority—especially the British Admiralty.

There are other points worth mention here. Notice first that Scott was not responsible for the invention of the basic instruments that made the reform in gunnery possible. This reform rested upon the gun itself, which as a rifle had been in existence on ships for at least forty years; the elevating gear, which had been, in the form Scott found it, a part of the rifled gun from the beginning; and the telescope sight, which had been on shipboard at least eight years. Scott's contribution was to bring these three elements, appropriately modified, into a combination that made continuous-aim firing possible for the first time. Notice also that he was allowed to bring these elements into combination by accident, by watching the unconscious action of a gun pointer endeavoring through the operation of his elevating gear to correct partially for the roll of his vessel.

The prepared mind is not enough

Scott, as we have seen, had been interested in gunnery; he had thought about ways to increase accuracy by practice and improvement of existing machinery; but able as he was, he had not been able to produce on his own initiative and by his own thinking the essential idea and modify instruments to fit his purpose. Notice here finally, the intricate interaction of chance, the intellectual climate, and Scott's mind. Fortune (in this case the unaware gun pointer) indeed favors the prepared mind, but even fortune and the prepared mind need a favorable environment before they can conspire to produce sudden change. No intelligence can proceed very far above the threshold of existing data or the binding combinations of existing data. . . .

Educating the Navy

It was in 1900 that Percy Scott went out to the China Station as commanding officer of H.M.S. *Terrible.* In that ship he continued his training methods and his spectacular successes in naval gunnery. On the China Station he met up with an American junior officer, William S. Sims. Sims had little of the mechanical ingenuity of Percy Scott, but the two were drawn together by temperamental similarities that are worth noticing here. Sims had the same intolerance for what is called spit-and-polish and the same contempt for bureaucratic inertia as his British brother officer. He had for some years been concerned, as had Scott, with what he took to be the inefficiency of his own Navy. Just before he met Scott, for example, he had shipped out to China in the brand new pride of the fleet, the battleship *Kentucky.* After careful investigation and reflection he had informed his superiors in Washington she was not a battleship at all—"but a crime against the white race."

The spirit with which he pushed forward his efforts to reform the naval service can best be stated in his own words to a brother officer: "I am perfectly willing that those holding views different from mine should continue to live, but with every fibre of my being I loathe indirection and shiftiness, and where it occurs in high place, and is used to save face at the expense of the vital interests of our great service (in which silly people place such a childlike trust), I want that man's blood and I will have it no matter what it costs me personally."

From Scott in 1900 Sims learned all there was to know about continuous-aim firing. He modified, with the Englishman's active assistance, the gear on his own ship and tried out the new system. After a few months' training, his experimental batteries began making remarkable records at target practice. Sure of the usefulness of his gunnery methods, Sims then turned to the task of educating the Navy at large. In 13 great official reports he documented the case for continuous-aim firing, supporting his arguments at every turn with a mass of factual data. Over a period of two years, he reiterated three principal points: First, he continually cited the records established by Scott's ships, the *Scylla* and the *Terrible,* and supported these with the accumulating data from his own tests on an American ship; second, he described the mechanisms used and the training procedures instituted by Scott and himself to obtain these records; third, he explained that our own mechanisms were not generally adequate without modification to meet the demands placed on them by continuous aim-firing. Our elevating gear, useful to raise or lower a gun slowly to fix it in position for the proper range, did not always work easily and rapidly enough to enable a gunner to follow a target with his gun throughout the roll of the ship. Sims also explained that such few telescope sights as there were on board our ships were useless. Their cross wires were so thick or coarse that they obscured the target, and the sights had been attached to the gun in such a way that the recoil system of the gun plunged the eyepiece against the eye of the gun pointer.

This was the substance not only of the first but of all the succeeding reports written on the subject of gunnery from the China Station. It will be interesting to see what response these met with in Washington. The response falls roughly into three easily identifiable stages.

First stage: no response. Sims had directed his comments to the Bureau of Ordnance and the Bureau of Navigation; in both bureaus there was dead silence. The thing—claims and records of continuous-aim firing—was not credible. The reports were simply filed away and forgotten. Some indeed, it was later discovered to Sims' delight, were half eaten away by cockroaches.

Second stage: rebuttal. It is never pleasant for any man to have his best work left unnoticed by superiors, and it was an unpleasantness that Sims suffered extremely ill. In his later reports, beside the accumulating data he used to clinch his argument, he changed his tone. He used deliberately shocking language because, as he said, "They were furious at my first papers and stowed them away. I therefore made up my mind I would give these later papers such a form that they would be dangerous documents to leave neglected in the files." To another friend he added, "I want scalps or nothing and if I can't have 'em I won't play."

Sims gets attention

Besides altering his tone, he took another step to be sure his views would receive attention. He sent copies of his reports to other officers in the fleet. Aware, as a result, that Sims' gunnery claims were being circulated and talked about, the men in Washington were then stirred to action. They responded—notably through the Chief of the Bureau of Ordnance, who had general charge of the equipment used in gunnery practice—as follows: (1) Our equipment was in general as good as the British; (2) Since our equipment was as good, the trouble must be with the men, but the gun pointer and the training of gun pointers were the responsibility of the officers on the ships; (3) And most significant—continuous-aim firing was impossible. Experiments had revealed that five men at work on the elevating gear of a six-inch gun could not produce the power necessary to compensate for a roll of five degrees in ten seconds. These experiments and calculations demonstrated beyond peradventure or doubt that Scott's system of gunfire was not possible.

Only one difficulty is discoverable in these arguments; they were wrong at important points. To begin with, while there was little difference between the standard British equipment and the standard U. S. equipment, the instruments on Scott's two ships, the *Scylla,* and the *Terrible,* were far better than the standard equipment on our ships. Second, all the men could not be trained in continuous-aim firing until equipment was improved throughout the fleet. Third, the experiments with the elevating gear had been ingeniously contrived at the Washington Navy Yard—on solid ground. It had, therefore, been possible in the Bureau of Ordnance calculation, to dispense with Newton's first law of motion, which naturally operated at sea to assist the gunner in elevating or depressing a gun mounted on a moving ship. Another difficulty was of course that continuous-aim firing was in use on Scott's and some of our own ships at the time the Chief of the Bureau of Ordnance was writing that it was a mathematical impossibility. In every way I find this second stage, the apparent resort to reason, the most entertaining and instructive in our investigation of the responses to innovation.

Third stage: name calling. Sims, of course, by the high temperature he was running and by his calculated overstatement, invited this. He was told in official endorsements on his reports that there were others quite as sincere and loyal as he and far less difficult; he was dismissed as a crack-brain egotist; he was called a deliberate falsifier of evidence.

Sims gets action

The rising opposition and the character of the opposition was not calculated to discourage further efforts by Sims. It convinced him that he was being attacked by shifty, dishonest men who were the victims, as he said, of insufferable conceit and ignorance. He made up his mind, therefore, that he was prepared to go to any extent to obtain the "scalps" and the "blood" he was after. Accordingly he, a lieutenant, took the extraordinary step of writing the President of the United States, Theodore Roosevelt, to inform him of the remarkable records of Scott's ships, of the inadequacy of our own gunnery routines and records, and of the refusal of the Navy Department to act. Roosevelt, who always liked to respond to such appeals when he conveniently could, brought Sims back from China late in 1902 and installed him as Inspector of Target Practice, a post the naval officer held throughout the remaining six years of the Administration.

With this sequence of events (the chronological account of the innovation of continuous-aim firing) in mind, it is possible now to examine the evidence to see what light it may throw on our present interest—the origins of and responses to change in a society.

First, the origins. We have already analyzed briefly the origins of the idea. We have seen how Scott arrived at his notion. We must now ask ourselves, I think, why Sims so actively sought, almost alone among his brother officers, to introduce the idea into his service. It is particularly interesting here to notice again that neither Scott nor Sims invented the instruments on which the innovation rested. They did not urge their proposal because of pride in the instruments of their own design.

The Engineer and the Entrepreneur

The telescope sight had first been placed on shipboard in 1892 by Bradley Fiske, an officer of great inventive capacity. In that year Fiske had even sketched out on paper the vague possibility of continuous-aim firing, but his sight was condemned by his commanding officer, Robley D. Evans, as of no use. Instead of fighting for his telescope Fiske turned his attention to a range finder. But six years later Sims took over and became the engineer of the revolution.

I would suggest, with some reservations, this explanation: Fiske, as an inventor, took his pleasure in great part from the design of the device. He lacked, not so much the energy as the overriding sense of social necessity, that would have enabled him to *force* revolutionary ideas on the service. Sims possessed this sense. In Fiske we may here find the familiar plight of the engineer who often enough must watch the products of his ingenuity being organized and promoted by other men. These other promotional men, when they appear in the world of commerce, are called entrepreneurs. In the world of ideas they are still entrepreneurs.

Sims was one, a middle-aged man caught in the periphery (as a lieutenant) of the intricate webbing of a precisely organized society. Rank, the exact definition and limitation of a man's capacity at any given moment in his own career, prevented Sims from discharging all his exploding energies into the purely routine channels of the peacetime Navy. At the height of his powers he was a junior officer standing watches on a ship cruising aimlessly in friendly foreign waters. The remarkable changes in systems of gunfire to which Scott introduced him gave him the opportunity to expend his energies quite legitimately against the encrusted hierarchy of his society. He was moved, it seems to me, in part by his genuine desire to improve his own profession but also in part by rebellion against tedium, against inefficiency from on high, and against the artificial limitations placed on his actions by the social structure, in his case junior rank.

Responding to change

Now having briefly investigated the origins of the change, let us examine the reasons for what must be considered the weird response we have observed to this proposed change. Here was a reform that greatly and demonstrably increased the fighting effectiveness of a service that maintains itself almost exclusively to fight. Why then this refusal to accept so carefully documented a case; a case proved incontestably by records and experience? Why should virtually all the rulers of a society so resolutely seek to reject a change that so markedly improved its chances for survival in any contest with competing societies?

There are the obvious reasons that will occur to everyone—the source of the proposed reform was an obscure junior officer 8000 miles away; he was, and this is a significant factor, criticizing gear and machinery designed by the very men in the bureaus to whom he was sending his criticisms. And furthermore, Sims was seeking to introduce what he claimed were improvements in a field where improvements appeared unnecessary. Superiority in war, as in other things, is a relative matter, and the Spanish-American War had been won by the old system of gunnery. Therefore, it was superior even though of the 9500 shots fired, at varying but close ranges, only 121 had found their mark.

A less obvious cause appears by far the most important one. It has to do with the fact that the Navy is not only an armed force; it is a society. In the forty years following the Civil War, this society had been forced to accommodate itself to a series of technological changes—the steam turbine, the electric motor, the rifled shell of great explosive power, case-hardened steel armor, and all the rest of it. These changes wrought extraordinary changes in ship design, and, therefore, in the concepts of how ships were to be used; that is, in fleet tactics, and even in naval strategy. The Navy of this period is a paradise for the historian or sociologist in search of evidence of a society's responses to change.

To these numerous innovations, producing as they did a spreading disorder throughout a service with heavy commitments to formal organization, the Navy responded with grudging pain. It is wrong to assume, as civilians frequently do, that this blind reaction to technological change springs exclusively from some causeless Bourbon distemper that invades the military mind. There is a sounder and more attractive base. The opposition, where it occurs, of the soldier and the sailor to such change springs from the normal human instinct to protect oneself and more especially one's way of life. Military organizations are societies built around and upon the prevailing weapon systems. Intuitively and quite correctly the military man feels that a change in weapon portends a change in the arrangements of his society.

Think of it this way. Since the time that the memory of man runneth not to the contrary, the naval society has been built upon the surface vessel. Daily routines, habits of mind, social organization, physical accommodations, convictions, rituals, spiritual allegiances have been conditioned by the essential fact of the ship. What then happens to your society if the ship is displaced as the principal element by such a radically different weapon as the plane? The mores and structure of the society are immediately placed in jeopardy. They may, in fact, be wholly destroyed. It was the witty cliché of the 20's that those naval officers who persisted in defending the battleship against the apparently superior claims of the carrier did so because the battleship was a more comfortable home. What, from one point of view, is a better argument?

This sentiment would appear to account in large part for the opposition to Sims; it was the product of an instinctive protective feeling, even if the reasons for this feeling were not overt or recognized. The years after 1902 proved how right, in their terms, the opposition was. From changes in gunnery flowed an extraordinary complex of changes: in shipboard routines, ship design, and fleet tactics. There was, too, a social change. In the days when gunnery was taken lightly, the gunnery officer was taken lightly. After 1903, he became one of the most significant and powerful members of a ship's company, and this shift of emphasis naturally was shortly reflected in promotion lists. Each one of these changes provoked a dislocation in the naval society, and with man's troubled foresight and natural indisposition to break up classic forms, the men in Washington withstood the Sims onslaught as long as they could. It is very significant that they withstood it until an agent from outside—outside and above—who was not clearly identified with the naval society, entered to force change.

This agent, the President of the United States, might reasonably and legitimately claim the credit for restoring our gunnery efficiency. But this restoration by *force majeure* was brought about at great cost to the service and men involved. Bitternesses, suspicions, wounds were caused that it was impossible to conceal or heal.

Now this entire episode may be summed up in five separate points:

(1) The essential idea for change occurred in part by chance, but in

an environment that contained all the essential elements for change, and to a mind prepared to recognize the possibility of change.

(2) The basic elements—the gun, gear, and sight—were put in the environment by other men; men interested in designing machinery to serve different purposes, or simply interested in the instruments themselves.

(3) These elements were brought into successful combination by minds not interested in the instruments for themselves, but in what they could do with them. These minds were, to be sure, interested in good gunnery, overtly and consciously. They may also, not so consciously, have been interested in the implied revolt that is present in the support of all change. Their temperaments and careers indeed support this view. From gunnery, Sims went on to attack ship designs, existing fleet tactics, and methods of promotion. He lived and died, as the service said, a stormy petrel, a man always on the attack against higher authority, a rebellious spirit.

(4) He and his colleagues were opposed on this occasion by men who were apparently moved by three considerations: honest disbelief in the dramatic but substantiated claims of the new process; protection of the existing devices and instruments with which they identified themselves; and maintenance of the existing society with which they were identified.

(5) The deadlock between those who sought change and those who sought to retain things as they were was broken only by an appeal to superior force; a force removed from and unidentified with the mores, conventions, devices of the society. This seems to me a very important point. The naval society in 1900 broke down in its effort to accommodate itself to a new situation. The appeal to Roosevelt is documentation for Mahan's great generalization that no military service should or can undertake to reform itself. It must seek assistance from outside.

(ELTING E. MORISON, "A Case Study of Innovation.") [7]

The following selection details an aspect of the struggle between orthodoxy and liberalism in Christianity as it was reflected in the life of Joseph Priestley, minister of the Gospel and renowned scientist, whose discoveries formed the foundation of our modern knowledge of the chemistry of gases.

From his experiments on oxygen, Priestley went on to further experiments with the other gases he had discovered, and was making his first trials of nitrous oxide upon the lower animals when God summoned him once more to his position in the pulpit, that he might fight in the cause of the true faith.

For the beginning of a new era was being revealed in various other domains as well as in that of science. Industry was on the march. Adam Smith had just published his *Wealth of Nations*—the bible of free trade—in Edinburgh. In the political field, dissent was gaining power, and was wrestling for the Rights of Man; Parliament was discussing the younger Pitt's schemes of reform; in the oratorical duels between Fox and Burke, liberalism and conservatism were fighting for supremacy. Across the Channel, in France, the great Revolution was developing, and Britain was taking time by the forelock with her advance along the liberal path.

So notable a revolution, transforming political and social life, could not leave Christianity fixed in orthodox rigidity. The spirit of liberalism made its way into the houses of the clergy, especially those of the non-conformists, separating divines into two camps, those who clung to the traditional faith, and the Unitarians who regarded liberal ideas and the Rights of Man as a new revelation.

Joseph Priestley, the renovator of chemistry, was wholly on the side of the Unitarians. For him, who in the depths of his own soul had experienced the working of the *Zeitgeist* on behalf of new creations, for him whom God had commissioned to reconstruct the extant views of the universe, for him there could be no doubt that the new, the coming, expressed the will of the Lord.

How was it possible to suppose that the Church, God's earthly habitation, would retain the obsolete forms which had come down through the ages? Another day had dawned, the Church was not to remain a mere museum of contemplation; it must be infused with the spirit of liberalism; evolution must play its part in shaping the new life.

Joseph Priestley was at work in his laboratory when the dispute between the orthodox and the Unitarians began to disintegrate the churches. He abandoned his researches, for the Lord had summoned him to play a part in bringing about the new dispensation. He was the apostle of progress. Thenceforward this religious struggle was to dominate Priestley's life and determine his destinies.

Priestley resigned his post as literary companion to Lord Shelburn and accepted a call to a dissenting pulpit in Birmingham. A number of noted men were then living in that Midland city, and Priestley joined their circle. He became a member of the Lunar Society, a friend of Erasmus Darwin, poet and scientist, grandfather of the famous Charles Darwin; of James Watt, the manufacturer of steam engines; of William Murdock, the discoverer of gaslighting; and of Richard L. Edgeworth, who was working at optical telegraphs.

His close association with these distinguished men made Priestley's life in Birmingham very agreeable. The only thing that troubled the harmony of his existence was that he became more and more immersed in theological disputes, and that his sympathies with revolutionary France aroused a great deal of enmity.

After the taking of the Bastille, a reaction against the ideas of the French Revolution had begun. Burke's policy gained the victory over that of Fox, and in the churches the orthodox got the upper hand. To these latter the Unitarian minister Joseph Priestley, who was also infected with liberal ideas, was a Son of Belial, against whom everyone must be warned, were it only for his soul's salvation.

Priestley regularly mounted the steps of his pulpit, but the pews were empty. Numbers of his congregation were married, children were born to them, deaths took place, but no one would have anything to do with the ill-famed minister. When he met any of his people in the street and said "good morning" to them, they gave him the cut direct. Street arabs ran after him shouting: "Priestley be damned, damned, damned forever, forever!"

Why should he stick any longer to his cure? The sidesmen refused to obey the heretic any longer, and threw up their jobs. His neighbors drew away from contact with this Son of Belial; they moved to other houses, in less "infected quarters."

As obstinate as they, he sat alone in his forsaken dwelling, shunned by all. But now, when Priestley could no longer do his work as minister of the Gospel, he returned to the experiments on which he had been engaged at Calne, and to the records of them he had been writing when on his travels with Lord Shelburn. Was it not possible that God's inscrutable will had only involved him in this dispute that he might have time to learn more about nitrous oxide, to make further experiments upon it and to convince a refractory age of the reality of progress by presenting it with irrefutable chemical formulae?

Priestley had tied one of the animals upon which he was experimenting to the laboratory table, and was preparing the nitrous oxide which he intended to administer by inhalation, when there came a knock at the door. A friend, the only one who still had courage to visit the discredited house, came breathless to inform Priestley that the mob was approaching to set the place on fire, and that the experimenter's only chance of escaping death in the conflagration was to flee with the utmost speed. He would gladly have saved the apparatus so laboriously constructed, the manuscript books filled with notes in which years of work were recorded. Impossible, it was too late. The raging mob rounded the corner and a crowd was already storming the house. The investigator had barely time to escape by the back door before the place was in flames, the notebooks had been reduced to ashes and the laboratory (the first chemical laboratory to be well equipped with modern apparatus) lay in ruins.

The fugitive attempted to reorganize a new laboratory at Hackney, then on the outskirts of London, and to start life afresh there. The plan miscarried, for feeling ran high against him: in various localities he was burned in effigy as a revolutionist. One day leaflets were showered into the streets denouncing him as an enemy of King and State. France, meanwhile, offered to build him a laboratory in Paris, hailed him as a "knight of progress" and appointed him a *citoyen de la République*. As soon as this news reached England, everyone began to howl for Priestley's trial and execution as a traitor.

There was nothing left for him to do but flee like a hunted beast. He decided to cross the Atlantic, and found repose at length on American soil. The liberal United States made this distinguished man of science welcome. A delegation called on him in New York; Philadelphia offered him a professorship, but the exhausted Priestley declined the honor.

For a time the experimenter went on with his work, his last discovery being carbonic oxide, and he also wrote a few theological pamphlets; but by this time the zealous theologian and the protagonist of modern science was a weary and a broken man. He lingered ten years, dying in 1804 at the age of 71, his declining days being passed in retirement as a farmer at the confluence of the northeast and west branches of the Susquehanna, in Northumberland, Pennsylvania.

(RENÉ FULOP-MILLER, *Triumph over Pain*.) [8]

CREATIVITY

Anyone who observes the process of social change soon realizes that an indispensable role is played by pioneers who break through barriers with new ideas, new aesthetic forms, new social, religious, or economic formulations. To recognize the crucial role played by the creative individual is not to deny the obvious fact that no person —no matter what his talents or his abilities—can really be creative if the environment in which he is forced to live denies him potentialities for growth. Nor does the recognition of the role of the difference between the highly creative individual and the more average person in any way deny the fact that the creative individual is a product of his times. But even when the times are "right," the creative individual by no means has an easy time of it.

Our concern here is not the concern of the geneticist who tries to ferret out what biological reasons there may be to help explain why some individuals have such unusual creative talents. Our concern is with the understanding of the creative process itself. What does it seem to be, what are its characteristics? We have gathered here a few excerpts from individuals who have taken an interest in the creative process as such and from other individuals who describe their own experience when their creative imagination was at work.

In these excerpts it is acknowledged that nearly all people are creative to some extent and that the creative activity of the outstanding genius is an enhancement of normal human processes. There is general agreement that originality is dependent upon man's capacity to feel frustration and a dissatisfaction with some aspect of the established order, a dissatisfaction usually coupled with the sense of a potentiality not yet brought out. This sense of potentiality gives rise to the typical feeling of vague and inexpressible restlessness, the state of nervous excitement as the creative process begins to brew.

While the creator must break through the past, the past cannot be completely sloughed off. Several writers emphasize that creation must be preceded by a period of preparation in which knowledge and relevant experience are accumulated and organized, and in which there is a self-conscious attempt to increase one's sensitivity and discrimination.

Important in the process, too, is a capacity and a need to isolate oneself from the immediate demands of life in order to get the perspective that is possible only if one is not bounded by considerations of space and time. For this reason the creative person is often regarded by others as aloof or non-conformist. Einstein expressed this when he wrote: "My passionate interest in social justice and social responsibility has always stood in curious contrast to a marked lack of desire for direct association with men and women. I am a horse for single harness, not cut for tandem or team work. I have never belonged wholeheartedly to any country or state, to my circle of friends, or even to my own family. These ties have always been accompanied by a vague aloofness, and the wish to withdraw into myself increases with the years. Such isolation is sometimes bitter, but I do not regret being cut off from the understanding and sympathy of other men. I lose something by it, to be sure, but I am compensated for it in being rendered independent of the customs, opinions, and prejudices of others, and am not tempted to rest my peace of mind upon such shifting foundations." [9]

The creator who effects social change does not seek the eccentric or the novel for its own sake. Rather, he is pulled ahead by some aim not wholly in view, and the highly selective and directed creative process is sustained by a sense of value in the doing itself and the potential satisfaction that will be brought about by the resolution of the restlessness. The creative process generally involves personal courage of a high order: the creator must be prepared to be misunderstood, unappreciated, and lonesome.

Almost every creative person who has written about the creative process has assigned a very significant role to a period of unconscious gestation or incubation after the first flash of insight or inspiration has provided a clue as to the direction thought or activity might take. The real creator somehow discovers how to make good use of his unconscious by not forcing himself and by cultivating moments, hours, or days of relaxed meditation, so that his whole being will be free to explore new lines of inquiry or weigh alternative value-satisfactions.

After reading first-person accounts of the creative process and the attempts of others to conceptualize it, one still feels faced with a mystery. There is in the process of creation something primordial and universal, and at the same time something highly refined and unique. It is the capacity of the creative person to combine these two dimensions into a single transaction which helps to keep alive a fruitful tension between form and flow, stability and change—both for himself and for his less gifted fellow human beings.

The first selection below describes how creative ideas were born in the minds of a few individual scientists; the second selection sketches the birth and development of a new musical form, namely American jazz.

. . . Helmholtz . . . the great German physicist, speaking in 1891 at a banquet on his seventieth birthday, described the way in which his most important new thoughts had come to him. He said that after previous investigation of the problem "in all directions . . . happy ideas come unexpectedly without effort, like an inspiration. So far as I am concerned, they have never come to me when my mind was fatigued, or when I was at my working table. . . . They came particularly readily during the slow ascent of wooded hills on a sunny day." Helmholtz here gives us three stages in the formation of a new thought. The first in time I shall call Preparation, the stage during which the problem was "investigated . . . in all directions"; the second is the stage during which he was not consciously thinking about the problem, which I shall call Incubation; the third, consisting of the appearance of the "happy idea" together with the psychological events which immediately preceded and accompanied that appearance, I shall call Illumination.

And I shall add a fourth stage, of Verification, which Helmholtz does not here mention. Henri Poincaré, for instance, in the book *Science and Method*, which I have already quoted . . . describes in vivid detail the successive stages of two of his great mathematical discoveries. Both of them came to him after a period of Incubation (due in one case to his military service as a reservist, and in the other case to a journey), during which no conscious mathematical thinking was done, but, as Poincaré believed, much unconscious mental exploration took place. In both cases Incubation was preceded by a Preparation stage of hard, conscious, systematic, and fruitless analysis of the problem. In both cases the final idea came to him "with the same characteristics of conciseness, suddenness, and immediate certainty." . . . Each was followed by a period of Verification, in which both the validity of the idea was tested, and the idea itself was reduced to exact form. "It never happens," says Poincaré, in his description of the Verification stage, "that unconscious work supplies *ready-made* the result of a lengthy calculation in which we have only to apply fixed rules. . . . All that we can hope from these inspirations, which are the fruit of unconscious work, is to obtain points of departure for such calculations. As for the calculations themselves, they must be made in the second period of conscious work which follows the inspiration, and in which the results of the inspiration are verified and the consequences deduced. The rules of these calculations are strict and complicated; they demand discipline, attention, will, and consequently, consciousness." . . . In the daily stream of thought these four different stages constantly overlap each other as we explore different problems. An economist reading a Blue Book, a physiologist watching an experiment, or a business man going through his morning's letters, may at the same time be "incubating" on a problem which he proposed to himself a few days ago, be accumulating knowledge in "preparation" for a second problem, and be "verifying" his conclusions on a third problem. Even in exploring the same problem, the mind may be unconsciously incubating on one aspect of it, while it is consciously employed in preparing for or verifying another aspect. And it must always be remembered that much very important thinking, done for instance by a poet exploring his own memories, or by a man trying to see clearly his emotional relation to his country or his party, resembles musical composition in that the stages leading to success are not very easily fitted into a "problem-and-solution" scheme. Yet, even when success in thought means the creation of something felt to be beautiful and true rather than the solution of a prescribed problem, the four stages of Preparation, Incubation, Illumination, and the Verification of the final result can generally be distinguished from each other.

(GRAHAM WALLAS, *The Art of Thought.*) [10]

Like other American cultural forms, indeed, like the American people themselves, jazz is hybrid. As everybody knows by now, especially through such energetic efforts as those of *Esquire Magazine* and the author of *Jazz Record Book* and *Jazzmen,* jazz originated in and around New Orleans. Its ultimate source is Negro folk-music, work-songs that lightened their labor, dances and shouts that expressed relief from labor, religious songs and chants that expressed their devotion, the dance rhythms brought over from Africa that were preserved in such institutions as the slave-holidays in Congo Square, and the field songs which, unknown to white overseers who interpreted them as indications of contentment, often conveyed from one group of field-hands to another secret messages aiding the escape of fugitive slaves and slaves in trouble. Even in these early stages, this folk-music was not purely Negro, since elements of Scottish, Irish, and English balladry and strains from Baptist and Methodist hymnals had been incorporated into the music.

It was in New Orleans that a great transformation overtook this folk-music. Enjoying more opportunities and more freedom there than in most other Southern cities, the Negroes got, in a somewhat backhanded way, the impact of the French musical culture of that city. As servants, they heard at social occasions the predominantly French dance tunes: polkas, mazurkas, quadrilles. In the streets they heard marches played by brass bands. Many Negroes acquired, by purchase or as hand-me-downs, second-hand musical instruments, such as cornets, trombones, and clarinets. Having at first little or no opportunity for formal musical training, they experimented with the instruments without instructions, and began to form bands of their own. The increasing Negro social life of the city created a demand for more Negro musicians. Gradually, there evolved in the late nineteenth and early years of the twentieth century, an entire new style of band playing, originated on the whole by Negro musicians who had never had formal musical training.

There are four outstanding points to be noted about this development. First is the fact that the folk-music background of these Negroes caused them to try to reproduce, in their harmonies and in their generous use of slurred and wailing notes, as well as in their marked rhythms, the styles of singing and group improvisation that characterized their earlier vocal efforts, such as spirituals, blues, and work-songs.

Secondly, having had few music lessons, these early instrumentalists were never instructed in what NOT to do. They tried all sorts of effects that teachers would have told them were "improper" or "sour" or even "beyond the range of the instrument." In other words, they took an entirely fresh view of these instruments and their possibilities. Not knowing that certain kinds of noises that came out of their instruments were regarded by teachers as "incorrect," they took delight in making them and finding places where they sounded right. Not knowing that it was supposed to be impossible to reach certain high notes on a cornet, they reached for them and got them. Not knowing that a trombone was supposed to be an accompanying instrument, they played solos with it. They broke all the rules, and therefore they made tremendous discoveries.

I am told that a delegation of the brass section of the London Philharmonic Orchestra waited on Louis Armstrong when he was appearing in London, and demanded that he show them how he got his effects (which they had heard on records) "without the aid of some mechanical contrivance." Armstrong promptly played a *glissando* for them, from the lowest possible tone to a note a fifth higher than they had ever heard before on a cornet, *and down again,* without a single pause or break in its magnificent fluid continuity.

Third, they restored to music something that Western music had all but lost a couple of hundred years ago as the result of the division of labor between composer and performer. In ordinary musical situations the performer, following a score, tries to interpret accurately the composer's intention. These early jazz musicians, however, had no score to follow and in many cases would not have been able to read it if they had. Partly because of the simplicity of the folk-themes they played, partly because the musicians sometimes didn't know what they were supposed to do and had to make something up for themselves as they went along, and partly out of sheer musical exuberance as they achieved greater mastery of their instruments, all jazz musicians improvised, both in solo and in group work. The skill and ingenuity of improvisation became more and more impressive as time went on. It was not long before every good band was a crew of skilled improvisers, each player influencing and being influenced by his fellows. Every performance of an old theme therefore became a new creation. In other words, the performer and composer were rolled back into one, restoring to music a spontaneity and zest which the white world had almost forgotten could exist.

Fourth, and this is perhaps the most important point: the work of these New Orleans musicians represents the first and perhaps only time in which a folk-music was enabled to continue to develop as folk-music, *but* with the technological advantages of modern instruments and their orchestral possibilities. If the Negroes had been left in the fields, their folk-music would have continued like other folk-music, Scottish, African, Western American, etc., primitive and charming, with no more technical resources than could be offered by bagpipes, tomtoms, crude string instruments, and the like. If, on the other hand, the Negroes had been fully assimilated into New Orleans life, they would have forgotten in a generation or two their folk backgrounds, and they would have been culturally assimilated into the white world, and their children's children would have struggled note by note over the compositions of Ethelbert Nevin.

What happened, of course, was neither of these things. In one way they shared the New Orleans culture, but in another way they didn't. They were both within the white culture and outside it. However unjust or unfortunate this situation may have been (and it continues so to this day), it meant that Negroes were forced back onto their older folk culture and pushed forward into a new culture at one and the same time. They therefore did the only possible thing: they fused the two strains of influence. In so doing, they unwittingly gave to American culture as a whole one of the greatest gifts any minority has brought: a new musical synthesis of urban sophistication with folk feeling.

(S. I. HAYAKAWA, "Reflections on the History of Jazz.)" [11]

LEADERSHIP

The leader is a particular kind of creator, a person who is able to generate confidence in himself under a particular set of circumstances, and who has an unusual ability to understand how other people see things. The leader senses certain common aspects of the reality-worlds of others and devises courses of action that dem-

onstrate to them a comforting or rewarding degree of correspondence between the interpretation he gives a situation and the consequences of action based on that interpretation.

Different kinds of situations or different historical eras generate
different types of leaders. The unique qualities of each individual
who becomes a leader seem to be brought into operation only in
those particular transactional situations that provide an opportunity
for them to emerge. A comparison of the kind of leadership described and advocated by Laotzu and that described and advocated
by Machiavelli brings into sharp relief the difference between democratic leadership based on common consensus and mutual trust
and leadership based on power, force, and cunning. But whatever
the circumstances and whatever the field within which the leader
operates, a common quality of all leaders is the capacity to make
value-judgments that other people perceive as likely to lead to
effective action—action which the leader implements and makes
possible through some scheme or organization.

While the followers of any leader may regard his pronounce-
ments as absolute and eternal, the leader himself is often quite
aware of the tentativeness of his assumptions. He may therefore be
unusually sensitive to outside impressions and clues which will help
him make better value-judgments based on more valid assumptions. Horace Greeley wrote of Lincoln: "He was not a born king
of men . . . but a child of the people, who made himself a great
persuader, therefore a leader, by dint of firm resolve, patient effort
and dogged perseverance. He slowly won his way to eminence and
fame by doing the work that lay next to him—doing it with all his
growing might—doing it as well as he could, and learning by his
failure, when failure was encountered, how to do it better. . . . He
was open to all impressions and influences, and gladly profited by
the teachings of events and circumstances, no matter how adverse
or unwelcome. There was probably no year of his life when he was
not a wiser, cooler and better man than he had been the year
preceding." [12]

In some of the readings below, the chief characteristic of the
leader is revealed as his capacity to make value-judgments concerned with what goals or aims to pursue—the type of value-judgments we called "what-for" judgments. The great leader generally

has the capacity to express these goals in language that people can readily understand. Even more important is his ability to show people what the abstractions and goals he is talking about actually refer to in concrete situations. For example, Lenin, writing in 1920 during the early years of the Russian Revolution, stressed that "without labor, and without struggle, book knowledge about Communism, obtained from Communist brochures and other writings, is absolutely worthless for it would continue the old gap between theory and practice. . . . The generation which is now fifteen years old and which in 10–20 years will live in a Communist society *must so conceive the aims of learning that every day in every village, in every city the young should actually perform some task of social labor, be it ever so small, be it ever so simple.*" [13]

If a person is to sustain a position of leadership, it is imperative that ways and means be found quickly to co-ordinate action so people will at least have a feeling that the leader's goals stand a good chance of being achieved. Here the leader's value-judgment is concerned with "how-to-do" decisions rather than "what-for" decisions. It should be stressed that goals and means are quite interdependent; if there is no confidence in the means proposed or no satisfaction obtained after taking action based on certain means, then the leader will lose his position in favor of someone else who appears better able to show the way.

Another quality of the great political, religious, or scientific leader is his capacity to judge immediate and short-term events in terms of long-range goals, exhibiting what may often be felt by his followers to be an exasperating patience or casualness in the face of frustrations or reversals. But it is this very quality of being able to keep his eye on long-range objectives that gives the leader perspective and resourcefulness in meeting new situations.

The passages below from Machiavelli and Plato describe the leader who rules by craft and cunning and are in sharp contrast to the excerpts from Laotzu. The final selection is an analysis of the "secret" of Gandhi's leadership.

HOW laudable it is for a prince to keep good faith and live with integrity, and not with astuteness, every one knows. Still the experience of our times shows those princes to have done great things who have had little regard for good faith, and have been able by astuteness to confuse men's brains, and who have ultimately overcome those who have made loyalty their foundation.

You must know, then, that there are two methods of fighting, the one by law, the other by force: the first method is that of men, the second of beasts; but as the first method is often insufficient, one must have recourse to the second. It is therefore necessary for a prince to know well how to use both the beast and the man. This was covertly taught to rulers by ancient writers, who relate how Achilles and many others of those ancient princes were given to Chiron the centaur to be brought up and educated under his discipline. The parable of this semi-animal, semi-human teacher is meant to indicate that a prince must know how to use both natures, and that the one without the other is not durable.

A prince being thus obliged to know well how to act as a beast must imitate the fox and the lion, for the lion cannot protect himself from traps, and the fox cannot defend himself from wolves. One must therefore be a fox to recognise traps, and a lion to frighten wolves. Those that wish to be only lions do not understand this. Therefore, a prudent ruler ought not to keep faith when by so doing it would be against his interest, and when the reasons which made him bind himself no longer exist. If men were all good, this precept would not be a good one; but as they are bad, and would not observe their faith with you, so you are not bound to keep faith with them. Nor have legitimate grounds ever failed a prince who wished to show colourable excuse for the non-fulfilment of his promise. Of this one could furnish an infinite number of modern examples, and show how many times peace has been broken, and how many promises rendered worthless, by the faithlessness of princes, and those that have been best able to imitate the fox have succeeded best. But it is necessary to be able to disguise this character well, and to be a great feigner and dissembler; and men are so simple and so ready to obey present necessities, that one who deceives will always find those who allow themselves to be deceived.

I will only mention one modern instance. Alexander VI did nothing else but deceive men, he thought of nothing else, and found the occasion for it; no man was ever more able to give assurances, or affirmed things with stronger oaths, and no man observed them less; however, he always succeeded in his deceptions, as he well knew this aspect of things.

It is not, therefore, necessary for a prince to have all the above-named qualities, but it is very necessary to seem to have them. I would even be bold to say that to possess them and always to observe them is dangerous, but to appear to possess them is useful. Thus it is well to seem merciful, faithful, humane, sincere, religious, and also to be so; but you must have the mind so disposed that when it is needful to be otherwise you may be able to change to the opposite qualities. And it must be understood that a prince, and especially a new prince, cannot observe all those things which are considered good in men, being often obliged, in order to maintain the state, to act against faith, against charity, against humanity, and against religion. And, therefore, he must have a mind disposed to adapt itself according to the wind, and as the variations of fortune dictate, and, as I said before, not deviate from what is good, if possible, but be able to do evil if constrained.

A prince must take great care that nothing goes out of his mouth which is not full of the above-named five qualities, and, to see and hear him, he should seem to be all mercy, faith, integrity, humanity, and religion. And nothing is more necessary than to seem to have this last quality, for men in general judge more by the eyes than by the hands, for every one can see, but very few have to feel. Everybody sees what you appear to be, few feel what you are, and those few will not dare to oppose themselves to the many, who have the majesty of the state to defend them; and in the actions of men, and especially of princes, from which there is no appeal, the end justifies the means. Let a prince therefore aim at conquering and maintaining the state, and the means will always be judged honourable and praised by every one, for the vulgar is always taken by appearances and the issue of the event; and the world consists only of the vulgar, and the few who are not vulgar are isolated when the many have a rallying point in the prince. A certain prince of the present time, whom it is well not to name, never does anything but preach peace and good faith, but he is really a great enemy to both, and either of them, had he observed them, would have lost him state or reputation on many occasions.

(MACHIAVELLI, *The Prince.*) [14]

Again, truth should be highly valued; if, as we were saying, a lie is useless to the gods, and useful only as a medicine to men, then the use of such medicines should be restricted to physicians; private individuals have no business with them.

Clearly not, he said.

Then if any one at all is to have the privilege of lying, the rulers of the State should be the persons; and they, in their dealings either with enemies or with their own citizens, may be allowed to lie for the public good. But nobody else should meddle with anything of the kind; and although the rulers have this privilege, for a private man to lie to them in return is to be deemed a more heinous fault than for the patient or the pupil of a gymnasium not to speak the truth about his own bodily illnesses to the physician or to the trainer, or for a sailor not to tell the captain what is happening about the ship and the rest of the crew, and how things are going with himself or his fellow sailors.

Most true, he said.

If, then, the ruler catches anybody beside himself lying in the State, "Any of the craftsmen, whether he be priest or physician or carpenter," he will punish him for introducing a practice which is equally subversive and destructive of ship or State.

Most certainly, he said, if our idea of the State is ever carried out.

(PLATO, *The Republic*) [15]

> A sound leader's aim
> Is to open people's hearts,
> Fill their stomachs,
> Calm their wills,
> Brace their bones
> And so to clarify their thoughts and cleanse their needs
> That no cunning meddler could touch them:
> Without being forced, without strain or constraint,
> Good government comes of itself.
>
> (LAOTZU, *The Way of Life*.) [16]

> A leader is best
> When people barely know that he exists,
> Not so good when people obey and acclaim him,
> Worst when they despise him.
> "Fail to honor people,
> They fail to honor you;"
> But of a good leader, who talks little,
> When his work is done, his aim fulfilled,
> They will all say, "We did this ourselves."
>
> (LAOTZU, *ibid.*) [17]

The less a leader does and says
The happier his people,
The more a leader struts and brags
The sorrier his people.
Often what appears to be unhappiness is happiness
And what appears to be happiness is unhappiness.
Who can see what leads to what
When happiness appears and yet is not,
When what should be is nothing but a mask

Disguising what should not be? Who can but ask
An end to such a stupid plot!
Therefore a sound man shall so square the circle
And circle the square as not to injure, not to impede:
The glow of his life shall not daze,
It shall lead.

(LAOTZU, *ibid.*) [18]

Why are rivers and seas lords of the waters?
Because they afford the common level
And so become lords of the waters.
The common people love a sound man
Because he does not talk above their level,
Because, though he lead them,
He follows them,
He imposes no weight on them;
And they in turn, because he does not impede them,
Yield to him, content:
People never tire of anyone
Who is not bent upon comparison.

(LAOTZU, *ibid.*) [19]

The secret of Gandhi's technique of influence, if not of his doctrine, seemed to me a little clearer after I had actually seen him practicing it at his prayer meeting. Not being able to understand his words was probably a help because the meaning of the non-verbal symbols was more apparent to me.

Gandhi is not merely trying to convert others to his opinions, in the normal Western way. He is obsessed with the notion of soul-force and tries both to use it himself to win over others to his beliefs and to generate it in them so that they can convert and activate still others. He has always preached that in the end this soul-force would take effect even upon his British enemies, and certainly now nobody is going to be able to prove that he was wrong.

The Gandhian concept of soul-force is a mystic one and seems to me basically unscientific. Yet the techniques based upon it are probably more effective than any techniques of mass influence that have been developed in our day. They not only win converts to a political cause, they not only generate enthusiasm and lasting morale, they not only produce zealous workers and volunteers for martyrdom, but they develop followers into dynamic leaders capable of attracting new followers —and they have totally refashioned the personalities of millions of Indians. This is no slight result and the man who has achieved it, the man who has perfected these techniques, is surely more than an exhibit in the sideshow of history.

It seems to me that without being able to describe in scientific terms
what he is doing, Gandhi operates in a most scientific manner. His
leadership is aimed at refashioning the personalities of those upon
whom it is exercised by modifying their central attitudes. It is not
enough that they believe in Indian independence. The attainment of
Indian independence must be their dominant interest in life and all
their lesser interests and attitudes must be rearranged to conform to the
psychic pattern of one who lives for Indian freedom. They must not
merely feel that violence is evil. Their whole mental field must be
colored by this intense central feeling about violence. They must not
merely support social reform but be dedicated to it as they are to
independence. They must breathe with a social reformer's lungs, see
with a social reformer's eyes, eat a social reformer's food.

How has Gandhi succeeded in imposing this pattern on the minds
of Indians? First of all, by becoming Gandhi, by adopting these central
attitudes himself. The Gandhi that the world knows today is not the
uxorious schoolboy husband who was once obsessed with his adolescent bride's body, the timid, awkward student in London, the sensitive,
bewildered young lawyer in South Africa wrestling with the problem
of religious belief. The present Gandhi is the result of years of rigorous
concentration on a few simple, emotionally significant ideas, of strict
self-discipline and intensive self-training.

This has produced the Gandhian personality, a combination of inner
peace, arising from a more total integration of all the elements in the
personality than most men achieve, with a tremendous, controlled release
of energy. One cannot talk to Gandhi or listen to him or even see him
from a distance without becoming aware both of the peace that is in
him and of the energy he radiates. They express themselves as well—
though necessarily less forcibly—in his literary style and even in the
structure of his thought. Because he is a poor semanticist and in many
ways a confused thinker, they express themselves best in certain non-
verbal symbols, chiefly in exemplary acts that are like propaganda and
sermons in action.

More than any other great leader of modern times, Gandhi follows
the sound rule of military leadership, that the best way to get men to
do anything is to show them by doing it yourself, to make them follow
by leading. At the first All-India Congress meeting that he attended as
a young man he was appalled by the filthy condition of the latrines and
suggested that this detracted from the dignity of the meeting. Everyone
agreed with him but said nothing could be done because the Untouchable latrine-cleaners were staging a protest strike. Gandhi, thereupon,

cleaned out the latrines himself, an unprecedented violation of caste rules as well as a gesture of religious humility and of leadership by example. He has never been able to define his views on Untouchability in words as clearly as he did by this gesture.

All his later life he has been startling, shocking, and ultimately capturing the imaginations of his compatriots by equally extraordinary exemplary acts, of which his symbolic gestures of passive resistance—like panning salt in violation of the excise laws—and his fasts in protest against the treatment of the Untouchable or the violation of his non-violent teachings by his own followers are the most famous.

Training by action, by deeds, another military principle, is also part of his secret. The convert to Gandhian ideas is immediately put to work developing a Gandhian personality by carrying on Gandhi-like activities. It is not enough for him to hold the right views and even to labor in the party cause. He must spin in his spare moments, because spinning is a personal act of satyagraha, which the individual can perform, while at the same time it helps the anti-British boycott. Direct, personal action, rather than mere participation in the general Congress campaign is one of the keynotes of Gandhi's teachings to his disciples. Help all you can on the big things but do some little thing yourself. Show that you are a real revolutionary not just by risking your life and going to jail, but by giving up tobacco, especially British tobacco, and alcohol. Learn Hindustani, your national tongue. Sit down to table with an Untouchable. . . .   (EDMOND TAYLOR, *Richer by Asia.*) [20]

SOCIAL CHANGE: ORDERLY OR VIOLENT?

Whether change will come about gradually and with a minimum of friction, or whether it will be accomplished by revolution or other forms of violence, depends in large part on the extent to which social leadership keeps a healthy balance between what the society can provide its people and their ever-increasing aspirations. Social change will be orderly only if individuals can preserve enough of their common reality-worlds to give direction to change. Whitehead wrote that "the major advances in civilization are processes which all but wreck the societies in which they occur:—like unto an arrow in the hand of a child. The art of free society consists first in the maintenance of the symbolic code; and secondly in fearlessness of revision, to secure that the code serves those purposes which satisfy an enlightened reason. Those societies which cannot combine reverence to their symbols with freedom of revision, must ultimately decay either from anarchy, or from the slow atrophy of a life stifled by useless shadows." [21] This principle was clearly recognized by Machiavelli, and was explicitly set forth in our own Declaration of Independence.

HE who desires or attempts to reform the government of a state, and wishes to have it accepted and capable of maintaining itself to the satisfaction of everybody, must at least retain the semblance of the old forms; so that it may seem to the people that there has been no change in the institutions, even though in fact they are entirely different from the old ones. For the great majority of mankind are satisfied with appearances, as though they were realities, and are often even more influenced by the things that seem than by those that are. The Romans understood this well, and for that reason, when they first recovered their liberty, and had created two Consuls in place of a king, they would not allow these more than twelve lictors, so as not to exceed the number that had served the king. Besides this, the Romans were accustomed to an annual sacrifice that could only be performed by the king in person; and as they did not wish that the people, in consequence of the absence of the king, should have occasion to regret the loss of any of their old customs, they created a special chief for that ceremony, whom they called the king of the sacrifice, and placed him under their high priest; so that the people enjoyed these annual sacrificial ceremonies, and had no pretext, from the want of them, for desiring the restoration of the kings. And this rule should be observed by all who wish to abolish an existing system of government in any state, and introduce a new and more liberal one. For as all novelties excite the minds of men, it is important to retain in such innovations as much as possible the previously existing forms. And if the number, authority, and duration of the term of service of the magistrates be changed, the titles at least ought to be preserved. This, as I have said, should be observed by whoever desires to convert an absolute government either into a republic or a monarchy; but, on the contrary, he who wishes to establish an absolute power, such as ancient writers called a tyranny, must change everything. . . .   (MACHIAVELLI, *The Discourses*.) [22]

We hold these truths to be self-evident: That all men are created equal; that they are endowed by their Creator with certain unalienable Rights; that among these are Life, Liberty and the pursuit of Happiness. That, to secure these rights, Governments are instituted among Men, deriving their just powers from the consent of the governed; That, whenever any Form of Government becomes destructive of these ends, it is the Right of the People to alter or to abolish it, and to institute a new Government, laying its foundation on such principles, and organizing its powers in such form, as to them shall seem most likely to effect their Safety and Happiness. Prudence, indeed, will dictate that Governments long established should not be changed for light and transient causes; and, accordingly, all experience hath shewn, that mankind are more disposed to suffer, while evils are sufferable, than to right themselves by abolishing the forms to which they are accustomed. But when a long train of abuses and usurpations, pursuing invariably the same Object, evinces a design to reduce them under absolute Despotism, it is their right, it is their duty, to throw off such Government, and to provide new Guards for their future security. . . .

(The Declaration of Independence.)

If change and the directed change that we believe to be progress are not experienced, if old assumptions fail to provide security, status, or the opportunities people think they deserve, then there are the makings of a mass movement or a revolution; old abstractions begin to lose all meaning and value; new symbols and slogans, created by new leaders, begin to take on new significances. History shows us how inevitable revolutions are when leaders or institutions insist upon defending and perpetuating old norms, refusing to modify or give way rapidly enough to social pressure that accumulates when hopes are long frustrated. Below are the ringing words of Tom Paine on the subject, followed by a program for revolution and a call to action by V. I. Lenin.

When we survey the wretched condition of Man, under the monarchical and hereditary systems of Government, dragged from his home by one power, or driven by another, and impoverished by taxes more than by enemies, it becomes evident that those systems are bad, and that a general Revolution in the principle and construction of Governments is necessary.

When is Government more than the management of the affairs of a Nation? It is not, and from its nature cannot be, the property of any particular man or family, but of the whole community, at whose expense it is supported; and though by force and contrivance it has been usurped into an inheritance, the usurpation cannot alter the right of things. Sovereignty, as a matter of right, appertains to the Nation only, and not to any individual; and a Nation has at all times an inherent indefeasible right to abolish any form of Government it finds inconvenient, and to establish such as accords with its interest, disposition, and happiness. The romantic and barbarous distinction of men into Kings and subjects, though it may suit the condition of courtiers, cannot that of citizens; and is exploded by the principle upon which Government are now founded. Every citizen is a member of the sovereignty; and, as such, can acknowledge no personal subjection: and his obedience can be only to the laws.

When men think of what Government is, they must necessarily suppose it to possess a knowledge of all the objects and matters upon which its authority is to be exercised. In this view of Government, the Republican system, as established by America and France, operates to embrace the whole of a Nation; and the knowledge necessary to the interest of all the parts, is to be found in the centre, which the parts by representation form; but the old Governments are on a construction that excludes knowledge as well as happiness; Government by monks, who know nothing of the world beyond the walls of a convent, is as inconsistent as Government by Kings.

What we formerly called Revolutions, were little more than a change of persons, or an alteration of local circumstances. They rose and fell like things of course, and had nothing in their existence or their fate that could influence beyond the spot that produced them. But what we now see in the world, from the Revolutions of America and France, is a renovation of the natural order of things, a system of principles as universal as truth and the existence of man, and combining moral with political happiness and national prosperity.

(Tom Paine, *The Rights of Man.*) 23

We base our faith entirely on Marx's theory; it was the first to transform socialism from a Utopia into a science, to give this science a firm foundation and to indicate the path which must be trodden in order further to develop this science and to elaborate it in all its details. It discovered the nature of present-day capitalist economy and explained the way in which the employment of workers—the purchase of labour power—the enslavement of millions of those possessing no property by a handful of capitalists, by the owners of the land, the factories, the mines, etc., is concealed. It has shown how the whole development of modern capitalism is advancing towards the large producer ousting the small one, and is creating the prerequisites which make a socialist order of society possible and necessary. It has taught us to see, under the disguise of ossified habits, political intrigues, intricate laws, cunning theories, the class struggle, the struggle between, on the one hand, the various species of the possessing classes, and, on the other hand, the mass possessing no property, the proletariat, which leads all those who possess nothing. It has made clear what is the real task of a revolutionary socialist party—not to set up projects for the transformation of society, not to preach sermons to the capitalists and their admirers about improving the position of the workers, not the instigation of conspiracies, but the organisation of the class struggle of the proletariat and the carrying on of this struggle, the final aim of which is the seizure of political power by the proletariat and the organisation of a socialist society.

. . . The class struggle of the proletariat is divided into: The economic fight (the fight against individual capitalists, or against the individual groups of capitalists by the improvement of the position of the workers) and the political fight (the fight against the Government for the extension of the rights of the people, i.e., for democracy, and for the expansion of the political power of the proletariat).

. . . Every economic fight of necessity turns into a political fight, and social-democracy must indissolubly combine the economic with the political fight into a united class struggle of the proletariat.

(V. I. LENIN, "Our Programme.") [24]

To be successful, the uprising must be based not on a conspiracy, not on a party, but on the advanced class. This is the first point. The uprising must be based on the revolutionary upsurge of the people. This is the second point. The uprising must be based on the *crucial point* in the history of the maturing revolution, when the activity of the vanguard of the people is at its height, when the *vacillations* in the ranks of the enemies, and *in the ranks of the weak, half-hearted, undecided friends of the revolution are at their highest point.* This is the third point. . . .

COMRADES!
I am writing these lines on the evening of the 6th. The situation is extremely critical. It is as clear as can be that delaying the uprising now really means death.

With all my power I wish to persuade the comrades that now everything hangs on a hair, that on the order of the day are questions that are not solved by conferences, by congresses (even by Congresses of Soviets), but only by the people, by the masses, by the struggle of armed masses. . . .

. . . We must at any price, this evening, to-night, arrest the Ministers, having disarmed (defeated if they offer resistance) the military cadets, etc.

We must not wait! We may lose everything!

Who should seize power?

At present this is not important. Let the Military Revolutionary Committee seize it, or "some other institution" which declares that it will relinquish the power only to the real representatives of the interests of the people, the interests of the Army (immediate offer of peace), the interests of the peasants (take the land immediately, abolish private property), the interests of the hungry.

It is necessary that all the boroughs, all regiments, all forces should be mobilised and should immediately send delegations to the Military Revolutionary Committee, to the Central Committee of the Bolsheviks, insistently demanding that under no circumstances is power to be left in the hands of Kerensky and Co. until the 7th, by no means!—but that the matter must absolutely be decided this evening or to-night.

History will not forgive delay by revolutionists who could be victorious to-day (and will surely be victorious to-day), while they risk losing much to-morrow, they risk losing all.

If we seize power to-day, we seize it not against the Soviets but for them.

Seizure of power is the point of the uprising; its political task will be clarified after the seizure.

It would be a disaster or formalism to wait for the uncertain voting of November 7. The people have a right and a duty to decide such questions not by voting but by force; the people have a right and duty in critical moments of a revolution to give directions to their representatives, even their best representatives, and not to wait for them.

This has been proven by the history of all revolutions, and the crime of revolutionists would be limitless if they let go the proper moment, knowing that upon them depends the *saving of the revolution,* the offer of peace, the saving of Petrograd, the saving from starvation, the transfer of the land to the peasants.

The government is tottering. We must *deal it the death blow* at any cost.

To delay action is the same as death.

Written November 6, 1917.
(V. I. Lenin, "On the Eve of October.") [25]

Change is inevitable, whether it comes about in orderly or violent fashion: all existence, including that of man, is an on-going process. But if the world which includes man is characterized by change, if the future is undetermined and undisclosed, if there is no such thing as absolute security or absolute peace of mind for any normal person who is plugged in to changing reality, how can man get along as well as he does without a crippling sense of doubt and anxiety? He apparently compensates for the probabilities of life by betting on certain constancies that sustain him. Our next and final chapter is concerned with the reality and function of man's faith.

8

Man's Faith [*][1]

> "Faith is the substance of things hoped for; the evidence of things not seen."   —Hebrews, XI:1

The experience of what we call "faith" is one of the most real, yet one of the most ineffable, that characterizes human living. If man did not have the capacity to maintain a faith, human nature would be far different from what it is; our thought and our behavior would lack a good deal of their consistency and conviction.

Faith plays a crucial role by holding our values together and integrating our various purposes. Without faith living would be a much more hit-and-miss affair. It would be directed much more by the contingencies of the immediate moment, and it would be empty of many of the value-overtones that we lump together as those that make our living "worthwhile."

Faith has turned notorious sinners into saints. By means of faith, ordinary men have performed extraordinary miracles. When faith has been aroused, dejected masses have been transformed into revolutionary crusaders. Faith, said the prophet, can move mountains.

Nearly all of us can testify to the reality of faith in our own lives —perhaps a faith we have experienced in something or someone, or that kept us plugging along when the going was unusually tough, or that altered our lives to some degree when we felt hopelessly bogged down. Perhaps we have experienced the feeling of emptiness and isolation when we have lost faith or had it shaken to its very roots.

* Notes to this chapter begin on p. 338.

MAN'S NEED FOR FAITH

Apparently one of the basic needs of most living organisms—certainly of human beings—is the need to preserve their sense of the worthwhileness of living. And with this need to preserve the worthwhileness of living goes a sense of responsibility to do so. Among other things, a person senses that he is a *chooser* of possibilities, an *experiencer* of situations where each flows into the next, a *fulfiller* of purposes whose ultimate destiny is beyond awareness and beyond description.

As we indicated much earlier, most individuals manage to preserve the sense of the worthwhileness of living by creating a reality-world—a system of interpretation—that functions with passable adequacy in an ever-changing cosmos. If the world and human behavior were entirely mechanistic and wholly predictable, there would of course be no need for faith. But, as we have repeatedly stressed, living is a process in which the future is undetermined, so that none of us can ever be completely certain about the next moment, the next day, or the next year. Living always involves some doubt, some risk.

We always have to do some guessing. All of us have to weigh some probabilities in a world which is an open system. In *The King and I* the bewildered King of Siam sings, "There are times I almost think I am not sure of what I absolutely know. Very often confusion in conclusion I concluded long ago." And the same idea was illustrated in an incident described by Carl Sandburg:

I have always enjoyed riding up front in a smoking car, in a seat back of the "deadheads," the railroaders going back to the home base. Their talk about each other runs free. . . . Once I saw a young fireman in overalls take a seat and slouch down easy and comfortable. After a while a brakeman in blue uniform came along and planted himself alongside the fireman. They didn't say anything. The train ran along. The two of them didn't even look at each other. Then the brakeman, looking straight ahead, was saying, "Well, what do you know today?" and kept on looking straight ahead till suddenly he turned and stared the fireman in the face, adding, "For sure." I thought it was a keen and intelligent question. "What do you know today—*for sure?*" I remember the answer. It came slow and honest. The fireman made it plain what he knew that day for sure: "Not a damn thing." [2]

Living therefore inevitably creates constant frustration. "Ye shall have tribulations," Jesus told his disciples. The frequency and severity of these frustrations, of course, depend upon the fortunes of our personal life histories, including our ability to meet frustrations. For millions of underprivileged people, there may be little other than frustration.

As we have constantly emphasized, our experience is so much a matter of probability, of the bets we are constantly making in a changing world as to the characteristics of things, of people, of events, that we *must* do something to put some order and predictability in the world in which we carry on our living. For we feel more comfortable if we think we can predict with a fair degree of accuracy the chain of events that will occur if we undertake a certain action. We crave certainty rather than doubt. We want a sense of direction in our thoughts and feelings. At the same time, we need to get along in the midst of some disorder and to accept human fallibility.

All of the constancies we create concerning things, people, and events help to provide us with enough interpretation to guess with fair accuracy the significances of the various signals that reach our sense organs. In this way we do not have to make fresh guesses at every turn. And all of these significances, we have seen, fuse and orchestrate together to give us our own unique reality-world: everything that has significance for us takes on its significance from our own personal reference center—in terms of *our own* purposes and *our own* actions. Samuel Butler makes the point in the following passage:

All our lives long, every day and every hour, we are engaged in the process of accommodating our changed and unchanged selves to changed and unchanged surroundings; living, in fact, is nothing else than this process of accommodation; when we fail in it a little we are stupid, when we fail flagrantly we are mad, when we suspend it temporarily we sleep, when we give up the attempt altogether we die. In quiet, uneventful lives the changes internal and external are so small that there is little or no strain in the process of fusion and accommodation; in other lives there is great strain, but there is also great fusing and accommodating power; in others great strain with little accommodating power. A life will be successful or not according as the power of accommodation is equal to or unequal to the strain of fusing and adjusting internal and external changes. [3]

Of particular importance to us in understanding what the concept of faith refers to is the function of the abstractions man has created through the ages in his perpetual attempt to bring order into disorder, to explain to himself various types of phenomena, or to find universal principles and guides for more ordered living, no matter what the unique purposes or circumstances of any one individual may be at the moment.

We have already observed that such abstractions as our scientific formulations, our maps, our legal, ethical, political, and religious systems, can be recalled by us or referred to at will, for they are spelled out, repeatable, and, for the time being, fixed. But just because these abstractions are by their very nature static, they can never be adequate substitutes for the personal meanings and significances assigned to events. The abstraction cannot take into account the unique contingency any unique individual is likely to meet in life, any more than a scientific formulation concerning the behavior of atoms can predict the behavior of a single atom. Nevertheless, these abstracted conceptions of reality that men have created play an indispensable role in helping us through our periods of frustration and doubt when our personal reality-world proves strained or inadequate.

When the tangibles of our personal reality-worlds break down, we can then turn to the intangibles, to certain relevant abstractions we have heard about that have been created by others and that seem to have proved useful to them in comparable situations. We can apply these abstractions to the problem we are faced with. We can make ourselves aware of creeds, beliefs, parables, maxims, symbols, and aesthetic representations of moods.

In this way we can bring some "universal truth," some moral principle, some creed or ideology to bear upon the unique situation with which we are involved at the moment. Men have the capacity to sense the experience of the immanent becoming transcendent, of the universal becoming particular, and the particular becoming universal, as some abstraction that is not bounded by intervals of time or units of space becomes relevant and functional in the concreteness of the "here-and-now" of their own personal reference center. For only when an abstraction becomes functional *for us*, can we experience what it refers to. Only then do we have a sense of its "reality."

It is then that we get an exciting or profound sense of a fleeting identity with something more lasting, more universal than our "selves"—a sense of identity with "truth," with "love," with "nature," with all mankind, or with "God." This sense of identification is reflected, for example, in the following Hindu prayer which is widely known and used in India:

> Thou art mother and thou art father,
> Thou art brother and thou art friend
> Thou art the bestower of knowledge
> Thou art all, my god of all gods. [4]

It is also illustrated in the well-known passage from Goethe's *Faust:*

FAUST: Who dares to say, my dear,
  "I believe in God?"
  Ask any priest or sage or seer,
  Their answer seems but mockery and fraud
  The inquirer to deride.
MARGARET: Then thou dost not believe?
FAUST: Sweet love, my meaning do not misconceive!
  Who dare Him name,
  Or who proclaim:
  "I believe in Him?"
  Who would care,
  Or who would dare,
  To say: "I believe Him not?"
  The All-embracing,
  The All-sustaining,
  Embraces and sustains He not
  Thee, me, Himself?
  Is not the vault of heaven above us?
  Lies the earth not firm beneath our feet?
  Do not with friendly glances
  Stars eternally arise?
  Gaze I not eye to eye on thee,
  And throng not all things
  To brain and heart of thee
  And weave in mystery eternal,
  Invisible, visible, near to thee?
  Fill thou thy heart, great as it is, with this,

And when this feeling gives thee perfect bliss,
Then call it what thou wilt,
Call it Bliss! Heart! Love! or God!
I have no name for it,
Feeling is all in all,
Name is but sound and smoke
Enshrouding heaven's glow. . . . [5]

Of course, most of us, most of the time, are not aware of faith or of the need for faith. For most of us, most of the time, seem able to cope with the routine problems of daily living in ways which do not require the support that faith can provide. The difference between those of us who carry on with life and the few who decide that life is not worth living and destroy themselves is reflected in a note written by a twenty-eight-year-old man just before he committed suicide.

Imagine a happy group of morons who are engaged in work. They are carrying bricks in an open field. As soon as they have stacked all the bricks at one end of the field, they proceed to transport them to the opposite end. This continues without stop and every day of every year they are busy doing the same thing. One day one of the morons stops long enough to ask himself what he is doing. He wonders what purpose there is in carrying the bricks. And from that instant on he is not quite as content with his occupation as he had been before.

I am the moron who wonders why he is carrying the bricks. The question, of course, has occurred to some of the other morons, but they have an ability which I lack. They are able to put it out of their minds, or to have faith that there *must* be a purpose though that purpose is unimaginable to them, or to get the feeling that life could be worthwhile though it had no purpose.

Most of us are so busy in the industry of living that we don't have time to ask ourselves what we are doing. . . .

Though I would avoid basing my suicide conclusion on the idea that life is unprofitable from a standpoint of happiness, I wish to bring out that our world can be miserable in spite of what is claimed by the romanticists.

First, let us acknowledge that there is not *one* world in which all of us live. There are billions of worlds: as many worlds as there are living organisms. Each world is different, as interpreted differently by the individual member of life—in accordance with whatever happens to be its own nervous structure, environment and background of experience.

There are some persons who live in beautiful worlds, others who live in worlds where suffering is in majority. And there are some, such as certain imbeciles, who live in worlds having neither pain nor pleasure to any considerable degree. No one can with validity claim his world to be the most real. We can observe, however, that the more a person studies his particular world—when his reasoning is in harmony with what we as a group judge to be sound—the more likely it is that he will grow discontent with what he sees around him. . . .

Upon re-reading this so-called essay, which has digressed into a personal note to a friend, I am disappointed that because of a lack of patience and ability I have so wretchedly treated a worthwhile subject. . . . As a final apology, I express my embarrassment for having written about life as if it were something of great significance when by all evidence it appears to be a farce. [6]

We seem to become aware of faith or the need for faith only under certain conditions; such as when some unexpected event negates some important aspect of our reality-world on which we have counted for constancy.

The nature of our reaction to the unexpected situation will, of course, depend on the nature of the occasion. And those situations that seem to invoke faith are situations where value, worth, and a sense of personal importance are involved. They are situations where we feel faced with some responsibility and some choice, situations where we feel personally isolated, or anxious, unless and until we can find something "beyond ourselves" to sustain us.

Sometimes we become aware of faith or of a need for faith when we lack confidence in our ability to cope with some *present* situation satisfactorily. At other times we become aware of faith or of a need for faith when we are haunted by the past, when we regret something we have or have not done, and when we blame ourselves for having made a mess of things. Sometimes we become aware of faith or of the need for faith when we are apprehensive about the *future,* when things look so uncertain that we do not know where to turn next or what to do to obtain now the confidence that we will do the right thing, i.e., that which will enable us to experience in the future what will prove most satisfying for us.

Under any of these conditions, we may come to doubt seriously the reliability of the reality-world we have built up so far—the only world we know. Our experience will become tinged with a sense of disappointment, of inadequacy, of incompleteness. We may feel a miserable inferiority, an overpowering depression, a gnawing guilt, or utter despair.

And yet far from being personal calamities, it is just such unpleasant or painful experiences that catalyze or increase faith. It is just such experiences that seem to be the preliminary conditions for faith. Faith is created and nourished by frustrations. The best-known statement of this in the Western world is found, of course, in Jesus' Sermon on the Mount, [7] where the multitude is told, among other things:

Blessed are the poor in spirit: for their's is the kingdom of heaven.
Blessed are they that mourn: for they shall be comforted.
Blessed are the meek: for they shall inherit the earth.
Blessed are they which do hunger and thirst after righteousness: for they shall be filled.
Blessed are they which are persecuted for righteousness' sake: for their's is the kingdom of heaven.
Blessed are ye, when men shall revile you, and persecute you, and shall say all manner of evil against you falsely, for my sake.

The relationship of frustrations to faith is also seen in the following excerpt from Schweitzer and the prayers of Fra Giovanni, Robert Louis Stevenson, and Tagore.

The most valuable knowledge we can have is how to deal with disappointments. All acts and facts are a product of spiritual power, the successful ones of power which is strong enough; the unsuccessful ones of power which is too weak. Does my behaviour in respect of love effect nothing? That is because there is not enough love in me. Am I powerless against the untruthfulness and the lies which have their being all around me? The reason is that I myself am not truthful enough. Have I to watch dislike and illwill carrying on their sad game? That means that I myself have not yet completely laid aside small-mindedness and envy. Is my love of peace misunderstood and scorned? That means that I am not yet sufficiently peace-loving.

The great secret of success is to go through life as a man who never gets used up. That is possible for him who never argues and strives with men and facts, but in all experience retires upon himself, and looks for the ultimate cause of things in himself.

No one who is always striving to refine his character can ever be robbed of his idealism, for he experiences in himself the power of the ideas of the good and the true. When he sees far too little of the external results at which he is aiming, he knows nevertheless that he is producing as much as his character allows; it is only that success has not yet begun, or that it is as yet hidden from him. Where there is power, there some result or other is produced. No ray of sunlight is ever lost, but the green which it wakes into existence needs time to sprout, and it is not always granted to the sower to live to see the harvest. All work that is worth anything is done in faith.

The knowledge of life, therefore, which we grown-ups have to pass on to the younger generation will not be expressed thus: "Reality will soon give way before your ideals," but "Grow into your ideals, so that life can never rob you of them." If all of us could become what we were at fourteen, what a different place the world would be!

As one who tries to remain youthful in his thinking and feeling, I have struggled against facts and experience on behalf of belief in the good and the true. At the present time when violence, clothed in life, dominates the world more cruelly than it ever has before, I still remain convinced that truth, love, peaceableness, meekness, and kindness are the violence which can master all other violence. The world will be theirs as soon as ever a sufficient number of men with purity of heart, with strength, and with perseverance think and live out the thoughts of love and truth, of meekness and peaceableness.

All ordinary violence produces its own limitations, for it calls forth an answering violence which sooner or later becomes its equal or its superior. But kindness works simply and perseveringly; it produces no strained relations which prejudice its working; strained relations which already exist it relaxes. Mistrust and misunderstanding it puts to flight, and it strengthens itself by calling forth answering kindness. Hence it is the furthest-reaching and the most effective of all forces.

All the kindness which a man puts out into the world works on the heart and the thoughts of mankind, but we are so foolishly indifferent that we are never in earnest in the matter of kindness. We want to topple a great load over, and yet will not avail ourselves of a lever which would multiply our power a hundred-fold.

There is an unmeasured depth of truth in that strange saying of Jesus: "Blessed are the meek, for they shall inherit the earth."

(ALBERT SCHWEITZER, *Memoirs of Childhood and Youth.*) [8]

I salute you:
There is nothing I can give you which you have not; but there is much, very much, that while I cannot give it you can take. No heaven can come to us unless our hearts find rest in it today. Take heaven! No peace lies in the future which is not hidden in this present little instant. Take peace! The gloom of the world is but a shadow. Behind it, yet

within our reach, is joy. There is radiance and glory in the darkness could we but see; and to see we have only to look. I beseech you to look.

Life is so generous a giver. Welcome it. Grasp it and you touch the angel's hand that brings it to you. Everything we call a trial, a sorrow, or a duty, believe me that angel's hand is there. The gift is there, and the wonder of an overshadowing presence.

Life is so full of meaning and purpose, so full of beauty beneath its covering, that you will find earth but cloaks your heaven. Courage then to claim it: that is all! But courage you have—and the knowledge that we are pilgrims together, wending through unknown country . . . home. And so at this time I greet you; not quite as the world sends greetings, but with profound esteem, and with the prayer that for you, now and forever, the day breaks and the shadows flee away.

(FRA GIOVANNI.)

Lord, behold our family here assembled. We thank Thee for this place in which we dwell; for the love that unites us; for the peace accorded us this day; for the hope with which we expect the morrow; for the health, the work, the food, and the bright skies, that make our lives delightful; for our friends in all parts of the earth, and our friendly helpers in this foreign isle. Let peace abound in our small company. Purge out of every heart the lurking grudge. Give us grace and strength to forbear and to persevere. Offenders, give us the grace to accept and to forgive offenders. Forgetful ourselves, help us to bear cheerfully the forgetfulness of others. Give us courage and gaiety and the quiet mind. Spare to us our friends, soften to us our enemies. Bless us, if it may be, in all our innocent endeavours. If it may not, give us the strength to encounter that which is to come, that we be brave in peril, constant in tribulation, temperate in wrath, and in all changes of fortune, and down to the gates of death, loyal and loving one to another. As the clay to the potter, as the windmill to the wind, as children to their sire, we beseech of Thee this help and mercy for Christ's sake.

(ROBERT LOUIS STEVENSON, *Prayers Written at Vailima*.) [9]

This is my prayer to Thee, my Lord—strike, strike at the root of
  penury in my heart.
Give me the strength lightly to bear my joys and sorrows.
Give me the strength to make my love fruitful in service.
Give me the strength never to disown the poor or bend my knees before
  insolent might.
Give me the strength to raise my mind high above daily trifles.
And give me the strength to surrender my strength to Thy will with
  love.   (RABINDRANATH TAGORE, "Gitanjali XXXVI.") [10]

WHAT FAITH INVOLVES

If the feeling, the process, or the state of mind we describe as "faith" is to become operationally real for us, certain conditions must be fulfilled. Among these conditions are the following:

1. Faith must be personal. It must be an experience that *you* can sense, that you can refer to in your *own* living, that *you* can act on. Otherwise it is only an abstract absolute which, while it may be intellectually understood or represented in the routine ritual you may go through, is still not a "substance" which will provide comfort, confidence, or direction.

2. Faith involves some active participation, some sense of the quality of experience to be obtained if you act in a certain way. It is only by experiencing the consequences of action that faith can be validated. Therefore, if faith is to be enduring, this process of participation must be such that one action will lead to another so that there is a never-ending process of activity with different phases which holds out the potentiality of even richer satisfaction.

3. Faith requires that you have a sense of confidence that ways can be found to achieve certain expectations or certain intended goals. While there can never be complete certainty, if faith is to survive you must have the feeling that there is at least an even chance that a goal can be achieved. Any goal that is too fanciful or too ambitious will sooner or later evaporate and disappear as a goal for *you*, because of the increasing frustration created as the goal appears to be increasingly unattainable.

4. And this means, as St. Paul said, that faith can be made real only if hopes are given substance. And hopes are given substance only if you have the satisfaction every now and then of realizing them, at least in part, through your own action, even though "action" may involve only a long period of waiting or of convalescence.

The role of some of these ingredients of faith is described in the following excerpts.

And an old priest said, Speak to us of Religion.
And he said:
Have I spoken this day of aught else?
Is not religion all deeds and all reflection,
And that which is neither deed nor reflection, but a wonder and a

surprise ever springing in the soul, even while the hands hew the stone or tend the loom?

Who can separate his faith from his actions, or his belief from his occupations?

Who can spread his hours before him, saying, "This for God and this for myself; This for my soul, and this other for my body"?

All your hours are wings that beat through space from self to self.

He who wears his morality but as his best garment were better naked.

The wind and the sun will tear no holes in his skin.

And he who defines his conduct by ethics imprisons his song-bird in a cage.

The freest song comes not through bars and wires.

And he to whom worshipping is a window, to open but also to shut, has not yet visited the house of his soul whose windows are from dawn to dawn.

Your daily life is your temple and your religion.

Whenever you enter into it take with you your all.

Take the plough and the forge and the mallet and the lute,

The things you have fashioned in necessity or for delight.

For in revery you cannot rise above your achievements nor fall lower than your failures.

And take with you all men:

For in adoration you cannot fly higher than their hopes nor humble yourself lower than their despair.

And if you would know God be not therefore a solver of riddles.

Rather look about you and you shall see Him playing with your children.

And look into space; you shall see Him walking in the cloud, outstretching His arms in the lightning and descending in rain.

You shall see Him smiling in flowers, then rising and waving His hands in trees.   (KAHLIL GIBRAN, *The Prophet*.) [11]

> Hope is the thing with feathers
> That perches in the soul,
> And sings the tune without the words,
> And never stops at all,
>
> And sweetest in the gale is heard;
> And sore must be the storm
> That could abash the little bird
> That kept so many warm.

I've heard it in the chillest land,
And on the strangest sea;
Yet, never, in extremity,
It asked a crumb of me.
(EMILY DICKINSON, "Hope Is the Thing with Feathers.") [12]

Almighty God whose Spirit has brought us to this new day, on this occasion help us recall the rock from which we are hewn, lest we forget who we are or what our destiny is. Refresh the roots of our memory that we may remember the faith and wisdom of the founding fathers out of which their dreams and visions arose and found transformation into reality. Grant that we too might stand firmly and dream for our time as great and worthy a vision—so it may be said of us—their young men dream dreams and see visions, "they mount up with wings as eagles, they run and are not weary, they walk and faint not."
(WILLIAM MATTHEWS, A Prayer for Founders' Day at Knox College.) [13]

If the conditions mentioned are fulfilled, the end product is, then, a value-sense of the worthwhileness of living. And this sense of the worthwhileness of living is itself dependent upon a sense of the worthwhileness of the reality-world which you yourself have built up with its constancies that serve as reliable guides to purposive action. And a most crucial aspect of faith, if it is to be an aspect of living that has reality, is the sense of identification which you, as an individual, have with the values faith represents and pulls together. If this identification is passive and provides only a one-way street leading from abstract values to your own personal life, then faith is likely to be only an escape, to involve no great sense of personal responsibility, and to require no active integration of your various purposes; nor will it demand of you any particular consistency between what you know and what you believe. Such a faith may become a blind idolatry with a worship of gods or images which may suddenly prove inadequate in some personal crisis. But if, on the other hand, faith plays an active role in living, then it takes on more the nature of an engagement, a commitment, a dedication to a set of principles or beliefs which it becomes your responsibility to try to apply and make real in the on-going, changing situations that constitute living.

We have repeatedly pointed out that the universe, as well as all human existence, is an on-going stream of events, constantly changing, constantly creative. And this means that any individual who is plugged in to the on-going events around him will have a sense that his own stable self-constancy will depend upon maintaining some continuous form of his reality-world within a changing matrix. He will sense that somehow he must continually transform and revise his reality-world to see himself through the frustrations and crises that are inevitably produced by the dialectical tension between form and flow, being and becoming, stability and change. Freedom itself can become a most frightening thing from which we will seek escape unless it is enmeshed in and directed by a faith in the reality of certain values that provide a compass to guide us in the direction that we are sure is worthwhile. In the short passage below, Amiel describes the "oscillations of feeling" that are an inevitable aspect of living. In the longer passage cited from Dostoevsky, the Grand Inquisitor accuses Jesus of urging men to seek a kind of freedom which they are unable to understand or to practice.

April 28, 1852. Do no violence to yourself, respect in yourself the oscillations of feeling. They are your life and your nature; One wiser than you ordained them. Do not abandon yourself altogether either to instinct or to will. Instinct is a siren, will a despot. Be neither the slave of your impulses and sensations of the moment, nor of an abstract and general plan; be open to what life brings from within and without, and welcome the unforeseen; but give to your life unity, and bring the unforeseen within the lines of your plan. Let what is natural in you raise itself to the level of the spiritual, and let the spiritual become once more natural. Thus will your development be harmonious, and the peace of heaven will shine upon your brow; always on condition that your peace is made, and that you have climbed your Calvary.

(*Amiel's Journal.*) [14]

Judge Thyself who was right—Thou or he who questioned Thee then? Remember the first question; its meaning, in other words, was this: "Thou wouldst go into the world, and art going with empty hands, with some promise of freedom which men in their simplicity and their natural unruliness cannot even understand, which they fear and dread—for nothing has ever been more insupportable for a man and a human society than freedom. But seest Thou these stones in this parched and barren wilderness? Turn them into bread, and mankind will run after Thee like a flock of sheep, grateful and obedient, though for ever trembling, lest Thou withdraw Thy hand and deny them Thy bread." But

Thou wouldst not deprive man of freedom and didst reject the offer, thinking, what is that freedom worth, if obedience is bought with bread? Thou didst reply that man lives not by bread alone. But dost Thou know that for the sake of that earthly bread the spirit of the earth will rise up against Thee and will strive with Thee and overcome Thee, and all will follow him, crying, "Who can compare with this beast? He has given us fire from Heaven!" Dost Thou know that the ages will pass, and humanity will proclaim by the lips of their sages that there is no crime, and therefore no sin; there is only hunger? "Feed men, and then ask of them virtue!" that's what they'll write on the banner, which they will raise against Thee, and with which they will destroy Thy temple. Where Thy temple stood will rise a new building; the terrible tower of Babel will be built again, and though, like the one of old, it will not be finished, yet Thou mightest have prevented that new tower and have cut short the sufferings of men for a thousand years; for they will come back to us after a thousand years of agony with their tower. They will seek us again, hidden underground in the catacombs, for we shall be again persecuted and tortured. They will find us and cry to us, "Feed us, for those who have promised us fire from Heaven haven't given it!" And then we shall finish building their tower, for he finishes the building who feeds them. And we alone shall feed them in Thy name, declaring falsely that it is in Thy name. Oh, never, never can they feed themselves without us! No science will give them bread so long as they remain free. In the end they will lay their freedom at our feet, and say to us, "Make us your slaves, but feed us." They will understand themselves, at last, that freedom and bread enough for all are inconceivable together, for never, never will they be able to share between them! They will be convinced, too, that they can never be free, for they are weak, vicious, worthless and rebellious. Thou didst promise them the bread of Heaven, but, I repeat again, can it compare with earthly bread in the eyes of the weak, ever sinful and ignoble race of man? And if for the sake of the bread of Heaven thousands and tens of thousands shall follow Thee, what is to become of the millions and tens of thousands of millions of creatures who will not have the strength to forego the earthly bread for the sake of the heavenly? Or dost Thou care only for the tens of thousands of the great and strong, while the millions, numerous as the sands of the sea, who are weak but love Thee, must exist only for the sake of the great and strong? No, we care for the weak too. They are sinful and rebellious, but in the end they too will become obedient. They will marvel at us and look on us as gods, because we are ready to endure the freedom which they have found so dreadful and to rule over them—so awful it will seem to them to be free. But we shall tell them that we are Thy servants and rule them in Thy name. We shall deceive them again, for we will not let Thee come to us again. That deception will be our suffering, for we shall be forced to lie.

This is the significance of the first question in the wilderness, and this is what Thou hast rejected for the sake of that freedom which Thou hast exalted above everything. Yet in this question lies hid the great secret of this world. Choosing "bread," Thou wouldst have satisfied the universal and everlasting craving of humanity—to find some one to worship. So long as man remains free he strives for nothing so incessantly and so painfully as to find some one to worship. But man seeks to worship what is established beyond dispute, so that all men would agree at once to worship it. For these pitiful creatures are concerned not only to find what one or the other can worship, but to find something that all would believe in and worship; what is essential is that all may be *together* in it. This craving for *community* of worship is the chief misery of every man individually and of all humanity from the beginning of time. For the sake of common worship they've slain each other with the sword. They have set up gods and challenged one another, "Put away your gods and come and worship ours, or we will kill you and your gods!" And so it will be to the end of the world, even when gods disappear from the earth; they will fall down before idols just the same. Thou didst know, Thou couldst not but have known, this fundamental secret of human nature, but Thou didst reject the one infallible banner which was offered Thee to make all men bow down to Thee alone—the banner of earthly bread; and Thou hast rejected it for the sake of freedom and the bread of Heaven. Behold what Thou didst further. And all again in the name of freedom! I tell Thee that man is tormented by no greater anxiety than to find some one quickly to whom he can hand over that gift of freedom with which the ill-fated creature is born. But only one who can appease their conscience can take over their freedom. In bread there was offered Thee an invincible banner; give bread, and man will worship Thee, for nothing is more certain than bread. But if some one else gains possession of his conscience—oh! then he will cast away Thy bread and follow after him who has ensnared his conscience. In that Thou wast right. For the secret of man's being is not only to live but to have something to live for. Without a stable conception of the object of life, man would not consent to go on living, and would rather destroy himself than remain on earth, though he had bread in abundance. That is true. But what happened? Instead of taking men's freedom from them, Thou didst make it greater than ever! Didst Thou forget that man prefers peace, and even death, to freedom of choice in the knowledge of good and evil? Nothing is more seductive for man than his freedom of conscience, but nothing is a greater cause of suffering. And behold, instead of giving a firm foundation for setting the conscience of man at rest for ever, Thou didst choose all that is exceptional, vague and enigmatic; Thou didst choose what was utterly beyond the strength of men, acting as though Thou didst not love them at all—Thou who didst come to give Thy life for them! Instead of taking possession of men's freedom, Thou didst increase it, and burdened the spiritual kingdom of mankind with its sufferings for ever. Thou didst desire man's free love, that he should follow Thee freely, enticed and taken captive by Thee. In place of the rigid ancient law, man must hereafter with free heart decide for himself what is good and what is evil, having only Thy image before him as his guide. But didst Thou not know he would at last reject even Thy image and Thy truth, if he is weighed down with the fearful burden of free choice? They will cry aloud at last that the truth is not in Thee, for they could not have been left in greater confusion and suffering than Thou hast caused, laying upon them so many cares and unanswerable problems.

(DOSTOEVSKY, *The Brothers Karamazov.*) [15]

KEEPING THE FAITH

The great majority of people in the world are, of course, born into a faith represented by some codified, institutionalized religion or some political ideology. They learn very early from their elders a particular pattern of values, and if they find that it "works" in their own lives they may get more satisfaction from it than they are often willing to acknowledge.

In order to perpetuate these formalized constancies and provide the possibility that they will acquire common and standardized significances and meanings, every institutionalized religion and every political creed has devised its own pattern of ritual and ceremony. Participation in such rituals enables the believer to associate himself through his own action with the abstraction the ritual symbolizes, whether it is telling his beads, saluting a flag, or bowing his head. And many of these rituals acquire a special significance when an individual performs them or participates in them with others for whom they are symbols. For example, the "silent prayer" that is so important a part of many religious services acquires a particular significance in the silent communal feeling of a congregation. In such a presence, one feels that one's own value-symbols are being confirmed by others.

While many people, to be sure, take part in such ceremonies with tongue in cheek or without really sensing any involvement or significance in what they are doing, still for many others there is a sense of being tuned in to more universal standards than we are normally conscious of. In the process, the individual's faith in his own standards—the standards he lives by—is confirmed. His faith is self-validated by repeating the constancies of a ritual.

From the beginning of time man has apparently sought some ultimate, universal constancy that would serve as a repository, protector, and fountainhead of all his most personal and most cherished values and aspirations. In all ages, men have apparently searched for some sort of God and have, in their search, brought forth all manner of deities according to their needs. The concept of "God" makes it easy for people to get hold of their value-constancies, hang on to them, and keep them fixed. It makes it possible for some people to get a feeling that there is an ultimate design, purpose, or destiny to life and the universe in which they are playing a useful role, but a role which is by the nature of things beyond their own comprehension.

In accounting for this search for God and in understanding the function God fulfills for the believer, we should recall some of the conditions that give rise to the need for faith: frustrations, disappointments, agonies, unfulfilled hopes. These conditions are also necessary to bring about the search for God.

Man's amazing capacity to help create an environment within which he can carry out his purposes and mitigate some of his problems enables him to obtain reassurance that his God is working with him. Hence, God *can* become part of human experience if he is sensed as a *process*. On the other hand, if God is a mere intellectual abstraction, he can never play a role in living, can never be demonstrated or experienced. "The Kingdom of God is in your midst," said Jesus.

ACQUIRING A PERSONAL FAITH

As man learns more and more about the universe of which he is a part, he may question more and more the validity of any faith which involves supernatural explanations.

But at the same time, the sense of being on his own without the aid of some outside friendly agent also increases man's feeling of helplessness and his sense of urgent need for something to believe in. If man's knowledge cannot of itself provide him with a faith, he does not wish it to prevent him finding a new faith. He continues to seek a set of beliefs—a set of beliefs consistent with what he knows.

The ardent Catholic or Buddhist can identify himself with beliefs that function for him and are confirmed by his daily rituals. The Communist militant faithfully follows the discipline of the party. But the individual who has no rigidly set institutionalized creed to adhere to must in a sense create his own faith and sustain this faith through his own transactions of living. And at the same time man's increasing knowledge of the world around him and of himself makes his craving for certainties and absolutes harder to satisfy and to justify. Tom Paine shows us one man's search for a personal faith.

It has been my intention, for several years past, to publish my thoughts upon religion; I am well aware of the difficulties that attend the subject, and, from that consideration, had reserved it to a more advanced period of life. I intended it to be the last offering I should make to my fellow-citizens of all nations, and that at a time when the purity of the motive that induced me to it, could not admit of a question, even by those who might disapprove the work.

The circumstance that has now taken place in France of the total abolition of the whole national order of priesthood, and of every thing appertaining to compulsive systems of religion, and compulsive articles of faith, has not only precipitated my intention, but rendered a work of this kind exceedingly necessary, lest, in the general wreck of superstition, of false systems of government, and false theology, we lose sight of morality, of humanity, and of the theology that is true.

As several of my colleagues, and others of my fellow-citizens of France, have given me the example of making their voluntary and individual profession of faith, I also will make mine; and I do this with all that sincerity and frankness with which the mind of man communicates with itself.

I believe in one God, and no more; and I hope for happiness beyond this life.

I believe in the equality of man; and I believe that religious duties consist in doing justice, loving mercy, and endeavouring to make our fellow creatures happy.

But, lest it should be supposed that I believe many other things in addition to these, I shall, in the progress of this work, declare the things I do not believe, and my reasons for not believing them.

I do not believe in the creed professed by the Jewish church, by the Roman church, by the Greek church, by the Turkish church, by the Protestant church, nor by any church that I know of. My own mind is my own church.

All national institutions of churches, whether Jewish, Christian, or Turkish, appear to me no other than human inventions, set up to terrify and enslave mankind, and monopolize power and profit.

I do not mean by this declaration to condemn those who believe otherwise; they have the same right to their belief as I have to mine. But it is necessary to the happiness of man, that he be mentally faithful to himself. Infidelity does not consist in believing, or in disbelieving; it consists in professing to believe what he does not believe.

It is impossible to calculate the moral mischief, if I may so express it, that mental lying has produced in society. When a man has so far corrupted and prostituted the chastity of his mind, as to subscribe his professional belief to things he does not believe, he has prepared himself for the commission of every other crime. He takes up the trade of a priest for the sake of gain, and in order to qualify himself for that trade, he begins with a perjury. Can we conceive any thing more destructive to morality than this?

Soon after I had published the pamphlet, "COMMON SENSE," in America, I saw the exceeding probability that a revolution in the system of government would be followed by a revolution in the system of religion. The adulterous connection of church and state, wherever it had taken place, whether Jewish, Christian, or Turkish, had so effectually prohibited, by pains and penalties, every discussion upon established creeds, and upon first principles of religion, that until the system of government should be changed, those subjects could not be brought fairly and openly before the world, but that whenever this should be done, a revolution in the system of religion would follow. Human inventions and priest-craft would be detected; and man would return to the pure, unmixed, and unadulterated belief of one God, and no more.

(Tom Paine, *Profession of Faith.*) [16]

The most widespread quest today seems to be for a "cause" that represents aspirations which men can share in a "scientific" age which they can dedicate themselves to and try to experience in their own living.

Circumstances seem to be forcing people to the realization that their relations with others are the crucial problem for their own well-being and for their survival. The question of faith seems to be becoming more and more a question of how to acquire faith in other people and how to instill in other people a faith in us. It is the ancient problem of acquiring and demonstrating compassion, charity, and love.

But we have already pointed out that when we look for constancies in other people and for some correspondence between what we think they are and how they turn out to be when we participate with them, a variety of complications is introduced. Other people have their own purposes, often difficult for us to understand. Their purposes will change as conditions change and as their behavior progresses from one goal to another. *Their* purposes and behavior are affected by *our* purposes and behavior, just as *ours* are affected by *theirs.* So when we deal with people, constancies and predictabilities are not easy to find.

As noted earlier, in an attempt to increase the meanings and significances people have in common, societies have developed all manner of customs, mores, conventions, laws, and other codes of behavior. And as people more and more sense their interdependence, both as individuals and as citizens of nations, old forms of behavior are revised, and new common links are devised in the attempt to keep purposes compatible with the new forms of behavior.

All of these social forms presumably serve the function of improving the degree of correspondence between what is in our awareness and what is potentially in the social environment to be aware of. And the reason for attempting to increase this correspondence is, of course, to provide purposeful action of a more predictable direction and with a greater chance of repeating itself in satisfying ways with more certain value-constancies.

The process is never-ending, for there can never be perfect correspondence between what we perceive in people and what we *might* perceive in them. Increased "correspondence" in our social perceptions of each other will inevitably be accompanied by increased satisfactions, which themselves will point to new potential satisfactions.

In this ceaseless process, the individual searching for faith gets support for his value-standards from others who seem to share them—his family, his friends, and the various groups he identifies himself with. As long as they help him carry out his purposes by their actions, help him maintain and develop his own self-constancy, he will find them fortifying his faith and deserving of it. But it is only in times of personal crisis and emergency that this faith in people is manifested and filters into awareness. At other times it is part of the relatively normal "neutral" world: it is *potentially* with us and we may take it into account in our behavior even though we are not aware of it.

A person will be able to become more aware of faith and to gain faith when he is able to see the *potential* values in living he has not sensed before *and* when he feels there is a good chance that he will be able to participate effectively in bringing about these potential value-satisfactions in his own experience. He may see himself and others as sharing in God's love or in some all-embracing universal force which guides human destiny and eternally provides the possibility of transformation, renewal, or relief.

But if his doubts and frustrations are continually unresolved through action, he is likely to find himself in a mental condition where he is uncertain about the present, or where he refuses to accept the past, or where he is unduly apprehensive about the future. In each case, faith and hope are abandoned and can only be re-established by painstaking relearning. Such relearning will require above all else a therapy which simplifies goals so that their accomplishment will be assured through the individual's own action, thereby rebuilding his confidence in himself. Once self-confidence is regained on a simple level, goals can gradually be raised.

And what holds for a single individual also holds for members of a group or culture.

So the problem of gaining faith is closely related to the ancient problem of insight. The recognition of our own adequacies and inadequacies in terms of the goals we have set for accomplishment can help restore faith in those whose self-assessment has been inaccurate and who consequently suffer from a constant sense of inadequacy because they are aiming at the wrong thing or looking in the wrong place for satisfaction to appear.

The process of self-examination can bring into awareness purposes we had heretofore not recognized were guiding our actions. It can also release latent abilities we have only vaguely sensed and insufficiently nurtured. The inquiry we must undertake in order to gain faith is the sort which we have earlier described as "value-inquiry" in contrast to logical or rational inquiry. It involves mulling things over, meditation, communion, or prayer. Its purpose is to allow us to sensitize ourselves to our feelings, to reflect on the priority and weight we should assign different value-standards, to get a sense of orchestration into the various aspirations and responsibilities we feel are right for us.

Only through learning and practicing value-inquiry can we get a sense of the full significances potentially available to us in our behavior. Only then can we guess the probable long-range consequences our actions will have on us and on the purposes of others. Only then can we see how to improve the quality of our satisfactions by improving the quality of our purposes and the quality of our actions. Only then can we begin to simplify our lives, learning that if we become sensitive to value-cues we can then become aware of how even our smallest daily actions hold a possibility of transcending the immediate moment and taking on more universal value-significance.

Thus by building up our value-standards, sensing their confirmation in action, discovering revisions that will make them more encompassing, we can develop a faith of sufficient power to weather the inevitable frustrations and deprivations we will encounter.

Faith enables us to feel that, come what may, life is still full of unpredictable and satisfying promises if we will only participate selflessly in the flow of events.

And faith makes it possible for us to get at least a vague sense of awareness that death itself is the beginning of the "everlasting life" we have as the result of the effects of our behavior on others and on still others yet to come in the long line of humanity ahead.

This need for insight and value-inquiry if we are to feel the richness of experience is beautifully stated in one of the prayers of St. Francis of Assisi:

Lord make me a channel of Thy peace
That where there is hatred—I may bring love,
That where there is wrong—I may bring the spirit of forgiveness.
That where there is discord—I may bring harmony.
That where there is error—I may bring truth,

That where there is doubt—I may bring faith,
That where there is despair—I may bring hope,
That where there are shadows—I may bring Thy light,
That where there is sadness—I may bring joy.
Lord, grant that I may seek rather
To comfort—than to be comforted;
To understand—than to be understood;
To love—than to be loved.

For
It is by giving—that one receives;
It is by self-forgetting—that one finds;
It is by forgiving—that one is forgiven;
It is by dying—that one awakens to eternal life.

Notes

NOTES TO CHAPTER 1

1. *Amiel's Journal*, (Mrs. Humphrey Ward, trans.). Second ed., n.p., A. L. Burt Co., n.d., p. 138.

2. *Ibid.*

3. Robert Henri, *The Art Spirit*, (Margery Ryerson, comp.). Philadelphia: J. B. Lippincott, 1923.

4. Alfred North Whitehead, *Modes of Thought.* New York: The Macmillan Company, 1938, p. 25.

5. Havelock Ellis, *The Dance of Life.* Boston: Houghton, Mifflin, 1923, pp. 101–102.

6. Aldous Huxley, *The Genius and the Goddess.* New York: Harper, 1955, pp. 35–36.

7. Charles Baudelaire, *My Heart Laid Bare and Other Prose Writings,* (Peter Quennel, ed.; Norman Cameron, trans.). New York: Vanguard Press, 1951, pp. 211–12.

8. *Ibid.*, pp. 31–33.

9. P. W. Bridgman, "New Vistas for Intelligence," *Physical Science and Human Values*, (E. P. Wigner, ed.). Princeton: Princeton University Press, 1947, pp. 144–45.

10. Allen Tate, "Preface to Reactionary Essays on Poetry and Ideas (1936)," *On the Limits of Poetry: Selected Essays: 1928–1948.* New York: Swallow Press & William Morrow, 1948, pp. xiv–xv.

11. *Conversations of Goethe with Eckermann*, (Ernest Rhys, ed.; John Oxenford, trans.). New York: E. P. Dutton, 1930, pp. 65–66.

12. Gilbert K. Chesterton, "Science and the Savages," *Heretics.* New York: John Lane, 1909, pp. 142–44.

13. *The Maxims of Marcel Proust*, (Justin O'Brien, ed. & trans.). New York: Columbia University Press, 1948, p. 209.

14. *The Confessions of Saint Augustine*, (Edward B. Pusey, trans.). New York: Pocket Books, 1952, pp. 67–68.

15. Albert Schweitzer, *Memoirs of Childhood and Youth*, (C. T. Campion, trans.). New York: The Macmillan Company, 1925, p. 73.

16. *Amiel's Journal*, (Mrs. Humphrey Ward, trans.). Second ed., n.p.: A. L. Burt Co., n.d., p. 151.

17. Albert Einstein and L. Infeld, *The Evolution of Physics*. New York: Simon & Schuster, 1942, p. 95.

18. Arnold J. Toynbee (trans.), *Greek Historical Thought from Homer to the Age of Heraclius*. New York: Mentor Books, 1952, p. 137.

19. This sketchy treatment of the nature of scientific inquiry may be supplemented by a study of H. Cantril *et al.*, "Psychology and Scientific Research," *Science*, CX (1949), pp. 461–64, 491–97, 517–22.

20. Alfred North Whitehead, *Adventures of Ideas*. New York: The Macmillan Company, 1954, p. 197.

21. Ralph Waldo Emerson, "Each and All," *The Oxford Book of American Verse*. New York: Oxford University Press, 1950, pp. 70–71.

22. Arnold J. Toynbee (trans.), *Greek Historical Thought from Homer to the Age of Heraclius*. New York: Mentor Books, 1952, pp. 44–46.

23. John Dewey and Arthur F. Bentley, *Knowing and the Known*. Boston: Beacon Press, 1949, pp. 107–109.

24. *Ibid.*, pp. 120–21.

25. W. H. Auden, "New Year Letter," *The Collected Poetry*. New York: Random House, 1945, p. 275.

26. *The Maxims of Marcel Proust*, (Justin O'Brien ed. & trans.). New York: Columbia University Press, 1948, p. 209.

27. Blaise Pascal, *"Pensées" and "The Provincial Letters."* New York: Modern Library, 1941, p. 7.

28. Charles Baudelaire, *My Heart Laid Bare and Other Prose Writings*, (Peter Quennel, ed.; Norman Cameron, trans.). New York: Vanguard Press, 1951, p. 147.

29. Aldous Huxley, *The Genius and the Goddess*. New York: Harper, 1955, p. 132.

30. Walt Whitman, "Song of Myself," *Poems*. New York: Modern Library, n.d., p. 38.

31. Kathleen McLaughlin, "East and West Differ at Movies Too, U. N. Finds," *New York Times*, March 25, 1953.

32. Alfred North Whitehead, *Science and the Modern World*. New York: The Macmillan Company, 1926.

33. Chester I. Barnard, *Organization and Management*. Cambridge, Massachusetts: Harvard University Press, 1948, pp. 129–32.

34. Anne Morrow Lindberg, *The Wave of the Future*. New York: Harcourt, Brace, 1940, pp. 6–7.

NOTES TO CHAPTER 2

1. William Blake, "The Everlasting Gospel," *Selected Poems*. London: Oxford University Press, 1927, p. 93.

2. Alfred North Whitehead, *Science and the Modern World*. New York: The Macmillan Company, 1926, p. 80.

3. Hans Vaihinger, *The Philosophy of "As If,"* (C. K. Ogden, trans.). New York: Harcourt, Brace, 1925, pp. 15–16.

4. *The Dialogues of Plato*, (Benjamin Jowett, trans.). New York: Boni and Liveright, 1927, pp. 380–81.

5. W. Macneile Dixon, *The Human Situation*. New York: St. Martin's Press, n.d. (The Gifford Lectures, University of Glasgow, 1935–1937), pp. 58–59.

6. *The Maxims of Marcel Proust*, (Justin O'Brien, ed. & trans.). New York: Columbia University Press, 1948, p. 37.

7. James Thurber, *Many Moons*. New York: Harcourt, Brace, 1943.

8. Since this is not meant to be a scientific treatise, a detailed discussion of the perceptual variables which have been isolated for investigation, the methods and techniques of investigation, and the specific data gathered would be out of order. Our interest is confined here to a general characterization of the process and analysis of its functional role in living.

9. The techniques by which the abstracted essential factors are investigated and manipulated as they relate to the central problem of perceiving need not be detailed here. Roughly speaking, the major approaches to the study of perceiving can be differentiated into the observational and clinical, and the laboratory and experimental. The many different methods and techniques employed in investigating the process of perceiving yield different, but complementary, forms of information. Here our main concern is with some of the important conclusions to be drawn from the evidence so far accumulated.

10. F. P. Kilpatrick, "Two Processes in Perceptual Learning," *Journal of Experimental Psychology*, XLVII (1954), pp. 362–70.

11. Martin Buber, *I and Thou*, (Ronald Gregor Smith, trans.). Edinburgh: T. & T. Clark; New York: Charles Scribner's Sons, 1937, pp. 25–26.

12. *The Maxims of Marcel Proust*, (Justin O'Brien, ed. & trans.). New York: Columbia University Press, 1948, p. 61.

13. Amy Lowell, "Meeting-House Hill," *The Oxford Book of American Verse*. New York: Oxford University Press, 1950, pp. 533–34.

14. Emily Dickinson, "The Brain Is Wider than the Sky," *The Oxford Book of American Verse*. New York: Oxford University Press, 1950, p. 424.

15. Marcus Aurelius Antoninus, *The Communings with Himself*, (C. R. Haines, trans.). New York: G. P. Putnam's Sons; London: W. Heineman, 1916, pp. 91–93.

16. Voltaire, *Candide or the Optimist*, (Henry Morley, trans.). London: George Routledge; New York: E. P. Dutton, n.d., p. 2.

17. Joost A. M. Meerloo, *Patterns of Panic*. New York: International Universities Press, 1950.

18. Carl Sandburg, *Good Morning, America*. New York: Harcourt, Brace, 1928, pp. 4–5.

19. William Blake, "The Everlasting Gospel," *Selected Poems*. London: Oxford University Press, 1927, p. 88.

20. Martin Buber, *I and Thou*, (Ronald Gregor Smith, trans.). Edinburgh: T. & T. Clark; New York: Charles Scribner's Sons, 1937, p. 29.

21. M. N. Dvivedi, *The Yoga-Sutras of Patanjali*. Madras, Adyar: Theosophical Publishing House, 1947.

22. *Amiel's Journal*, (Mrs. Humphrey Ward, trans.). Second ed., n.p.: A. L. Burt Co., n.d., pp. 372–73.

23. W. H. Auden, "True Enough," *The Collected Poetry*. New York: Random House, 1954, p. 54.

24. Walt Whitman, "Song of Myself," *Poems*. New York: Modern Library, n.d., pp. 40–41.

NOTES TO CHAPTER 3

1. Walter B. Cannon, *The Wisdom of the Body*. New York: W. W. Norton, 1932.

2. W. Macneile Dixon, *The Human Situation*. New York: St. Martin's Press, n.d. (The Gifford Lectures, University of Glasgow, 1935–1937), pp. 195–97.

3. *Amiel's Journal*, (Mrs. Humphrey Ward, trans.). Second ed., n.p.: A. L. Burt Co., n.d., p. 68.

4. E. B. White, "Heavier than Air," *The Second Tree from the Corner*. New York: Harper, 1954, pp. 118–21.

5. Blaise Pascal, *"Pensées" and "The Provincial Letters."* New York: Modern Library, 1941, pp. 47–48.

6. *Ibid.*, pp. 60–61.

7. Walt Whitman, "Song of Myself," *Poems.* New York: Modern Library, n.d., p. 73.

8. E. B. White, "Quo Vadimus?" *Quo Vadimus or The Case of the Bicycle.* New York: Harper, 1927, pp. 23–29.

9. Feodor Dostoevsky, *Letters from the Underworld,* (C. J. Hogarth, trans.). New York: E. P. Dutton, n.d., pp. 38–42.

10. Learned Hand, "A Plea for the Freedom of Dissent," *New York Times Magazine,* February 6, 1955, pp. 12, 33, 35.

11. William James, "On a Certain Blindness in Human Beings," *Talks to Teachers on Psychology: and to Students on Some of Life's Ideals.* New York: Henry Holt, 1901, pp. 255–57.

12. Edmond Taylor, *Richer by Asia.* Boston: Houghton Mifflin Co., 1947, pp. 280–81.

13. *The Maxims of Marcel Proust,* (Justin O'Brien, ed. & trans.). New York: Columbia University Press, 1948, p. 197.

14. Richard Eberhart, "If I Could Only Live at the Pitch That Is Near Madness," *Mid-Century American Poets,* (John Ciardi, ed.). New York: Twayne Publishers, 1950, p. 235.

15. William Wordsworth, "Lines Composed a Few Miles above Tintern Abbey," *British Poets of the Nineteenth Century,* (C. H. Page, ed.). New York: Sanborn, 1925, p. 11.

16. Chester I. Barnard, *Organization and Management.* Cambridge, Massachusetts: Harvard University Press, 1948, pp. 14–15.

17. William James, *The Principles of Psychology.* New York: Henry Holt, 1890, I, 309–16.

18. Laotzu, *The Way of Life,* (Witter Bynner, trans.). New York: John Day, 1944, p. 43.

19. Cleveland Amory, *The Last Resorts.* New York: Harper, 1948, pp. 174–79.

20. Della Yoe and Jennette Edwards, "Till the River Rises," *These Are Our Lives.* (Federal Writers' Project, Works Progress Administration.) Chapel Hill: University of North Carolina Press, 1939, pp. 372–80.

21. William O. Douglas, *Of Men and Mountains.* New York: Harper, 1950, p. 15.

22. Alfred North Whitehead, *The Aims of Education.* New York: Mentor Books, 1949, p. 51.

23. Horace M. Kallen, *Human Beings and Psychological Systems.* Princeton: privately printed for Perception Demonstration Center, Princeton University, 1954, p. 18.

NOTES TO CHAPTER 4

1. *The Confessions of St. Augustine*, (Edward B. Pusey, trans.). New York: Pocket Books, 1952, pp. 185, 188.

2. James Thurber, "The Scotty Who Knew Too Much," *The Thurber Carnival*. New York: Harper, 1945, p. 185.

3. *The Panchatantra*, (Arthur W. Ryder, trans.). Chicago: University of Chicago Press, 1925, pp. 159–60.

4. *Aesop's Fables*, (Thomas James and George Tyler Townsend, trans.). Philadelphia: J. B. Lippincott, 1949, p. 25.

5. William Shakespeare, "Sonnet 148."

6. Mr. Justice Jackson, *United States v. Ballard*, 322 U. S. 78.

7. Oliver Wendell Holmes, *Collected Legal Papers*. New York: Harcourt, Brace, 1920, pp. 304–305.

8. Albert Schweitzer, *Memoirs of Childhood and Youth*, (C. T. Campion, trans.). New York: The Macmillan Company, 1925, pp. 39–44.

9. Nadezhda K. Krupskaya, *Memories of Lenin*, (E. Verney, trans.). New York: International Publishers, n.d., I, 5–6.

10. George S. Counts and Nucia P. Lodge (trans.), *I Want to Be Like Stalin*. New York: John Day, 1947, pp. 58–62.

11. Edmond Taylor, *Richer by Asia*. Boston: Houghton Mifflin Co., 1947, pp. 134–39.

12. A. J. Liebling, "A Reporter at Large: The Neutral Corner Art Group," *The New Yorker*, December 18, 1954, p. 72.

13. R. S. Lillie, "Randomness and Directiveness in the Evolution and Activity of Living Organisms," *American Naturalist*, LXXXII (1948), No. 802, 17ff.

14. *See* Hadley Cantril, *The Invasion from Mars*. Princeton: Princeton University Press, 1940.

15. James Thurber, "The Day the Dam Broke," *The Thurber Carnival*. New York: Harper, 1945, pp. 139–43.

16. Leo N. Tolstoy, "How Much Land a Man Needs," *What Shall We Do Then?; Collected Articles, etc.*, (Leo Wiener, trans.). Boston: L. C. Page, 1904, pp. 459–69.

17. Carl Sandburg, "Happiness," *Oxford Book of American Verse*. New York: Oxford University Press, 1952, p. 587.

18. Alexis de Tocqueville, *Democracy in America*. New York: Alfred A. Knopf Inc., 1945, II, Book 2, pp. 136–39.

19. F. C. Bartlett, *Remembering*. London: Cambridge University Press, 1932, pp. 44–45.

20. Santha Rama Rau, *East of Home*. New York: Harper, 1950, pp. 75–76.

21. Corey Ford, "How to Guess Your Age," *Collier's*, February 12, 1949, p. 52.

22. Carl Sandburg, *The People, Yes*. New York: Harcourt, Brace, 1936, p. 29.

NOTES TO CHAPTER 5

1. Albert Einstein, *The World as I See It*, (Alan Harris, trans.). New York: Covici, Friede, 1934, p. 238.

2. Dante, *Divine Comedy*. New York: Thomas Y. Crowell, 1897, pp. 246–47.

3. W. Macneile Dixon, *The Human Situation*. New York: St. Martin's Press, n.d. (The Gifford Lectures, University of Glasgow, 1935–1937), pp. 362–63.

4. Joseph Needham, *The Sceptical Biologist*. New York: W. W. Norton, 1930, pp. 138–40.

5. P. W. Bridgman, "Science and Common Sense," *The Scientific Monthly*, LXXIX (1954), pp. 35–36.

6. We are using the word "matrix" to mean the "enveloping element within which something originates, takes form or develops." (Webster.)

7. *The Confessions of St. Augustine*, (Edward B. Pusey, trans.). New York: Pocket Books, 1952, pp. 227–29.

8. Robert Frost, "The Road Not Taken," *The Oxford Book of American Verse*. New York: Oxford University Press, 1952, pp. 556–57.

9. Albert Einstein, *Out of My Later Years*. New York: Philosophical Library, 1950, pp. 21–22.

10. *Gandhi's Autobiography*. Washington: Public Affairs Press, 1948, pp. 269–72.

11. George Sava, *A Surgeon Remembers*. London: Faber & Faber, 1953.

12. Christopher Fry, *The Lady's Not for Burning*. London: Oxford University Press, 1950, pp. 81–83.

13. Carl Sandburg, *The People, Yes*. New York: Harcourt, Brace, 1936, pp. 18–19.

14. *Doctor Johnson's Prayers*. New York: Harper, 1945, p. 4.

15. William Henry Roberts, *The Problem of Choice*. Boston: Ginn & Company, 1941, p. 19.

16. Charles Morris, *The Open Self*. New York: Prentice-Hall, 1948, pp. 13–14.

17. Herman Melville, *Moby Dick or The Whale*. New York: Random House, 1930, pp. 54–56.

18. Louis Fischer, *The Life of Mahatma Gandhi*. New York: Harper, 1950, pp. 273–75.

19. *The Wisdom of Wu Ming Fu,* (Stanwood Cobb, ed.). New York: Henry Holt, 1931, p. 3.

20. *Gandhi's Autobiography*. Washington: Public Affairs Press, 1948, p. 575.

21. Oscar Wilde, *De Profundis*. Second ed., New York: G. P. Putnam's Sons, 1905, pp. 45–47.

22. Thomas Paine, *The Selected Work of Tom Paine*. New York: Duell, Sloan & Pearce, 1946, p. 47.

23. Girolamo Savonarola, in: *The Golden Book of Prayer,* (Donald B. Aldrich, ed.). New York: Dodd, Mead, 1945, p. 209.

24. Chester I. Barnard, *The Functions of the Executive*. Cambridge: Harvard University Press, 1946.

25. *The Wisdom of Wu Ming Fu,* (Stanwood Cobb, ed.). New York: Henry Holt, 1931, p. 38.

26. Walt Whitman, "Song of the Open Road," *Poems*. New York: Modern Library, n.d., p. 128.

27. Euripides, *The Bacchae of Euripides,* (Gilbert Murray, trans.). New York: Longmans, Green, n.d., p. 19.

28. John Jay Chapman, *Emerson and Other Essays*. London: David Nutt, 1898, pp. 10–11.

29. Louis Fischer, *The Life of Mahatma Gandhi*. New York: Harper, 1950, pp. 28–29.

30. D. G. Mukerji, *The Song of God: Translation of the Bhagavad-Gita*. New York: Dutton, 1931, pp. 30–34.

31. Leo N. Tolstoy, *Resurrection*. New York: Thomas Y. Crowell, 1911, II, 161–66.

32. Chester I. Barnard, *Organization and Management*. Cambridge: Harvard University Press, 1948, p. 57.

33. Robert Bridges, *The Testament of Beauty*. New York: Oxford University Press, 1929, pp. 157–58.

NOTES TO CHAPTER 6

1. *Aesop's Fables*, (Thomas James and George Tyler Townsend, trans.). Philadelphia: J. B. Lippincott, 1949, p. 128.

2. Carl Sandburg, *The People, Yes*. New York: Harcourt, Brace, 1936, pp. 251–54.

3. Martin Buber, *I and Thou*, (Ronald Gregor Smith, trans.). Edinburgh: T. & T. Clark; New York: Charles Scribner's Sons, 1937, pp. 8–9.

4. Alexis de Tocqueville, *Democracy in America*. New York: Alfred A. Knopf Inc., 1945, II, 1068.

5. Learned Hand, *The Spirit of Liberty*. New York: Alfred A. Knopf, Inc., 1952, pp. 189–91.

6. I Corinthians, 13.

7. Luigi Pirandello, "It Is So! (If You Think So)," *Naked Masks*, (Eric Bentley, ed.). New York: E. P. Dutton, 1952, pp. 68–71.

8. Marcel Proust, *Swann's Way*, (C. K. Scott Moncrieff, trans.). New York: Modern Library, 1928, p. 21.

9. American Oriental Society, *The Study of Human Abilities: The Jen Wu Chih of Liu Shao*. New Haven: American Oriental Society, 1937, pp. 124–26.

10. Laotzu, *The Way of Life*, (Witter Bynner, trans.). New York: John Day, 1944, pp. 41–42.

11. *Ibid.*, p. 56.

12. *Ibid.*, pp. 68–69.

13. Anton Chekov, "To Whom Shall I Tell My Grief?" *The Stories of Anton Chekov*, (Robert N. Linscott, ed.). New York: Modern Library, 1932, pp. 103–109.

14. D. G. Mukerji, *The Song of God: Translation of the Bhagavad-Gita*. New York: Dutton, 1931, pp. 23, 35, 152.

15. Chester I. Barnard, *Organization and Management*. Cambridge: Harvard University Press, 1948, p. 71.

16. Konrad Lorentz, *King Solomon's Ring*. New York: Thomas Y. Crowell, 1952, p. 127.

17. We are deliberately omitting any review of or illustrations from the rich literature accumulated by the ethnologists concerning the many different forms loyalties take among different people. Examples of these will be found in Frazer's *Golden Bough*, Sumner's *Folkways*, or, more recently, the popular writings of Ruth Benedict, Margaret Mead, *et al.*

18. Kenneth Grahame, *The Wind in the Willows.* New York: Charles Scribner's Sons, 1908, pp. 118–19.

19. Oliver Wendell Holmes, *Collected Legal Papers.* New York: Harcourt, Brace, 1920, pp. 311–12.

20. Bill Mauldin, *Up Front.* New York: Henry Holt, 1945, pp. 58–60.

21. Ralph Waldo Emerson, "Give All to Love," *The Oxford Book of American Verse.* New York: Oxford University Press, 1950, pp. 105–107.

22. Conrad Aiken, "Music I Heard with You," *The Oxford Book of American Verse.* New York: Oxford University Press, 1950, p. 862.

23. John Donne, "A Valediction: Forbidding Mourning," *The Oxford Book of Seventeenth Century Verse.* London: Oxford University Press, 1934, p. 105.

24. Eugene O'Neill, *Strange Interlude.* New York: Boni & Liveright, 1928, pp. 34–35.

25. Kahlil Gibran, *The Prophet.* New York: Alfred A. Knopf, Inc., 1923, pp. 66–67.

26. Emily Dickinson, "Much Madness Is Divinest Sense," *The Oxford Book of American Verse.* New York: Oxford University Press, 1950, p. 415.

27. Mark Twain, *The Adventures of Huckleberry Finn.* New York: Harper, 1896, pp. 9–14, 17–20.

28. William Manning, *The Key of Libberty, etc.* Billerica, Massachusetts: The Manning Association, 1922, pp. 14–15, 20.

29. Ralph Waldo Emerson, "Self-Reliance," *The Complete Essays & Other Writings of Ralph Waldo Emerson,* (Brooks Atkinson, ed.). New York: Modern Library, 1940, pp. 145–52.

30. Albert Einstein, *The World as I See It,* (Alan Harris, trans.). New York: Covici, Friede, 1934, pp. 246–47.

31. *Amiel's Journal,* (Mrs. Humphrey Ward, trans.). Second ed., n.p.: A. L. Burt Co., n.d., pp. 34–35.

32. James Thurber, "The Secret Life of Walter Mitty," *The Thurber Carnival.* New York: Harper, 1945, pp. 34–37.

33. *Amiel's Journal,* (Mrs. Humphrey Ward, trans.). Second ed., n.p.: A. L. Burt Co., n.d., pp. 272–73.

34. Thorstein Veblen, *The Theory of the Leisure Class.* New York: Modern Library, 1934, pp. 75, 76–85.

35. Louis Fischer, *The Life of Mahatma Gandhi.* New York: Harper, 1950, pp. 221–22.

36. *The Maxims of Marcel Proust,* (Justin O'Brien, ed. & trans.). New York: Columbia University Press, 1948, p. 39.

37. John Steinbeck, *Cannery Row.* New York: Viking, 1945, p. 14.

38. Lewis Carroll, *Through the Looking-Glass*. Mt. Vernon: Peter Pauper Press, n.d., p. 114.

39. Oliver Wendell Holmes, *The Autocrat of the Breakfast Table*. Boston: Houghton Mifflin Co., 1894, pp. 51–54.

40. Charles Baudelaire, *My Heart Laid Bare and Other Prose Writings*, (Peter Quennel, ed.; Norman Cameron, trans.). New York: Vanguard Press, 1951, pp. 139–40.

41. Anatole France, *The Garden of Epicurus*, (Alfred Allinson, trans.). London: John Lane, The Bodley Head; New York: Dodd, Mead, 1923, p. 71.

42. John Dewey, *Art as Experience*. New York: Minton, Balch & Company, 1934, p. 106.

43. A. Parker Nevin, "Subject: The Crisis (or any other topic)," *Princeton Alumni Weekly*, October 29, 1948, p. 7.

NOTES TO CHAPTER 7

1. W. H. Mallock, *Lucretius on Life and Death*. New York: John Lane, 1900, pp. 15–16.

2. Thomas à Kempis in: *The Golden Book of Prayer*, (Donald B. Aldrich, ed.). New York: Grosset, 1941, p. 127.

3. Arthur Koestler, *Darkness at Noon*, (Daphne Hardy, trans.). New York: The Macmillan Company, 1945, pp. 224–25.

4. Horace M. Kallen, *The Liberal Spirit*. Ithaca, N. Y.: Cornell University Press, 1948, pp. 17–21.

5. Adolf Hitler, *Mein Kampf*. New York: Reynal & Hitchcock, 1939, pp. 227–34.

6. George S. Counts, *The Challenge of Soviet Education*. New York: McGraw-Hill, 1957, pp. 131–35.

7. Elting E. Morison, "A Case Study of Innovation," *Engineering and Scientific Monthly*, April, 1950.

8. René Fülöp-Miller, *Triumph over Pain*. New York: Literary Guild of America, 1938, pp. 44–47.

9. Phillip Frank, *Einstein: His Life and Times*, (George Rosen, trans.). New York: Alfred A. Knopf, Inc., 1947, pp. 49–50.

10. Graham Wallas, *The Art of Thought*. New York: Harcourt, Brace, 1926, pp. 79–92.

11. S. I. Hayakawa, "Reflections on the History of Jazz," (Poetry

Magazine Modern Arts Series Lecture, at the Arts Club of Chicago, March 17, 1945).

12. Benjamin P. Thomas, *Abraham Lincoln.* New York: Alfred A. Knopf Inc., 1953, pp. 497–98.

13. Quoted in George S. Counts, *The Challenge of Soviet Education.* New York: McGraw-Hill, 1957, p. 63.

14. Niccolo Machiavelli, *"The Prince" and "The Discourses."* New York: Modern Library, 1940, pp. 63–66.

15. *The Republic of Plato,* (Benjamin Jowett, trans.). Third ed., Oxford: Clarendon Press, 1921/1922, I, 389ff.

16. Laotzu, *The Way of Life,* (Witter Bynner, trans.). New York: John Day, 1944, pp. 26–27.

17. *Ibid.,* pp. 34–35.

18. *Ibid.,* p. 62.

19. *Ibid.,* p. 68.

20. Edmond Taylor, *Richer by Asia.* Boston: Houghton Mifflin Co., 1947, pp. 411–13.

21. Alfred North Whitehead, *Symbolism: Its Meaning and Effect.* New York: The Macmillan Company, 1927, p. 88.

22. Niccolo Machiavelli, *"The Prince" and "The Discourses."* New York: Modern Library, 1940, pp. 182–83.

23. Thomas Paine, *The Selected Work of Tom Paine,* (Howard Fast, ed.). New York: Duell, Sloan & Pearce, 1945, pp. 180–81.

24. V. I. Lenin, "Our Programme," *A Handbook of Marxism,* (Emile Burns, ed.). New York: International Publishers, 1935, pp. 571–75.

25. V. I. Lenin, "On the Eve of October," *A Handbook of Marxism,* (Emile Burns, ed.). New York: International Publishers, 1935, pp. 800, 808–810.

NOTES TO CHAPTER 8

1. Portions of the textual material of this chapter have been taken from an article, "The Nature of Faith," by Hadley Cantril, which appeared in the *Journal of Individual Psychology,* XIII (1957), pp. 24–37.

2. Carl Sandburg, *Always the Young Strangers.* New York: Harcourt, Brace, 1952, pp. 145–46.

3. Samuel Butler, *The Way of All Flesh.* New York: E. P. Dutton, 1916, pp. 343–44.

4. Translated from the Sanskrit for us by Dr. Kali Prasad.

5. Johann W. V. Goethe, *Faust,* (W. H. Van der Smissen, trans.).

London: J. M. Dent, 1926, Act IV, Scene 11, pp. 109–110.

6. Curtis Reynolds, *Suicide Note*. Los Angeles: New Age Publishing Co., 1948, pp. 57, 62, 66.

7. St. Matthew, chapter V.

8. Albert Schweitzer, *Memoirs of Childhood and Youth*. New York: The Macmillan Company, 1925, pp. 101–103.

9. Robert Louis Stevenson, *Prayers Written at Vailima*. New York: Charles Scribner's Sons, 1904, p. 1.

10. Rabindranath Tagore, "Gitanjali XXXVI," *Collected Poems and Plays of Rabindranath Tagore*. London: The Macmillan Company, 1936, p. 17.

11. Kahlil Gibran, *The Prophet*. New York: Alfred A. Knopf Inc., 1923, pp. 87–89.

12. Emily Dickinson, "Hope Is the Thing with Feathers," *The Oxford Book of American Verse*. New York: Oxford University Press, 1952, p. 419.

13. William Matthews, "A Prayer for Founders' Day at Knox College," (unpublished).

14. *Amiel's Journal*, (Mrs. Humphrey Ward, trans.). Second ed., n.p.: A. L. Burt Co., n.d., pp. 26–29.

15. Feodor Dostoevsky, *The Brothers Karamazov*, (Constance Garnett, trans.). New York: Modern Library, n.d., pp. 262–64.

16. Thomas Paine, *The Selected Work of Tom Paine*, (Howard Fast, ed.). New York: Duell, Sloan & Pearce, 1945, pp. 285–86.

Index of Quotations